SHORTHAND WRITTEN
BY JEROME P. EDELMAN

GREGG SHORTHAND FOR COL

VOLUME TWO

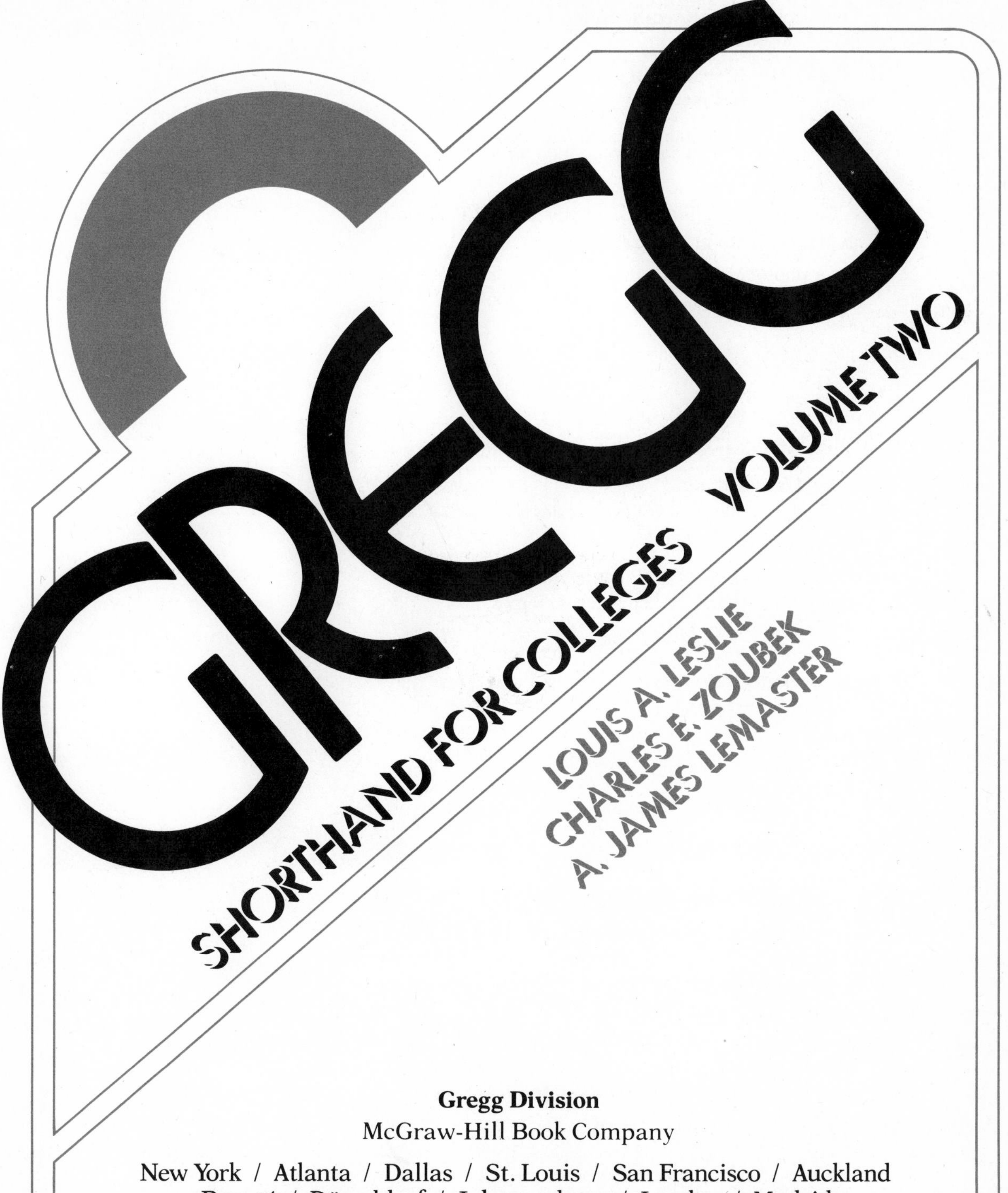

Gregg Division
McGraw-Hill Book Company

New York / Atlanta / Dallas / St. Louis / San Francisco / Auckland
Bogotá / Düsseldorf / Johannesburg / London / Madrid
Mexico / Montreal / New Delhi / Panama / Paris / São Paulo
Singapore / Sydney / Tokyo / Toronto

This text was prepared by members of the Gregg Shorthand staff:

Editorial: Barbara J. Hann, Diana M. Johnson, Albert H. Rihner

Production: Jerome P. Edelman, Mary C. Buchanan, Michael S. Valentine

Art & Design Coordinators: Tracy A. Glasner, Karen T. Mino

Designer: A Good Thing Inc.

Cover photo: Martin Bough/Studios Inc.

Chapter photos: Ken Karp

Library of Congress Cataloging in Publication Data

Leslie, Louis A. date.

Gregg shorthand for colleges, series 90.

Includes index.

1. Shorthand–Gregg. I. Zoubek, Charles E., date. joint author. II. Lemaster, A. James, joint author. III. Title.

Z56.2.G7L48 1980 653'.427 79-12060

ISBN 0-07-037749-9 (v. 1)

ISBN 0-07-037754-5 (v. 2)

Gregg Shorthand for Colleges,

Volume Two, Series 90

2 3 4 5 6 7 8 9 0 DODO 8 8 7 6 5 4 3 2 1 0

Preface

In *Gregg Shorthand for Colleges, Volume One, Series 90,* all the word-building principles of Gregg Shorthand were introduced. In addition, many nonshorthand elements were included. *Volume Two,* as its title indicates, is designed to be used following *Volume One.* The reading level of *Volume Two* is 7-8.

Objectives

Volume Two has the following major objectives:

1 To review the principles of Gregg Shorthand.

2 To develop the students' ability to construct outlines for unfamiliar words under the stress of dictation.

3 To develop the students' dictation speed to the highest point possible.

4 To extend the students' knowledge of the basic nonshorthand elements of transcription.

5 To give the students the ability to transcribe mailable correspondence.

6 To teach the students to handle simple problems of office-style dictation.

Organization

Volume Two is organized into 16 chapters, each containing 5 lessons, for a total of 80 lessons. Each lesson consists of 3 parts:

☐ Developing Word-Building or Phrasing Power

☐ Building Transcription Skills

☐ Reading and Writing Practice

Developing Word-Building or Phrasing Power

The five lessons comprising each of the 16 chapters contain a carefully planned cycle of word-building or phrasing drills that provide a quick, intensive recall in list form of the important elements of Gregg Shorthand.

The first lesson in each chapter concentrates on brief forms. It contains a chart of 36 brief forms and derivatives. The brief forms of the system are reviewed thoroughly. The first letter in the Reading and Writing Practice of each first lesson contains many brief forms.

The second lesson in each chapter concentrates on Useful Business-Letter Phrases. The first letter in the Reading and Writing Practice of each second lesson is a letter containing a high concentration of useful phrases. In addition, each second lesson contains a drill on cities, states, and other geographical expressions.

The third lesson in each chapter is devoted to shorthand Word Families. These shorthand Word Families enable the students to take advantage of a very effective aid in word building—analogy. Shorthand Word Families are an important factor in helping the students construct outlines for unfamiliar words.

The fourth lesson in each chapter is devoted to an intensive drill on Word Beginnings and Endings. Through these drills, the students review the word beginnings and endings of the system.

The fifth lesson in each chapter contains a Shorthand Vocabulary Builder that provides drills on major principles of Gregg Shorthand—blends, vowel combinations, omission of vowels, and so on.

Building Transcription Skills

Transcription teachers agree that one of the basic problems in shorthand classes is the difficulty that students have in handling the mechanics of the English language. Business executives frequently comment that stenographers cannot spell, cannot punctuate, and have no grasp of correct grammar.

To cope with this basic problem, a number of transcription skill-building features were introduced in *Volume One*. In *Volume Two* the emphasis on the mechanics of the English language has been intensified, beginning with the first lesson. *Volume Two* contains the following transcription skill-building features.

Spelling

Two types of spelling exercises are provided:

Marginal Reminders Words have been selected from the Reading and Writing Practice for special spelling attention. These words are printed in a second color in the shorthand and appear in type, correctly syllabicated, in the margins of the shorthand.

Spelling Families Each spelling family contains a list of words that present common spelling problems—for example, words ending in *-cial, -tial; -ance, -ence;* and so on.

Punctuation

In *Volume One* the students studied nine of the most frequent uses of the comma. In *Volume Two* they continue to drill on those uses of the comma. In addition, they study other important punctuation marks, including the semicolon, the hyphen, and the apostrophe.

To test the students' grasp of the punctuation rules studied, each lesson (except the fifth lesson in each chapter) contains a Transcription Quiz in which the students must supply all internal punctuation. The Transcription Quiz also teaches the students to supply from context words that have been omitted in the shorthand.

Vocabulary Development

Three types of drills are provided to help the students expand their vocabulary and develop their understanding of words:

Business Vocabulary Builders In each lesson the students study several words or expressions, selected from the Reading and Writing Practice, with which they may not be familiar. Each word or expression is briefly defined as it is used in the lesson.

Similar-Words Drills The Similar-Words Drills make the students aware of groups of words that sound alike or almost alike—words that are responsible for many transcription errors. Examples of similar words are *farther, further* and *thought, though, through.* In *Volume Two* there are eleven groups of similar words.

Common Prefixes An effective device to aid the students increase their understanding of words is the study of common prefixes. In *Volume Two* the students study six common prefixes.

Grammar Checkups

Six lessons contain drills dealing with common errors in grammar that the unwary stenographer often makes.

Typing Style Studies

In the Typing Style Studies the students are taught how to transcribe dates, street addresses, amounts of money, times of day, and so on. In Lessons 41 and 52 the students are taught how to type short and average-length letters; in Lesson 56 the students are taught how to type memorandums.

Introductory Transcription

Beginning with Lesson 41 the students are introduced step by step to elementary transcription. The *Instructor's Handbook for Gregg Shorthand for Colleges, Volume Two, Series 90,* includes letters for the students to transcribe in letter form.

Office-Style Dictation

In Chapters 13 through 16 the students learn how to handle some of the office-style dictation problems they will meet when they take dictation on the job—insertions, deletions, and changes during dictation. Each problem is explained and illustrated.

Reading and Writing Practice

An extremely important part of a students' practice program is the reading and copying of large quantities of well-written shorthand. This reading and copying provides a constant, automatic review of the principles of the system. In addition, it stocks the students' minds with the shapes of individual shorthand characters and with the correct joinings of characters so that they can effectively construct a shorthand outline for any word that is dictated.

Volume Two contains thousands of words of practice material on business letters and on interesting, informative articles. All of the practice material in this edition is new.

The publishers are confident that *Gregg Shorthand for Colleges, Volume Two, Series 90,* will enable the teacher to do an even more effective job of training accurate and rapid transcribers.

The Publishers

CONTENTS

You are now beginning the second, and very important, phase of your shorthand program — the development of shorthand speed. Take a few moments to review what you have already accomplished. Upon completion of *Gregg Shorthand for Colleges, Volume One, Series 90,* you have learned the alphabet of Gregg Shorthand; consequently, you can construct a legible outline for any word in the English language. You have also learned many useful abbreviating devices such as brief forms, word beginnings and endings, and phrases that will help you write shorthand easily and quickly. In addition, you have improved your command of the nonshorthand elements of transcription — spelling, punctuation, word usage, and grammar.

You now have an excellent foundation for the work ahead — developing your ability to take dictation and transcribe accurately on the typewriter. With this foundation, you will experience the thrill of watching your shorthand speed grow and your ability to handle the mechanics of the English language improve daily.

Your Practice Program—Outside of Class

Your assignments outside of class will consist largely of reading and copying well-written shorthand from *Gregg Shorthand for Colleges, Volume Two, Series 90*. Reading and copying shorthand will help your shorthand speed develop rapidly. This part of your practice program should be easy and pleasant; you have no new shorthand to learn.

To get the most from your out-of-class practice, follow these suggestions:

Read the drills at the beginning of each lesson. Cover the key as you read. The moment you cannot read an outline, refer to the key.

Read and study the material in the Building Transcription Skills section.

Read and copy the Reading and Writing Practice in each lesson in this way:

1 Read a letter or article from the shorthand. When you cannot read an outline, spell the shorthand characters in it; this spelling will often give you the meaning. If it does not, refer to your transcript. If you do not have a transcript, make a note of the outline you cannot read. Do not spend more than a few seconds trying to decipher an outline. The next day in class find out the meaning of the outline.

2 After you have read the material from the shorthand, make a shorthand copy of it in your notebook. Read a convenient group of words—aloud if possible—and then write that group in your notebook. Write as rapidly as you can, but be sure that what you write is legible. (You may be called on to read from your shorthand notes in class.)

3 Read what you have written.

4 Complete the corresponding lesson in the *Workbook for Gregg Shorthand for Colleges, Volume Two, Series 90,* if you have one.

Your Practice Program—in Class

Most of your time in class will be devoted to taking dictation at constantly increasing speeds. Your instructor will see that you get the proper kind of dictation at the proper speeds so that your skill will increase easily and rapidly.

1
SALES

COMMA BRUSHUP

As you learned in *Gregg Shorthand for Colleges, Volume One, Series 90*, secretaries must be able to punctuate correctly if they are to turn out letters that their employers will have no hesitation in signing. In *Volume One* you studied nine of the simpler uses of the comma as they occurred in the Reading and Writing Practice.

In *Gregg Shorthand for Colleges, Volume Two, Series 90*, you will take up new and more advanced points of punctuation. Before you are introduced to these new points, however, you will "brush up" on the uses of the comma that you studied in *Volume One*. In Chapter 1 of *Volume Two* you will review five of those uses; in Chapter 2, the remaining four.

PRACTICE PROCEDURES

To be sure that you get the greatest benefit from your study of punctuation and spelling in each Reading and Writing Practice, follow these suggestions:

1 Read carefully each punctuation rule and the examples.

2 Continue to read each Reading and Writing Practice as you have always done.

3 Each time you see a circled comma, note the reason for its use, which is indicated directly above it.

4 As you copy the Reading and Writing Practice, insert the commas in your shorthand notes, encircling them.

, parenthetical

In order to make the meaning clearer, a writer sometimes inserts a comment or an explanation that could be omitted without changing the meaning of the sentence. These added comments and explanations are called *parenthetical* and are separated from the rest of the sentence by commas.

If the parenthetical word or expression occurs at the end of a sentence, only one comma is needed.

His main responsibility, of course, *is to his family.*

We are sure, Mrs. Withers, *that you will like our new store.*

We will send your order by return mail, of course.

Each time a parenthetical expression occurs in the Reading and Writing Practice, it will be indicated as shown in the margin:

par

(,)

, apposition

Sometimes a writer mentions a person or thing and then, in order to make the meaning perfectly clear, says the same thing again in different words. This added explanation is known as an expression in *apposition.*

An expression in apposition is set off by two commas, except at the end of a sentence, when only one comma is necessary.

Our consultant, Miss Nancy Brown, *will visit your store soon.*

The conference will be held on Tuesday, September 9, *at the Hotel Lexington.*

This is my associate, Pedro Suarez.

Each time an expression in apposition occurs in the Reading and Writing Practice, it will be indicated as shown in the margin:

ap

(,)

, series

When the last member of a series of three or more items is preceded by *and, or,* or *nor,* place a comma before the conjunction as well as between the other items.

Miss Taylor is a worker of initiative, imagination, and dedication.

The convention is scheduled for December 16, 17, and 18.

My responsibilities are typing letters, filing correspondence, and answering the telephone.

Each time a series occurs in the Reading and Writing Practice, it will be indicated as shown in the margin:

ser ,

, conjunction

A comma is used to separate two independent clauses that are joined by a conjunction.

I wrote to him several weeks ago, but *I have not received a reply.*

He enjoyed traveling in Europe, and *he plans to return there in the future.*

Each time this use of the comma occurs in the Reading and Writing Practice, it will be indicated as shown in the margin:

conj ,

, and omitted

When two or more adjectives modify the same noun, they are separated by commas.

Don gave a thorough, convincing *argument.*

However, the comma is not used if the first adjective modifies the combined idea of the second adjective plus the noun.

Kay bought a beautiful red *car.*

Each time this use of the comma occurs in the Reading and Writing Practice, it will be indicated as shown in the margin:

and o ,

Developing Word-Building Power

1 Brief Forms The following chart contains 36 brief forms. You have practiced these brief forms many times, and you should be able to read them rapidly. First read each line from left to right; then read each line from right to left. Finally, read down each column.

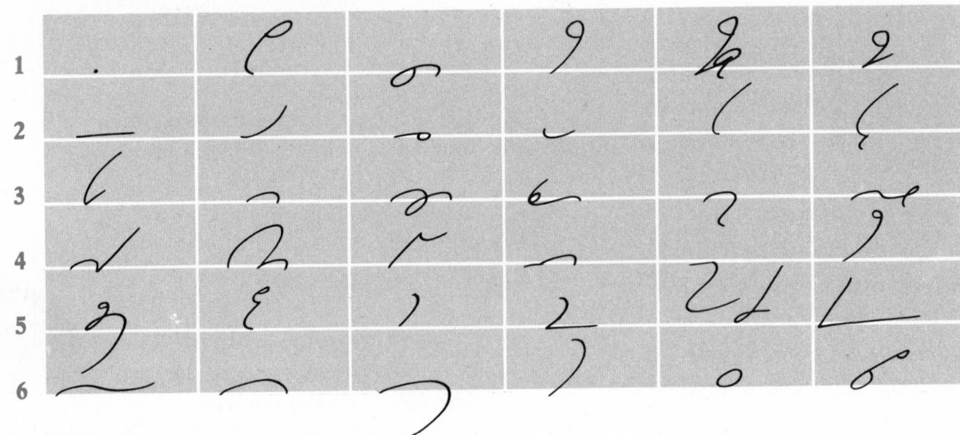

1 A-an, about, acknowledge, advantage, advertise, after.
2 Am, and, any, are-our-hour, be-by, business.
3 But, can, character, circular, company, correspond-correspondence.
4 Could, difficult, doctor, enclose, envelope, ever-every.
5 Executive, experience, for, from, general, gentlemen.
6 Glad, good, govern, have, I, idea.

Building Transcription Skills

2 Business Vocabulary Builder The better command you have of the English language, the more efficient a secretary you will be. In each lesson a Business Vocabulary Builder will help you to continue to expand your language skills.

Study each Business Vocabulary Builder before you begin your work on the Reading and Writing Practice of each lesson.

Business Vocabulary Builder	**apparel**	Clothing.
	deleted	Eliminated; erased.
	metrics	A standard of measurement.
	reimburse	To pay back.

Reading and Writing Practice

3 Brief-Form Letter The following letter contains many brief forms and derivatives. Read and copy it several times.

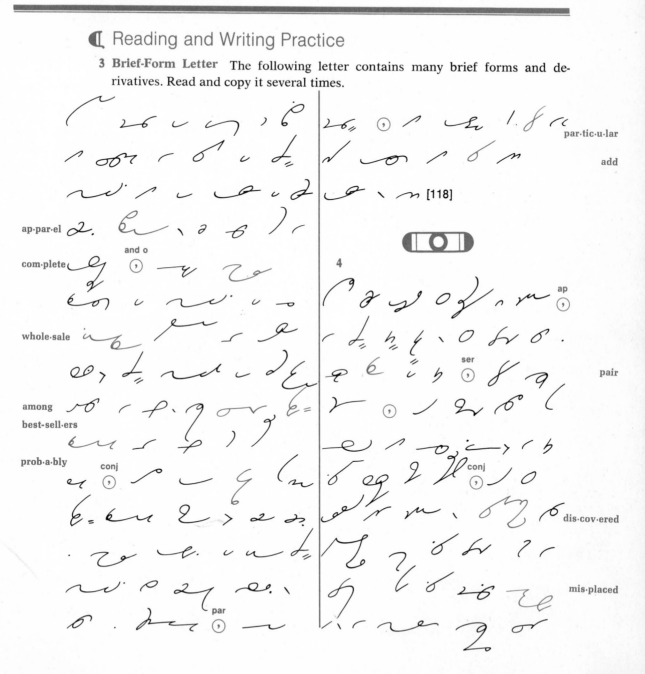

ap·par·el

and o

com·plete

whole·sale

ser

among

best-sell·ers

prob·a·bly

conj

par

par·tic·u·lar

add

[118]

4

ap

pair

conj

dis·cov·ered

mis·placed

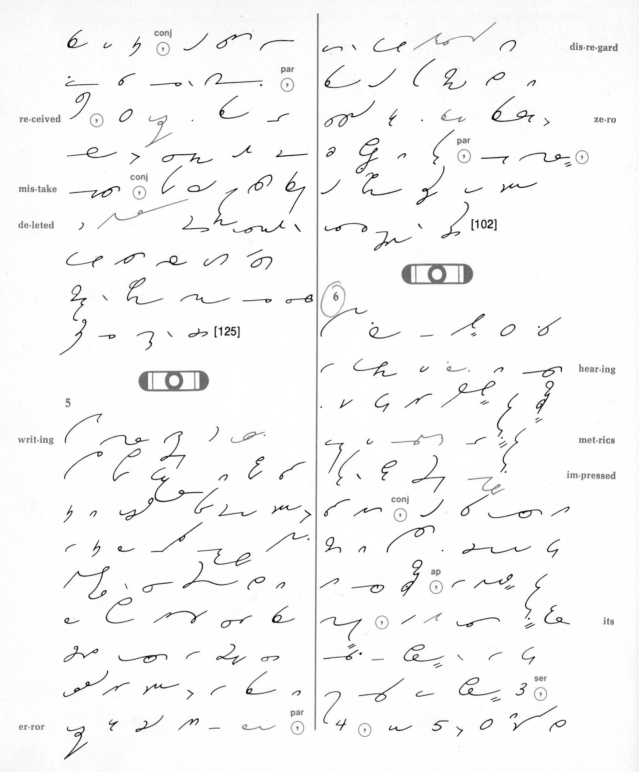

conj

par

re·ceived

mis·take

conj

de·leted

[125]

5

writ·ing

er·ror

par

dis·re·gard

ze·ro

par

[102]

6

hear·ing

met·rics

im·pressed

conj

ap

its

ser

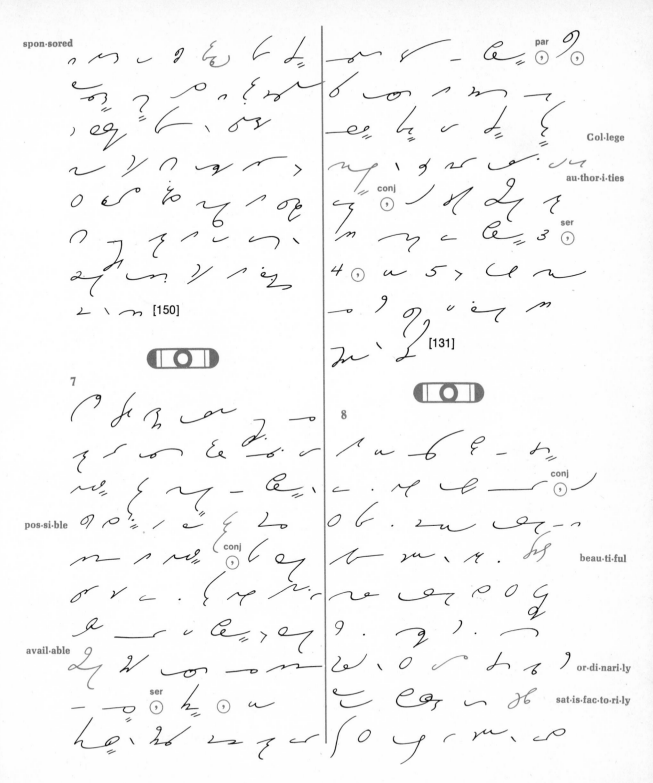

spon·sored

par

Col·lege

au·thor·i·ties

conj

ser

[150]

[131]

7

8

pos·si·ble

conj

conj

beau·ti·ful

avail·able

or·di·nari·ly

sat·is·fac·to·ri·ly

ser

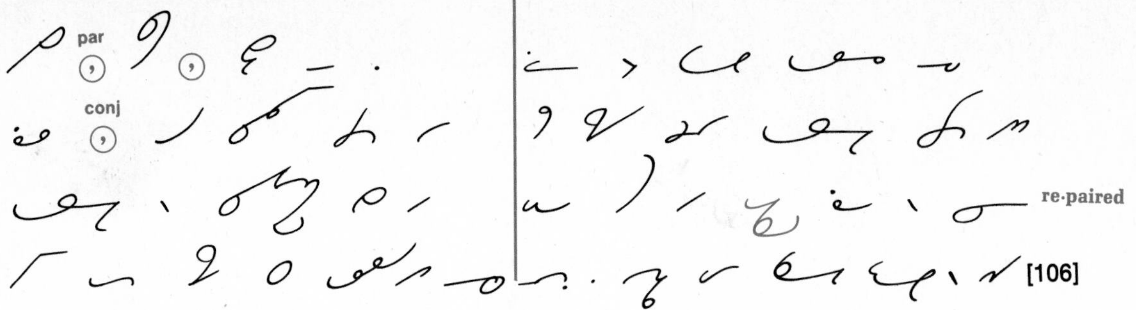

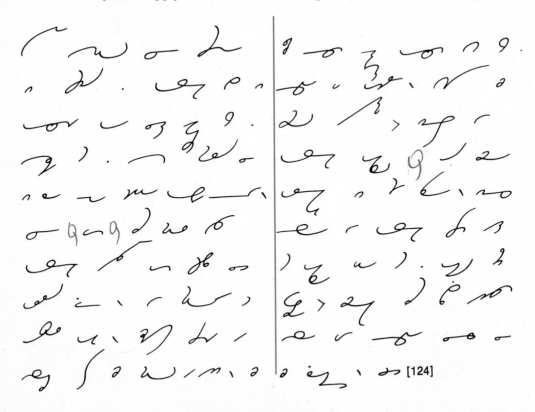

9 Transcription Quiz You are already familiar with the Transcription Quiz from your work in *Volume One.* The Transcription Quiz gives you an opportunity to see how well you can apply the comma rules you have studied.

In Chapters 1 and 2 of *Volume Two,* the Transcription Quiz will contain the same type of problems as those in *Volume One.* In later chapters, as new points of punctuation are introduced, the quizzes will become more advanced.

As you read the letter, decide what punctuation should be used. Make a shorthand copy of it, and insert the correct punctuation marks in the proper places in your notes.

For you to supply: 3 commas—2 commas parenthetical, 1 comma conjunction.

[124]

Building Phrasing Skill

1 **Useful Business-Letter Phrases** Below are a number of phrases that are used frequently in business correspondence. Can you read the entire list in 40 seconds?

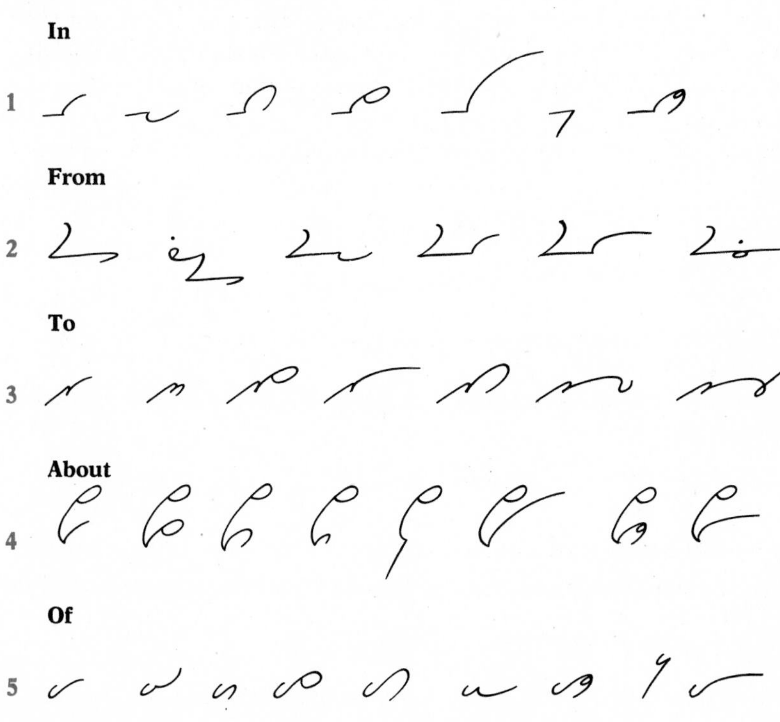

1 In the, in our, in this, in that, in time, in which, in these.
2 From you, hear from you, from our, from the, from them, from him.
3 To the, to you, to that, to them, to this, to go, to get.
4 About the, about that, about this, about your, about which, about time, about these, about them.
5 Of the, of their, of your, of that, of this, of our, of these, of which, of them.

2 Geographical Expressions

1 Boston, Des Moines, Miami, Indianapolis, Minneapolis, St. Paul, Philadelphia.
2 Massachusetts, Iowa, Florida, Indiana, Minnesota, Ohio, Pennsylvania.

Building Transcription Skills

3 SPELLING FAMILIES ● ie, ei

One of the most troublesome letter combinations in the English language is the *ie, ei* pair. A few basic rules cover most of the words.

□ 1 *i* comes before *e*:	con•ve•nient	chief	friend
	niece	piece	be•lieve
□ 2 Except:			
(a) after *c*	re•ceive	de•ceit	re•ceipt
(b) when the combination has the sound of *a*			
	eight	heir	neigh•bor

However, there are some exceptions:

ei•ther   ef•fi•cient   lei•sure

Watch for the *ie, ei* combinations in the Reading and Writing Practice.

4 Business Vocabulary Builder

complement To fill; to make complete.
elegant Of a high quality; splendid.
sturdy Firm; strong.
liquidation The determination and disposition of assets in order to pay debts.

Reading and Writing Practice

5 Phrase Letter The following letter contains many useful phrases. Read it first, then copy it several times.

ap·peal

me·chan·i·cal

ser

your·self [104]

quite

conj

ex·cept

conj

gar·ment

par

[103]

6

sweat·er

niece

ap

cloth·ing

conj

7

neigh·bor·hood

and o

fur·ni·ture

swiv·el

pos·ture

ser

ex·ec·u·tive

com·ple·ment

suite

[130]

8

con·fer·ence

conj

de·signed

stur·dy

conj

ser·vice·able

too

conj

trade-in

[136]

9

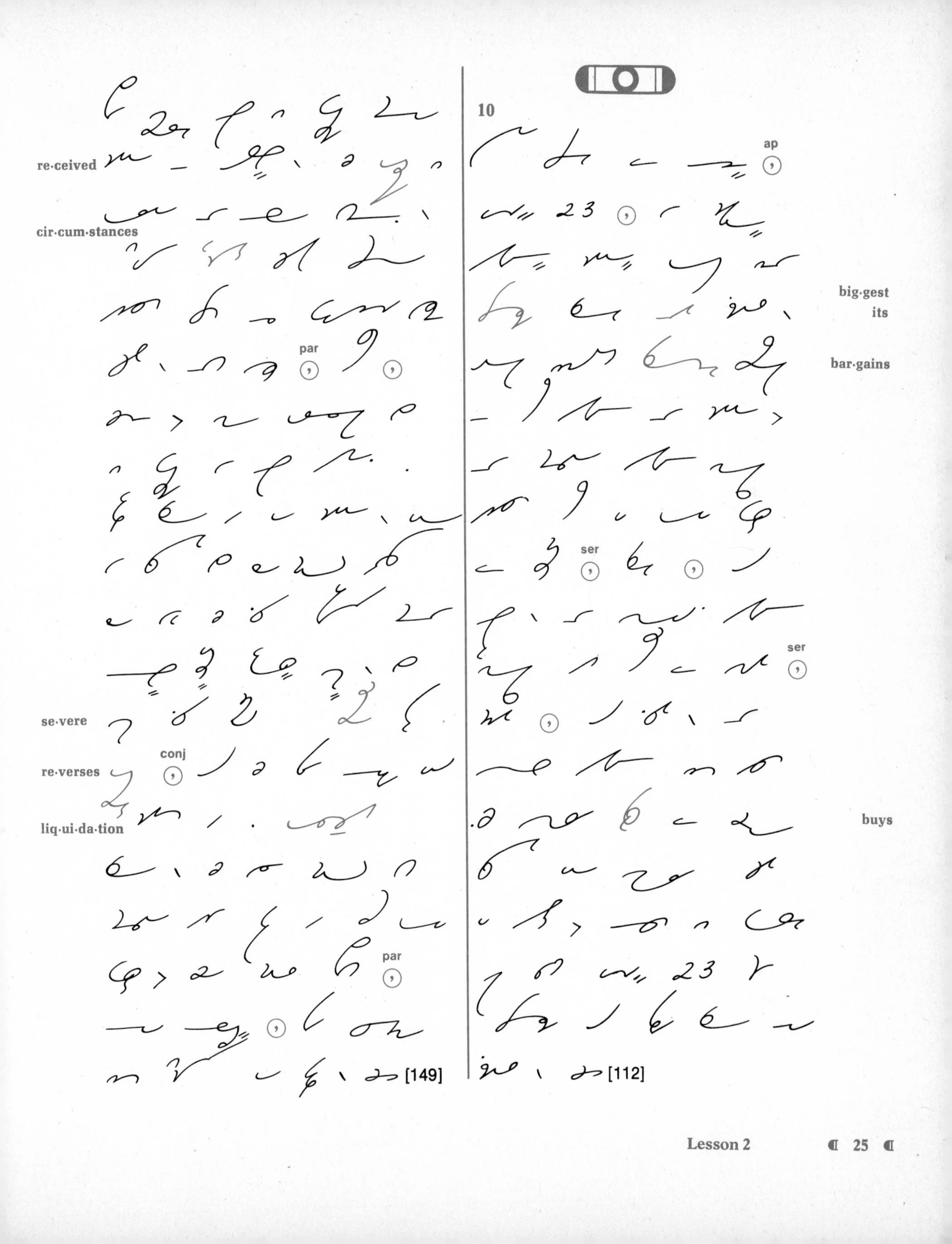

re·ceived

cir·cum·stances

par

se·vere

conj

re·verses

liq·ui·da·tion

par

[149]

10

ap

23

big·gest
its

bar·gains

ser

ser

buys

23

[112]

11 Transcription Quiz For you to supply: 6 commas—2 commas apposition, 2 commas series, 2 commas parenthetical.

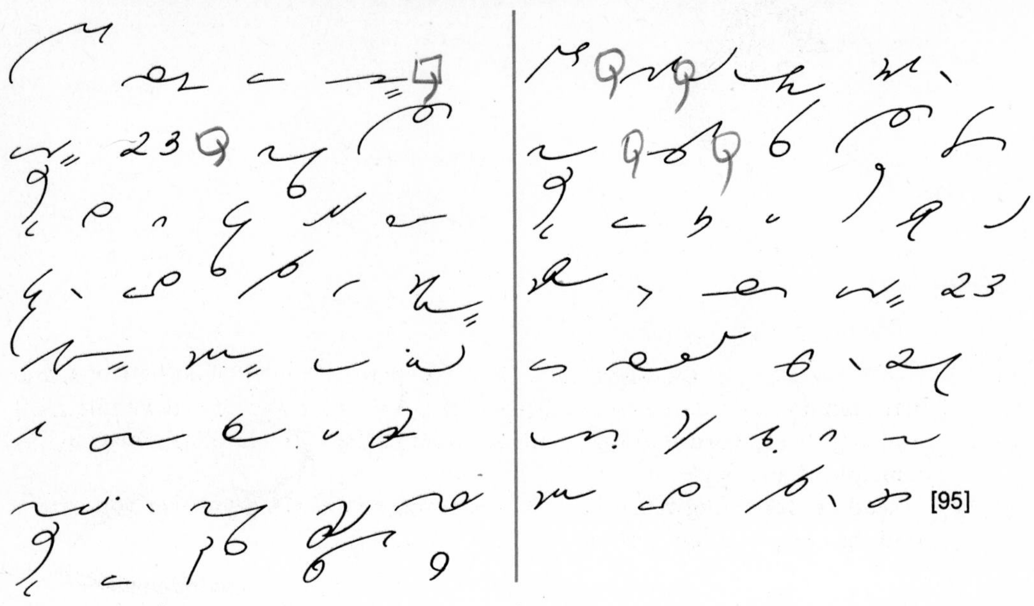

A secretary should never mail a letter that is less than perfect. An accurate, attractive, and neatly typed letter tells the reader that the company is concerned about quality in every detail.

Developing Word-Building Power

1 **Word Families** In the third lesson of each chapter you will find lists of words that contain a similar element. These elements are called Word Families. By studying these Word Families you will learn to construct similar words by the principle of analogy.

Read the following Word Families, referring to the key whenever you cannot read the word in a few seconds.

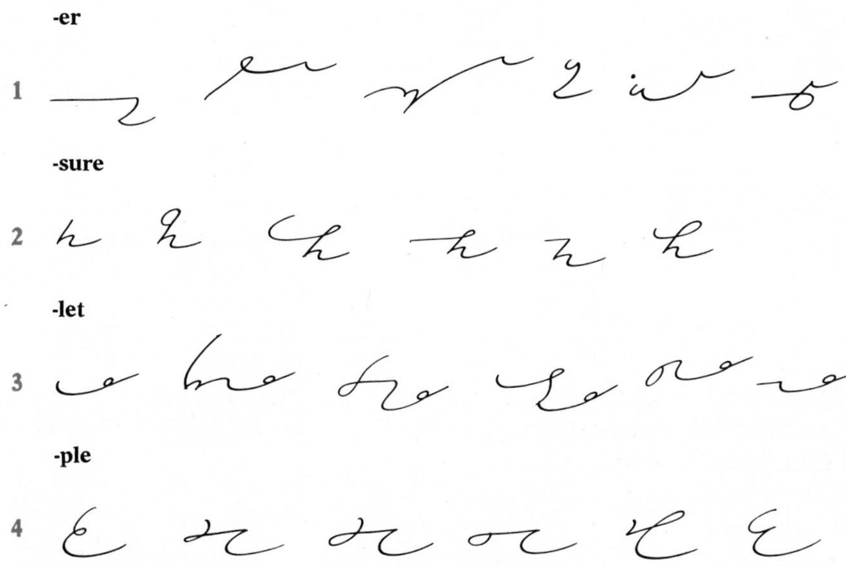

1 Manufacturer, dealer, customer, offer, holder, matter.
2 Sure, assure, pleasure, measure, ensure, reassure.
3 Let, booklet, pamphlet, leaflet, outlet, inlet.
4 People, simple, sample, ample, staple, purple.

Building Transcription Skills

2 **GRAMMAR CHECKUP ● pronouns**

A pronoun must agree with its antecedent in person, number, and gender.

The general clothing store *is closing* its *doors.*
All customers *can save money on* their *purchases.*
Each person *must complete* his or her *own application.*

Business Vocabulary Builder

3 **wardrobe** A collection of clothes.
previous Earlier; before.
open stock Merchandise available on an individual basis; not sold as a set.

Reading and Writing Practice

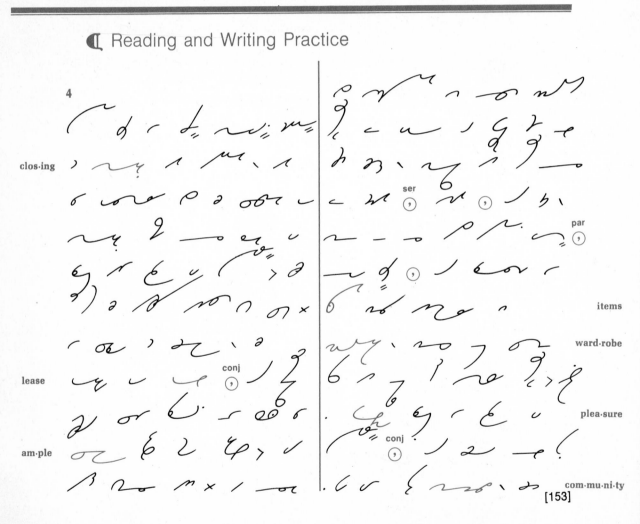

4

clos·ing

ser

par

items

ward·robe

lease

conj

plea·sure

am·ple

conj

com·mu·ni·ty

[153]

5

its

conj

sales·peo·ple

ser

pre·vi·ous

simply

ser

per·son·al

[104]

6

choos·ing

and o

shop·ping

pro·cess·ing

conj

par

us·ing

ma·jor

[112]

7

ser

pot·tery

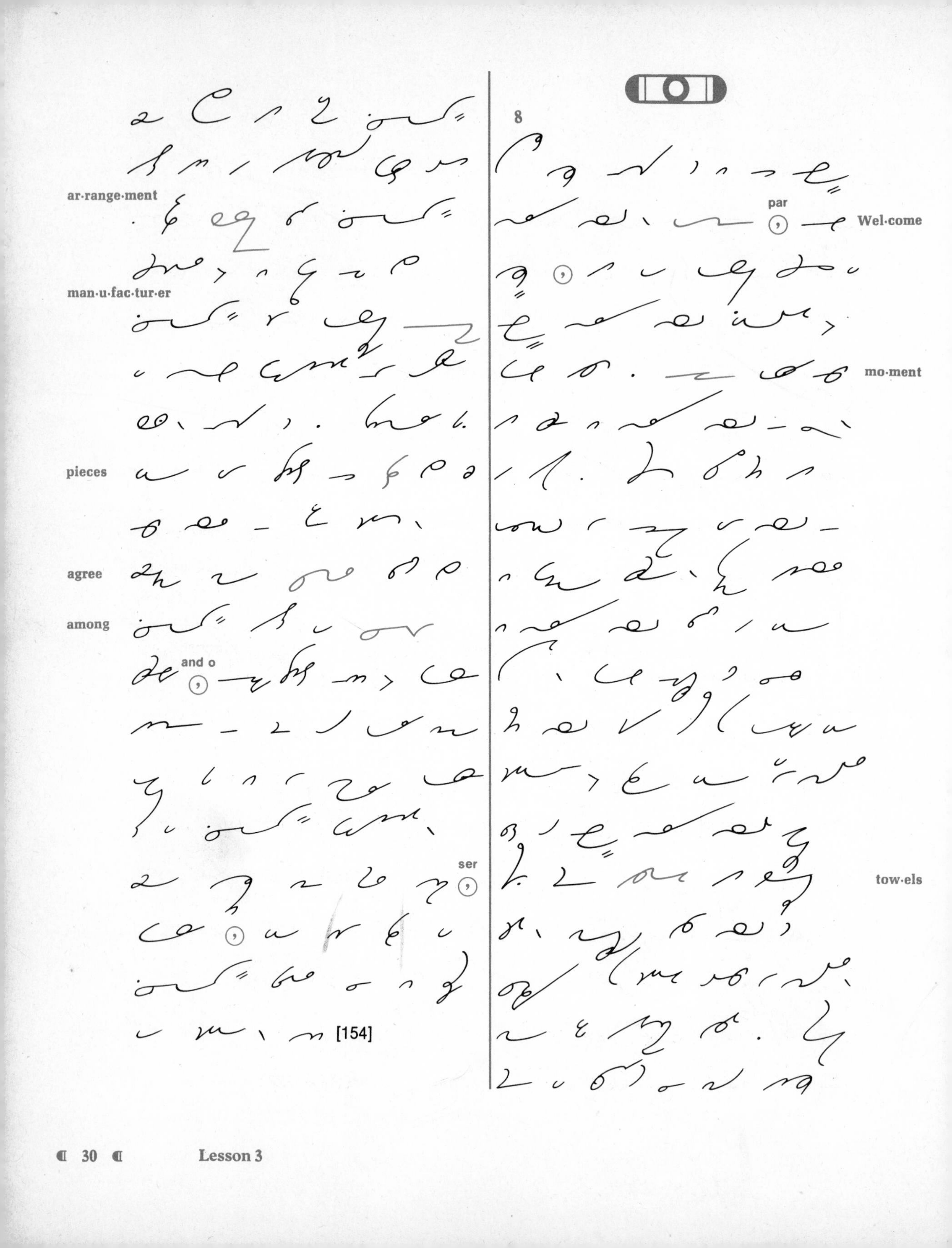

ar·range·ment

man·u·fac·tur·er

pieces

agree

among

and o

ser

[154]

8

par

Wel·come

mo·ment

tow·els

con·fi·dence

[159]

9

par

conj

pro·cess

par

mean·time

[87]

10 Transcription Quiz For you to supply: 3 commas—2 commas parenthetical, 1 comma conjunction.

[114]

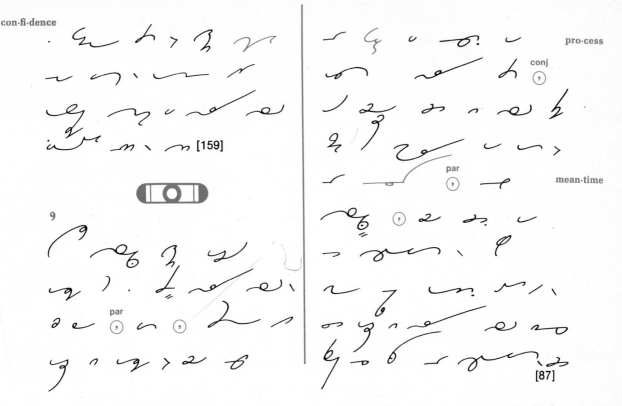

Developing Word-Building Power

1 Word Beginnings and Endings

Re-

1

De-

2

-ing

3

-ly

4

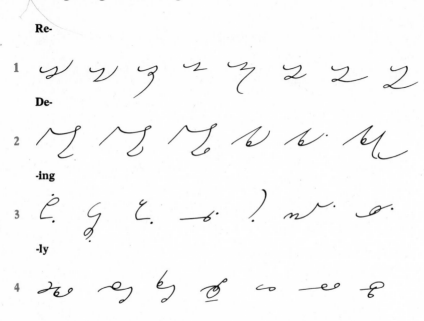

1 Recent, refund, receive, reason, reasonable, refer, refill, reveal.
2 Deliver, delivered, delivery, depend, depending, dependability.
3 Happening, purchasing, opening, meeting, having, wondering, writing.
4 Sincerely, carefully, cheerfully, quietly, only, merely, nicely.

Building Transcription Skills

2 SIMILAR-WORDS DRILL

In *Gregg Shorthand for Colleges, Volume Two, Series 90,* you will continue to study similar words—words that sound alike and words that sound or look *almost* alike. Sometimes these words are mistranscribed by stenographers.

Study each definition carefully. As you read the Reading and Writing Practice, watch for the words.

SIMILAR-WORDS DRILL ● advice, advise

advice *(noun)* Recommendation; suggestion; guidance.

Here is some good *advice* for you.

advise *(verb)* To guide; to suggest; to inform.

Please *advise* me on the matter.

3 Business Vocabulary Builder

imperfection Flaw; blemish.

characteristic A distinguishing trait or quality.

varying Changing.

Reading and Writing Practice

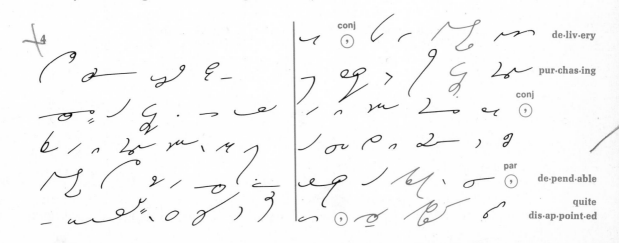

4

conj

de·liv·ery

pur·chas·ing

conj

par

de·pend·able

quite

dis·ap·point·ed

def·i·nite

[115]

5

brief

suede

im·per·fec·tion

sleeves

ad·vise

[81]

6

ad·vis·ing

ap·pears

char·ac·ter·is·tic

vary·ing

grain

al·most

par

ser

in·sure

cheer·ful·ly

[134]

7

ad·vice

ser

rea·son·able

their

conj

re·ceive

[128]

8

ap

conj

ad·vice

ex·cep·tion

life·time

prac·ti·cal·ly

ser

kitch·en

un·beat·able

par

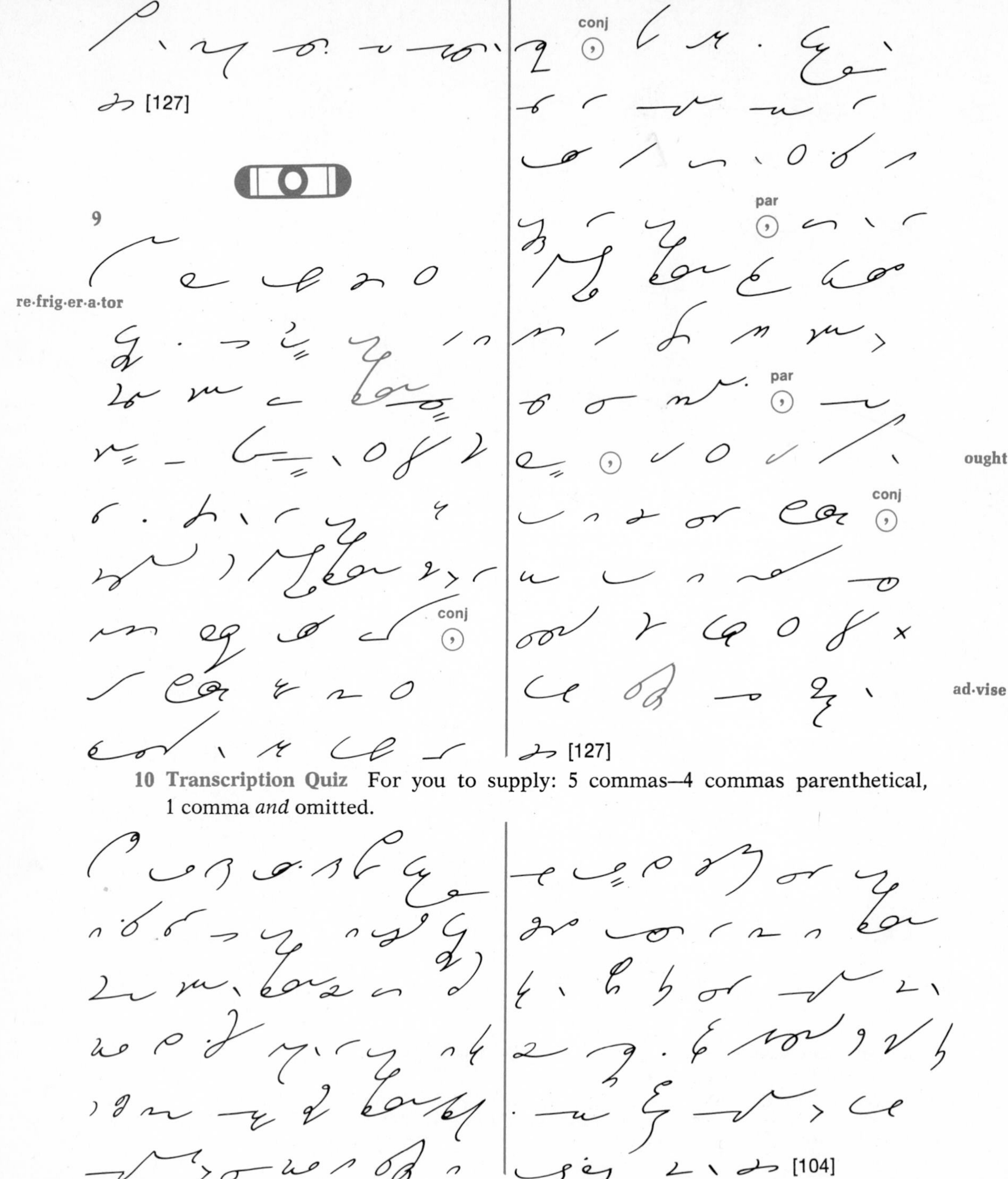

10 Transcription Quiz For you to supply: 5 commas—4 commas parenthetical, 1 comma *and* omitted.

Developing Word-Building Power

1 Shorthand Vocabulary Builder

Ng

1

Ngk

2

Mt

3

Md

4

Nd

5

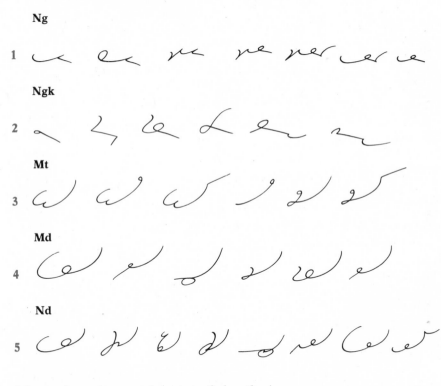

1 Long, along, strong, string, strength, length, ring.
2 Ink, function, frank, bank, tanker, uncle.
3 Prompt, promptly, prompted, empty, exempt, exempted.
4 Blamed, deemed, named, seemed, framed, termed.
5 Planned, found, opened, find, mind, trend, blend, render.

Building Transcription Skills

2 Business Vocabulary Builder

misfortune Bad luck.

surly Irritable; sullen.

vital Important; essential.

Reading and Writing Practice

3 The Art of Selling

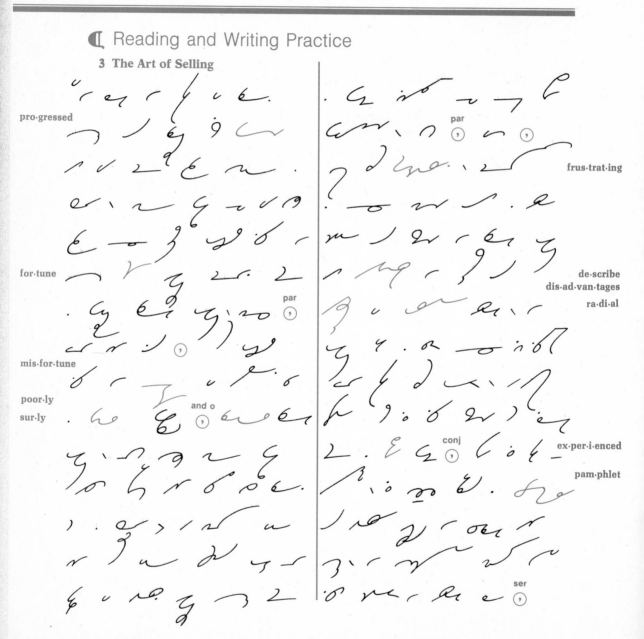

pro·gressed

for·tune

par

mis·for·tune

poor·ly

sur·ly

and o

par

frus·trat·ing

de·scribe

dis·ad·van·tages

ra·di·al

conj

ex·per·i·enced

pam·phlet

ser

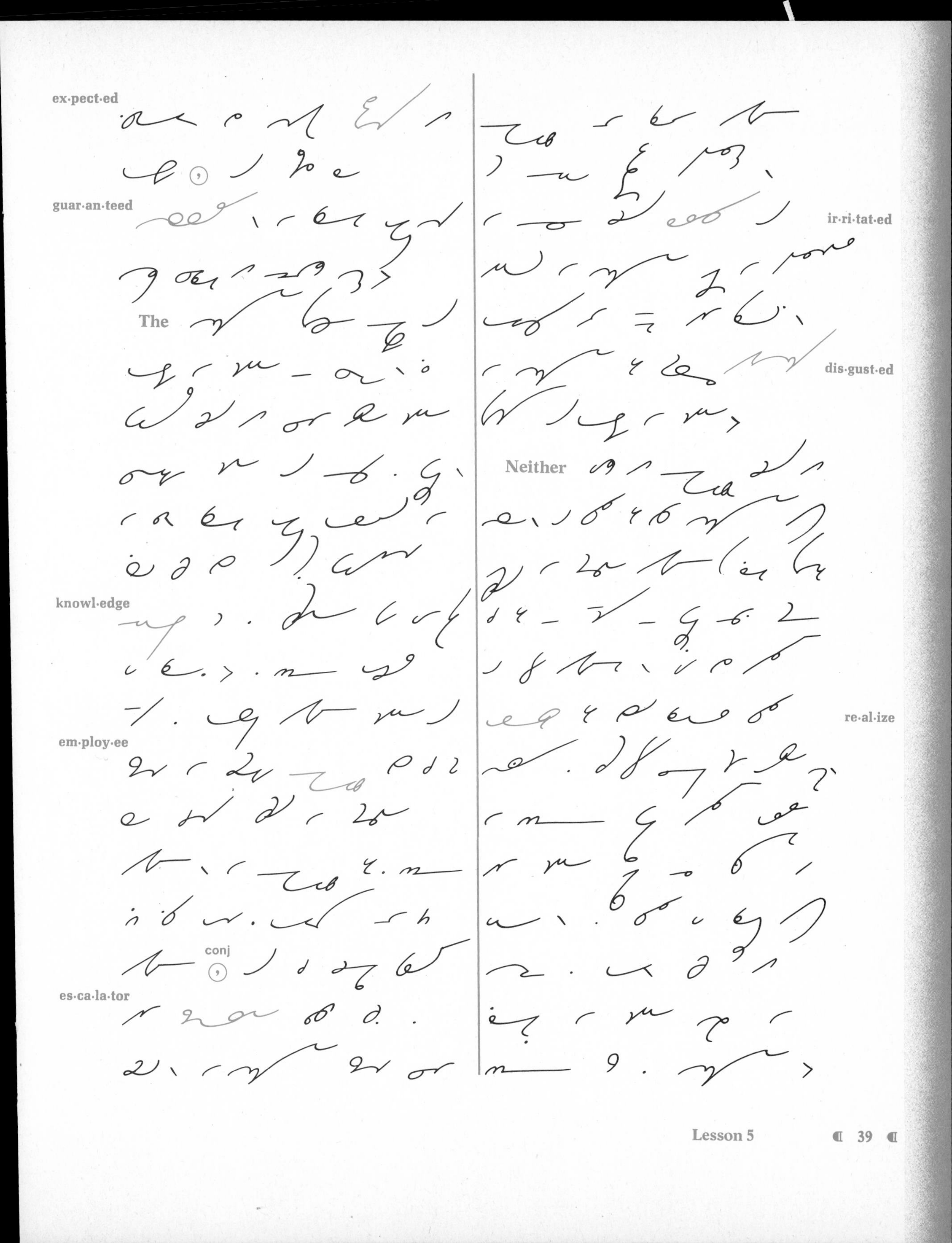

ex·pect·ed

guar·an·teed

The

knowl·edge

em·ploy·ee

conj

es·ca·la·tor

ir·ri·tat·ed

dis·gust·ed

Neither

re·al·ize

paid

ag·gres·sive

clev·er

par

conj

po·ten·tial

A few

Al·though

ob·vi·ous

me·chan·ic

lose

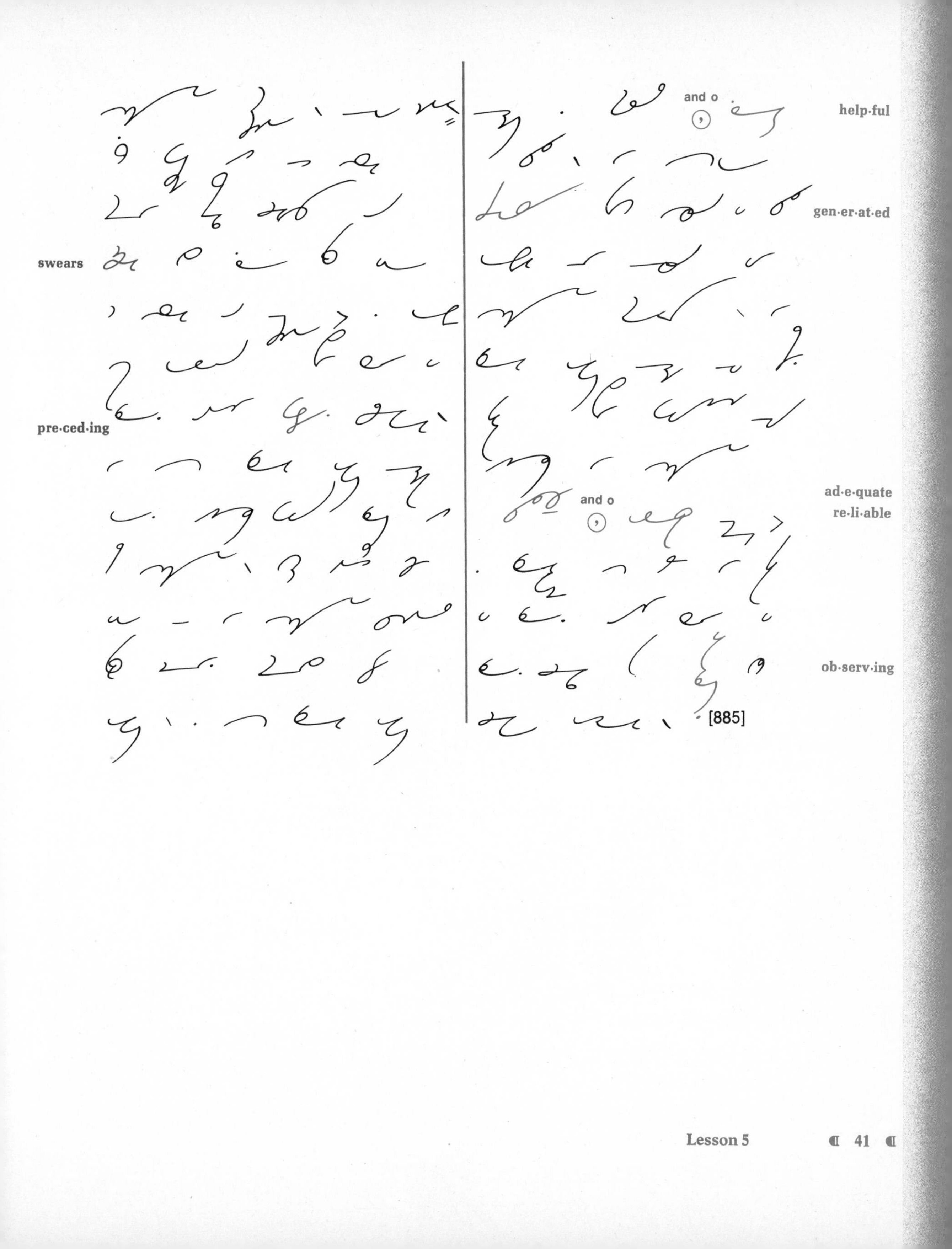

and o

help·ful

gen·er·at·ed

swears

pre·ced·ing

and o

ad·e·quate
re·li·able

ob·serv·ing

[885]

2
EDUCATION

COMMA BRUSHUP (Concluded)

Introductory Commas

In Chapter 2 you will review the remaining four uses of the comma that you studied in *Volume One*—commas with introductory expressions. Introductory commas will be treated under the four headings given below. Below each heading is the indication that will appear in the shorthand of the Reading and Writing Practice for that use of the comma.

, when clause
when
(,)

, if clause
if
(,)

, as clause
as
(,)

, introductory
intro
(,)

Introductory dependent clauses beginning with words other than *when, as,* and *if* will be classified as "introductory."

When we hear from you, *we will send your order.*

As you probably know, *I have been transferred.*

If you want me to do the work, *please let me know.*

Until we receive the equipment, *we will not be able to do the work.*

When the main clause comes first, however, no comma is usually necessary between the main clause and the dependent clause.

We will not be able to do the work *until we receive the equipment.*

Please let me know *if you want me to do the work.*

A comma is also required after introductory words and explanatory expressions such as *frankly, consequently, on the contrary,* and *for instance.*

Frankly, *I am disappointed.*

On the contrary, *I do not believe he is right.*

Developing Word-Building Power

1 Brief Forms Can you read these brief forms in 35 seconds or less?

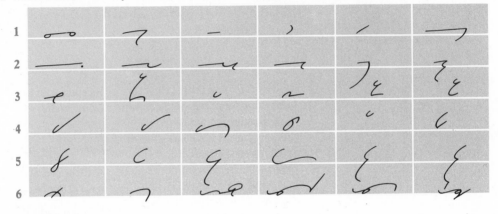

1 Immediate, important-importance, in-not, is-his, it-at, manufacture.
2 Morning, Mr., Mrs., Ms., never, newspaper.
3 Next, object, of, one (won), opinion, opportunity.
4 Order, ordinary, organization, out, over, part.
5 Particular, present, probable, progress, public, publish-publication.
6 Quantity, question, recognize, regard, regular, request.

Building Transcription Skills

2 Business Vocabulary Builder

avail *(noun)* Advantage; use.
brochure A small pamphlet; a booklet.
process *(verb)* To perform a series of actions.
verify To confirm.

Reading and Writing Practice

3 Brief-Form Letter

tried

avail

Speak·ing

plan·ning

op·por·tu·ni·ty

if

intro

conj

[149]

fur·ther

4

grad·u·a·tion

if

tech·ni·cal

choose

and o

ex·cit·ing

ser

me·chan·i·cal

if

[115]

5

grad·u·ate

intro

mi·nor

dis·crep·an·cy

trans·ferred

when

en·rolled

conj

if

cur·rent

[137]

6

pur·sue

Ap·par·ent·ly

intro

if

ver·i·fy

res·o·lu·tion

intro

[120]

7

in·com·plete

cleared

ap

reg·is·trar

if

[77]

8

de·scrib·ing

conj

fur·ther

intro

col·lege

par

par

conj

coun·sel·ors

par

re·ceiv·ing

[204]

9 Transcription Quiz For you to supply: 5 commas—2 commas parenthetical, 2 commas *if* clause, 1 comma conjunction.

[120]

Building Phrasing Skill

1 Useful Business-Letter Phrases The following groups contain a number of phrases. Can you read them in 55 seconds?

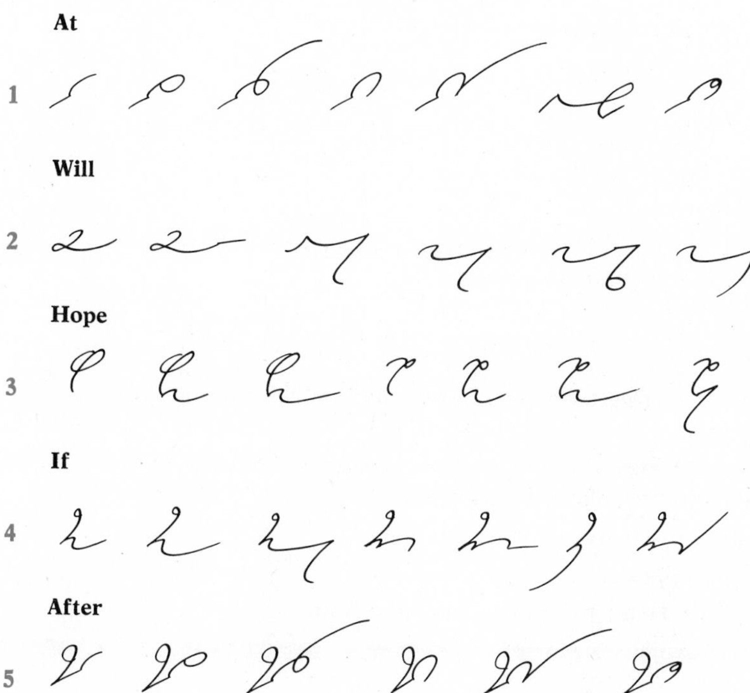

1 At the, at that, at that time, at this, at this time, at last, at these.
2 We will, we will not, there will be, you will be, you will not be able, you will have.
3 I hope, I hope you are, I hope you will, we hope, we hope you are, we hope you will, we hope to be.
4 If you are, if you will, if you will be, if you can, if you cannot, if you have, if you could.
5 After the, after that, after that time, after this, after this time, after these.

2 Geographical Expressions

1 Atlanta, Denver, Albuquerque, Phoenix, Dallas, Salt Lake City.
2 Alabama, Colorado, Utah, Idaho, New Mexico, Texas, Georgia, Arizona.

Building Transcription Skills

3 SIMILAR-WORDS DRILL ● farther, further

farther Greater distance from a point.

She lives *farther* from the school than I do.

further Moreover; to a greater degree or extent.

He advanced *further* than the other students in his reading skills.

4 Business Vocabulary Builder

accredited Having official recognition.
consent *(verb)* To give approval; to agree.
evaluate To appraise; to study.
review copies Items furnished for evaluation.

Reading and Writing Practice

5 Phrase Letter

de·ci·sion

col·lege

if

trav·el

far·ther

ap

its

ac·cred·it·ed

man·age·ment

ser

if

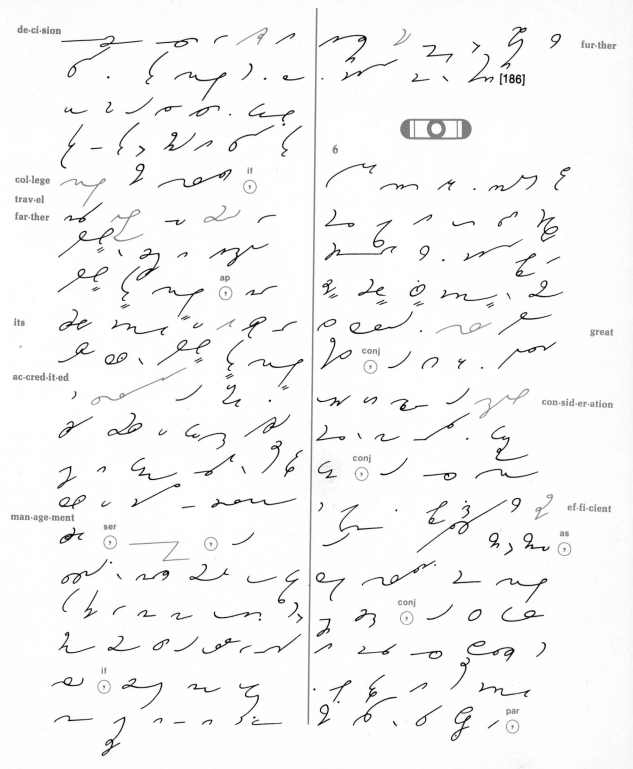

fur·ther

[186]

6

great

conj

con·sid·er·ation

conj

ef·fi·cient

as

conj

par

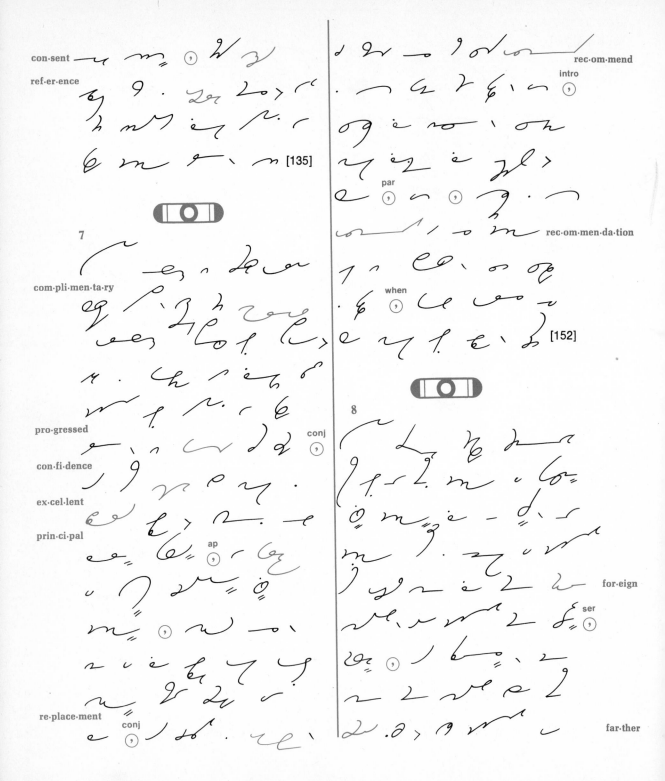

con·sent

ref·er·ence

[135]

7

com·pli·men·ta·ry

pro·gressed

conj

con·fi·dence

ex·cel·lent

prin·ci·pal

ap

re·place·ment

conj

rec·om·mend

intro

par

rec·om·men·da·tion

when

[152]

8

for·eign

ser

far·ther

intro

and o

in·for·ma·tive

if

eval·u·ate

el·e·men·ta·ry

[158]

9 Transcription Quiz For you to supply: 5 commas—2 commas series, 1 comma *and* omitted, 1 comma introductory, 1 comma *if* clause.

[161]

Developing Word-Building Power

1 Word Families

Pro-

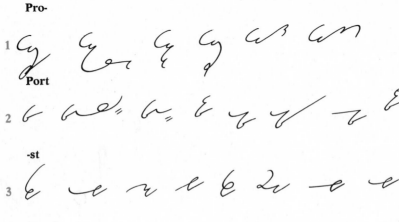

1

Port

2

-st

3

-pend

4

1 Provide, problems, propose, provision, produce, production.
2 Port, Portland, Porter, sport, report, reported, import, export.
3 Best, least, cost, test, passed, first, missed, rest.
4 Depend, dependence, independence, spend, expend, expended.

Building Transcription Skills

2 SPELLING FAMILIES ● -ance, -ence

Words Ending in -ance

as-sis-tance	**al-low-ance**	**as-sur-ance**
guid-ance	**in-sur-ance**	**ac-cep-tance**
per-for-mance	**clear-ance**	**ac-cor-dance**

Words Ending in -ence

con-fi-dence	con-fer-ence	ev-i-dence
pref-er-ence	ref-er-ence	ab-sence
in-sis-tence	in-ci-dence	con-se-quence

3 **Business Vocabulary Builder**

opposition Difference of opinions or ideas.

issuance Giving out; making available.

aligned On the side of; connected with.

Reading and Writing Practice

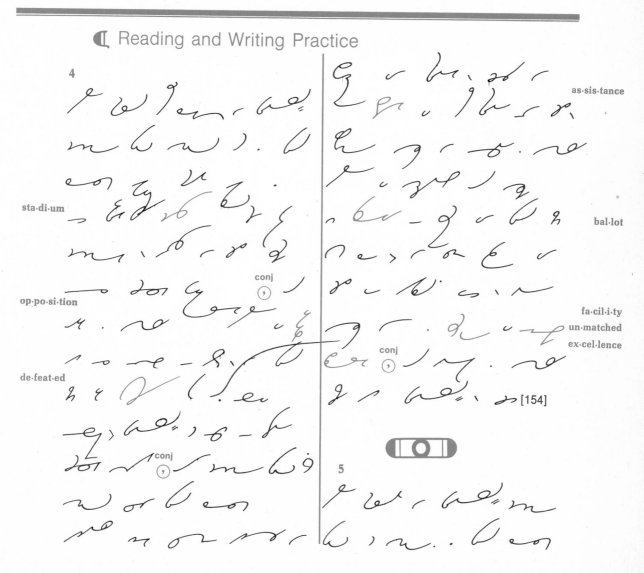

4

sta·di·um

op·po·si·tion

conj

de·feat·ed

conj

as·sis·tance

bal·lot

fa·cil·i·ty

un·matched

ex·cel·lence

conj

[154]

5

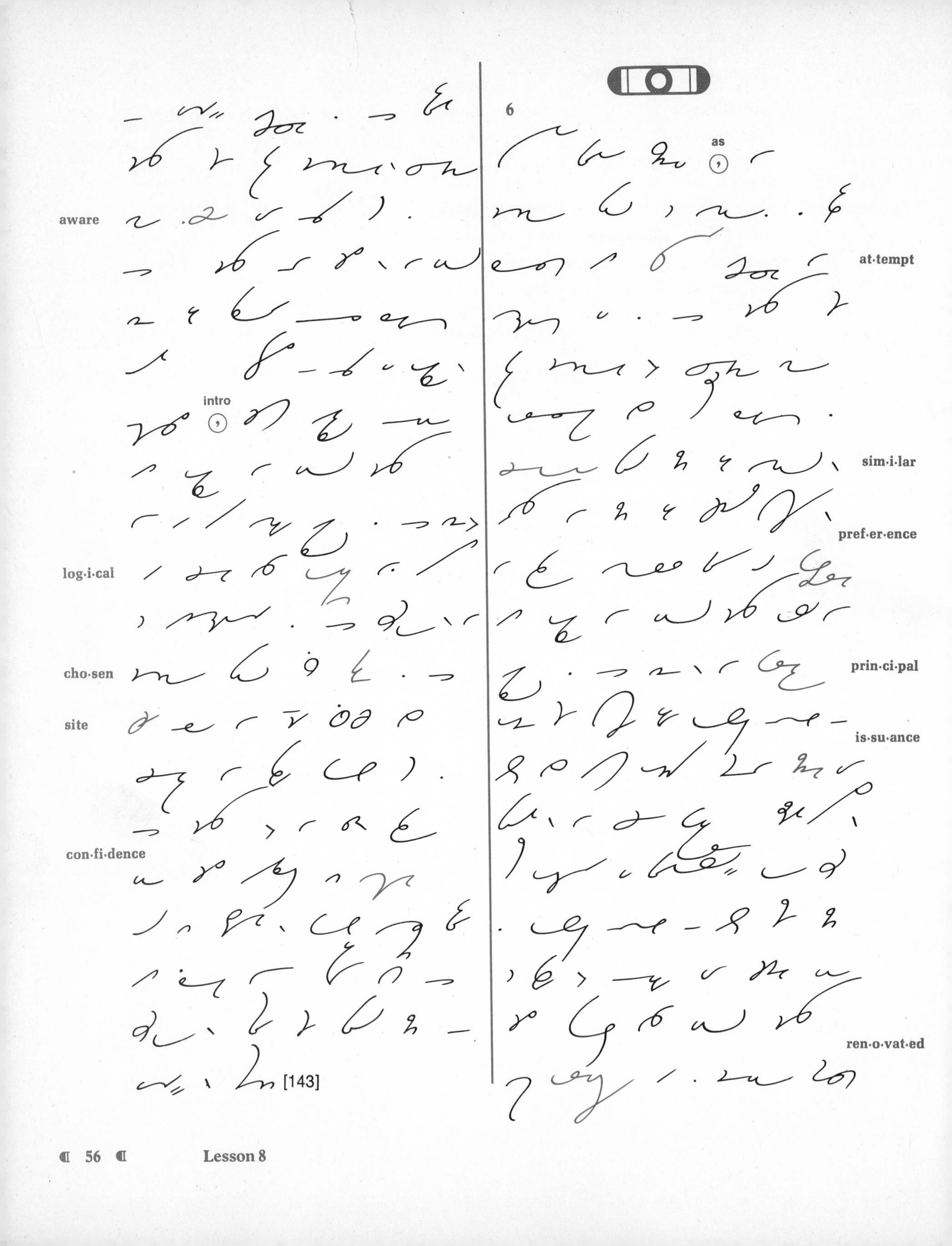

aware

intro

log·i·cal

cho·sen

site

con·fi·dence

[143]

6

as

at·tempt

sim·i·lar

pref·er·ence

prin·ci·pal

is·su·ance

ren·o·vat·ed

vi·tal·ly

[191]

7

main·tained

res·i·dence

intro

intro

intro

ser

fi·nance

ded·i·ca·tion

ed·u·ca·tion

in·de·pen·dent

aligned

[149]

8

as·sis·tance

as

conj

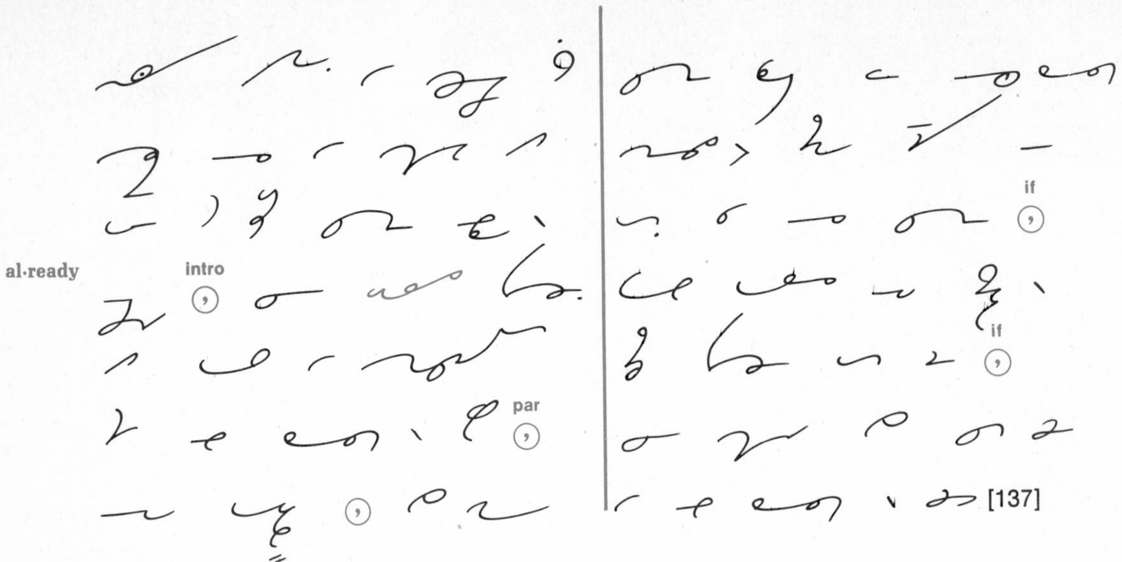

9 Transcription Quiz For you to supply: 3 commas—1 comma *as* clause, 1 comma apposition, 1 comma conjunction.

[114]

Developing Word-Building Power

1 Word Beginnings and Endings

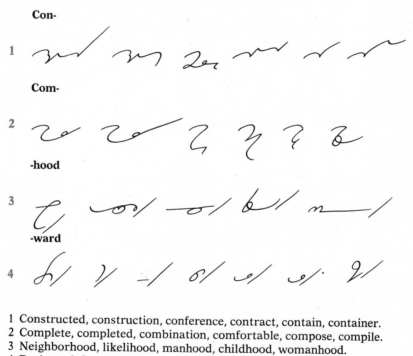

1 Constructed, construction, conference, contract, contain, container.
2 Complete, completed, combination, comfortable, compose, compile.
3 Neighborhood, likelihood, manhood, childhood, womanhood.
4 Backward, forward, inward, outward, reward, rewarding, afterward.

Building Transcription Skills

2 GRAMMAR CHECKUP ● between, among

Between is used when referring to two things or persons; *among*, when referring to more than two.

We will divide the work between *the two students.*
The books will be divided among *the five boys and girls.*

3 **decade** Ten years.
Business Vocabulary Builder
disseminate To distribute.
carrels Partitioned tables used for individual study.

Reading and Writing Practice

4

con·struct

el·e·men·ta·ry

as

neigh·bor·hood

res·i·dents

conj

over·crowd·ed

il·lus·trat·ed

ten·ta·tive

if

[134]

5

fi·nance

for·wards

conj

jus·ti·fied

par

en·cour·age

plan·ning

dis·sem·i·nate

if

[109]

6

as

intro

Out·ward·ly

intro

intro

de·creas·ing

Ob·vi·ous·ly

intro

intro

waste

Un·for·tu·nate·ly

intro

if

intro

com·pelled

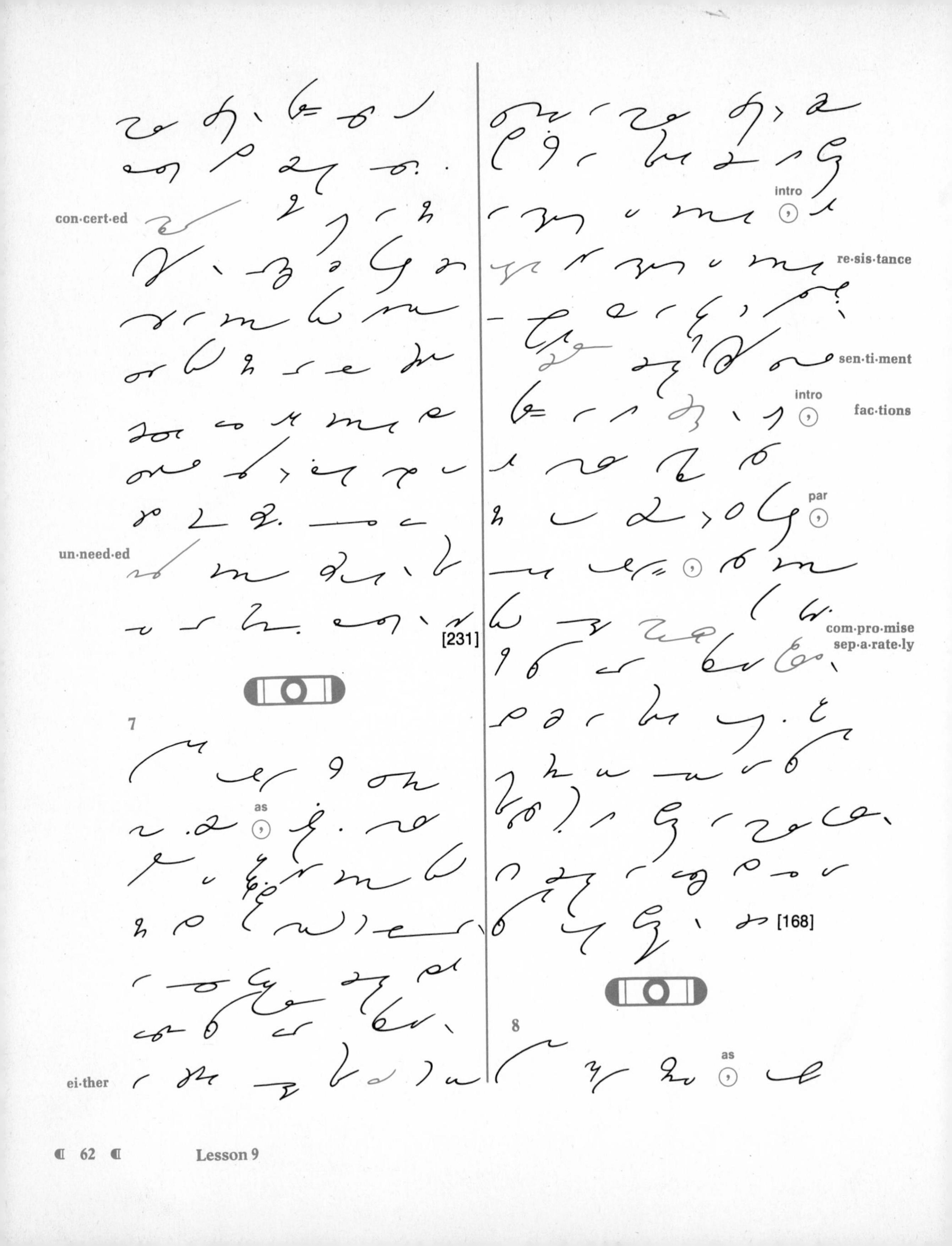

con·cert·ed

un·need·ed

[231]

7

as

ei·ther

intro

re·sis·tance

sen·ti·ment

intro

fac·tions

par

com·pro·mise

sep·a·rate·ly

[168]

8

as

el·e·men·ta·ry

ar·chi·tect

intro

res·i·dents

ser

ad·vice

par

[261]

9 Transcription Quiz For you to supply: 5 commas—1 comma conjunction, 4 commas series.

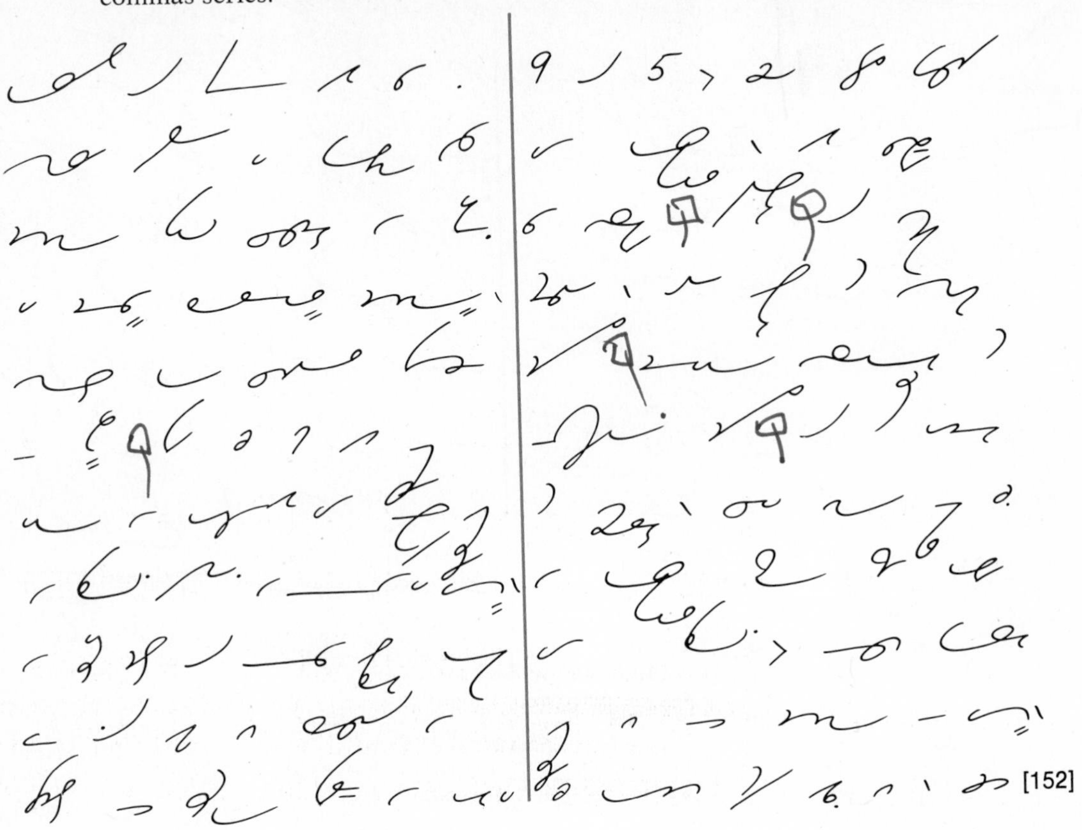

[152]

REVIEW TIP

In the Appendix you will find complete lists of the word beginnings, word endings, and brief forms of Gregg Shorthand.

You are already familiar with the words in these lists, but to be sure that they do not become hazy in your mind, you should review them frequently. Plan to set aside a few minutes each day to read from these lists. At this stage of your shorthand course, you should be able to read the lists very rapidly.

Time spent on this exercise will be time well spent.

Developing Word-Building Power

1 Shorthand Vocabulary Builder

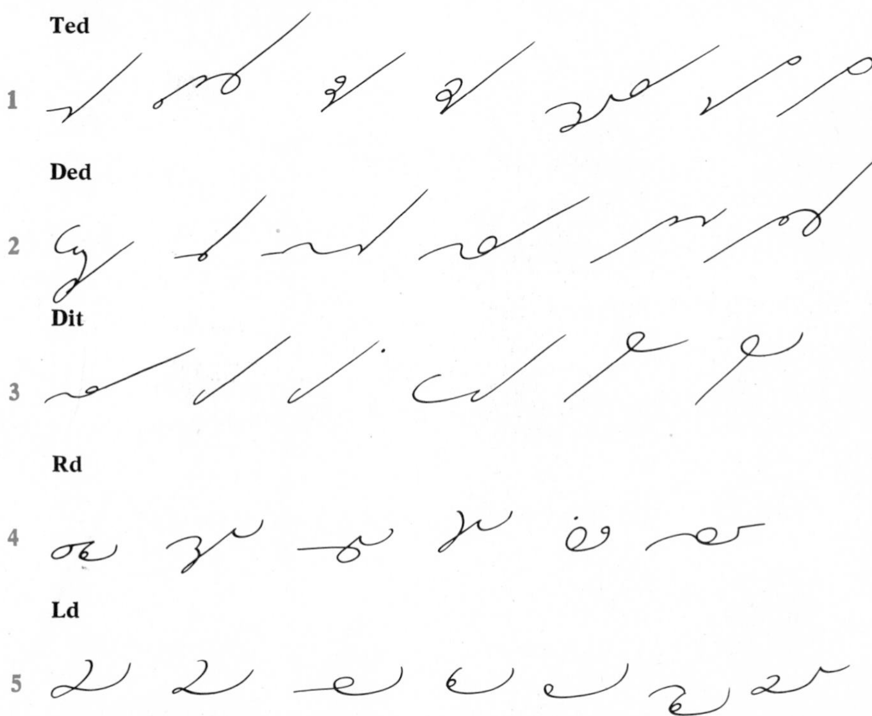

1 Instead, educated, existed, wasted, concentrated, study, today.
2 Provided, needed, included, graded, deduct, dedicated.
3 Credit, audit, auditing, plaudit, detail, detailed.
4 Answered, considered, mattered, featured, hardly, garden.
5 Failed, field, mailed, sealed, yield, concealed, welder.

Building Transcription Skills

2 Business Vocabulary Builder

rigorous Extremely accurate; exact; demanding.

compulsory Required; enforced.

populace People.

diligently Earnestly; steadily.

Reading and Writing Practice

3 Modern Education

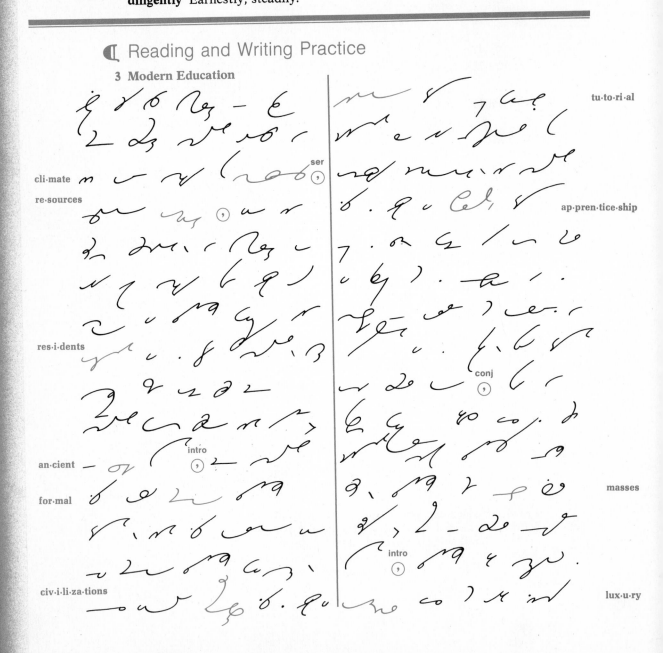

ser

cli·mate

re·sources

res·i·dents

intro

an·cient

for·mal

civ·i·li·za·tions

tu·to·ri·al

ap·pren·tice·ship

conj

masses

intro

lux·u·ry

intro

rig·or·ous

for·eign

intro

lan·guages

ser

par

In more

intro

conj

au·to·mo·tive

cur·ric·u·lum

ap·pear

when

lev·el

scorned

intro

cul·tur·al

ser

intro

sec·re·tari·al

au·dit·ing

ser

Education

intro

com·pul·so·ry

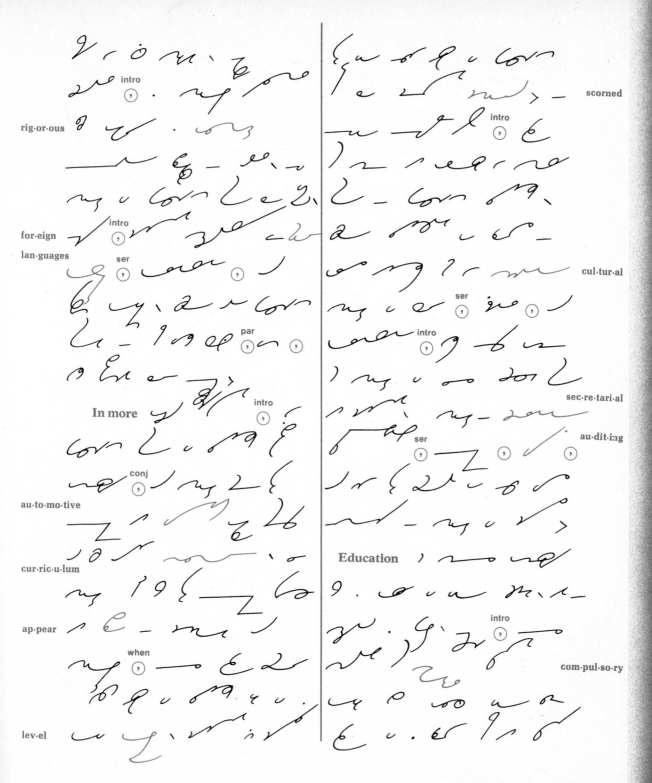

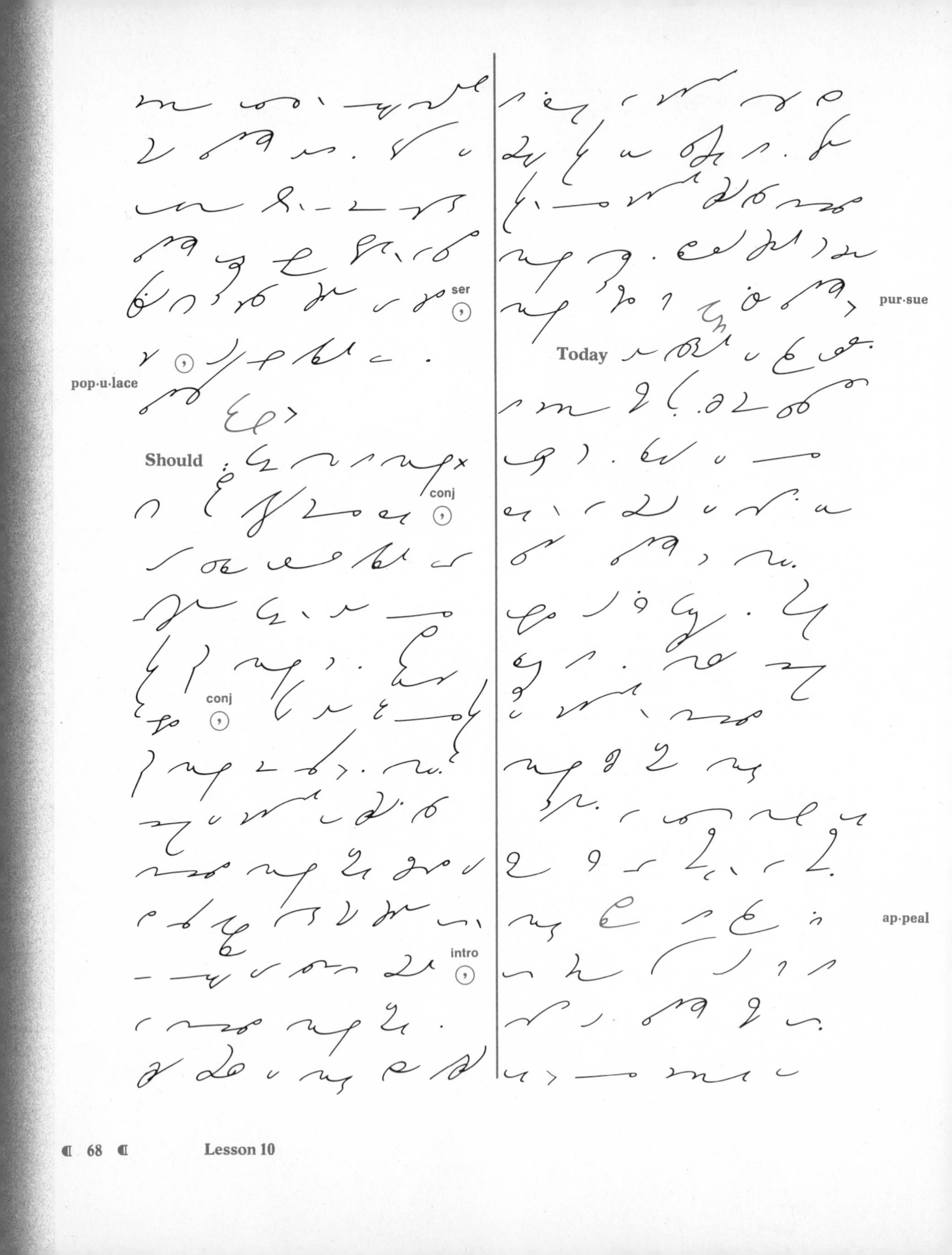

ser

pop·u·lace

Should

conj

conj

intro

pur·sue

Today

ap·peal

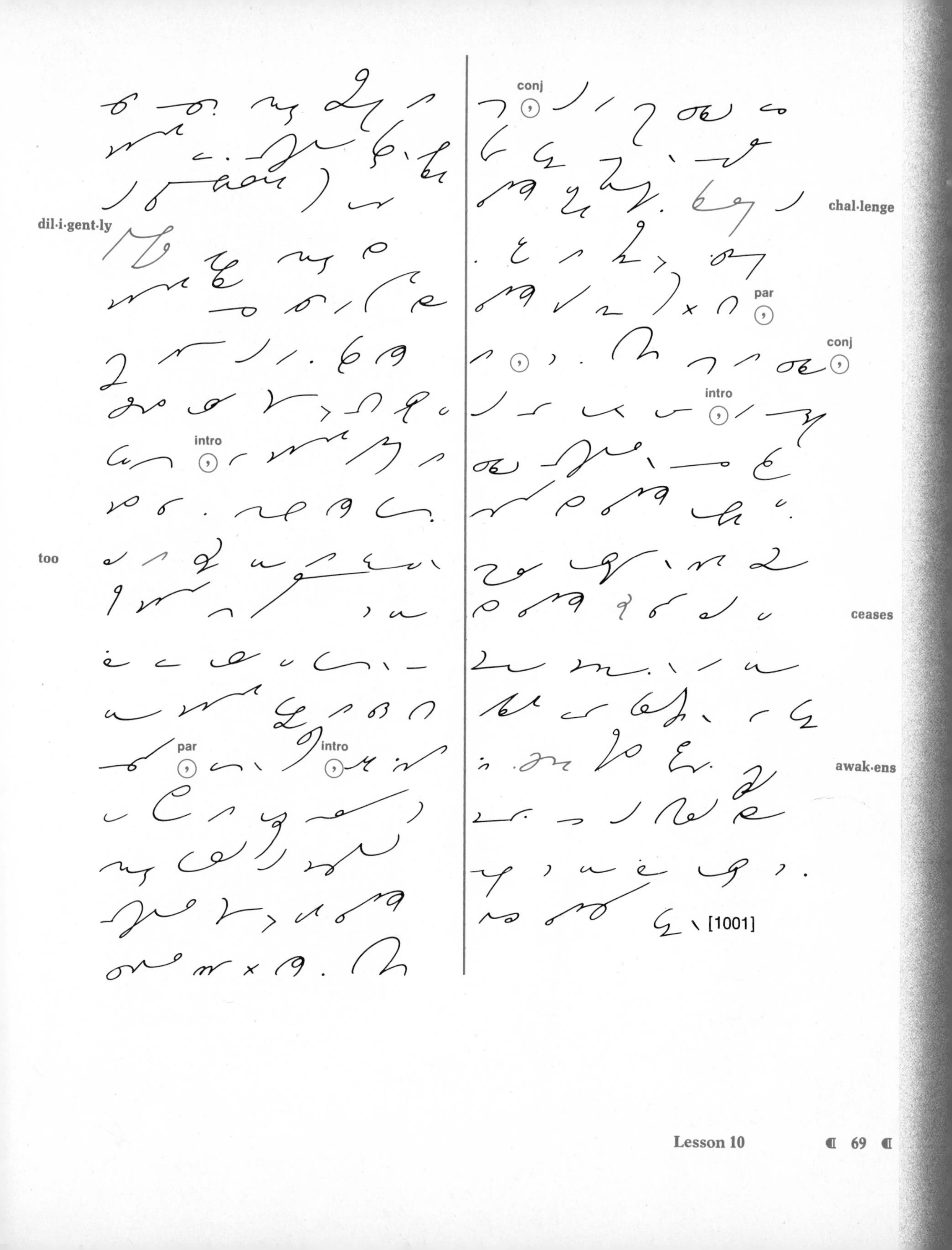

conj

chal·lenge

dil·i·gent·ly

par

conj

intro

intro

too

ceases

par intro

awak·ens

[1001]

3 CREDIT

Developing Word-Building Power

1 Brief Forms Can you read these brief forms in 35 seconds or less?

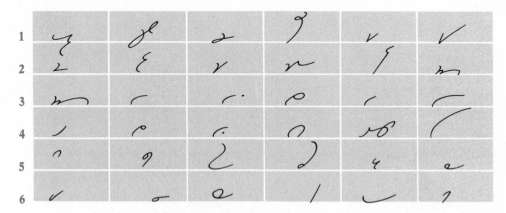

1 Responsible, satisfy-satisfactory, send, several, short, should.
2 Soon, speak, state, street, subject, success.
3 Suggest, than, thank, that, the, them.
4 There (their), they, think-thing, this, throughout, time.
5 Under, usual, value, very, was, were.
6 What, when, where, which, will-well, wish.

Building Transcription Skills

2 PUNCTUATION PRACTICE

You have reviewed all the uses of the comma that you studied in *Volume One*. In this lesson and in a number of lessons that follow, you will take up new, more advanced punctuation pointers.

PUNCTUATION PRACTICE ●, nonrestrictive

A nonrestrictive (or nonessential) clause or phrase is one that may be omitted without changing the meaning of the sentence. Nonrestrictive clauses are set off with commas and may be considered parenthetical. It is very important that you follow the meaning of the sentence exactly in order to determine if a clause is nonrestrictive.

Lee Smith, who is registering in college, *should have a physical examination.*

In this sentence the clause *who is registering in college* is not necessary to identify Lee Smith, the particular person who should have an examination. The clause could be omitted without changing the meaning of the sentence. Therefore, it is *nonrestrictive; commas are used* to set it off.

All persons who are enrolling in college *should have a physical examination.*

In this sentence the clause *who are enrolling in college* is necessary to identify the particular persons who should have a physical examination. It is *restrictive; no commas* are needed.

When a nonrestrictive comma appears in the Reading and Writing Practice, it will be indicated in the shorthand thus: nonr (,)

3 Business Vocabulary Builder

wholesale Items sold in quantity, usually for resale.

reputation A place in public esteem; a good name.

turnout A gathering of people.

Reading and Writing Practice

4 Brief-Form Letter

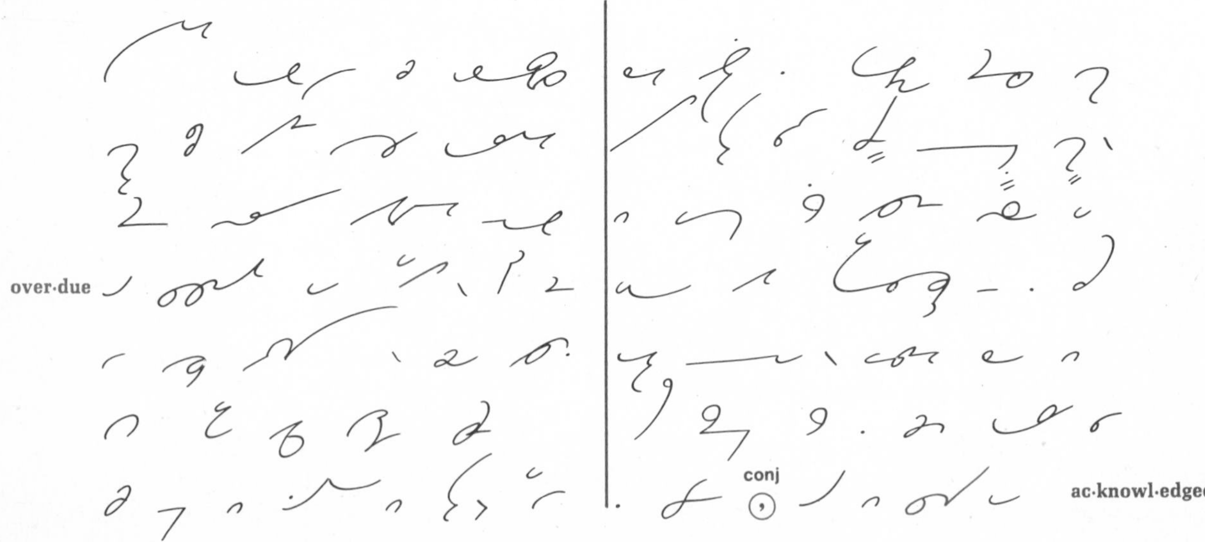

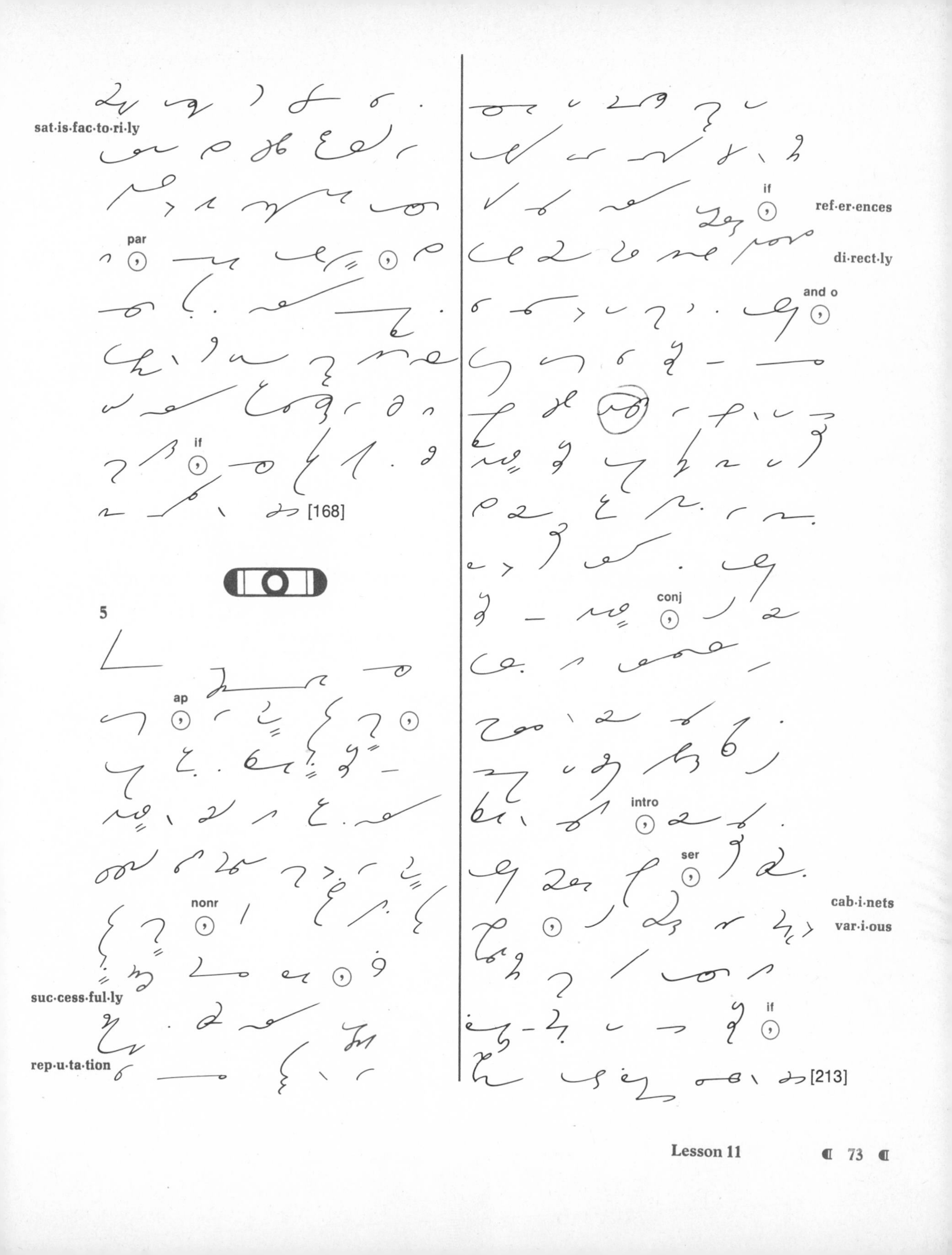

sat·is·fac·to·ri·ly

par

if

[168]

5

ap

nonr

suc·cess·ful·ly

rep·u·ta·tion

if

ref·er·ences

di·rect·ly

and o

conj

intro

ser

cab·i·nets

var·i·ous

if

[213]

6

an·nu·al con·fer·ence

conj

ac·cept

par

nonr

dis·cuss

intro

per·ti·nent

if

grate·ful

[149]

7

as·sets

conj

lose

Whole·sale

nonr

conj

intro

al·ter·na·tive

if

col·lec·tion

en·dan·ger

par

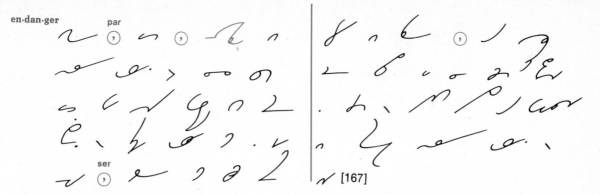

ser

[167]

8 **Transcription Quiz** In this lesson and in those that follow, the Transcription Quizzes will contain a new factor. In addition to supplying the necessary punctuation, you will have to supply a number of words that have been omitted from the shorthand.

Occasionally a secretary will leave out a word when taking dictation. The secretary must read the sentence for sense before transcribing. As the meaning of the sentence becomes clear, the secretary can usually supply the missing word with little difficulty.

You should have no trouble supplying the missing words in the Transcription Quiz. In each case only one possible word makes sense.

For you to supply: 5 commas—2 commas nonrestrictive, 1 comma *as* clause, 2 commas introductory; 2 missing words.

[170]

Building Phrasing Skill

1 **Useful Business-Letter Phrases** Here are a number of useful phrases. Can you read them in 50 seconds?

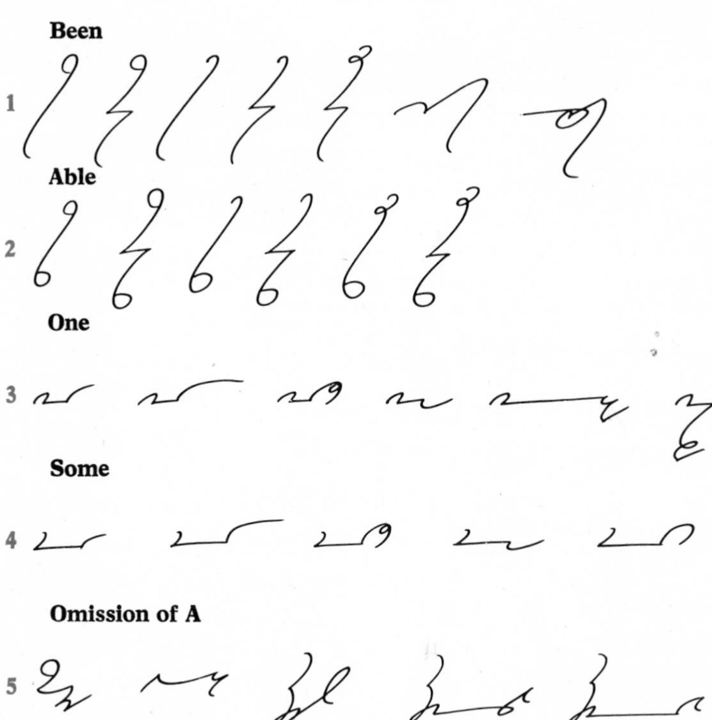

1 I have been, I have not been, you have been, you have not been, we have not been, could have been, might have been.
2 I have been able, I have not been able, you have been able, you have not been able, we have been able, we have not been able.
3 One of the, one of them, one of these, one of our, one of the most, one of the best.
4 Some of the, some of them, some of these, some of our, some of this.
5 As a result, at a loss, for a few days, for a few minutes, for a few months.

2 Geographical Expressions

1 San Francisco, New York, Newark, Hartford, Seattle, Chicago, Los Angeles.
2 California, Oregon, New Jersey, Connecticut, Kentucky, Illinois, Tennessee, Washington.

Building Transcription Skills

3 TYPING STYLE STUDY ● Numbers

1 Spell out numbers 1 through 10.

We made four *telephone calls.*

2 Use figures for numbers above 10.

They expect 25 *people at the picnic.*

3 If several numbers both below and above 10 are used in the same sentence, use figures for all numbers.

The vote was 4 *for Mark,* 12 *for Marian, and* 5 *for Kay.*

4 Spell out a number at the beginning of a sentence.

Twelve *students were absent.*

5 Express percentages in figures and spell out the word *percent.*

We offer a 6 percent *discount to our customers.*

6 To express even millions or billions in business correspondence, use the following style:

14 million *215 billion*

The correct form for typing numbers will occasionally be called to your attention in the margins thus: **Transcribe: 500**

4 Business Vocabulary Builder

rectify To correct; to set right.
entitled Have a right to.
entice To tempt.
initial First; beginning.

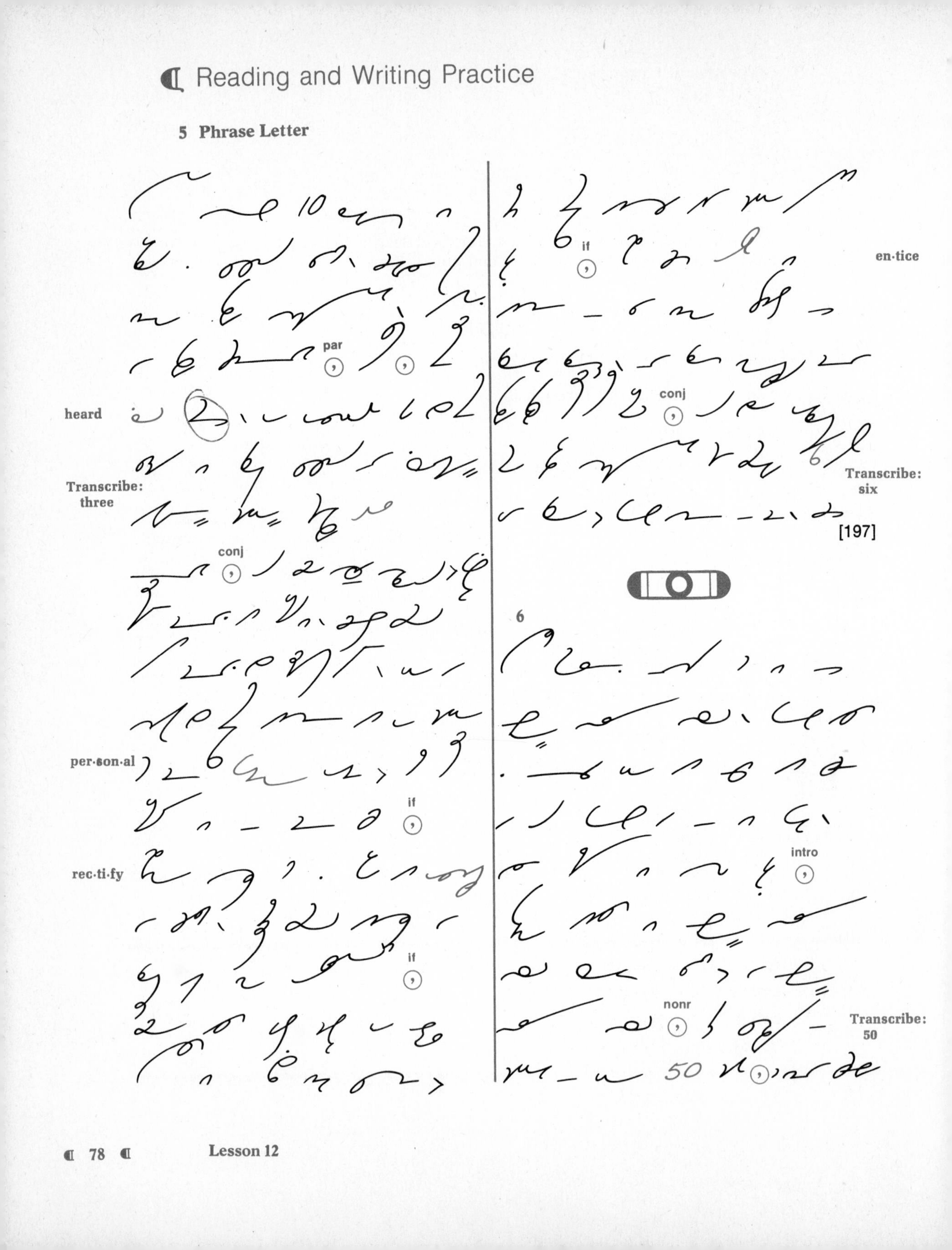

Reading and Writing Practice

5 Phrase Letter

heard

Transcribe: three

per·son·al

rec·ti·fy

en·tice

Transcribe: six

[197]

6

Transcribe: 50

Wheth·er

rec·og·nized

intro

in·teg·ri·ty

Transcribe: 1 percent

agree·ment

when

Wel·come

par

[187]

7

conj

trav·el·ing

ser

10

12

intro

iden·ti·fi·ca·tion

Transcribe: 800

ser

car·ries

reg·is·tered

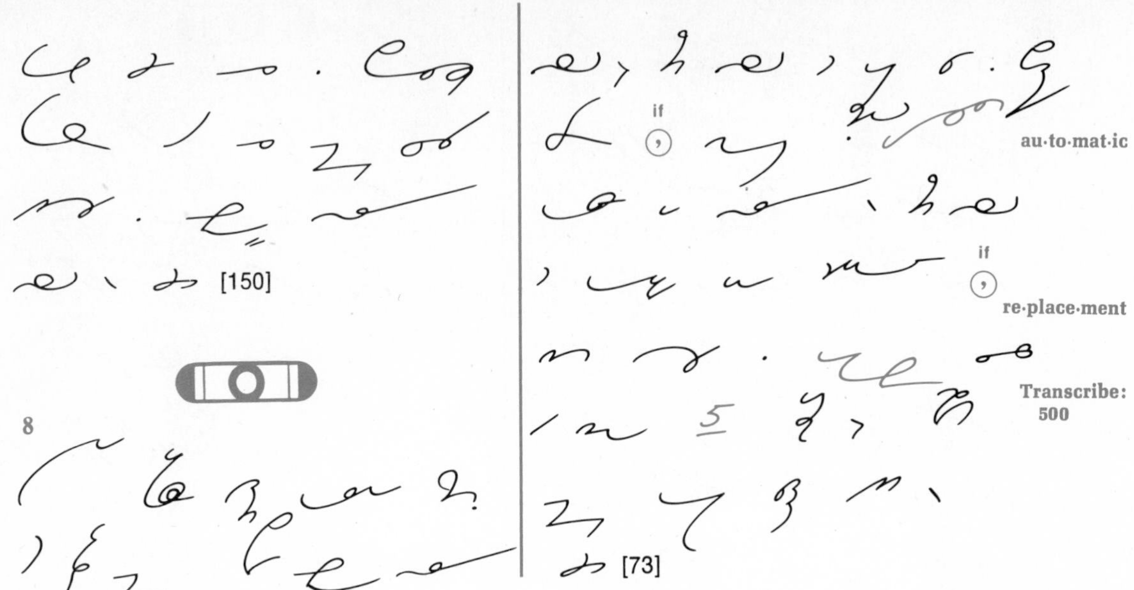

9 Transcription Quiz For you to supply: 5 commas—2 commas nonrestrictive, 2 commas parenthetical, 1 comma introductory; 2 missing words.

[130]

Developing Word-Building Power

1 Word Families

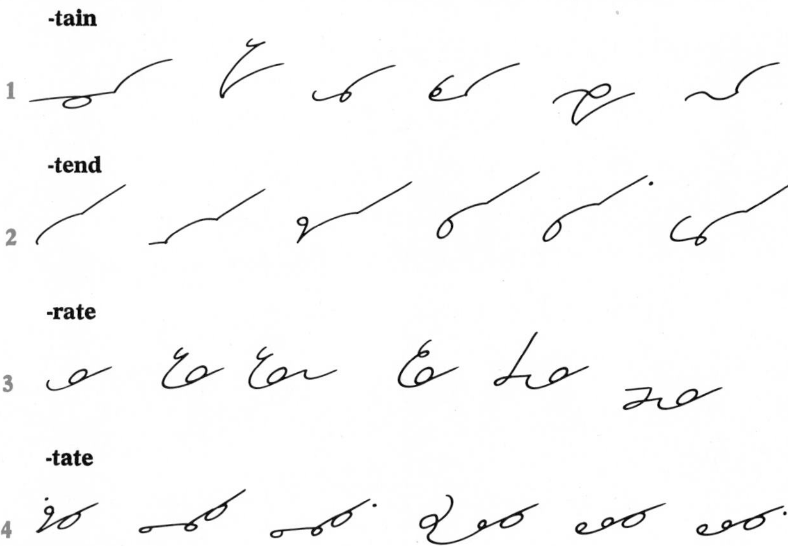

1 Maintain, obtain, retain, certain, captain, curtain.
2 Tend, intend, extend, attend, attending, pretend.
3 Rate, operate, operator, separate, generate, incinerate.
4 Hesitate, imitate, imitating, facilitate, irritate, irritating.

Building Transcription Skills

2 PUNCTUATION PRACTICE ● commas in numbers

1 When a number contains four or more digits, a comma is generally used to separate thousands.

2,000 *541,872* *850,000*

2 Commas are not used in serial numbers, house or store numbers, telephone numbers, page numbers, ZIP Codes, or between the digits of a year.

No. 61812	*3158 Park Avenue*	*Telephone Number 555-8107*
page 1670	*New York, NY 10020*	*the year 1888*

The recommended usage will be called to your attention in the margin of the Reading and Writing Practice thus: **Transcribe: 2,000** **Transcribe: 1888**

3 **Business Vocabulary Builder**

facilitate To make easy.

accounts receivable The balance due from debtors.

attentive Observant; mindful.

Reading and Writing Practice

4

Transcribe: 1,000

intro

fa·cil·i·tate

pa·tients

intro

intro

when

par

hes·i·tate

touch

Transcribe: 1800 South Main

77704

[110]

5

1950

res·i·dents

as

prob·a·bly

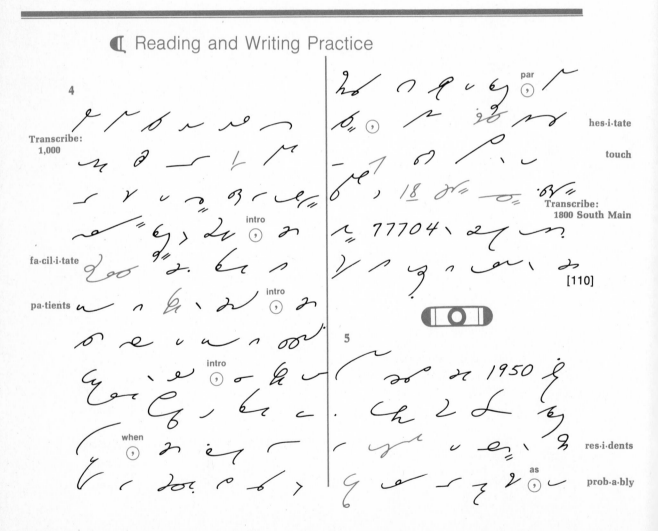

Transcribe: seven

and o

ex·pe·ri·enced

com·pa·ny's

intro

ad·e·quate

bor·row

intro

Transcribe: 2 million eight

fi·nan·cial

and o

at·ten·tive

al·ways

when

555-1871 [205]

6

ser

Transcribe: 5 10 20

course

if

ex·act·ly

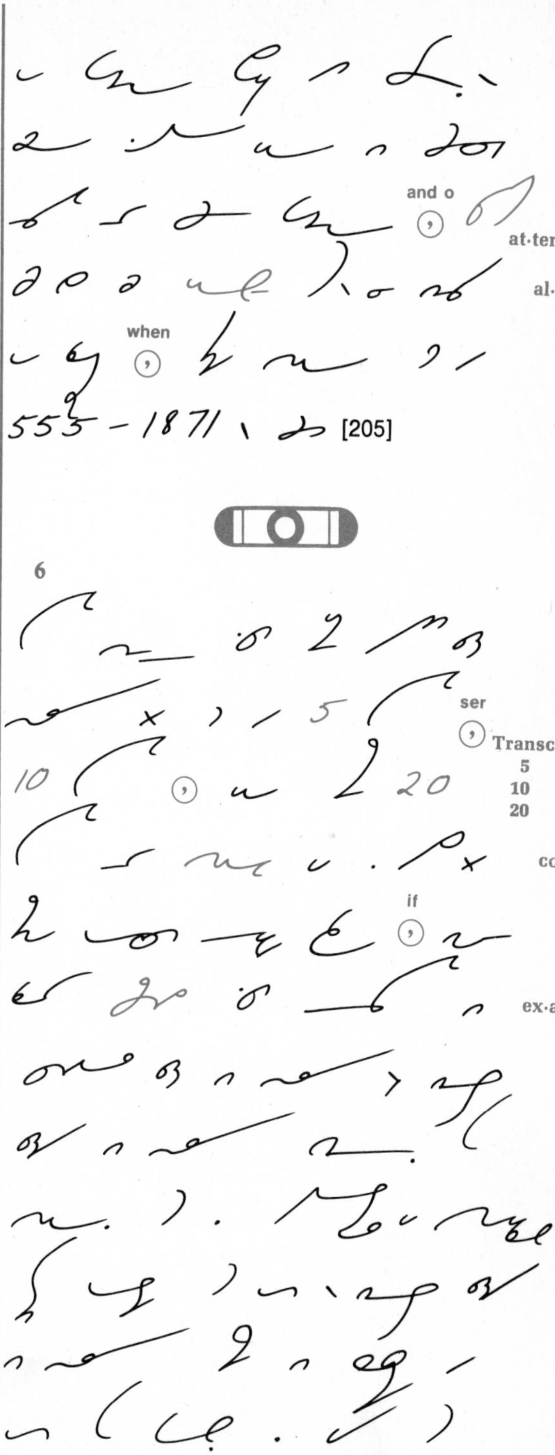

Transcribe:
4209 Main Street

[221]

7

if

as

par

as

conj

conj

intro

Transcribe:
1,000
2,000

adds

owed

Transcribe:
four

4

4209

1976

4

ex·ceed·ing·ly

priv·i·lege

Transcribe:
four

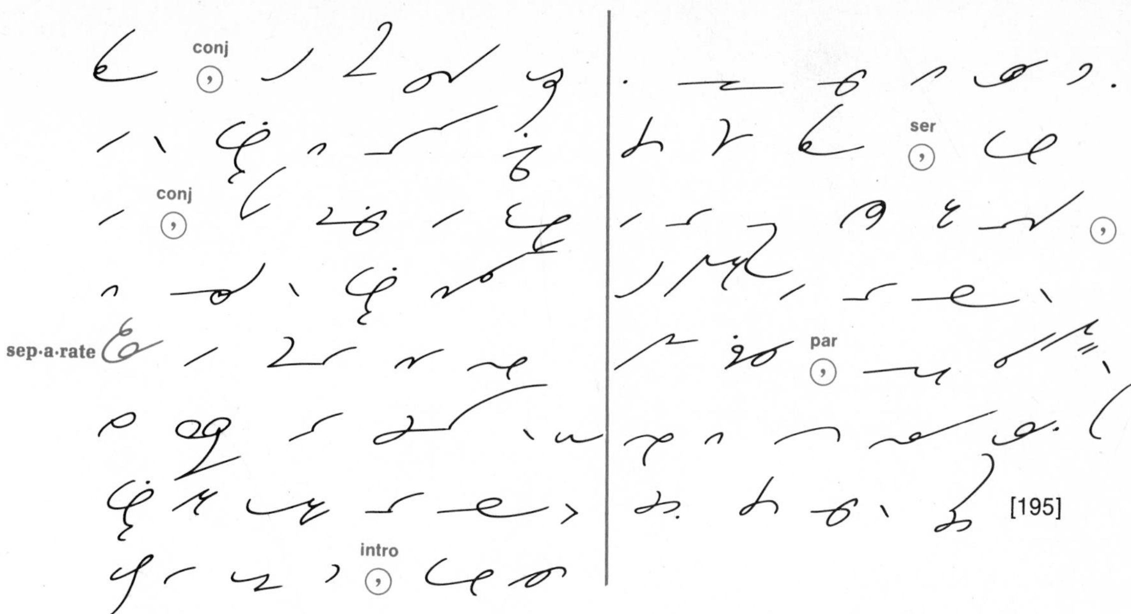

Transcription Quiz For you to supply: 7 commas—2 commas introductory, 2 commas series, 1 comma *when* clause, 2 commas conjunction; 2 missing words.

[145]

Developing Word-Building Power

1 Word Beginnings and Endings

Super-

1

For-, Fore-

2

Per, Pur-

3

-ment

4

-ly

5

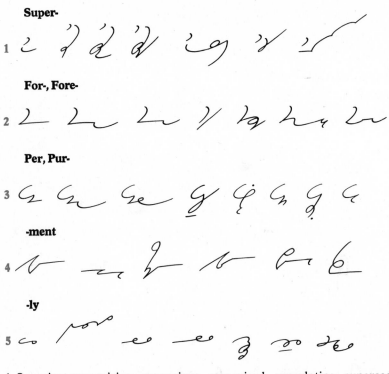

1 Superior, supervision, supervisor, supervised, superlative, supersede, superintendent.
2 Form, formal, former, forward, forecast, foreclose, forerunner.
3 Person, personal, personnel, persuade, perhaps, pursue, purchasing, purse.
4 Department, moments, adjustment, deportment, apartments, basement.
5 Only, directly, nearly, merely, concisely, quickly, sincerely.

Building Transcription Skills

2 PUNCTUATION PRACTICE ● ; no conjunction

A semicolon is used to separate two independent but closely related clauses when no conjunction is used between them.

Your account is overdue; please send us your check immediately.

The above sentence could have been written as two sentences.

Your account is overdue. Please send us your check immediately.

Because the two thoughts are closely related, the semicolon is more appropriate than the period.

Each time this use of the semicolon appears in the Reading and Writing Practice, it will be indicated in the shorthand thus: nc (;)

3 Business Vocabulary Builder

formerly At an earlier time.

relocate To move to a new place.

superior Of higher quality.

Reading and Writing Practice

4

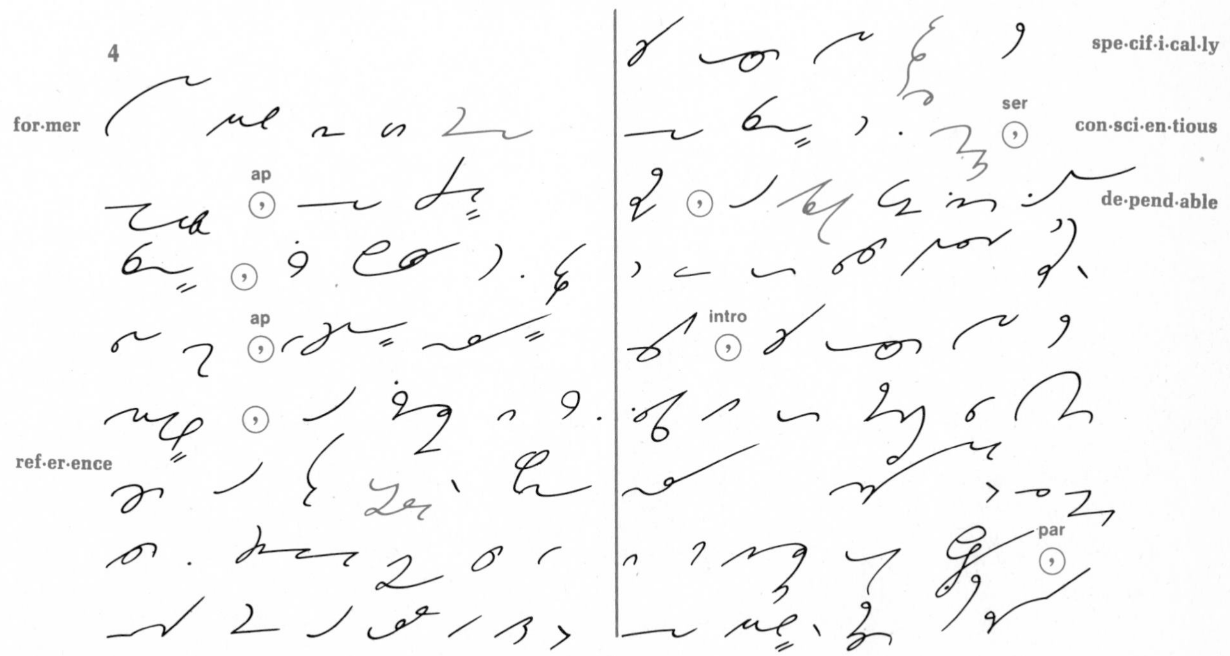

sim·i·lar

if

ap·pre·ci·ate

nc

[158]

5

for·mer·ly

nonr

conj

intro

ini·tia·tive

per·son·nel

nc

per·son·al·ly

if

555-1798

[109]

6

nc

su·per·vi·sor

intro

cli·mate

nc

re·lo·cate

pur·sue

intro

intro

ob·serve

com·plete

[129]

7

Transcribe: two

conj

occasions

paid

par

intro

intro

al·most

nc

un·til

intro

if

for·ward

nc

[188]

8

conj

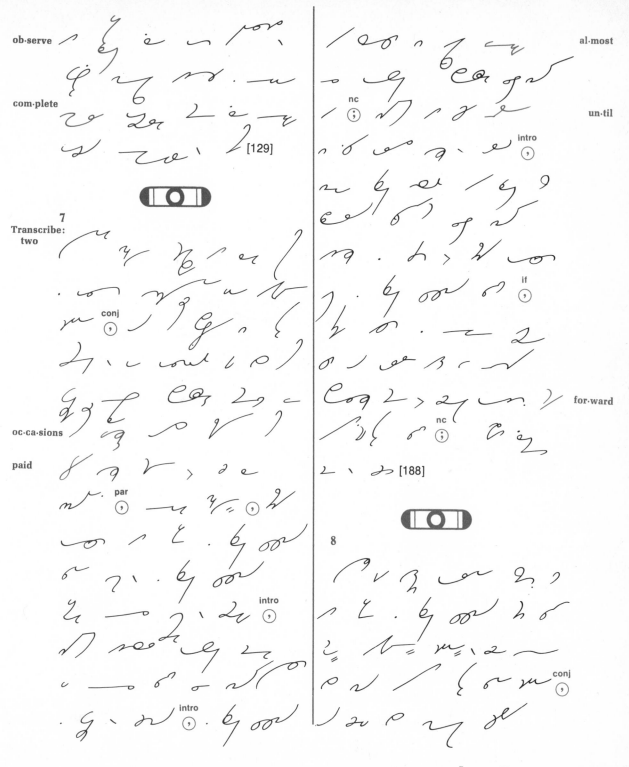

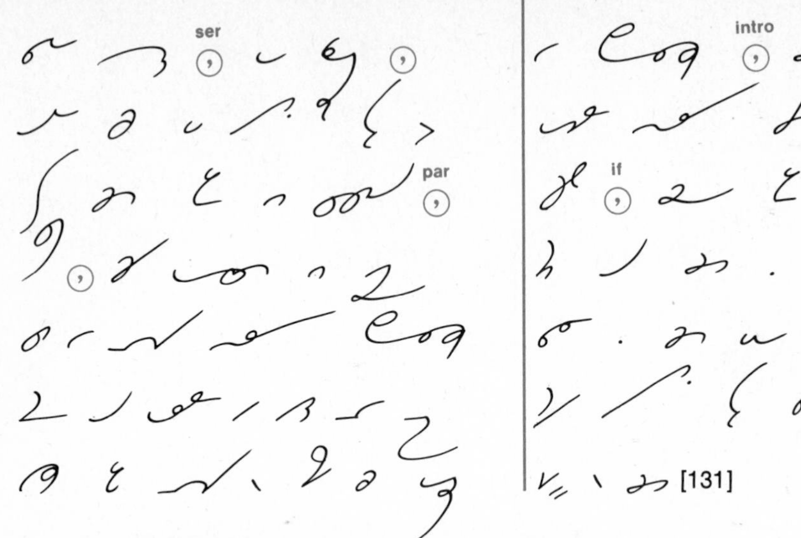

9 Transcription Quiz For you to supply: 4 commas—1 comma *and* omitted, 1 comma introductory, 2 commas series; 2 missing words.

[114]

Developing Word-Building Power

1 Shorthand Vocabulary Builder

Mon, Men, Etc.

1

OO for U After M and N

2

-tition, Etc.

3

Omission of Minor Vowel

4

1 Money, monthly, common, meant, examination, minute.
2 Municipal, music, communicate, continue, continues.
3 Condition, institution, sanitation, addition, edition, reputation, foundation, expectation.
4 Various, serious, obvious, genuine, courteous, ideal, union.

Building Transcription Skills

2 Business Vocabulary Builder

fiscal Relating to financial matters.

scale A series of ranks by which something is measured.

revolving charge account A continuing charge account for which monthly payments are made and which includes a service charge.

Reading and Writing Practice

3 The World Buys on Credit

conj

ex·tent

chief

its

ma·chin·ery

ser

rep·u·ta·tion

bor·row

Many

cit·i·zens

ser

when

ser

ex·empt

nonr

in·vest·ment

The

an·tic·i·pate

due

intro

nonr

re·ceiv·able

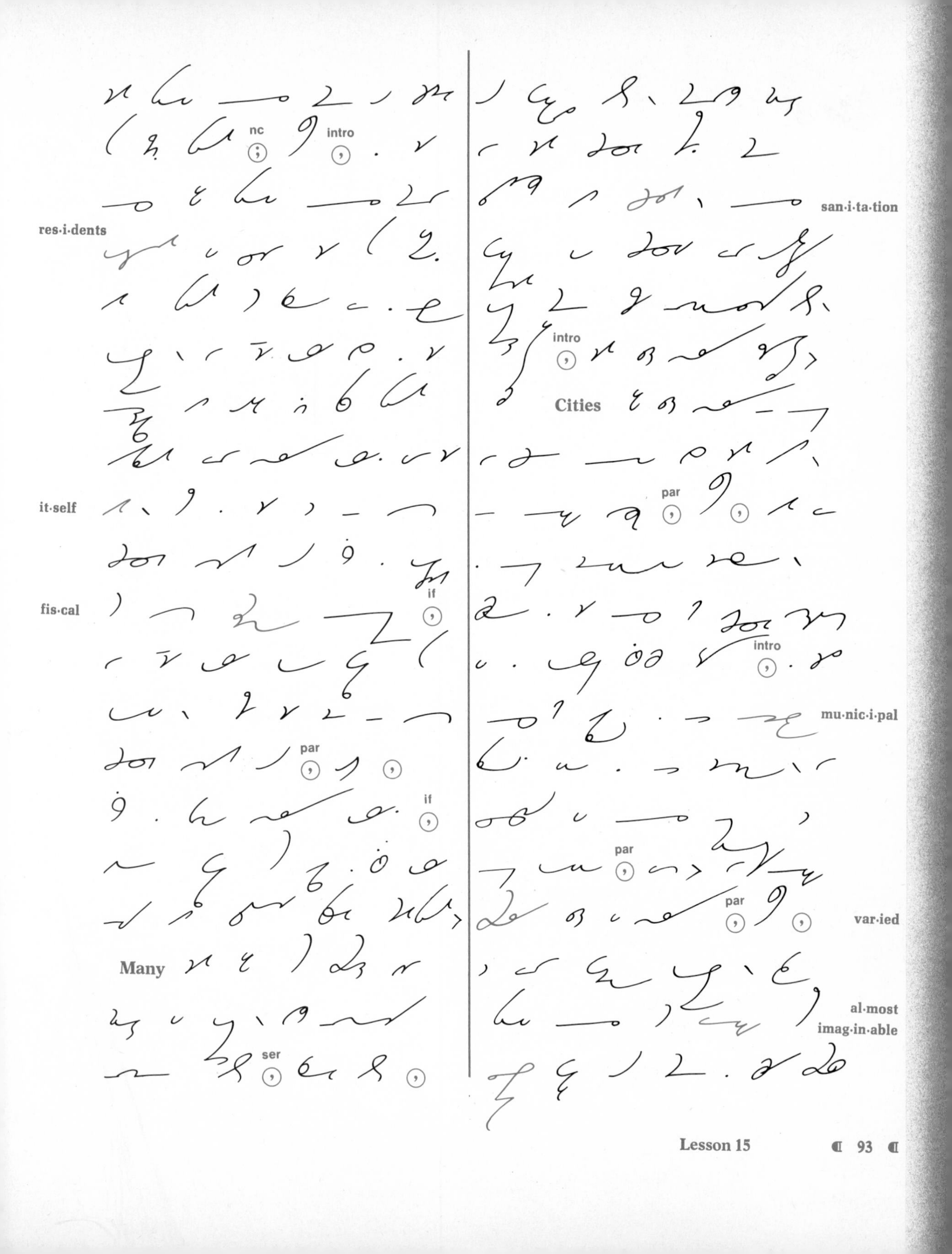

nc ; intro ,

res·i·dents

it·self

fis·cal

if ,

par , ,

if ,

Many

ser , ,

san·i·ta·tion

intro ,

Cities

par , ,

intro ,

mu·nic·i·pal

par ,

par , ,

var·ied

al·most

imag·in·able

mort·gages

prin·ci·pal

intro

Many

ser

col·lege

ser

It is

[797]

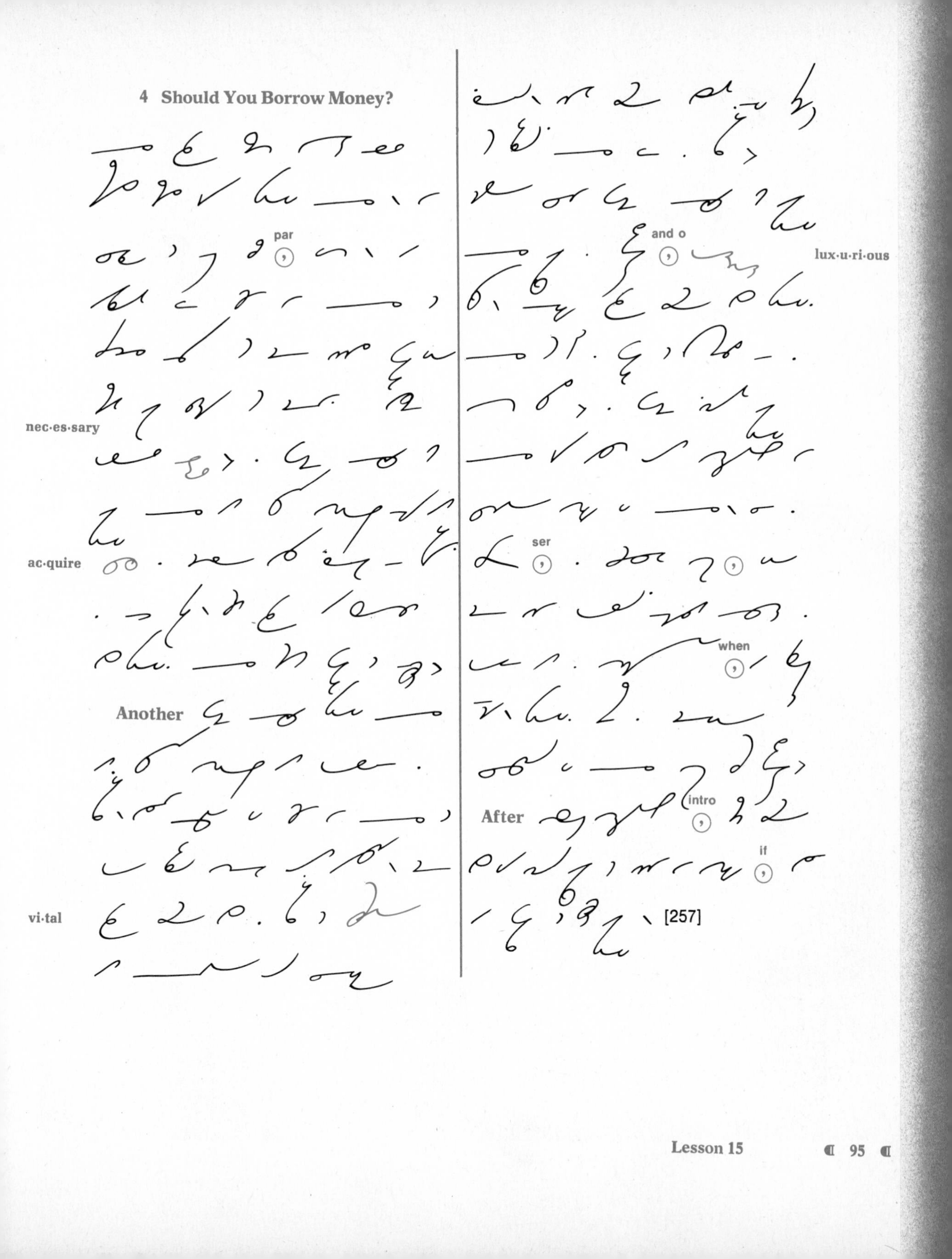

4 Should You Borrow Money?

par

and o

lux·u·ri·ous

nec·es·sary

ser

acquire

when

Another

intro

After

if

vi·tal

[257]

4 PERSONNEL

Developing Word-Building Power

1 **Brief Forms and Derivatives** Can you read these brief forms and derivatives in 40 seconds or less?

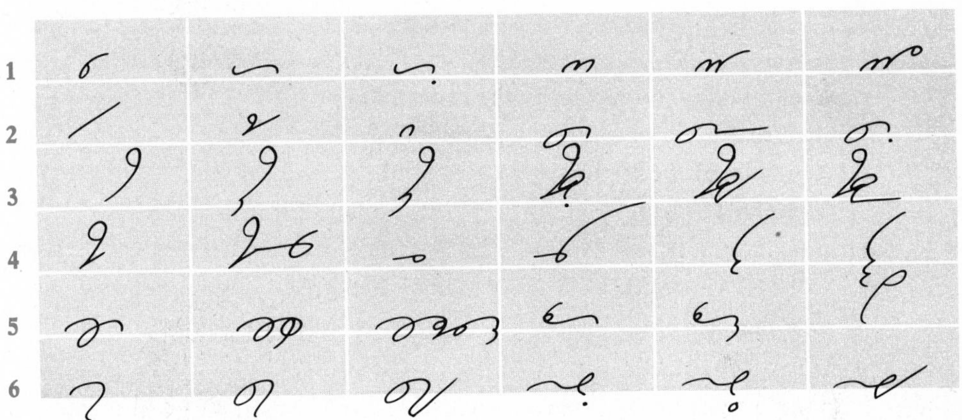

1 With, work, working, world, worth, worthy.
2 Would, yesterday, you-your, acknowledge, acknowledgment, acknowledging.
3 Advantage, advantages, advantageous, advertising, advertised, advertisement.
4 After, aftermath, any, anytime, business, businesses.
5 Character, characterize, characteristics, circular, circulars, about.
6 Company, accompany, accompanied, corresponding, correspondingly, corresponded.

Building Transcription Skills

2 **PUNCTUATION PRACTICE ● . courteous request**

One business executive may wish to persuade another to take some definite action. The request could be made as a direct statement.

I want your check by return mail.

However, a direct statement of this kind is very blunt and is likely to anger the reader. Many executives, therefore, prefer to make the request in the form of a question, which is much less blunt.

May I have your check by return mail.

When such a question is actually a courteous request, a period is used rather than a question mark. Here is how you can tell whether to use a period or a question mark.

□ 1 When a question calls for *definite action,* a period is used at the end of the sentence.

□ 2 When a question calls for a *yes-or-no answer,* a question mark is used at the end of the sentence.

Whenever a period is used at the end of a courteous request in the Reading and Writing Practice, it will be indicated in the following manner: cr (.)

3 Business Vocabulary Builder

reciprocate To respond in the same manner.

tenure A term of holding a position.

semiannual Occurring every six months or twice a year.

comply To obey.

Reading and Writing Practice

4 Brief-Form Letter

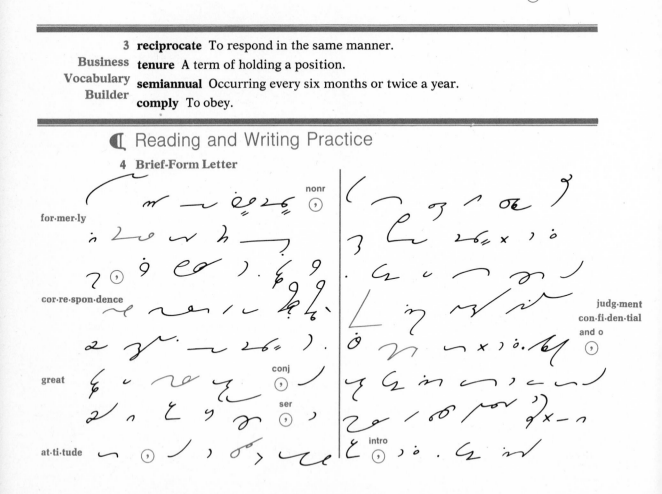

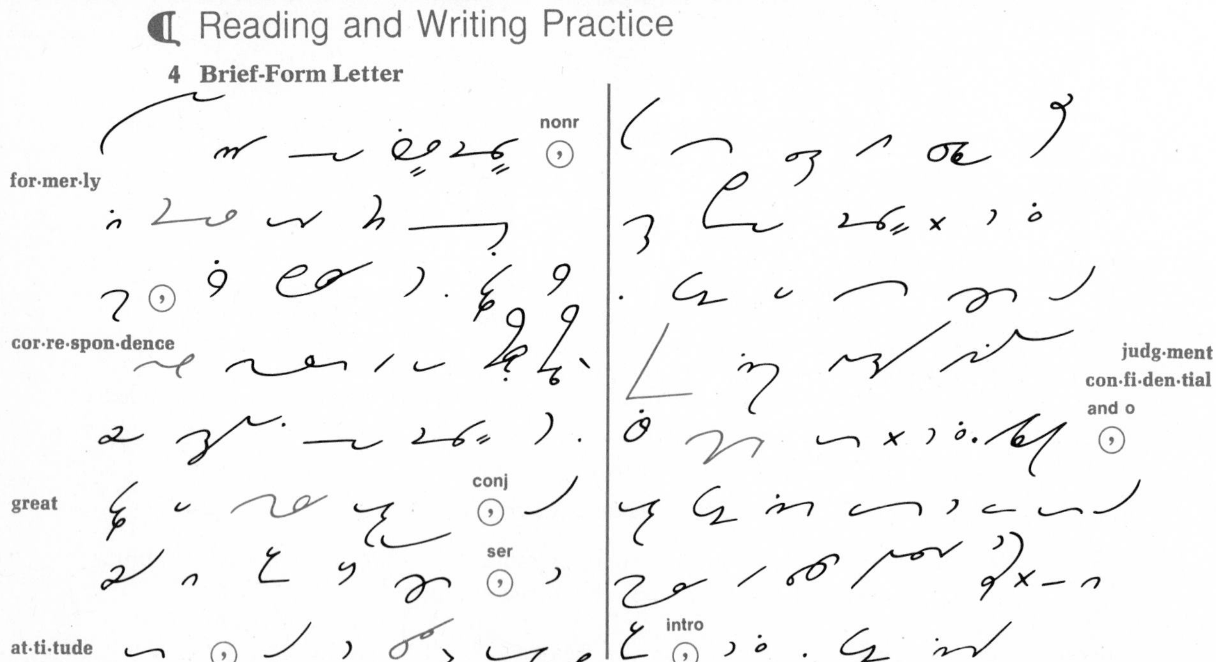

ours

cr

sim·i·lar

if

nc

re·cip·ro·cate

[191]

5

rec·om·mend·ing

as

Transcribe:
ten

10

ex·cel·lent

conj

su·per·vi·sion

conj

re·ceived

ten·ure

oc·ca·sion

intro

ad·vance·ment

tal·ents

conj

oc·curred

when

par

if

ef·fi·cient

hire

cr [247]

6

re·gion·al

if

as

suc·cess·ful

and o

Transcribe:
12
15
5
5

12

15

ser

5 5

ad·ver·tise·ments

intro

main·te·nance

cus·to·di·al

semi·an·nu·al

if

touch

nonr

there

555-
9436

[240]

7 Transcription Quiz In addition to the commas and missing words you have been supplying up to this point, you will now have to supply periods indicating courteous requests.

For you to supply: 7 commas—1 comma introductory, 1 comma *and* omitted, 2 commas parenthetical, 1 comma *when* clause, 2 commas apposition; 1 period courteous request; 2 missing words.

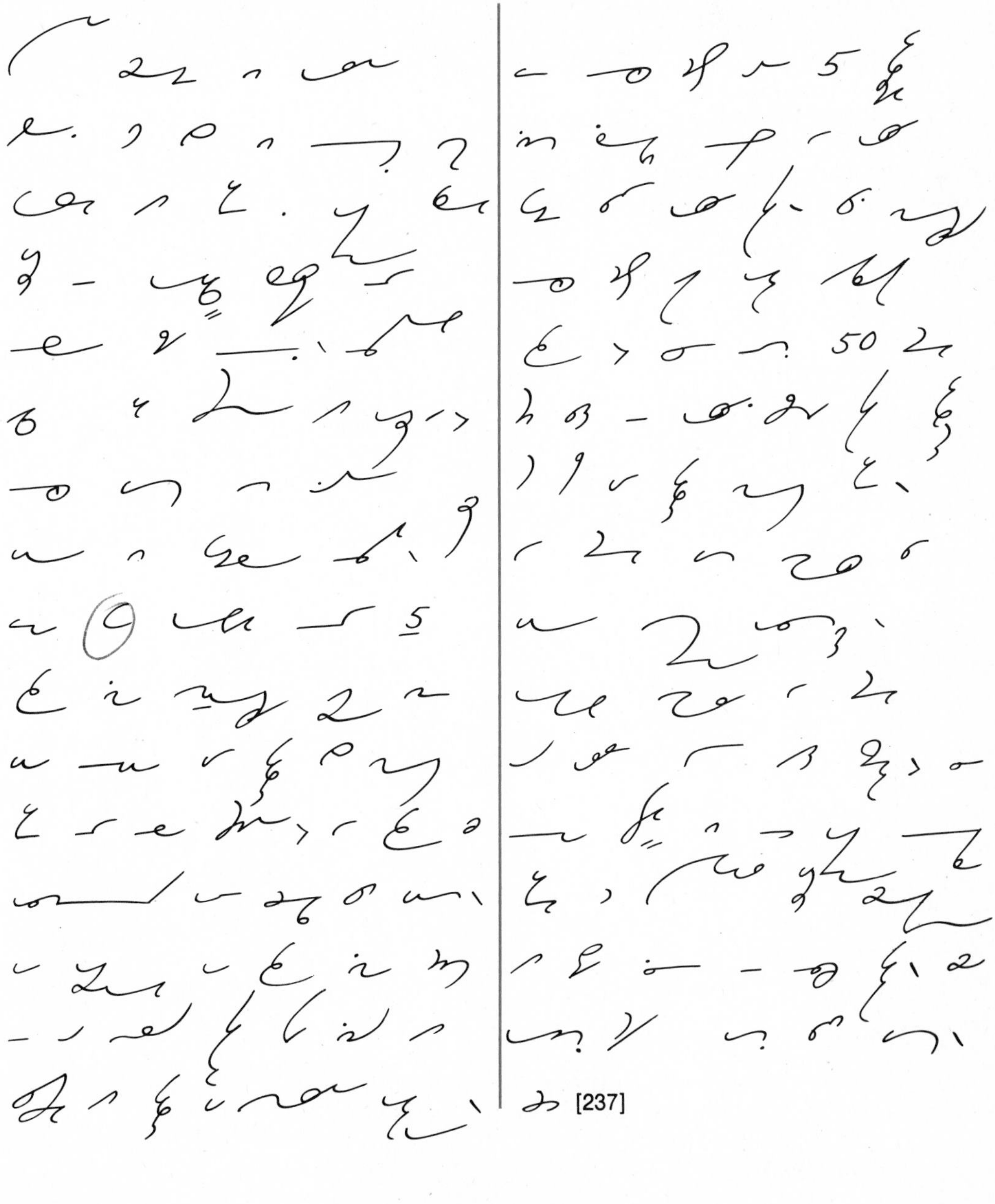

[237]

Building Phrasing Skill

1 **Useful Business-Letter Phrases** The following groups contain a number of phrases. Can you read the entire list in 45 seconds?

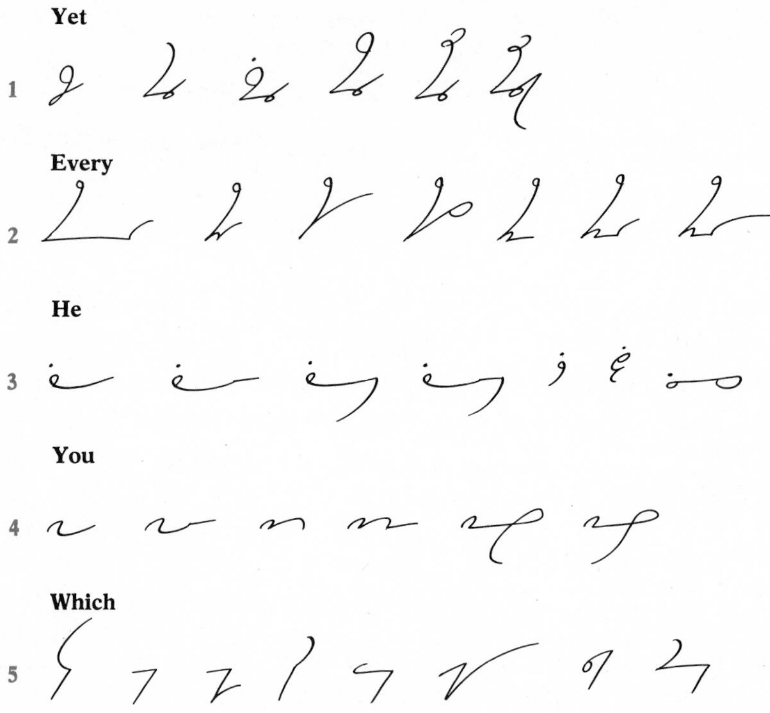

1 As yet, have not yet, has not yet, I have not yet, we have not yet, we have not yet been.
2 Every month, every other, every time, every day, every one, every one of the, every one of them.
3 He will, he will not, he will have, he will not have, he is, he was, he may.
4 You are, you are not, you can, you cannot, you may be, you may have.
5 By which, in which, in which the, for which, on which, at which time, with which, from which.

2 Geographical Expressions

1 Little Rock, Milwaukee, Providence, New Orleans, Jackson.
2 Arkansas, Wisconsin, Rhode Island, Louisiana, Mississippi, Washington, Indiana.

Building Transcription Skills

3 PUNCTUATION PRACTICE ● hyphens

Compound expressions often call for hyphens in the English language. You can decide whether to use a hyphen in a compound expression like *past due* or *well educated* by observing these rules:

1 If a noun follows the expression, use a hyphen.

Our well-educated *representatives* (noun) *are ready to serve you.*

When a hyphenated expression occurs in the Reading and Writing Practice, it will be called to your attention thus: **well-ed·u·cat·ed hyphenated before noun**

2 If no noun follows the compound expression, a hyphen is not generally used.

Our representatives are well educated.

Occasionally, these expressions will be called to your attention in the Reading and Writing Practice in the following manner: **well ed·u·cat·ed no noun, no hyphen**

3 If the first word in the compound modifier is an adverb ending in *ly*, do not use a hyphen.

It is a beautifully illustrated *book.*

To be sure that you do not put hyphens in such expressions, your attention will occasionally be called to them in the following way: **beau·ti·ful·ly il·lus·trat·ed no hyphen after ly**

4 There are a few compound expressions that must be read as a unit to make sense. These are "one-thought modifiers" that must be hyphenated before or after a noun.

We sell tax-exempt *bonds.*
The bonds are tax-exempt.

4 Business Vocabulary Builder

interoffice Between the offices of a company.

management trainee A person being educated for a supervisory position.

diversified Varied; made up of different parts.

compatible Related; in harmony.

Reading and Writing Practice

5 Phrase Letter

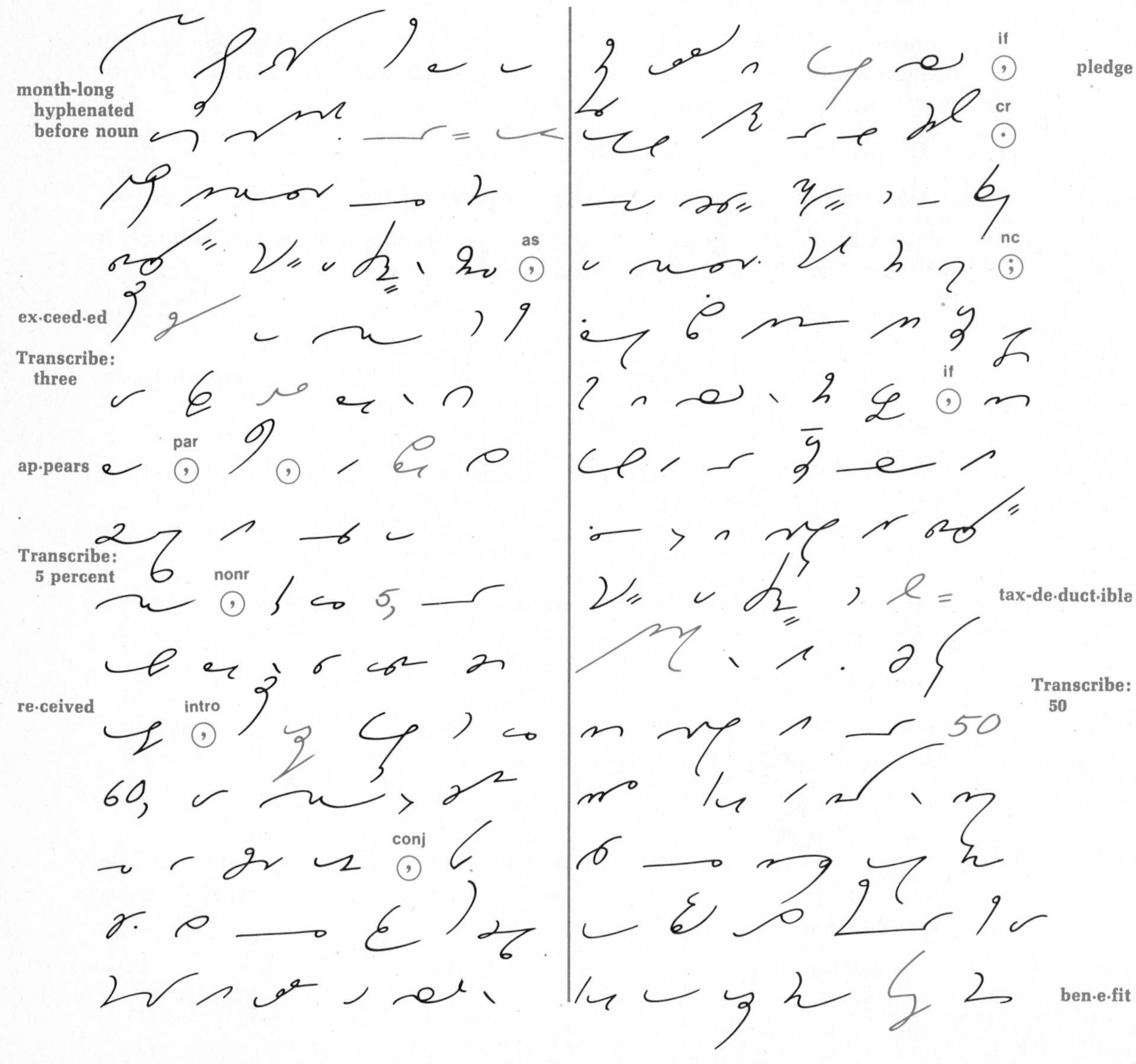

[209]

[141]

6

Transcribe: three

po·ten·tial

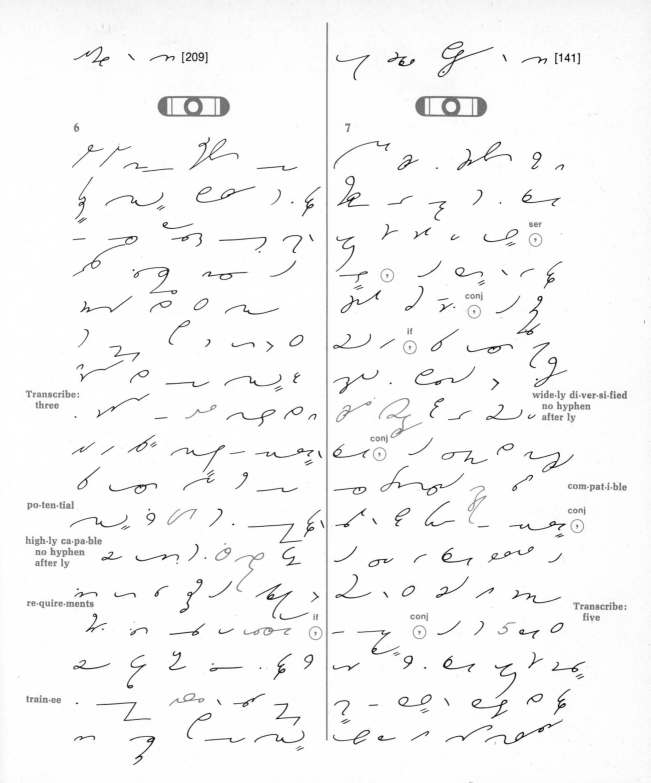

high·ly ca·pa·ble no hyphen after ly

re·quire·ments

if

train·ee

7

ser

conj

if

wide·ly di·ver·si·fied no hyphen after ly

conj

com·pat·i·ble

conj

Transcribe: five

conj

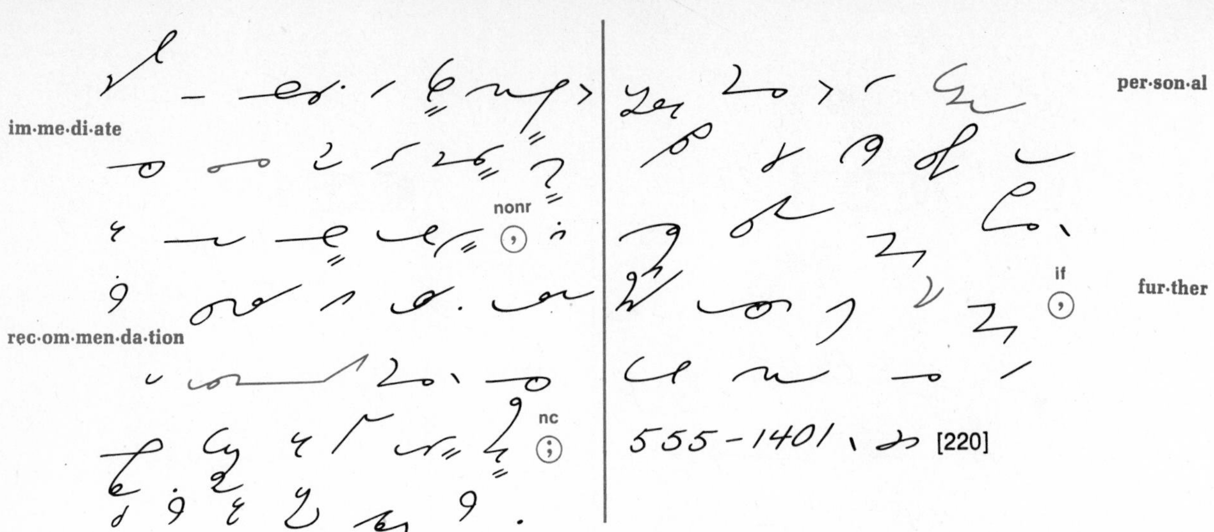

8 Transcription Quiz For you to supply: 7 commas—4 commas series, 1 comma conjunction, 1 comma *if* clause, 1 comma *and* omitted; 1 period courteous request; 2 missing words.

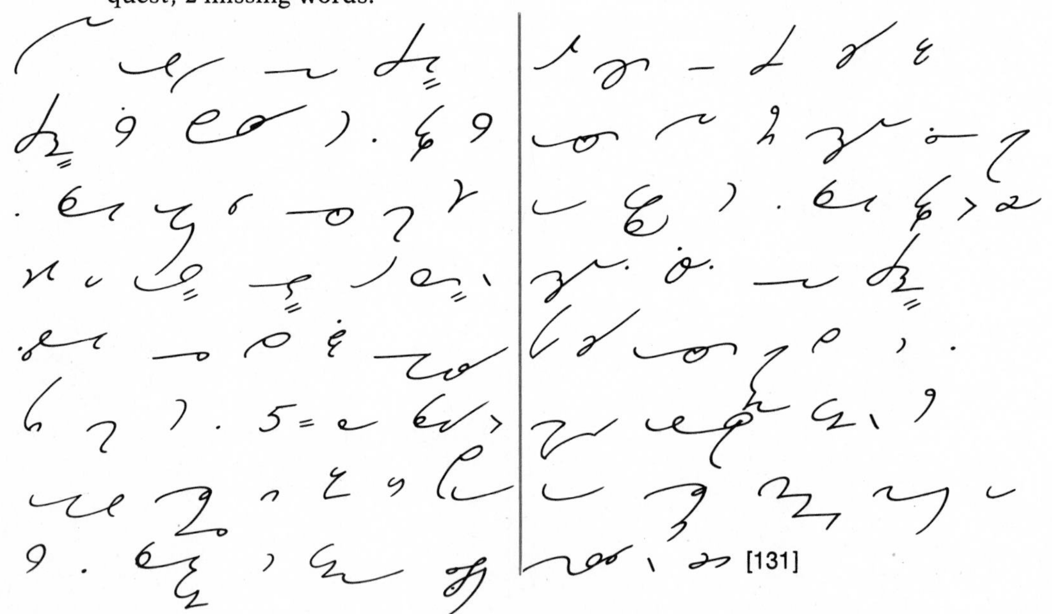

Developing Word-Building Power

1 Word Families

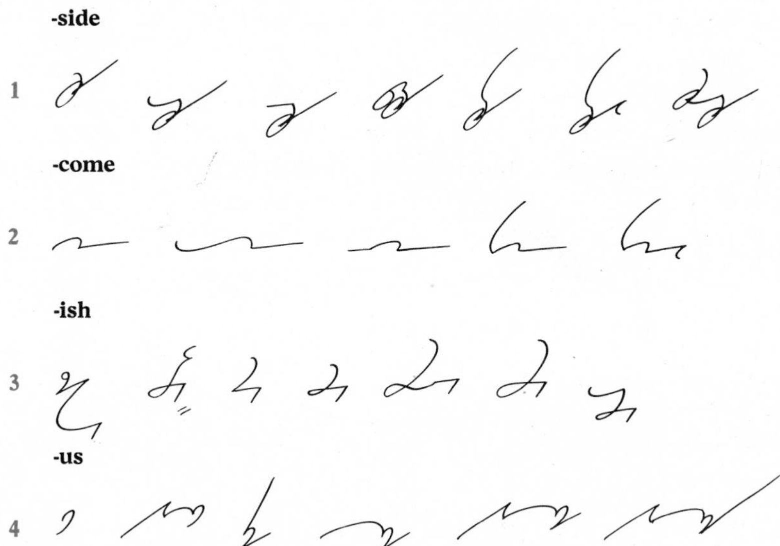

1 Side, reside, inside, outside, beside, besides, fireside.
2 Come, welcome, income, become, becomes.
3 Establish, Spanish, furnish, finish, varnish, vanish, refinish.
4 Us, discuss, just, gust, disgust, disgusted.

Building Transcription Skills

2 PUNCTUATION PRACTICE ● the apostrophe

☐ **1** A noun ending in an *s* sound and followed by another noun is usually a possessive, calling for an apostrophe before the *s* when the word is singular.

One person's *work is done.*

☐ **2** A plural noun ending in *s* calls for an apostophe *after* the *s* to form the possessive.

Several students' *books were lost.*

☐ **3** An irregular plural calls for an apostrophe *before* the *s* to form the possessive.

The store sells children's *clothing.*

☐ **4** The possessive forms of pronouns do not require an apostrophe.

This book is not yours; *it is* ours.
The company keeps its *files in good condition.*

---

3 Business Vocabulary Builder

retroactive To be made effective as of a preceding date.
animosity Ill will; resentment.
rescind To take back; to cancel.
detrimental Harmful.

Reading and Writing Practice

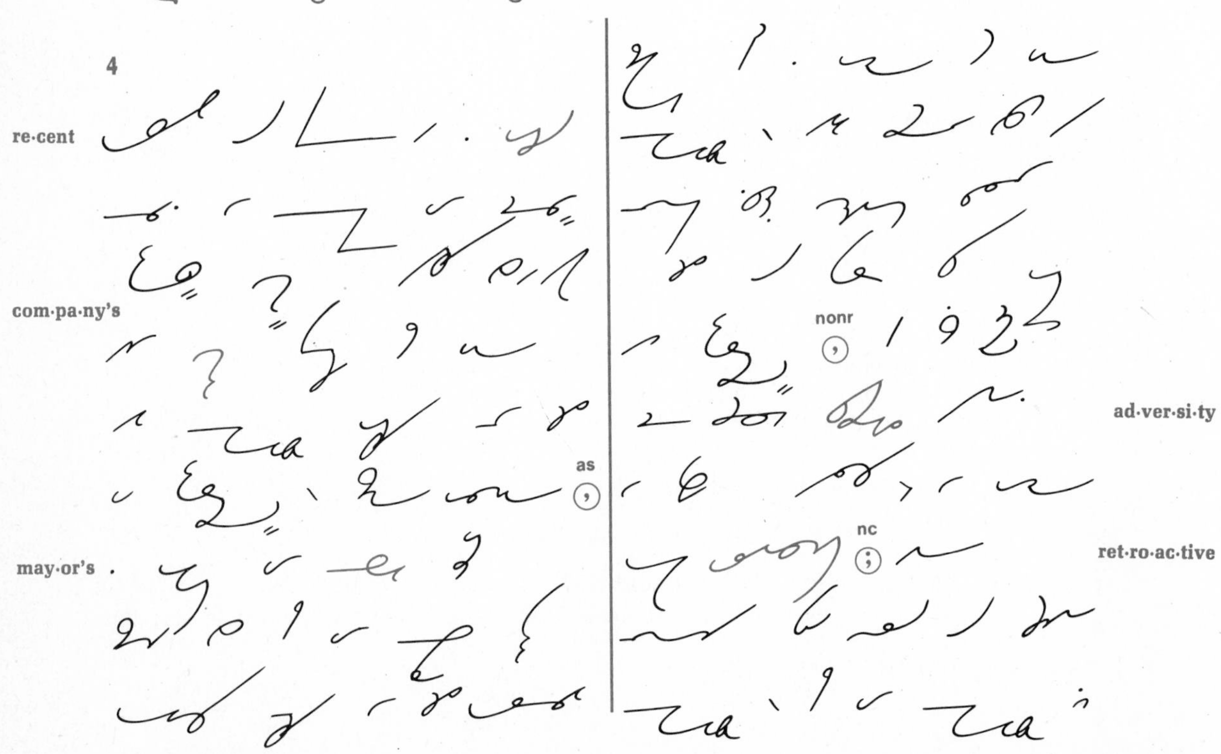

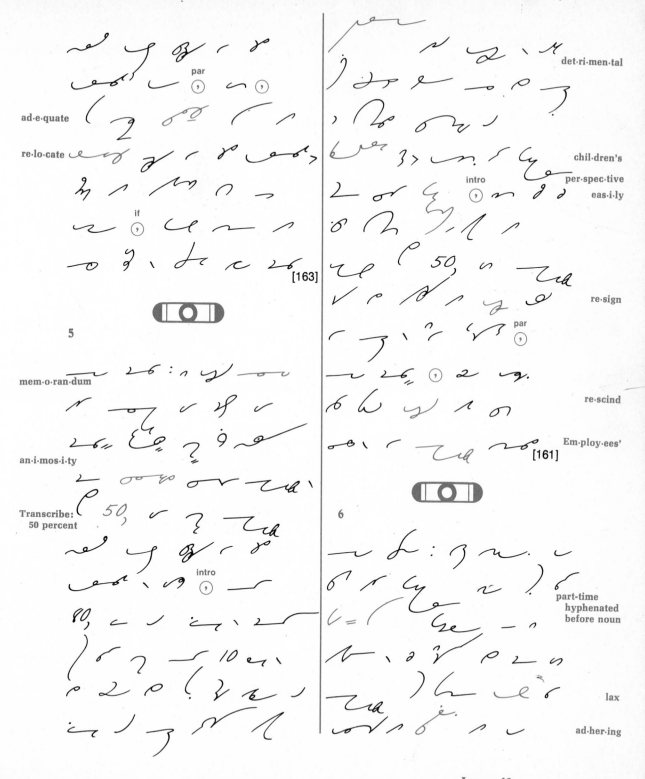

par

ad·e·quate

re·lo·cate

if

[163]

5

mem·o·ran·dum

an·i·mos·i·ty

Transcribe:
50 percent

intro

det·ri·men·tal

chil·dren's

intro

per·spec·tive

eas·i·ly

re·sign

par

re·scind

Em·ploy·ees'

[161]

6

part-time
hyphenated
before noun

lax

ad·her·ing

intro

ours

theirs

com·pa·nies'

conj

par

[123]

7

conj

if

can·di·date

conj

an·nu·al

three-year hyphenated before noun

com·mit·ment

par

[130]

8

nc

if

[38]

9 Transcription Quiz For you to supply: 7 commas—1 comma *as* clause, 1 comma conjunction, 1 comma introductory, 4 commas parenthetical; 2 missing words.

[177]

Developing Word-Building Power

1 Word Beginnings and Endings

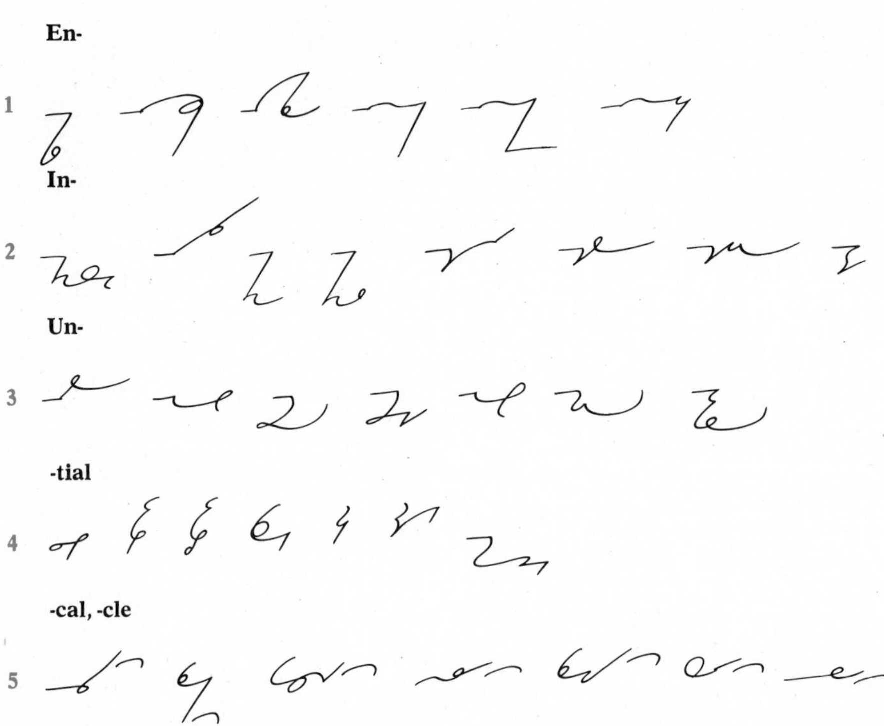

1 Enjoy, engage, endanger, encourage, encouragement, encroach.
2 Insurance, indeed, injure, injury, instant, instill, install, insist.
3 Until, unless, unfilled, unfinished, unwrap, unsold, unspoiled.
4 Initial, special, specially, partial, social, substantial, influential.
5 Medical, surgical, practical, critical, periodical, article, miracle.

Building Transcription Skills

2 PUNCTUATION PRACTICE ● geographical

Place a comma between the name of a city and state.

She lives in Boise, Idaho.

If the name of the state does not end the sentence, a comma follows the name of the state also.

He visited Reno, Nevada, *on his way home.*

Whenever this use of the comma appears in the Reading and Writing Practice, it will be called to your attention thus: geo ,

3 Business Vocabulary Builder

mutually Commonly shared.

commitment An agreement or pledge to do something.

cease To come to an end; to stop.

Reading and Writing Practice

4

yes·ter·day's

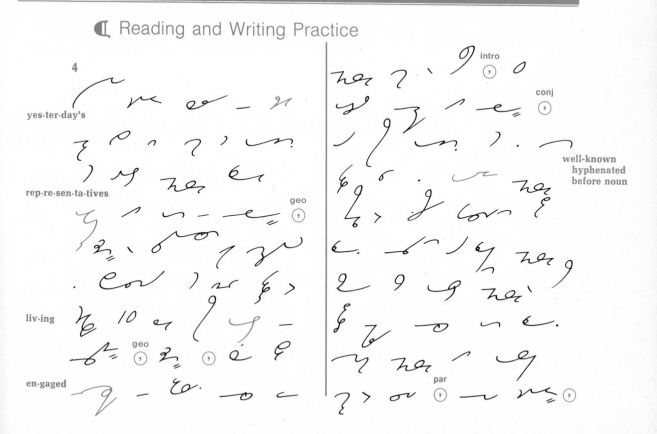

rep·re·sen·ta·tives

geo ,

liv·ing

geo , ,

en·gaged

intro ,

conj ,

well-known hyphenated before noun

par , ,

op·por·tu·ni·ty

fur·ther

if

555-17

for·ward

[201]

5

cho·sen

conj

equal·ly

as

com·pa·ny's

years'

conj

re·quire·ment

par

six-month
long-term
hyphenated
before noun

com·mit·ment

intro

cease

em·bar·rass·ment

nonr

nc

per·son·nel

min·utes'

ar·ti·cle

when

touch

[235]

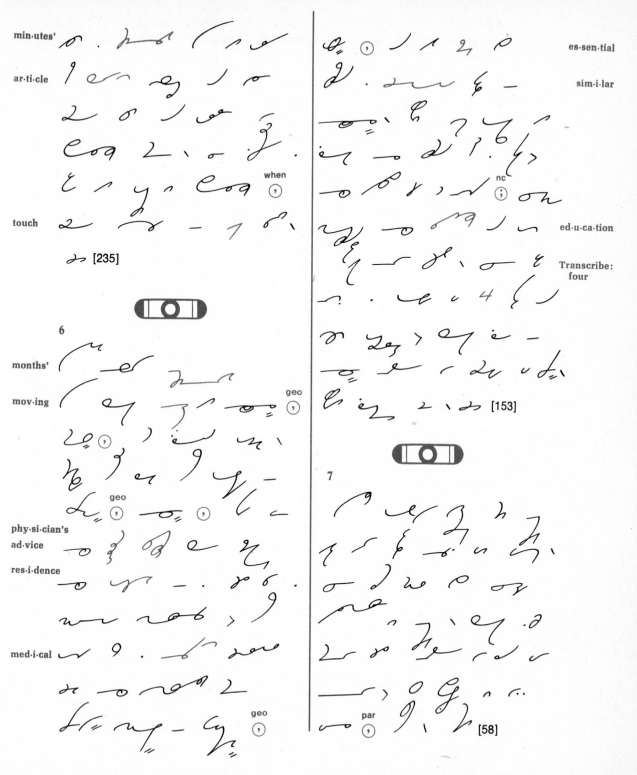

6

months'

mov·ing

geo

geo

phy·si·cian's

ad·vice

res·i·dence

med·i·cal

geo

es·sen·tial

sim·i·lar

nc

ed·u·ca·tion

Transcribe: four

4

[153]

7

par

[58]

8 Transcription Quiz For you to supply: 6 commas—2 commas *if* clause, 2 commas geographical, 1 comma *and* omitted, 1 comma parenthetical; 2 missing words.

[158]

Developing Word-Building Power

1 Shorthand Vocabulary Builder

Dif-, Div-, Etc.

1 [shorthand outlines]

Omission of Short U

2 [shorthand outlines]

Ind-, Int-

3 [shorthand outlines]

Ses

4 [shorthand outlines]

1 Difficult, difference, divide, division, definite, definitely, develop, developing.
2 Much, such, budget, touch, rush, lunch, luncheon.
3 Industry, indecision, indelible, intellect, intelligent, integrity.
4 Services, offices, process, versus, sister, assist, persist, consist, necessary.

Building Transcription Skills

2 Business Vocabulary Builder

hinder To make slow or difficult; to prevent.
indifference A lack of interest.
prosper To succeed; to do well.

Reading and Writing Practice

3 Personnel—A Valuable Asset

in·dus·try's

com·pa·ny's

its

ser

in·tel·li·gent

de·pend·able

and o

if

suc·ceed

char·ac·ter

in·teg·ri·ty

if

intro

if

Per·son·nel

par

em·ploy·ees

and o

con·trib·ut·ing

if

in·dif·fer·ence

de·vel·op

par

breaks

ef·fect

em·ploy·ees'

if

ex·clud·ed

fost·er

if

People

dai·ly

short-term hyphenated before noun

conj

The

or·ga·ni·za·tion's

ser

Transcribe:
5
10
20

short-range
long-range
hyphenated before noun

if

its

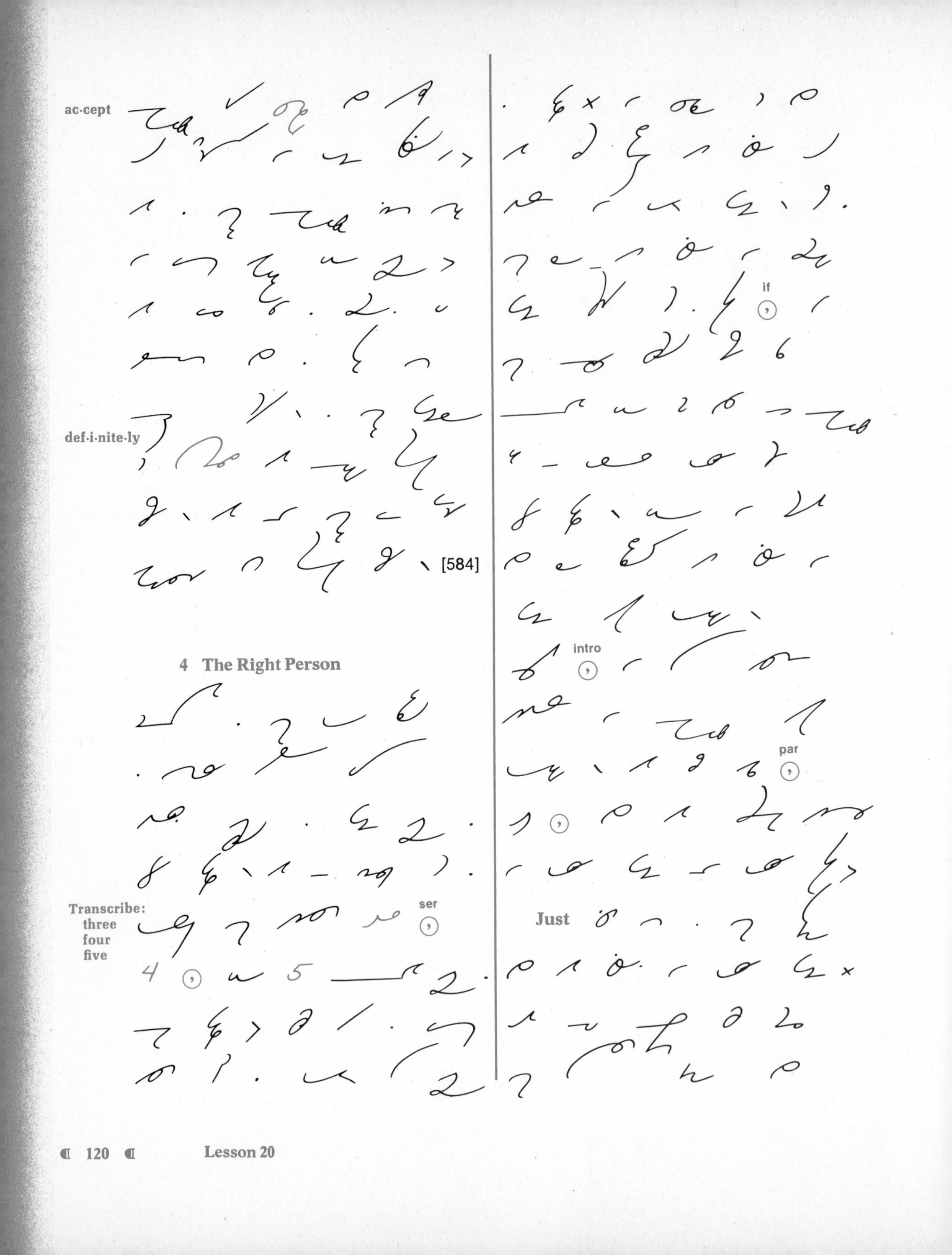

ac·cept

def·i·nite·ly

[584]

4 The Right Person

Transcribe:
three
four
five

ser

if

intro

par

Just

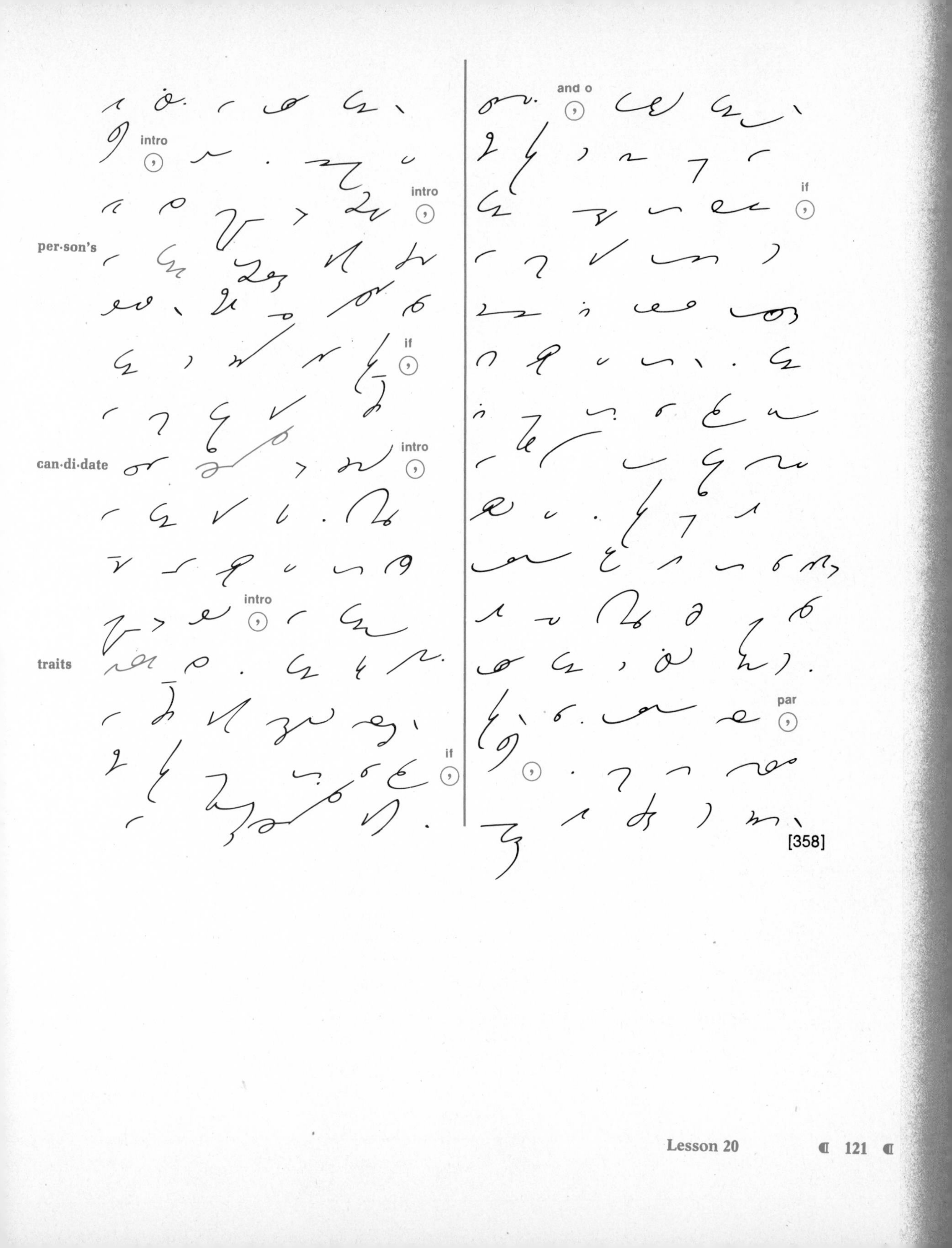

intro

intro

per·son's

if

can·di·date

intro

intro

traits

if

and o

if

par

[358]

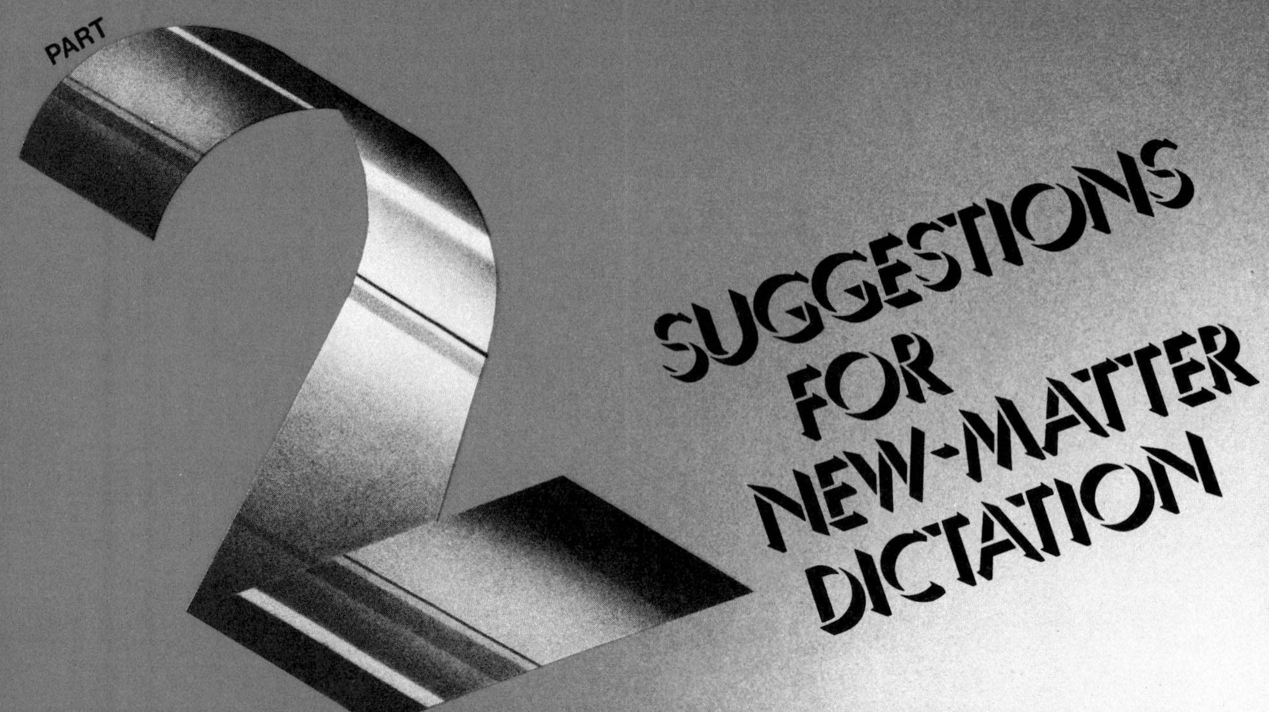

You have no doubt been taking dictation on unfamiliar material, that is, material that you have not previously practiced. As you have probably discovered, developing skill in the writing of unfamiliar material presents several problems. Here are some suggestions that will help you meet those problems.

Unfamiliar Words

Every shorthand writer — even the most experienced — will occasionally have to write a word that is unfamiliar. In your work hardly a day will pass that you will not encounter a new word. When this happens, try to write it in full; write all the sounds that you hear. If this is not possible, try to write at least the beginning of the word. Often this beginning, with the help of context, will help you find the word in the dictionary.

If the word completely escapes you, leave a space in your notes — perhaps skip a line — and continue writing. Don't spend so much time trying to construct an outline that the dictation gets too far ahead of you. When you transcribe, you will probably be able to fill in the word or supply an acceptable substitute.

Words You Do Not Hear

When you do not hear — or mishear — a word, leave a space in your notes. When you transcribe, you may be able to determine the meaning of the word from the context.

If you think you hear a word but know from the context that it could not possibly be the correct one, write the word that you think you hear and circle it. If you are too pressed for time to circle it, skip a line. Often this outline will help you supply the correct word.

Occasionally the word you did not hear—or misheard—will occur to you later during dictation. Do not take the time to insert it in the proper place. Instead, jot the word in the margin of your notes or just remember it and fill it in immediately upon the completion of the dictation.

Poorly Written Outlines

No matter how skillful shorthand writers may be, they will occasionally write a poor outline during dictation. When this happens to you, don't scratch out that outline and write a better one. The dictator will not stop while you are correcting your notes, and you may find yourself hopelessly behind. Once you have written an outline, leave it. Even though you may have written it poorly, the chances are that, with the help of context, you will be able to read it.

Phrasing

Using good phrases is a great help in developing shorthand speed. However, the dictators may not always say a phrase as one piece. They may say one word in a phrase and then pause before saying the remaining words. When that occurs, you will probably have the first word written before you hear the rest of the phrase. Do *not* stop to scratch out the word you have written and substitute the phrase. This takes time, and time is precious in speed development. Rather, write the remaining words of the phrase as though a phrase were not involved.

5
GOVERNMENT

Developing Word-Building Power

1 Brief Forms and Derivatives

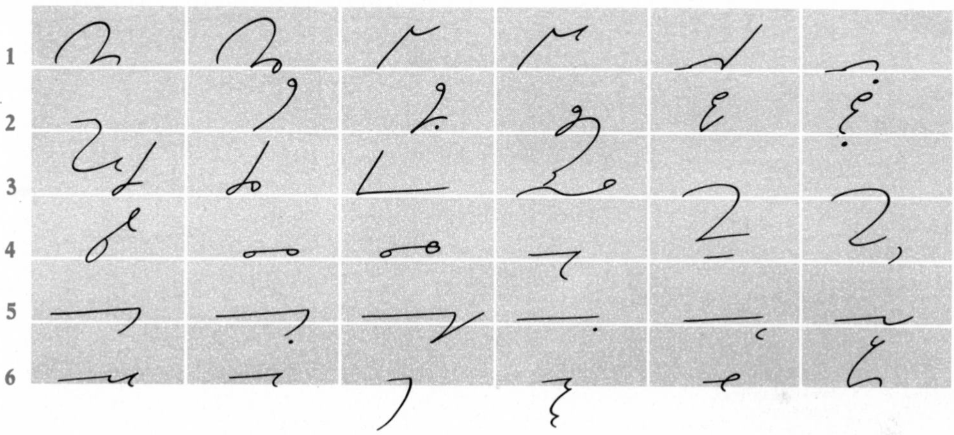

1 Difficult, difficulty, doctor, doctors, enclosed, enclosing.
2 Envelopes, ever-every, everything, executives, experienced, experiencing.
3 General, generally, gentlemen, gladly, government, governor.
4 Ideas, immediate, immediately, important-importance, in-not, his-is.
5 Manufacture, manufacturing, manufactured, morning, mornings, Mr.
6 Mrs., Ms., never, newspapers, next, object.

Building Transcription Skills

2 TYPING STYLE STUDY ● dates

1 If the month precedes the day, do not use *th*, *st*, or *d* after the number.

On August 21, 1979, *we opened our doors for business.*

When a date is expressed this way, place a comma both before and after the year.

2 If the day precedes the month or if the day stands alone, *th, st,* or *d* should be included.

On the 3d *of January we will visit our friends.*
We plan to be out of town on the 25th.

3 Business Vocabulary Builder

succession Sequence; one after the other.
meritorious Deserving of regard or honor.
dynamic Powerful.

Reading and Writing Practice

4 Brief-Form Letter

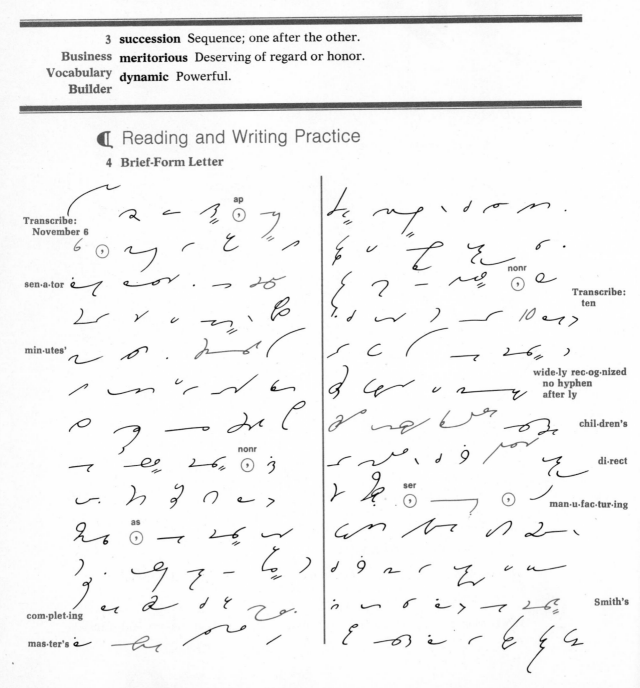

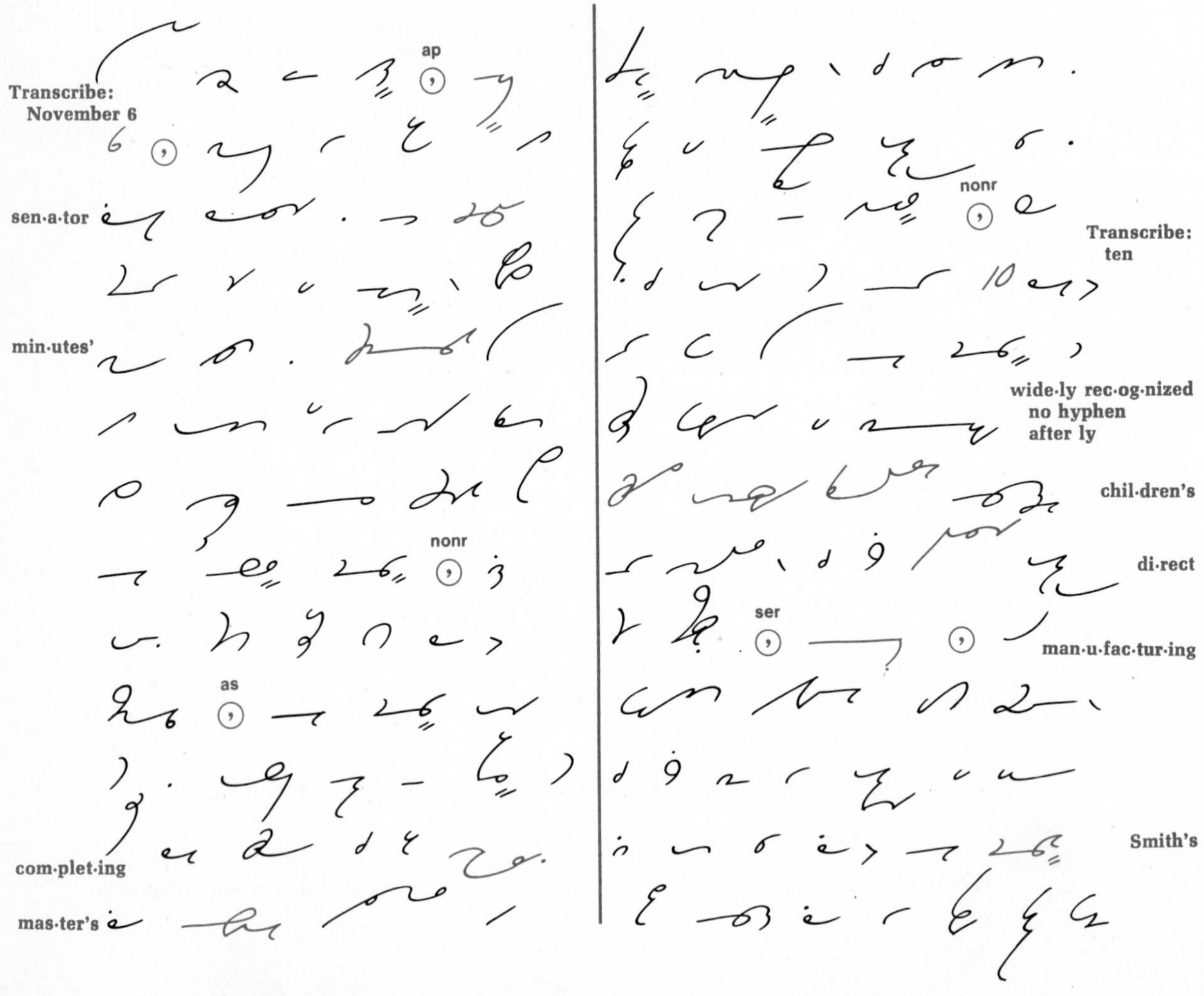

nc

[203]

5

polls

as

choose

well-qual·i·fied hyphenated before noun.

nc

intro

opin·ion

ser

con·fi·dence

years'

Transcribe: June 1, 1965,

when

1965

intro

chose

suc·ces·sion

ser

mer·i·to·ri·ous

or·di·nary

nc

def·i·nite·ly

cr

[267]

6

Transcribe: 7th

as

na·tion's

de·vel·op·ing

dy·nam·ic

when

[113]

7

morn·ing's

geo

Coun·cil

intro

par

conj

well qual·i·fied no noun, no hyphen

nonr

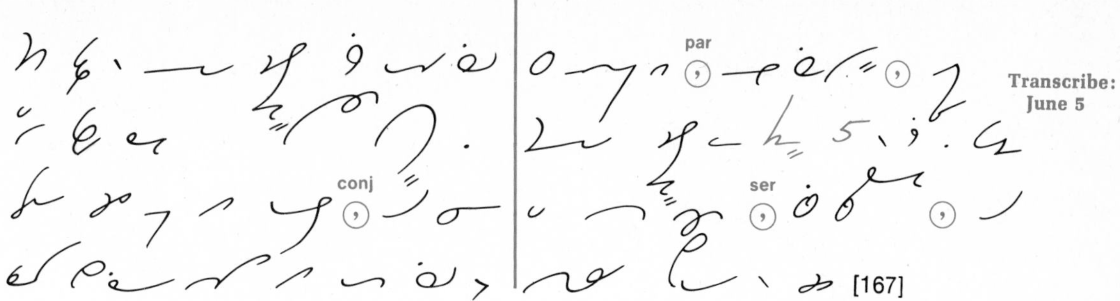

Transcribe: June 5

8 Transcription Quiz Beginning with this lesson the transcription quizzes will be a greater challenge to you. Thus far you have had to supply only commas, periods indicating courteous requests, and missing words; hereafter you will also have to supply semicolons.

For you to supply: 8 commas—3 commas *if* clause, 1 comma *and* omitted, 1 comma introductory, 2 commas series, 1 comma conjunction; 1 semicolon no conjunction; 2 missing words.

[154]

A NOTE FROM A CHAMPION

When Martin J. Dupraw won the world's shorthand championship, he established some remarkable records for accuracy. On a speech dictated at 200 words a minute for five minutes, he made only one error. On court testimony dictated at 280 words a minute for five minutes, he made only two errors. These and many other records that he has established are the result, in large measure, of the amazing legibility of his shorthand notes.

When you examine Mr. Dupraw's shorthand notes on the opposite page, one thing will immediately impress you—the careful attention to proportion.

Notice, for example, how large he makes the *a* circles and how small he makes the *e* circles. Notice, too, how much larger his *l's* are than his *r's*.

Another thing that will strike you is the way he rounds off angles. He does not consciously do this; rounding angles comes naturally to him as a result of his high speed. As your speed increases, you, too, will find that you will naturally round off angles.

In the page that Mr. Dupraw has written in his beautiful shorthand, he discusses the size of notes. Note that he has fairly large shorthand style, just as he has a large longhand style.

Don't try to imitate Mr. Dupraw's style of writing; take the advice he gives in his article, "How Big Should My Shorthand Be?"

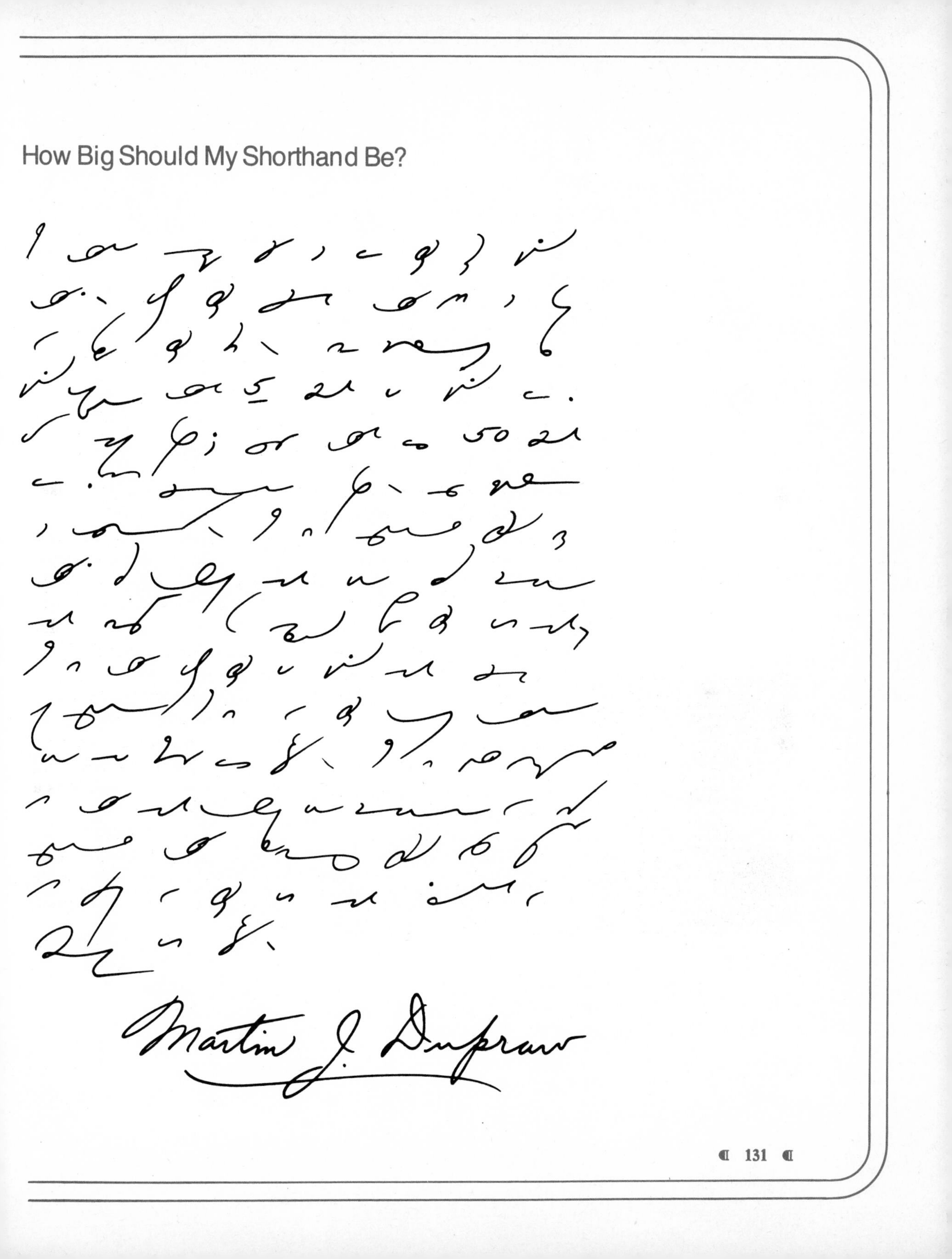

How Big Should My Shorthand Be?

Martin J. Dupraw

Building Phrasing Skill

1 Useful Business-Letter Phrases

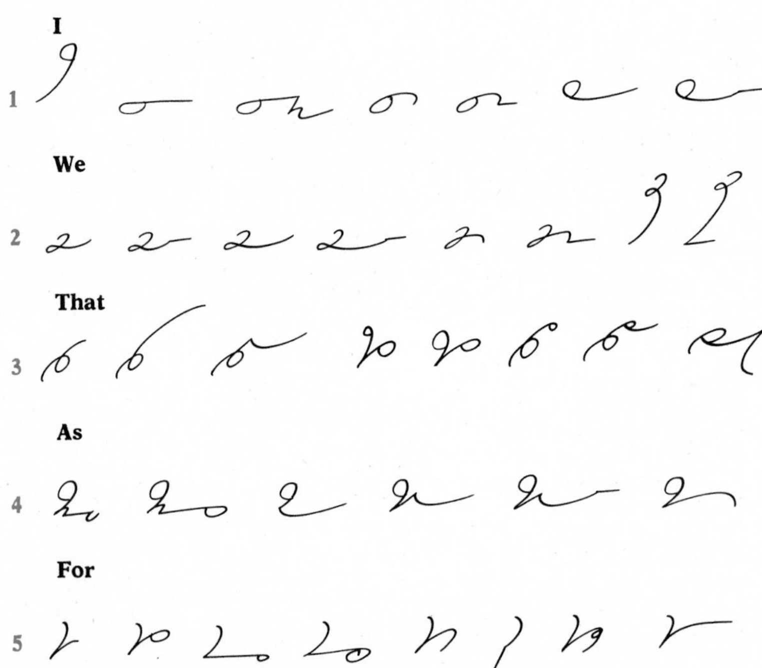

1 I have, I am, I am sure, I can, I cannot, I will, I will not.
2 We are, we are not, we will, we will not, we can, we cannot, we have, we have not.
3 That the, that time, that it will, if that, as that, that they, that they are, that will be.
4 As you know, as you may, as well, as it will, as it will not, as good.
5 For the, for that, for me, for my, for this, for which, for these, for them.

2 Geographical Expressions

1

2

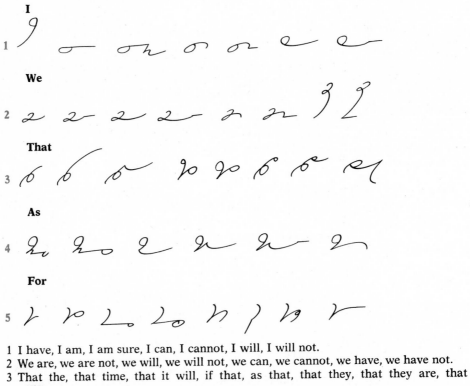

1 Oklahoma City, Fargo, Tulsa, Lincoln, Omaha, Wichita.
2 Oklahoma, Kansas, Montana, Nebraska, North Dakota, South Dakota.

Building Transcription Skills

3 TYPING STYLE STUDY ● addresses in sentences

□ **1** Use figures for house numbers.

He lives at 742 *Main Street.*

□ **2** Spell out numbers below 11 in street names.

She works at 800 Third *Avenue.*

□ **3** Use figures for street names above ten.

My new address is 228 East 38 *Street, New York, New York 10030.*

Note: □ **1** Spell out *Street, Road, Drive,* etc.
□ **2** If a direction indicator such as *East* occurs before a numbered street name, *th, st,* or *d* may be omitted.

4 Business Vocabulary Builder

intensify To increase in degree; to aggravate; to heighten.
density The quantity per unit of space.
congestion A condition of overcrowding.
inadequate Not enough; insufficient.

Reading and Writing Practice

5 Phrase Letter

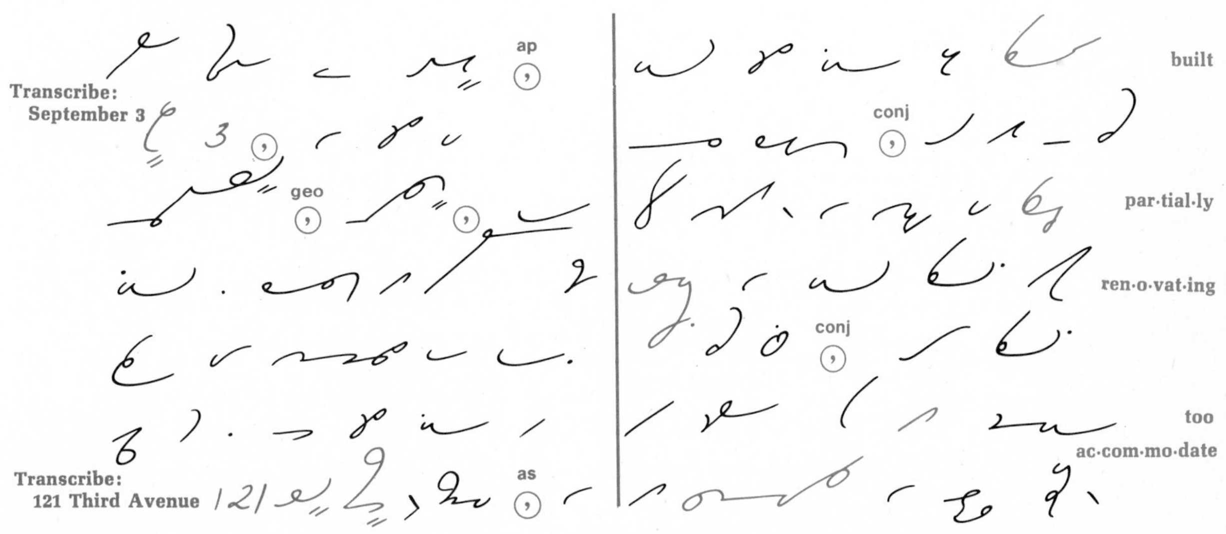

sites

intro

waste

conj

au·tho·rized

if

up-to-date hyphenated before noun

and o

well spent no noun, no hyphen

nc

[181]

6

Transcribe: 742 24th Street

742 24

geo

height

frame·work

intro

your·self

cr

in·ten·si·fy

con·ges·tion

al·ready

den·si·ty

[158]

7

mid·dle

se·ri·ous

par

intro

Coun·cil

drain·age

cr

[78] al·le·vi·ate

8 **Transcription Quiz** For you to supply: 5 commas—2 commas introductory, 1 comma *as* clause, 2 commas conjunction; 1 semicolon no conjunction; 2 missing words.

[165]

Developing Word-Building Power

1 Word Families

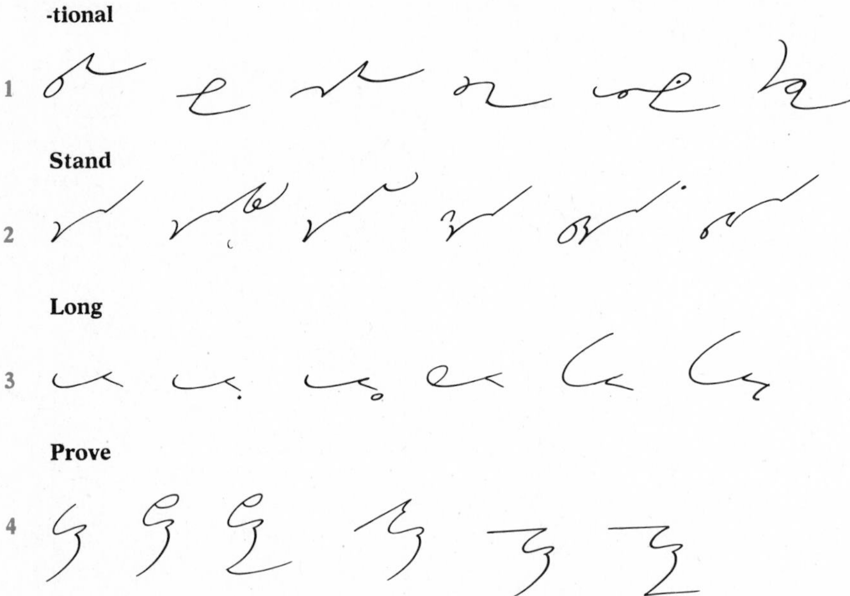

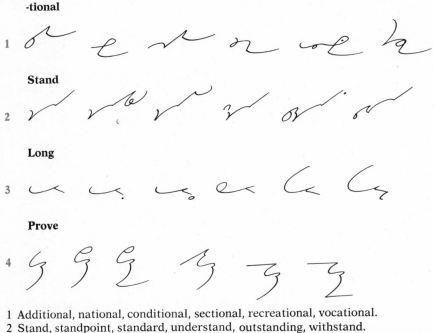

1 Additional, national, conditional, sectional, recreational, vocational.
2 Stand, standpoint, standard, understand, outstanding, withstand.
3 Long, longing, longingly, along, belong, belongs.
4 Prove, approve, approval, disprove, improve, improvement.

Building Transcription Skills

2 TYPING STYLE STUDY ● amounts of money

☐ **1** When transcribing whole dollar amounts in business correspondence, do not add a decimal point or zeros.

The bill for $75 (*not* $75.00) *was received today.*

□ **2** In business correspondence use the word *cents* in amounts under $1.

The cost was only 39 cents (*not* $.39).

□ **3** Even millions and billions of dollars may be transcribed in numbers and words for easier reading.

The building cost $18 million.

When amounts such as the above appear in the Reading and Writing Practice, they will occasionally be called to your attention in the margin of the shorthand thus: **Transcribe: $1 million**

3 Business Vocabulary Builder

annex *(verb)* To take possession or control of.

adjacent Next to.

pending Not yet decided or acted upon.

unanimously Agreed to by all.

Reading and Writing Practice

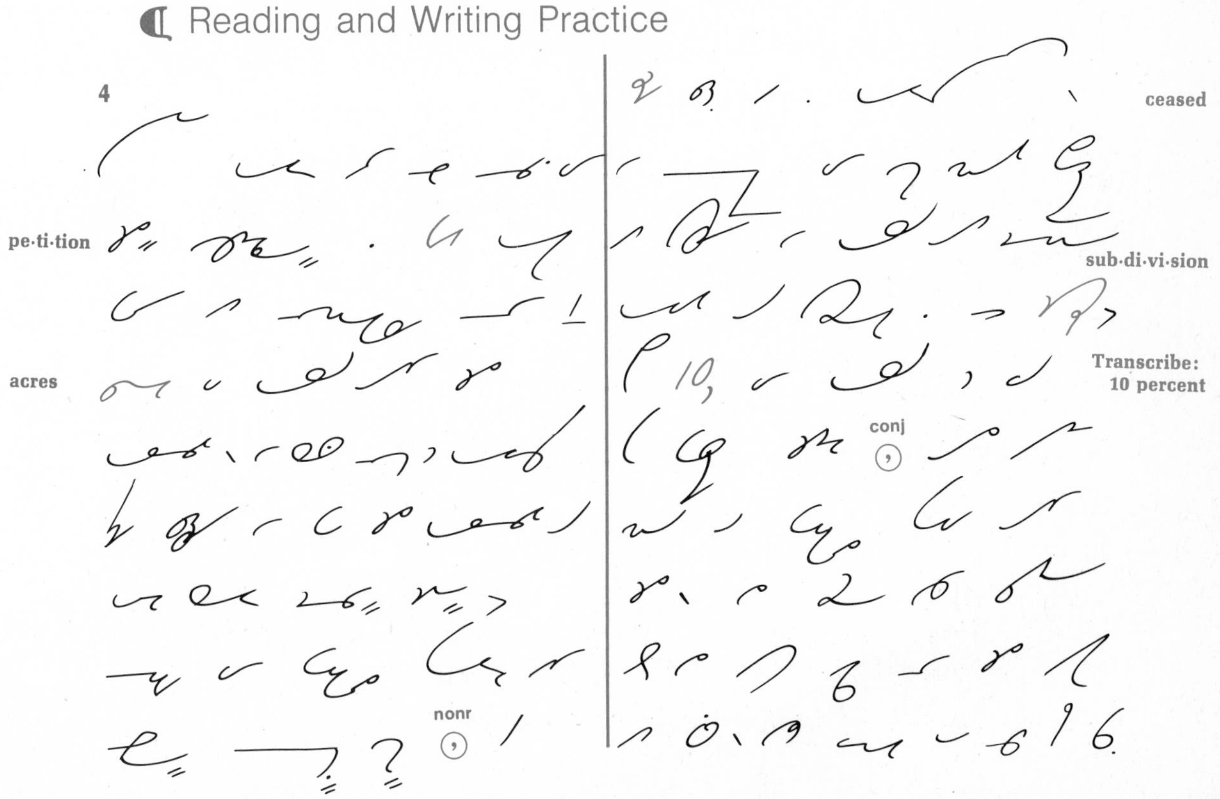

Transcribe: $200

conj

if

Transcribe: $300

intro

cir·cum·stances

sched·uled

cr

[197]

5

geo

an·nex

par

intro

as

nonr

ad·ja·cent

yours

Transcribe: $3 million

if

Transcribe: $5,000

ap

Transcribe: 42 East 46 Street

par

gov·ern·ment

thor·ough·ly

[239]

6

back·ing

nonr

bad·ly

conj

sub·mit·ted

com·plete

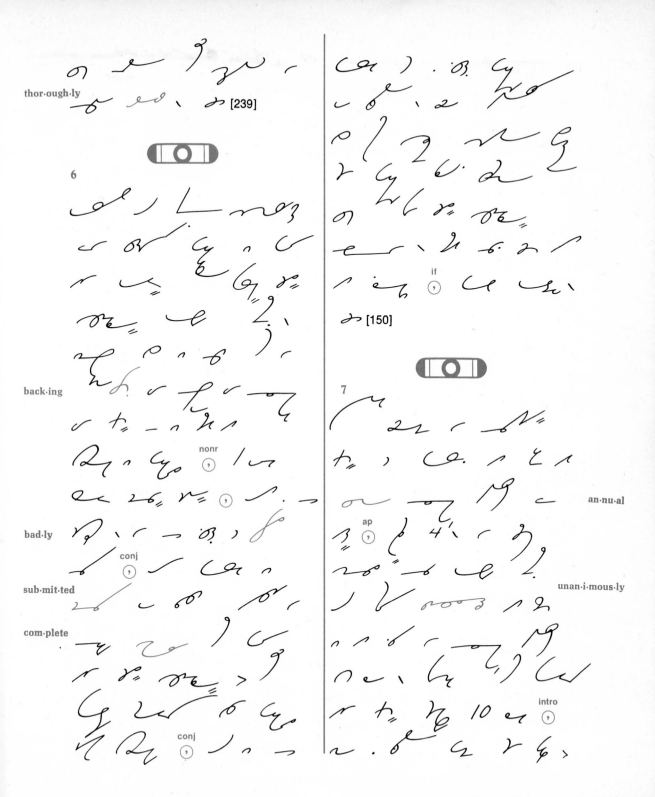

conj

if

[150]

7

an·nu·al

ap

unan·i·mous·ly

intro

add

50

50

Transcribe: $2,000

par

par

ac·cept

[159]

8 Transcription Quiz For you to supply: 5 commas—4 commas parenthetical, 1 comma *if* clause; 1 semicolon no conjunction; 2 missing words.

25

50

10

[173]

Developing Word-Building Power

1 Word Beginnings and Endings

Dis-, Des-

Al-

Electric-

-ful

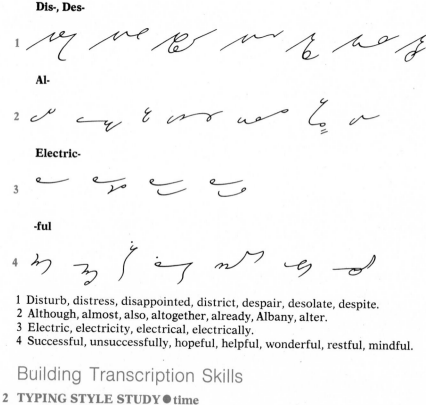

1 Disturb, distress, disappointed, district, despair, desolate, despite.
2 Although, almost, also, altogether, already, Albany, alter.
3 Electric, electricity, electrical, electrically.
4 Successful, unsuccessfully, hopeful, helpful, wonderful, restful, mindful.

Building Transcription Skills

2 TYPING STYLE STUDY ● time

☐ **1** Use figures to express time with *o'clock.* (Remember the apostrophe.)

We arrived at 9 *o'clock (not* nine *o'clock).*

☐ **2** Use figures to express time with *a.m.* and *p.m.*

They left at 10:15 *a.m. and returned at* 11 *p.m.*

Note: Type *a.m.* and *p.m.* with small letters and no space after the first period.

☐ **3** Spellout time if *a.m., p.m.,* or *o'clock* is not used.

We are open from nine *to* six.

Occasionally these expressions of time will be called to your attention in the margins of the shorthand in the Reading and Writing Practice thus:

Transcribe:
9 a.m.

3 Business Vocabulary Builder

dismayed Disappointed; upset.

inflation Reduction in buying power because of increased prices.

radical Extreme; unusual.

Reading and Writing Practice

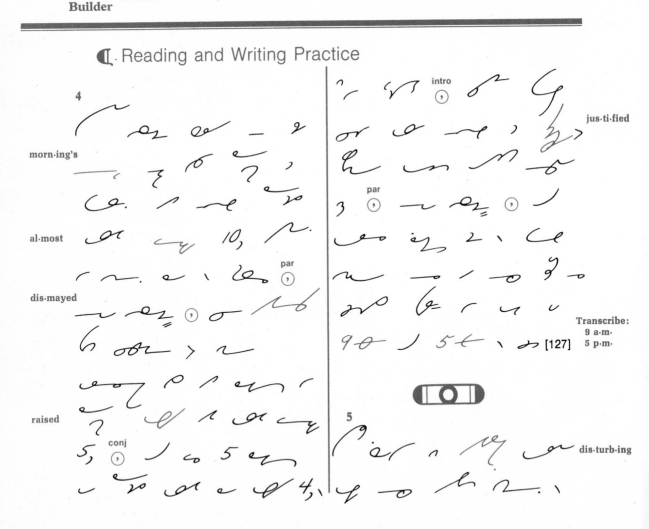

4

morn·ing's

al·most

dis·mayed

raised

conj

par

intro

jus·ti·fied

par

Transcribe:
9 a.m.
5 p.m.

[127]

5

dis·turb·ing

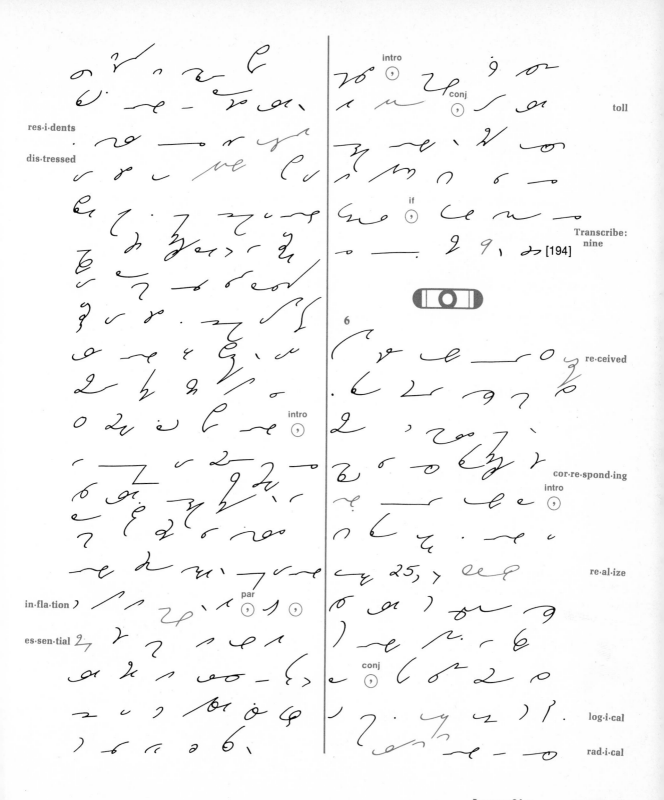

res·i·dents

dis·tressed

intro

in·fla·tion

par

es·sen·tial

intro

conj

toll

if

Transcribe: nine

[194]

6

re·ceived

cor·re·spond·ing

intro

re·al·ize

25,

conj

log·i·cal

rad·i·cal

intro

hope·ful

when

nc

555-1746

Transcribe:
9 o'clock
5 o'clock

9 5

[151]

7

as

zon·ing

geo

des·ig·nate

nonr

intro

suc·cess·ful

conj

dis·ap·point·ed

at·tempt

by·pass

con·ges·tion

ad·vi·so·ry

[193]

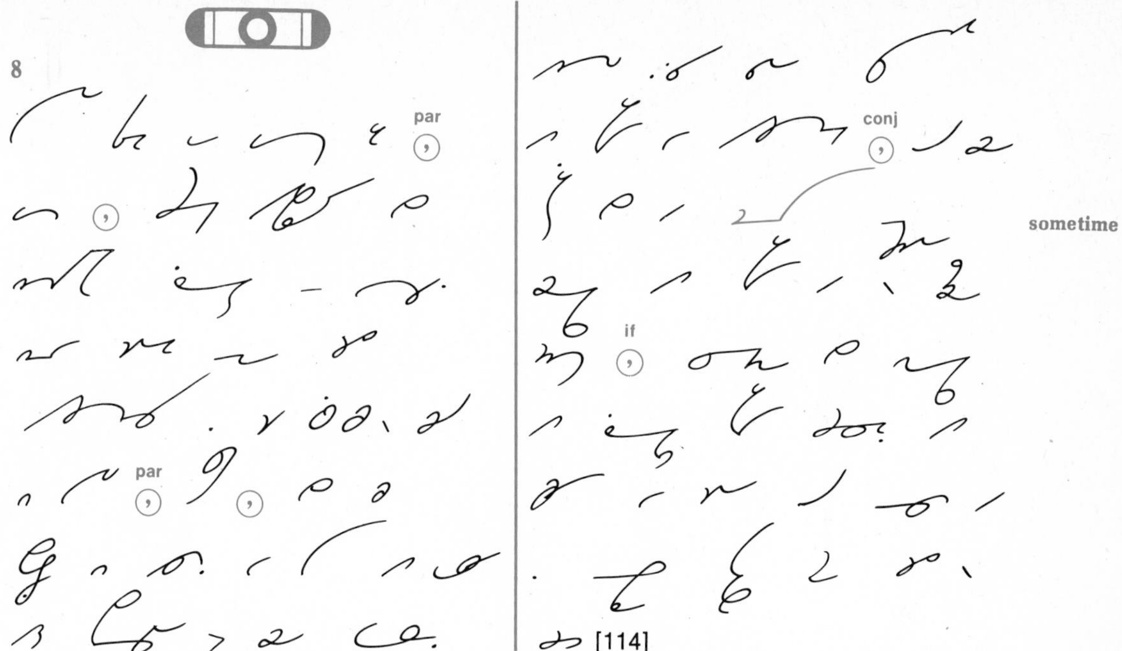

9 Transcription Quiz For you to supply: 4 commas—3 commas apposition, 1 comma introductory; 1 semicolon no conjunction; 2 missing words.

[121]

Developing Word-Building Power

1 Shorthand Vocabulary Builder

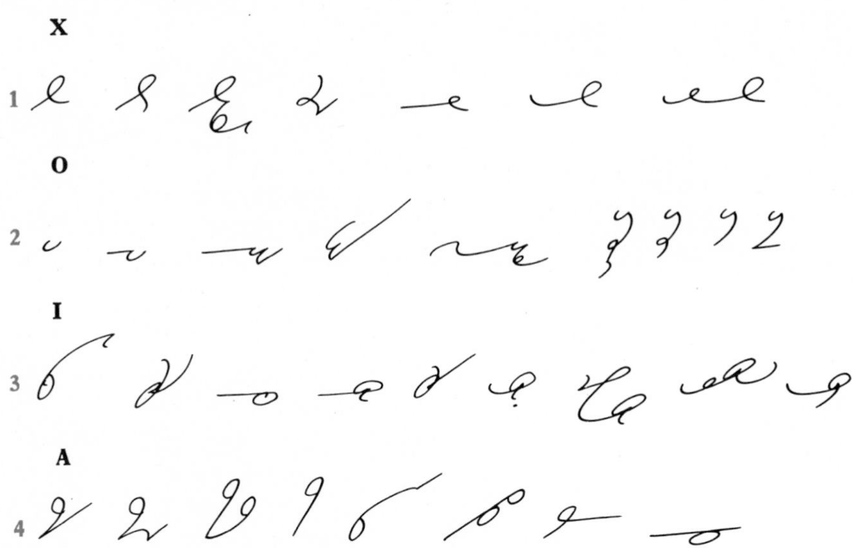

1 Tax, taxes, taxpayers, fixed, mix, lax, relax.
2 Owe, no, most, posted, closer, officials, office, off, often.
3 Items, find, my, myself, side, rising, stabilize, retired, life.
4 Afford, affect, agenda, age, attempt, data, tame, main.

Building Transcription Skills

2 Business Vocabulary Builder

assemble To meet together; to gather.
fraud An act of trickery; deception.
unscrupulous Lacking in moral integrity.

Reading and Writing Practice

3 Government—How Big Is Big?

an·swer

par

when

dis·agree

par

The

ser

in·ter·pret·ing

en·forc·ing

Transcribe: three

conj

intro

rep·re·sen·ta·tive

intro

par

intro

well fi·nanced no noun, no hyphen

conj

The

ed·u·ca·tion

ar·gue

peo·ple's

theft

van·dal·ism

when

writ·ten

speech

ser

as·sem·ble

when

for·mer·ly

Some

con·sum·er·pro·tec·tion
en·vi·ron·men·tal·con·trol
hyphenated
before noun

fraud
un·scru·pu·lous

ser

con·ges·tion

conj

intro

Just

ser

nonr

[519]

4 The Branches of Government

leg·is·la·tive

ser

ju·di·cial

Each of

and o

[202]

6 BANKING

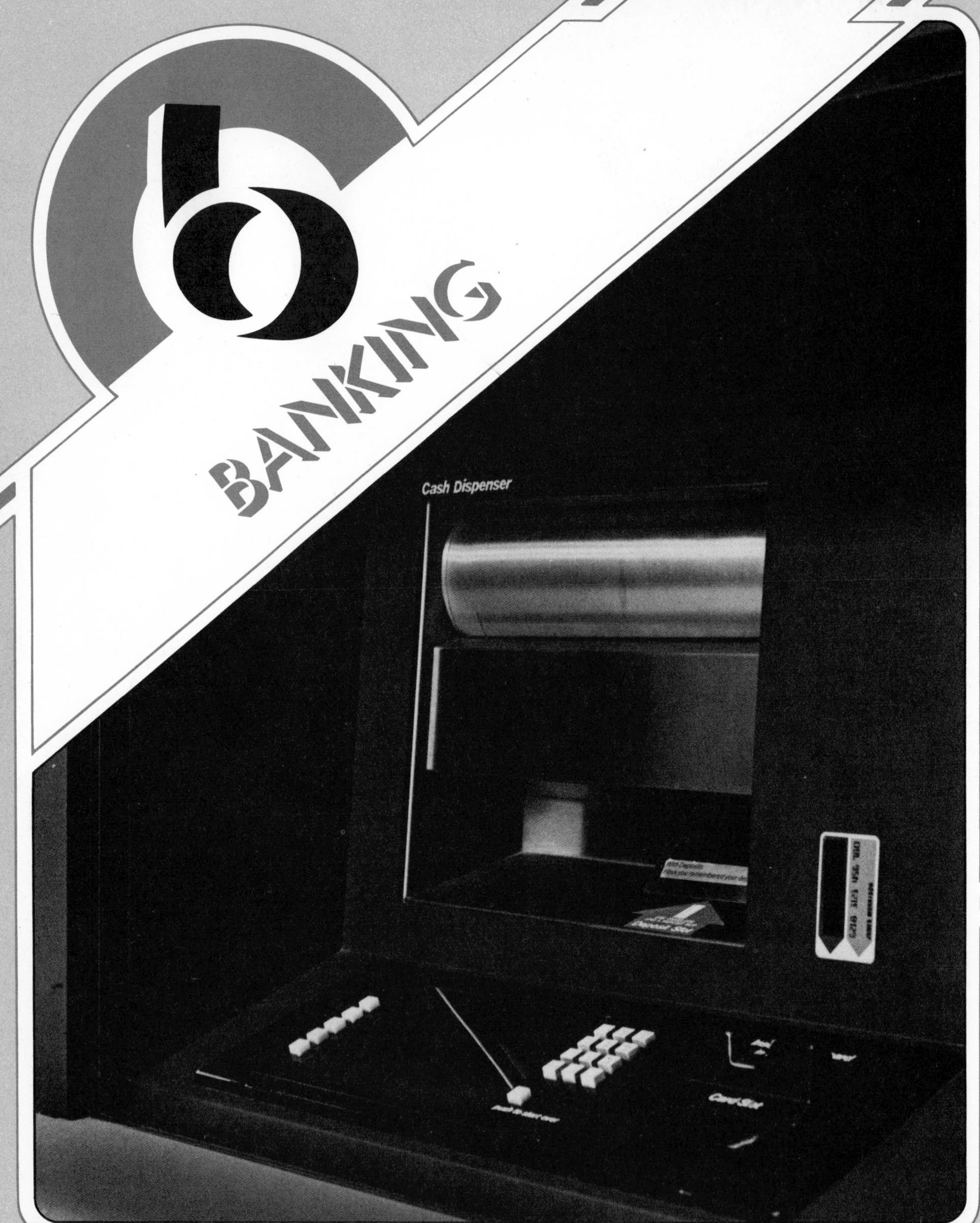

Developing Word-Building Power

1 Brief Forms and Derivatives

1 Objected, objective, one (won), once, opinion, opinions.
2 Opportunity, opportunities, order, orders, ordered, ordering.
3 Ordinary, ordinarily, organize, organized, organization, organizational.
4 Out, outside, over, overcome, overtake, part.
5 Department, apartment, particular, particularly, present, represent.
6 Representative, probable, probably, probability, progressed, progressive.

Building Transcription Skills

2 TYPING STYLE STUDY ● capitalization

Company Names

Divisions in an Organization

□ 1 Capitalize the first letter in the main words of a company name. Capitalize the word *the* only when it is part of the legal name of the organization. (Check the letterhead of the company to be sure.)

He works for The General Manufacturing Company.
She worked for the State National Bank.

□ **2** Common organizational terms, such as *advertising department, manufacturing division, finance committee,* and *board of directors,* are not ordinarily capitalized.

> *The* board of directors *will not meet this month.*
> *She heads the* finance committee.
> *He works in the* advertising department.

---

3 Business Vocabulary Builder

assets Resources; property that can be sold for cash.
yield To give back; to return.
substantial Considerable; major.

Reading and Writing Practice

4 Brief-Form Letter

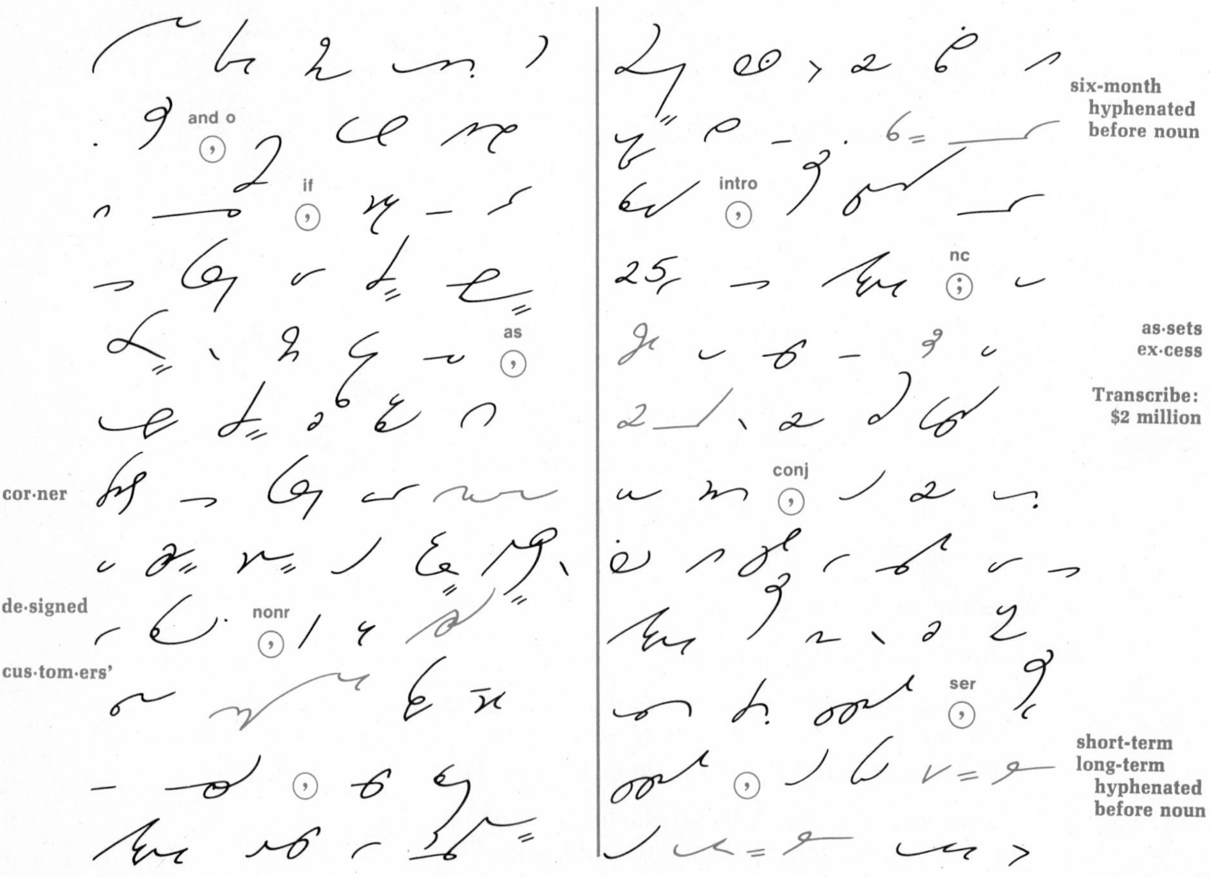

intro

nc

[168]

[118]

5

when

sum

intro

bear

Transcribe:
5 percent

yield

Transcribe:
200 State Street

6

ap

par

and o

ap·pre·ci·ate

prompt

ef·fi·cient

oc·curred

if

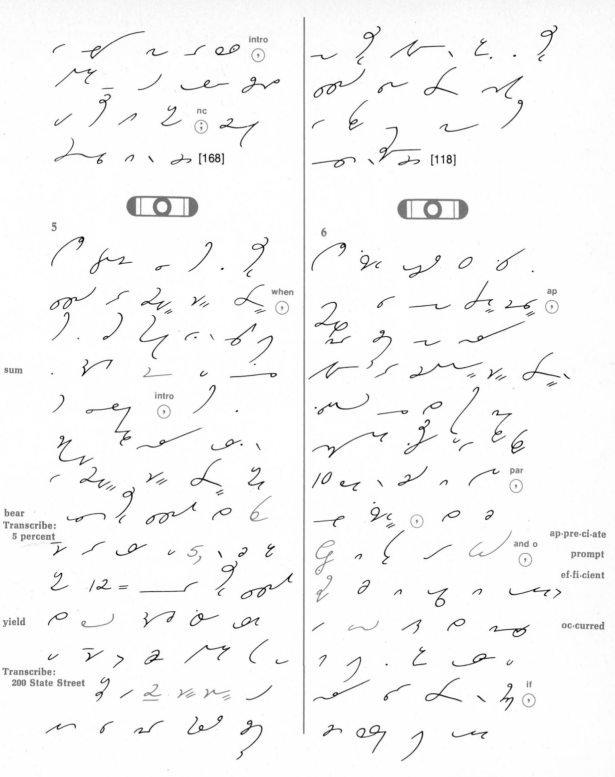

Transcribe: $1,000

ser

nc

[147]

7

to·day's

re·ceived

as

de·vices
ac·cept·ed

nc

intro

out-of-town
hyphenated
before noun

conj

pro·cess·ing

rou·tine

cr

when

[144]

touch

8

re·gard

nc

nc ; intro ,

intro ,

mov·ing

cur·rent

book·keep·ing

if ,

[130]

9

ap ,

, conj , de·pos·it Transcribe: $500

re·ceive

dup·li·cate

cr .

par ,

,

[93]

10

em·ploy·ees

ap ,

conj ,

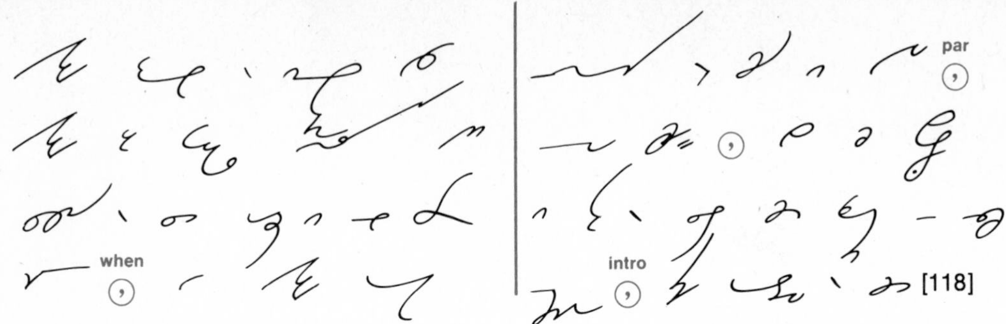

11 Transcription Quiz For you to supply: 4 commas—1 comma conjunction, 1 comma *if* clause, 2 commas parenthetical; 1 semicolon no conjunction; 2 missing words.

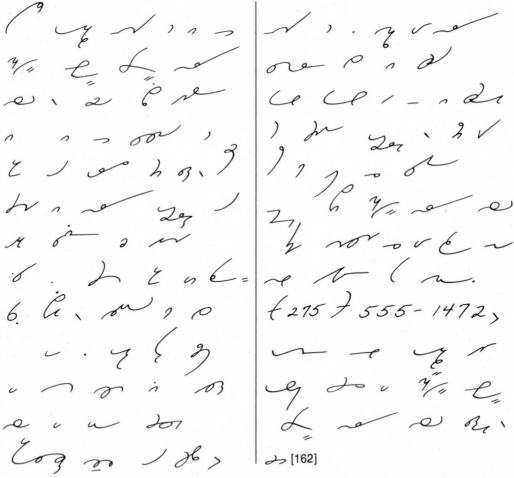

(275) 555-1472

[162]

Building Phrasing Skill

1 Useful Business-Letter Phrases

Few

Thank

Sure

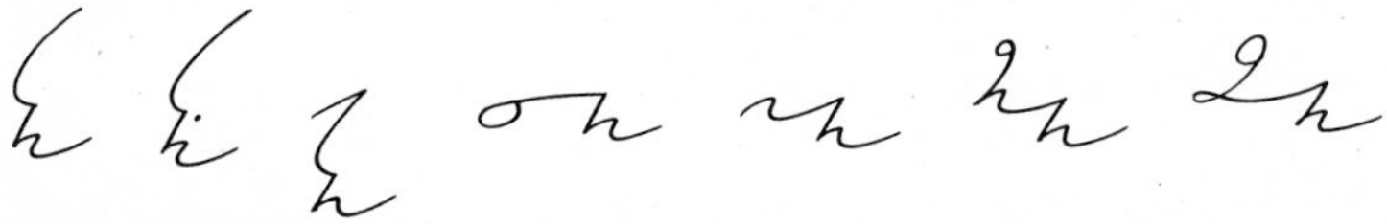

Miscellaneous

1 Few days, few days ago, few months, few months ago, few minutes.
2 Thank you, thank you for, thank you for your, thank you for the, thank you for your order, thank you for this, thank you for these, thank you for that.
3 Be sure, being sure, to be sure, I am sure, you are sure, if you are sure, I feel sure.
4 As soon as, as soon as possible, to me, to know, to make, to do, let us, let me.

2 Geographical Expressions

1 Juneau, Honolulu, St. Louis, Kansas City, Jefferson City.
2 Alaska, Hawaii, Missouri, Wyoming, America, American.

Building Transcription Skills

3 SIMILAR-WORDS DRILL ● through, thought, though

through From one point to another.

I drove *through* the state of Wyoming.

thought Past tense of *think*.

He told me he *thought* the problem could be solved easily.

though In spite of; however.

Even *though* the amount of the deposit was small, I was concerned.

---

4 Business Vocabulary Builder

blunder *(noun)* Mistake; error.

eventuality Something that may happen.

innovations New ideas, methods, or devices.

Reading and Writing Practice

5 Phrase Letter

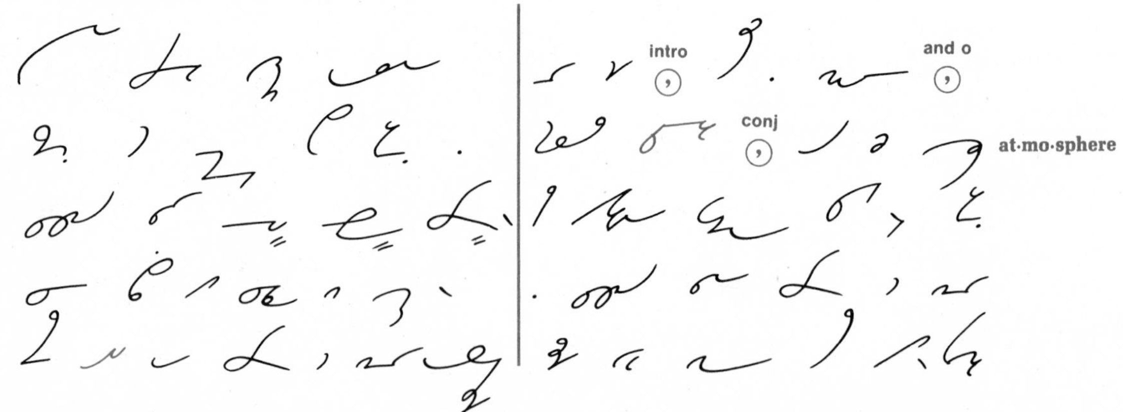

though

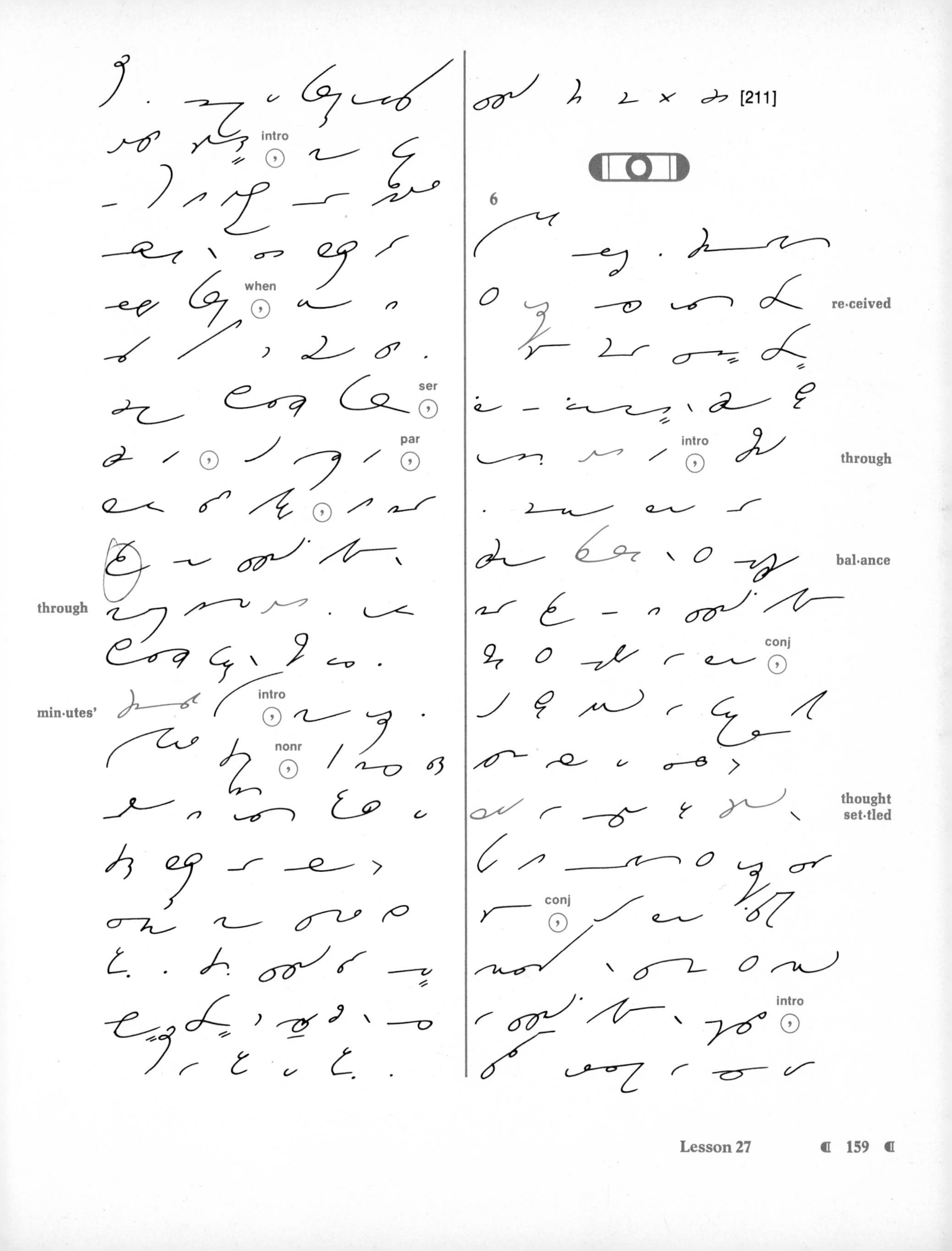

intro
when
ser
par
through
min·utes'
intro
nonr

[211]

6

re·ceived
intro
through
bal·ance
conj
thought
set·tled
conj
intro

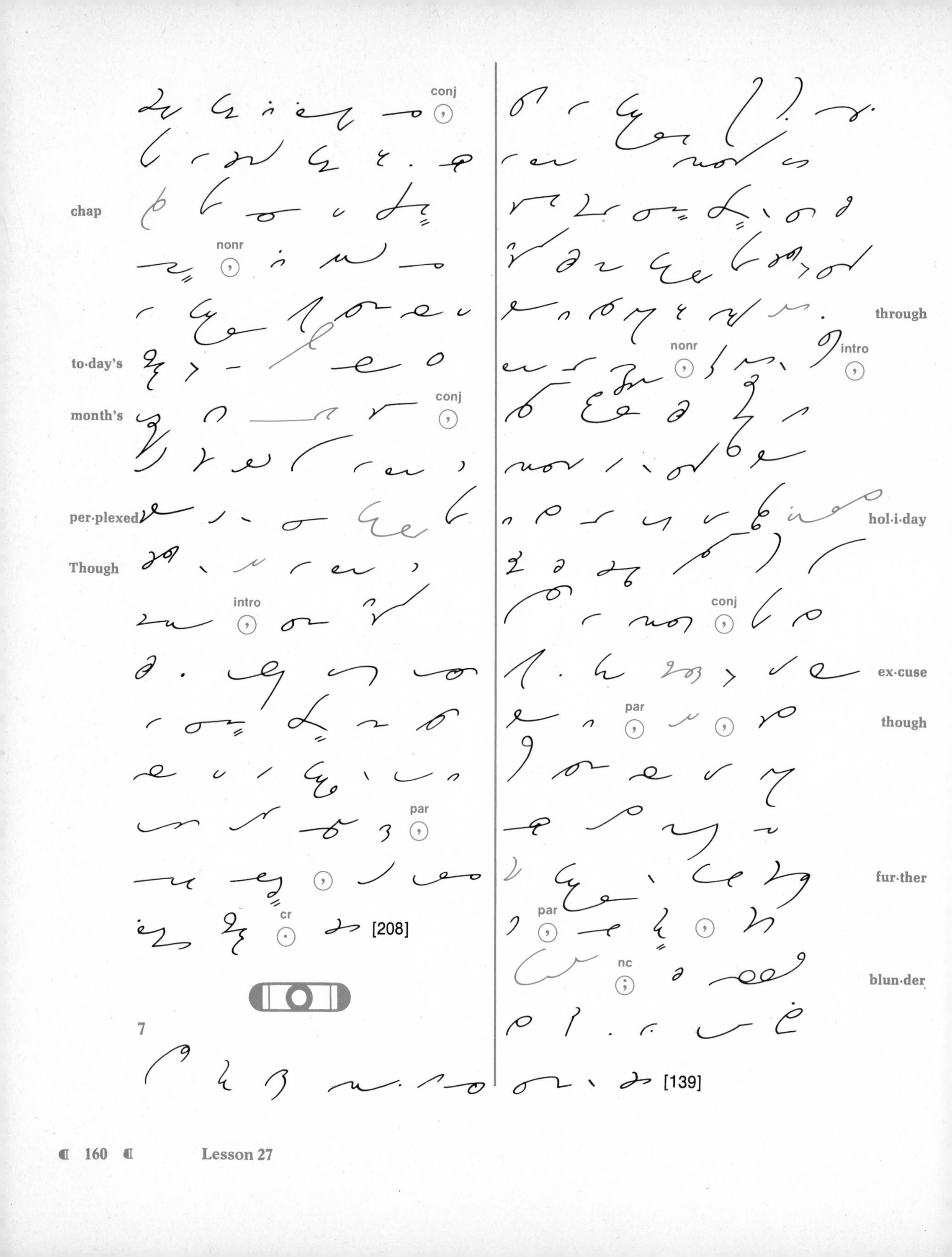

chap

to·day's

month's

per·plexed

Though

[208]

7

through

hol·i·day

ex·cuse

though

fur·ther

blun·der

[139]

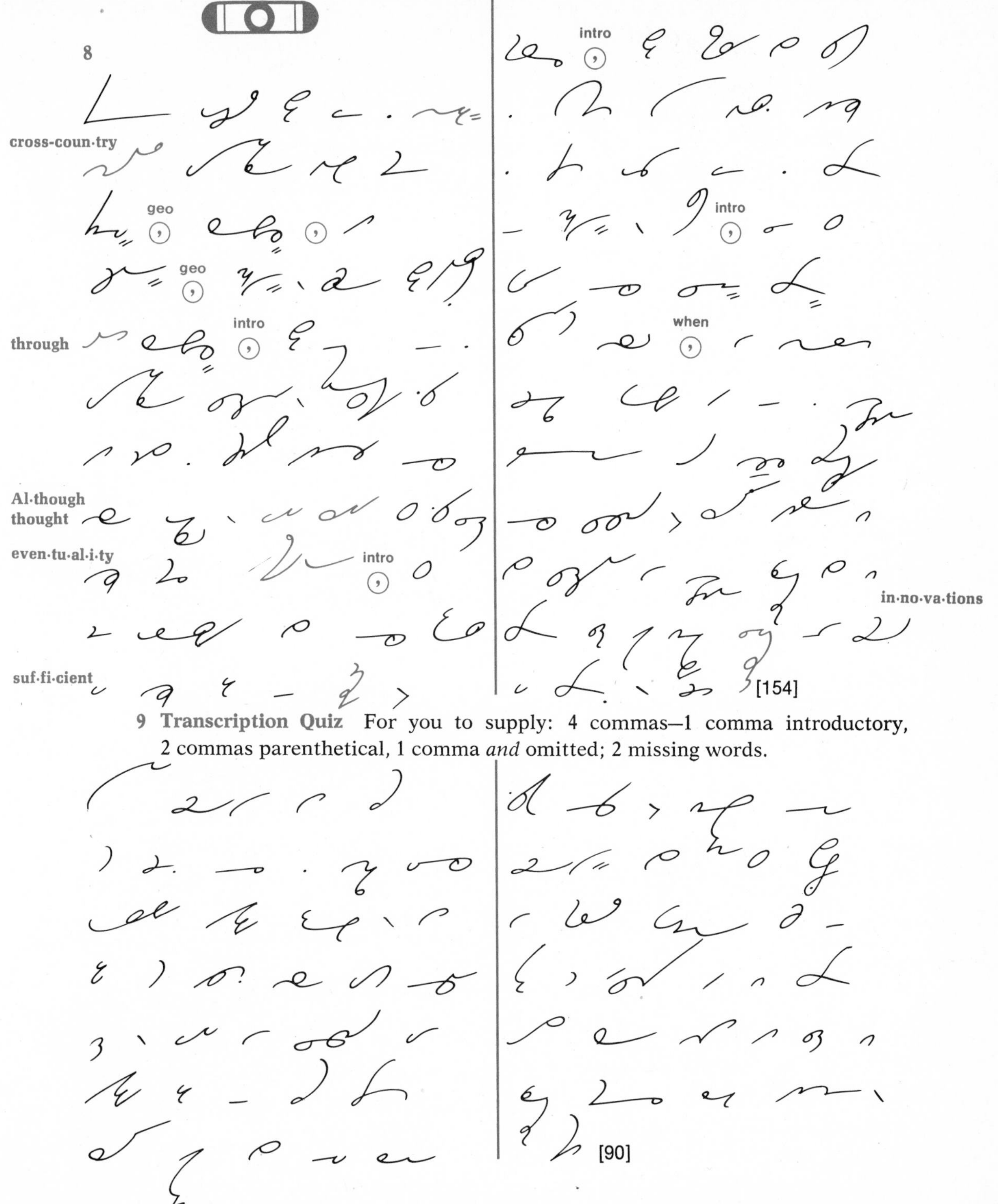

9 Transcription Quiz For you to supply: 4 commas—1 comma introductory, 2 commas parenthetical, 1 comma *and* omitted; 2 missing words.

Developing Word-Building Power

1 Word Families

-tment

1

-nted

2

-val, -vel

3

-ger

4

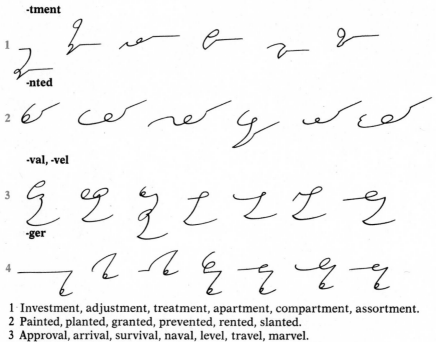

1 Investment, adjustment, treatment, apartment, compartment, assortment.
2 Painted, planted, granted, prevented, rented, slanted.
3 Approval, arrival, survival, naval, level, travel, marvel.
4 Manager, danger, endanger, passenger, messenger, larger, merger.

Building Transcription Skills

2 GRAMMAR CHECKUP ● possessive with gerund

A gerund is a verbal noun ending in *ing*.

Verb	*Gerund*
leave	leaving
do	doing
send	sending

Be sure you use the possessive case for nouns and pronouns that precede gerunds.

Bill's leaving *caused us to be late with the work.*

The pay depends on our (*not* us) doing *a satisfactory job.*

Be very careful when you transcribe *you* and *your.* Before a gerund *your* is the proper pronoun to use.

I will appreciate your (*not* you) sending *me the papers.*

3 Business Vocabulary Builder

real estate broker One who acts as a go-between in the sale and purchase of property and buildings.

precisely Exactly.

job description A record of the tasks involved in performing a job.

Reading and Writing Practice

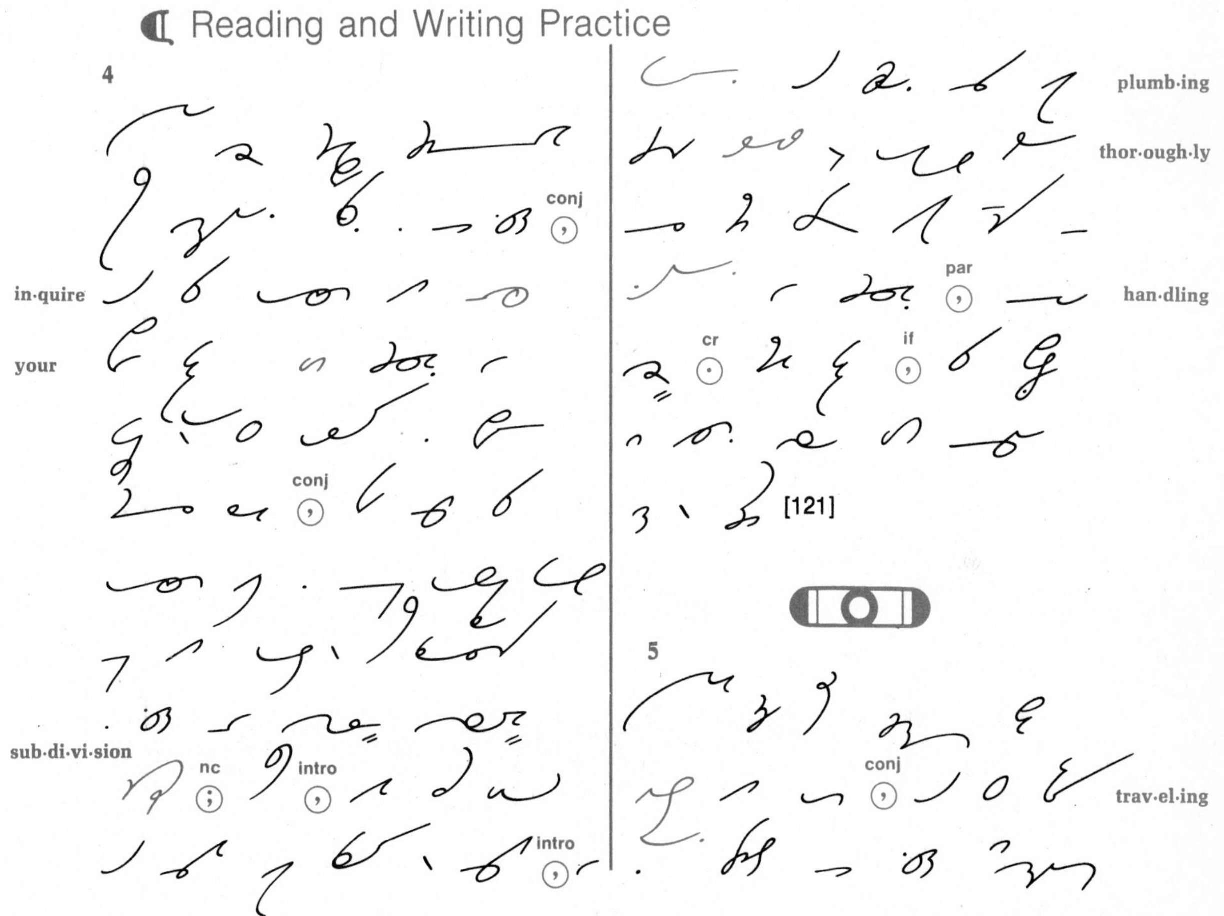

sit·u·at·ed

conj

al·ready

bro·ker

conj

ser

cr

conj

5 555-

9408 [138]

6

as

ap

three-month hyphenated before noun

my fi·nal·iz·ing

par

par

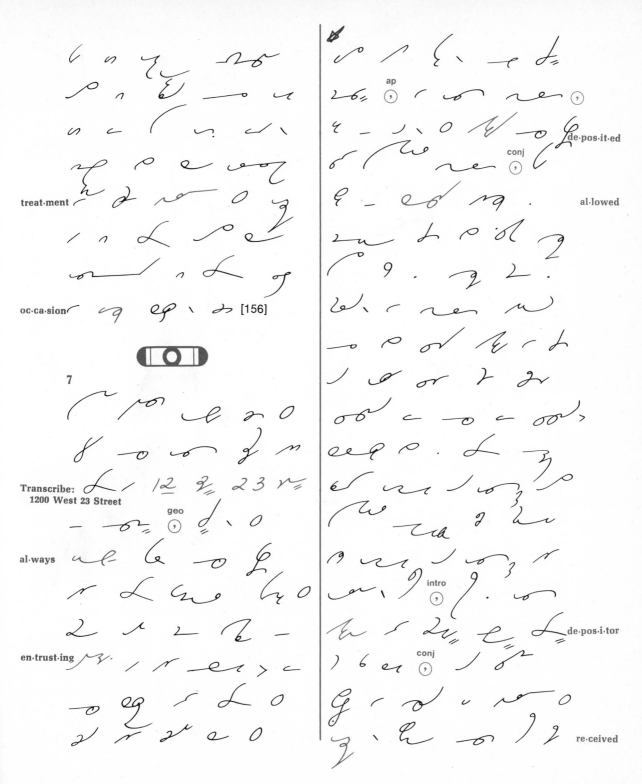

treat·ment

oc·ca·sion [156]

7

Transcribe:
1200 West 23 Street

geo

al·ways

en·trust·ing

ap

de·pos·it·ed

conj

al·lowed

intro

de·pos·i·tor

conj

re·ceived

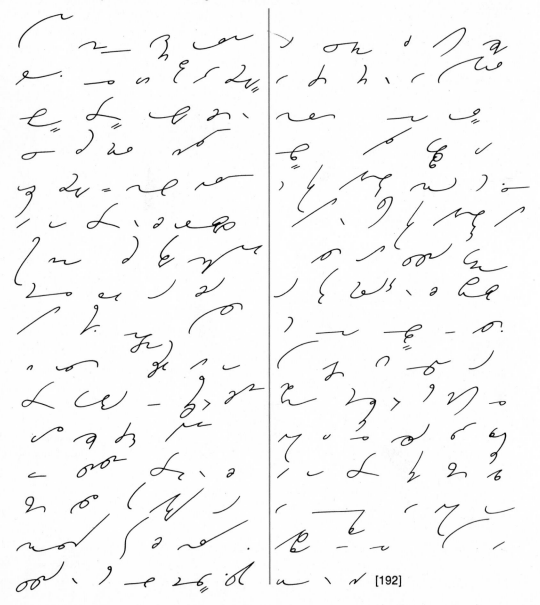

[194]

8 **Transcription Quiz** For you to supply: 7 commas—2 commas conjunction, 2 commas *if* clause, 2 commas apposition, 1 comma introductory; 1 semicolon no conjunction; 2 missing words.

[192]

Developing Word-Building Power

1 Word Beginnings and Endings

Im-

1

Em-

2

-ble

3

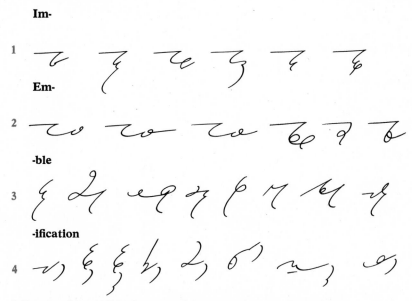

-ification

4

1 Import, impossible, impressed, improve, impose, imposition.
2 Employ, employment, employer, embarrass, emphasis, empire.
3 Possible, available, reliable, sensible, payable, trouble, dependable, noticeable.
4 Notification, specification, specifications, justification, verification, identification, qualifications, ratification.

Building Transcription Skills

2 COMMON PREFIXES ● im-

A knowledge of the common prefixes in the English language will help you to be a better worker and a better secretary. In *Volume One* you studied several prefixes. In *Volume Two* you will study several more.

im- As a prefix, *im* frequently means *not.*

impossible Not possible; not capable of occurring.

improbable Not probable.

impolite Not polite.

imperfect Not perfect.

immobile Not movable; fixed; stationary.

3 Business Vocabulary Builder

devastating Having the power to ruin or cause disorder.

facade The front of a building.

outmoded Out of date; no longer sufficient.

Reading and Writing Practice

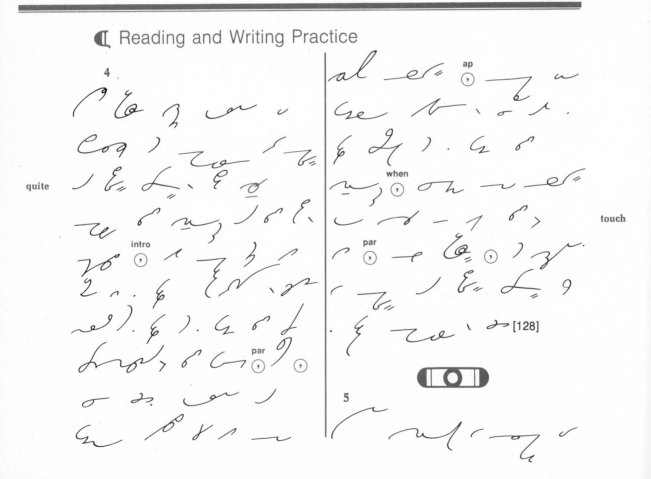

4

quite intro par ap when touch par [128]

5

too

suit·able

site

conj

in·con·ve·nience

intro

sub·ur·ban

nonr

conj

im·pact

dis·trict

par

sur·vey

em·ploy·ees' mo·rale

if

[230]

6

com·pre·hen·sive

intro

dev·as·tat·ing
ef·fect

conj

your

intro

ter·ri·ble

in·con·sis·tent

Transcribe:
five

struc·tur·al

fa·cade

al·ter·na·tives

[228]

7

its

intro

ten·ta·tive·ly

re·mod·el
in·te·ri·or

conj

in·ef·fi·cient

intro

when

and o

up-to-date hyphenated before noun

[147]

8 Transcription Quiz For you to supply: 7 commas—2 commas apposition, 1 comma *and* omitted, 2 commas nonrestrictive, 1 comma introductory, 1 comma *if* clause; 1 semicolon no conjunction; 2 missing words.

13

[150]

Developing Word-Building Power

1 Shorthand Vocabulary Builder

U

1

U

2

Ea, Ia

3

Compounds

4

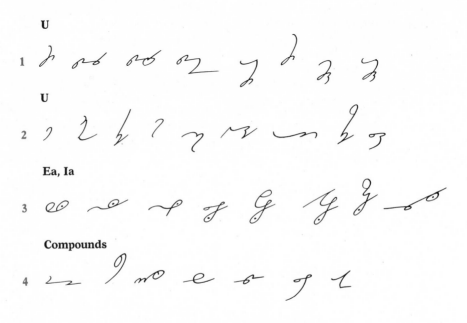

1 Few, unit, unite, uniform, review, view, confuse, refuse.
2 Us, suffer, just, up, cup, trust, luck, adjust, enough.
3 Area, create, creation, initiate, appreciate, depreciate, associate, mediate.
4 Someone, however, worthwhile, anywhere, anyone, whenever, thereupon.

Building Transcription Skills

2 Business Vocabulary Builder

initiated Started; began.
advent Coming; arrival.
boon A benefit.

Reading and Writing Practice

3 The Changing Banking Industry

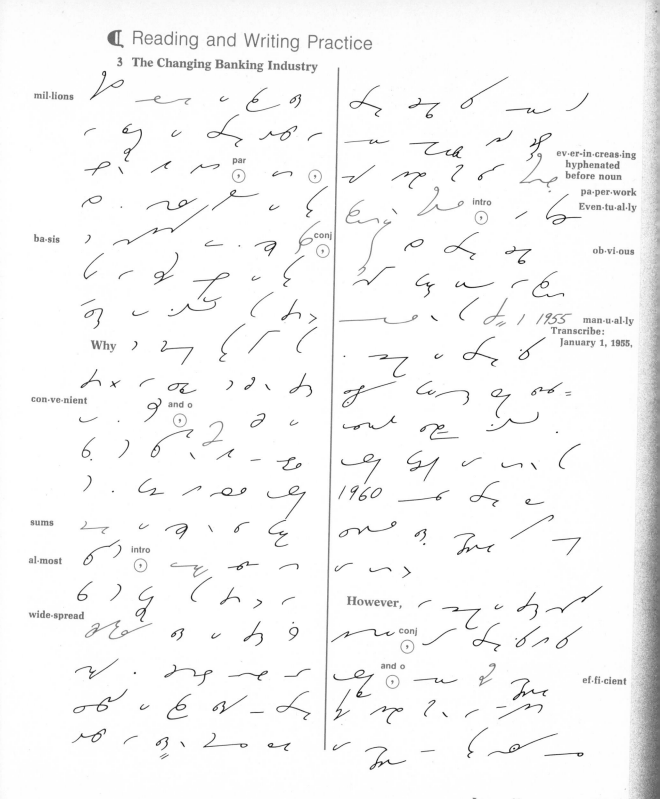

mil·lions

par

conj

ba·sis

Why

con·ve·nient

and o

sums

al·most

intro

wide·spread

ev·er-in·creas·ing hyphenated before noun

pa·per·work

intro

Even·tu·al·ly

ob·vi·ous

1955

man·u·al·ly

Transcribe: January 1, 1955,

1960

However,

conj

and o

ef·fi·cient

key·punch

com·put·er-re·lat·ed hyphenated before noun

intro

ad·vent Even intro

pro·ce·dures

al·le·vi·ate

bur·den

At first,

par

person's

intro

conj

writ·ten cre·at·ed

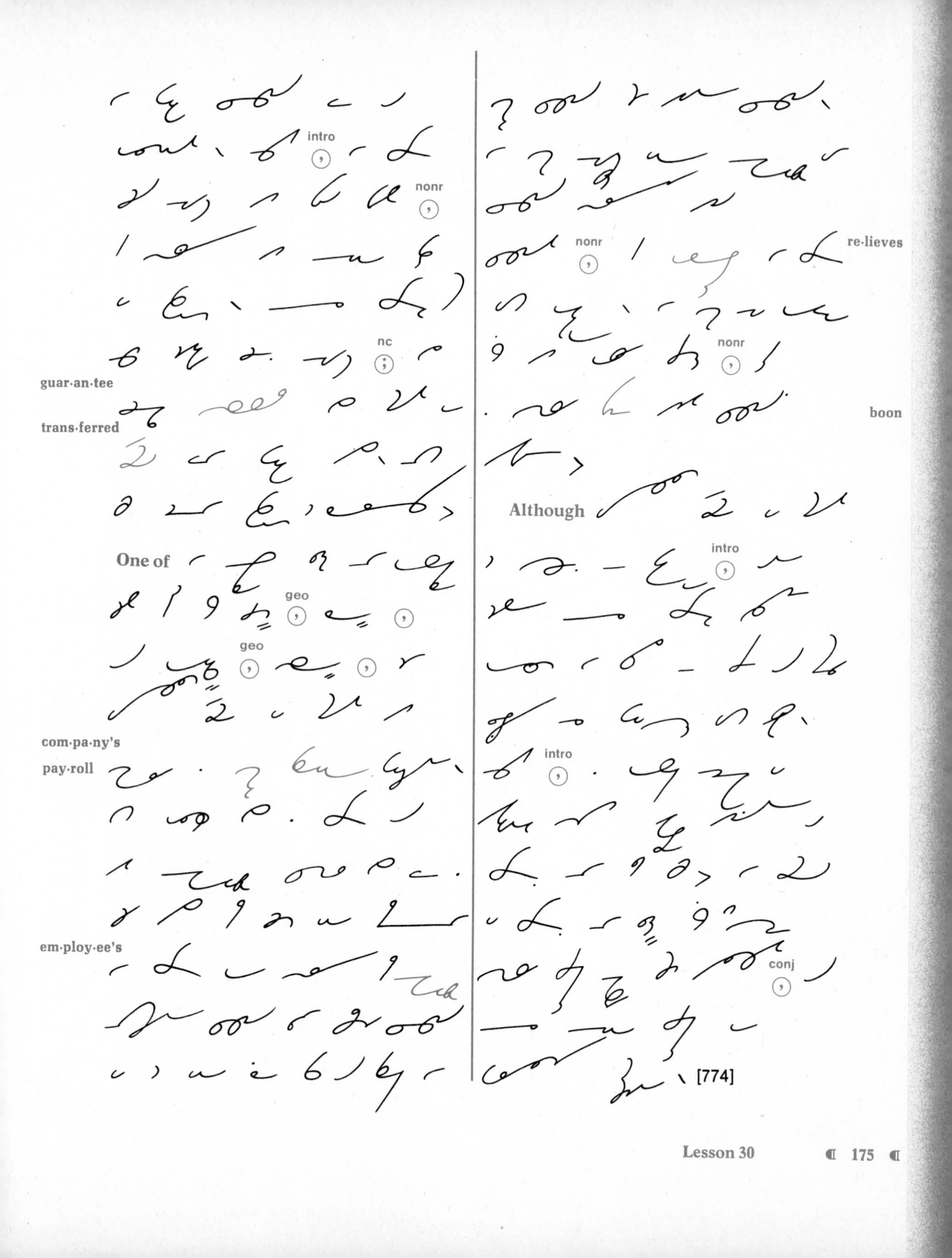

intro

nonr

nc

guar·an·tee

trans·ferred

One of

geo

geo

com·pa·ny's

pay·roll

em·ploy·ee's

nonr

re·lieves

nonr

boon

Although

intro

intro

conj

[774]

7 ENERGY

Developing Word-Building Power

1 Brief Forms and Derivatives

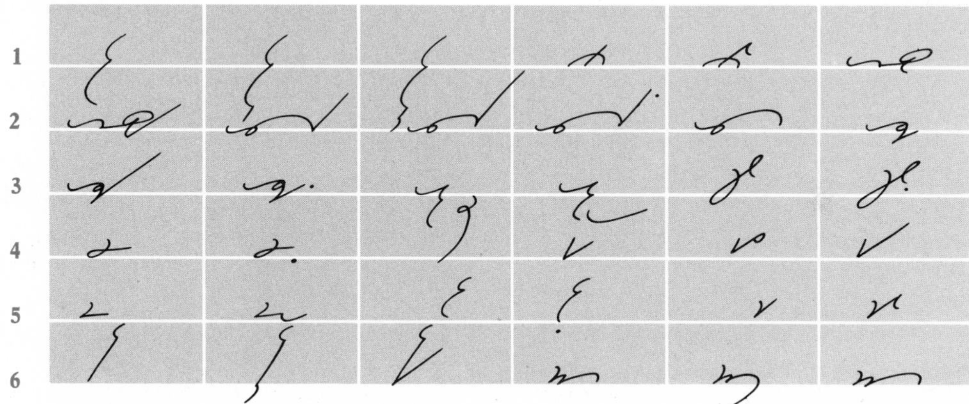

1 Public, publish-publication, publications, quantity, quantities, recognize.
2 Recognized, regard, regarded, regarding, regular, request.
3 Requested, requesting, responsible, responsibility, satisfy-satisfactory, satisfying.
4 Send, sending, several, short, shortly, should.
5 Soon, sooner, speak, speaking, state, states.
6 Subject, subjects, subjected, success, successful, suggest.

Building Transcription Skills

2 TYPING STYLE STUDY ● capitalization

Compass Points

Capitalize *north, south, east, west,* etc., only when they designate definite regions or when they are an integral part of a proper name.

I live in North Carolina.
Her home is in southern *Utah.*
We drove east.
He likes the weather in the West.

3 Business Vocabulary Builder

solar Having to do with the sun.
disposition Final action taken.
compelled Forced; urged strongly.

Reading and Writing Practice

4 Brief-Form Letter

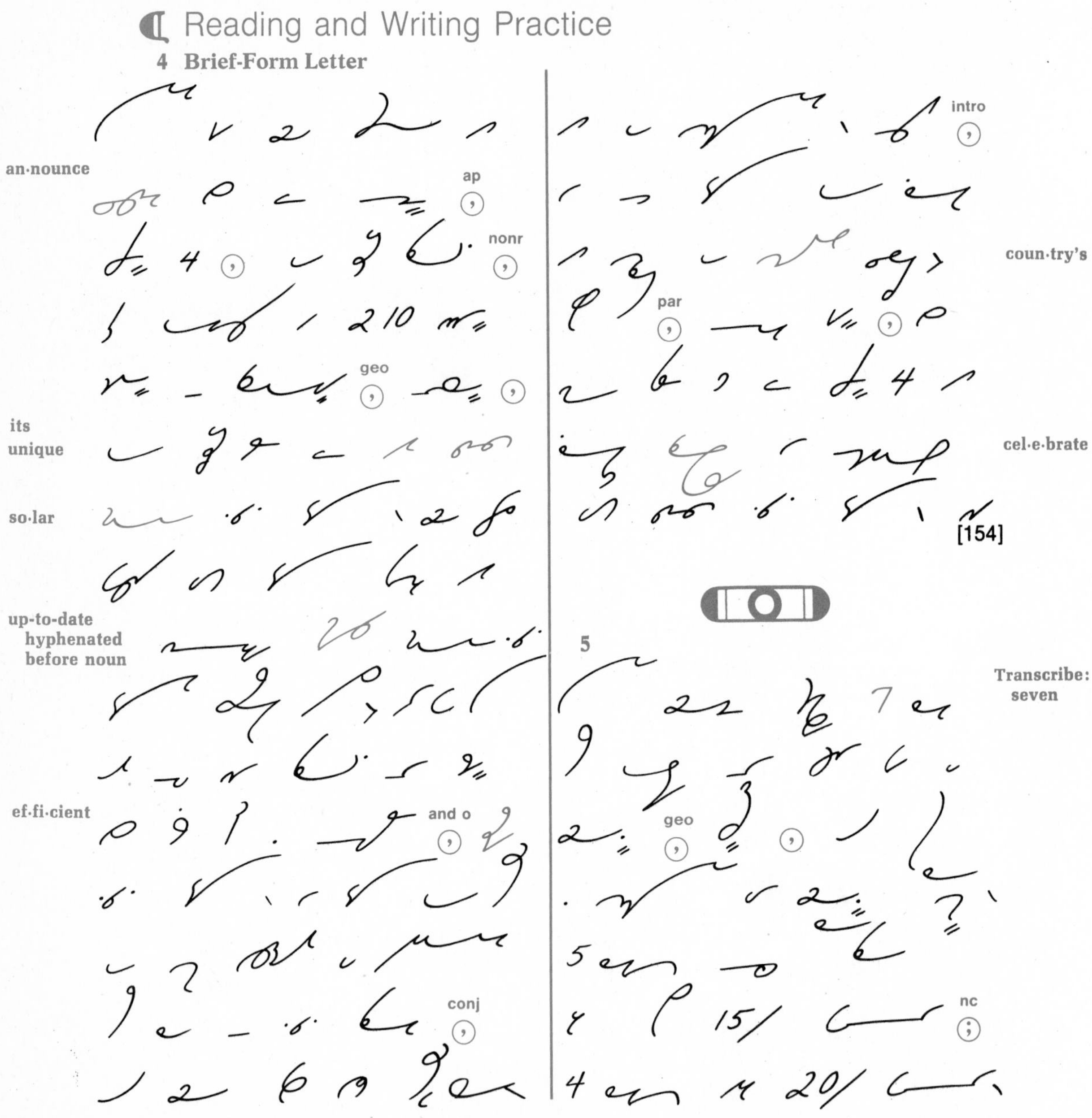

intro

ris·en

Transcribe:
5 percent

par

conj

cr [109]

6

driv·ing

conj

ly·ing

at·tached

conj

de·fec·tive

conj

ev·i·dence

conj

dis·po·si·tion

cr [138]

7

nc

intro

com·pelled

412

trench

as

dis·rupts

haz·ard

intro

conj

conj

re·ceived

one-month hyphenated before noun

if

cr

[170]

8

geo

months'

when

intro

bank·rupt·cy

conj

wait

[122]

9 Transcription Quiz In the Transcription Quizzes in previous lessons you have had to supply missing words that were obvious; they were the only words that made sense. From now on, however, several words will make sense, and it will be your responsibility to supply the word you think fits best in the sentence.

For example:

In this sentence, *happy, delighted,* or *glad* all make sense. If you decide that *glad* is the best word, place the word in your shorthand notes in this manner:

We are glad that you will be working for our company.

Always be sure that the word you choose makes good sense in the sentence.

For you to supply: 10 commas—2 commas geographical, 1 comma *as* clause, 4 commas series, 1 comma introductory, 1 comma conjunction, 1 comma nonrestrictive; 2 missing words.

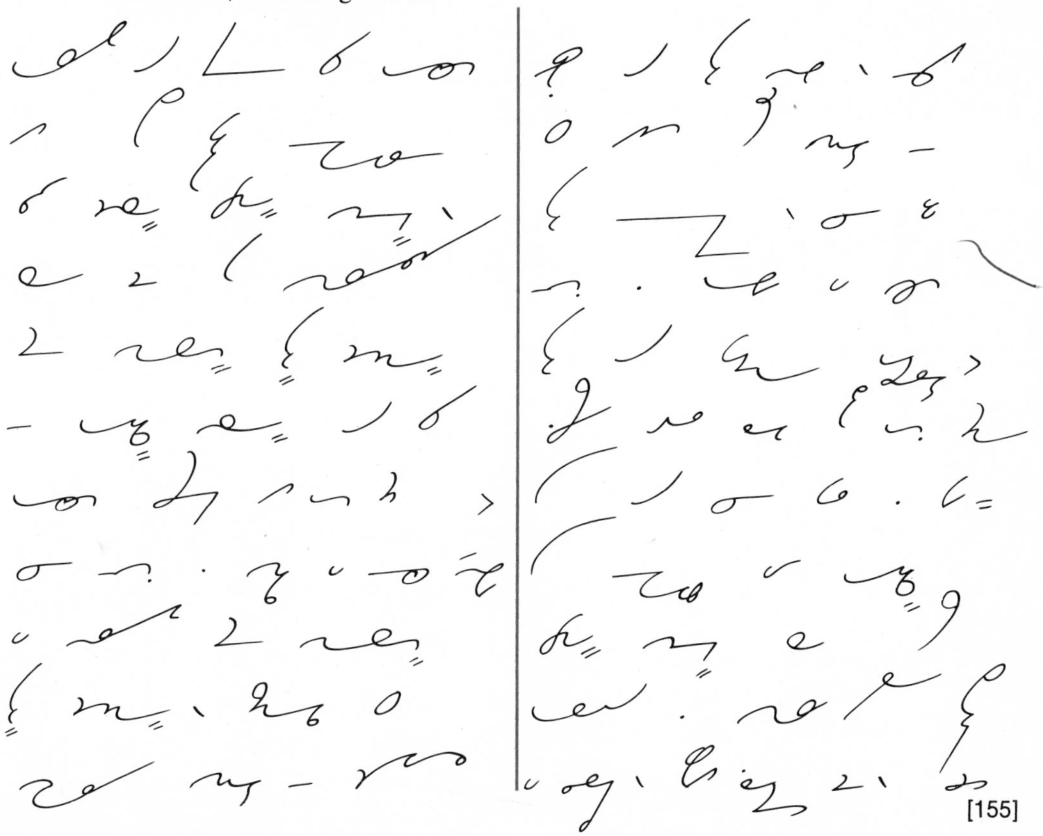

[155]

Building Phrasing Skill

1 Useful Business-Letter Phrases

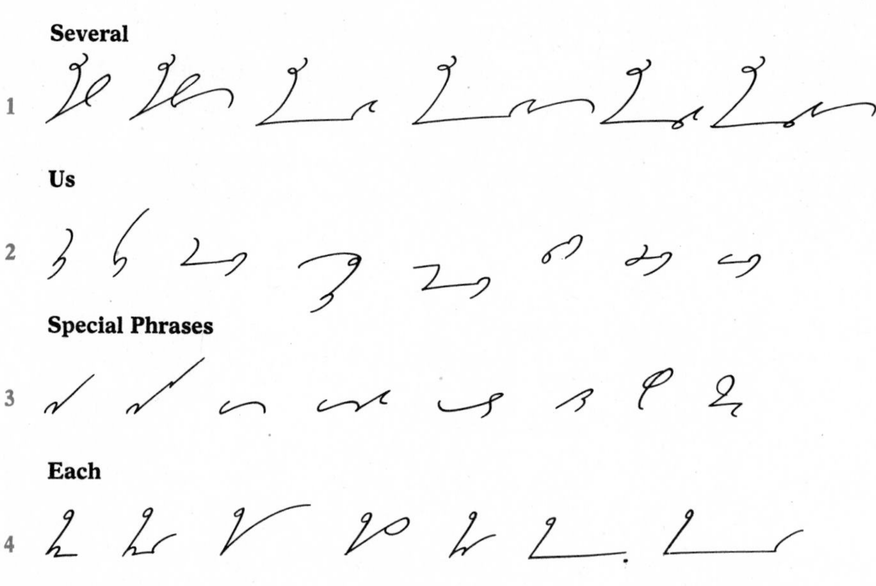

1 Several days, several days ago, several months, several months ago, several minutes, several minutes ago.
2 For us, by us, from us, give us, inform us, with us, send us, on us.
3 Your order, you ordered, of course, of course it is, let us, to us, I hope, as soon as.
4 Each one, each one of the, each time, each day, each other, each morning, each month.

2 Geographical Expressions

1

2

1 Detroit, Reno, Rochester, Troy, Bangor, Montpelier.
2 Michigan, Nevada, New York, Maine, New Hampshire, Vermont, Oregon, Florida.

Building Transcription Skills

3 SIMILAR-WORDS DRILL ● billed, build

billed (past tense of *bill*) Charged.

You will be *billed* once a month.

build To construct; to produce.

We plan to *build* a new house.

4 Business Vocabulary Builder

prospect *(noun)* A possibility; a chance.

agenda A list of things to be done.

status The current state of affairs; the situation.

Reading and Writing Practice

5 Phrase Letter

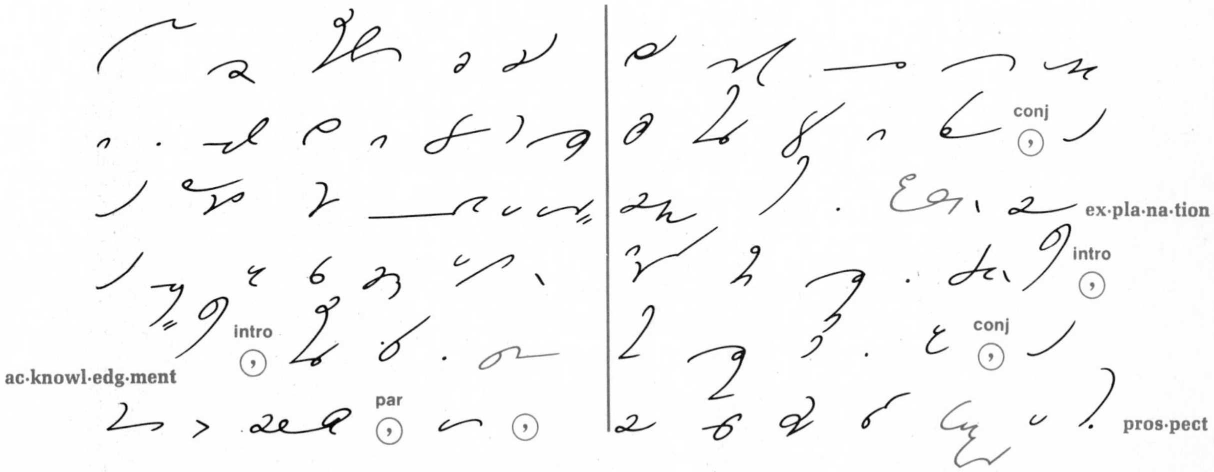

at·tor·neys

if

jeop·ar·dy

if

par·tial

[164]

6

heard
build

nat·u·ral
pipe·line

geo

geo

if

ap

sta·tus

cr

in·de·pen·dent

[110]

7

to·day's

geo

wel·come

ser

Transcribe: 800 West 14 Street

min·utes'

intro

Transcribe: $50

de·pos·it

par

billed

util·i·ty

nc

pay·able

par

cho·sen

conj

[199]

8

nonr

conj

intro

conj

touch

par

hear

if

de·prive

conj

[153]

9

if

nonr

514

10

[154]

10

com·pa·ny's

when

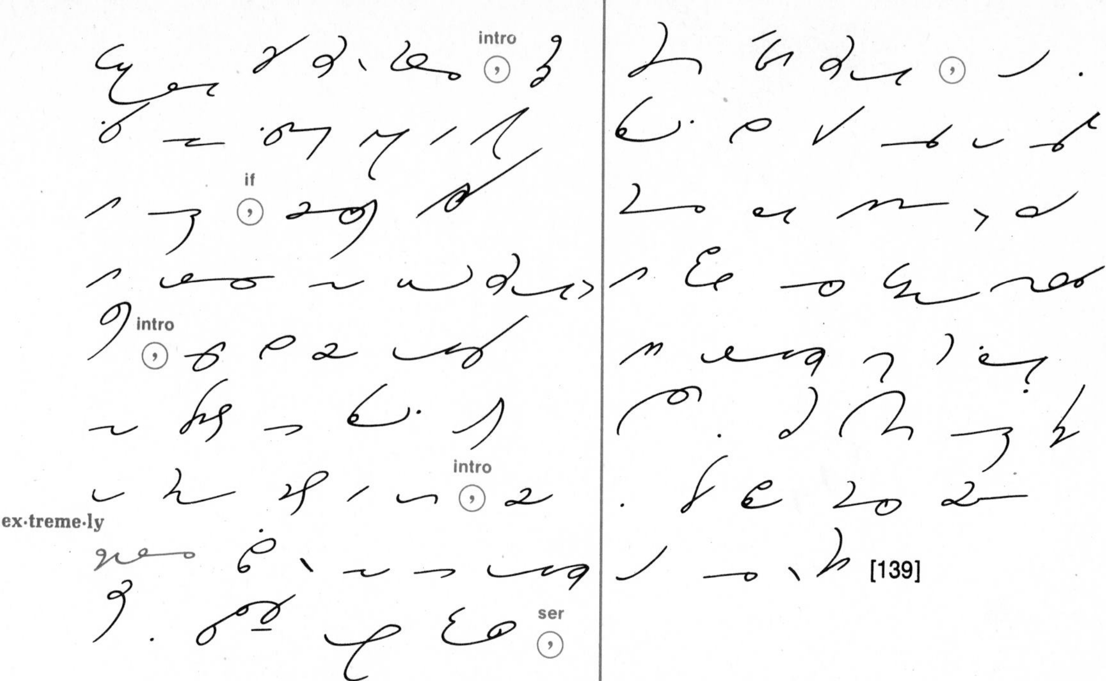

11 Transcription Quiz For you to supply: 4 commas—1 comma *as* clause, 2 commas apposition, 1 comma *if* clause; 1 semicolon no conjunction; 2 missing words.

[121]

Developing Word-Building Power

1 Word Families

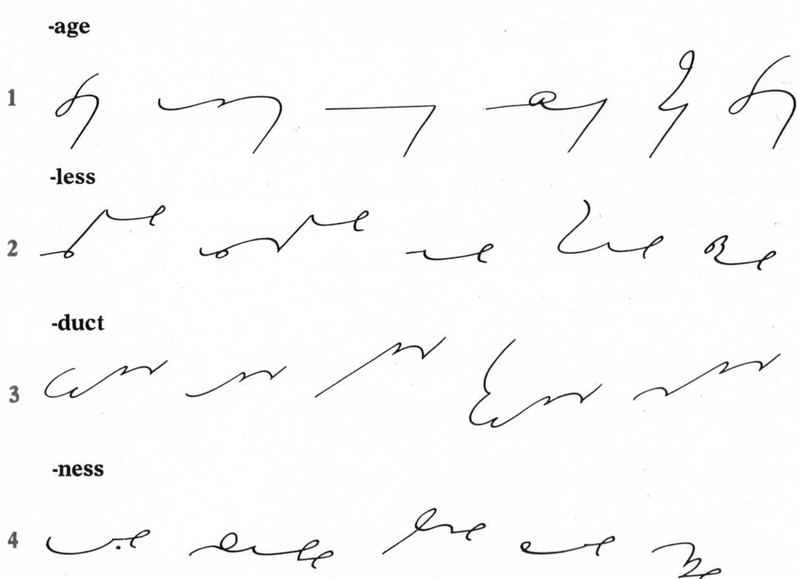

1 Package, luggage, manage, mileage, average, baggage.
2 Needless, regardless, unless, valueless, useless.
3 Product, induct, deduct, by-product, conduct.
4 Willingness, carelessness, darkness, illness, consciousness.

Building Transcription Skills

2 SPELLING FAMILIES ● -cial, -tial

Be very careful when you transcribe a word ending in the sound *shul.* Sometimes the word will be spelled *cial;* other times it will be spelled *tial.*

-cial

spe-cial **so-cial** **ben-e-fi-cial**
com-mer-cial **fi-nan-cial** **su-per-fi-cial**
es-pe-cial **ar-ti-fi-cial** **cru-cial**

-tial

es-sen-tial **con-fi-den-tial** **res-i-den-tial**
ini-tial **par-tial** **po-ten-tial**
spa-tial **sub-stan-tial** **mar-tial**

3 Business Vocabulary Builder

imposing *(verb)* Taking unwarranted advantage.
grudgingly Unwillingly.
radius The circular area around a given point.
thoroughfare Street; road; highway.

Reading and Writing Practice

4

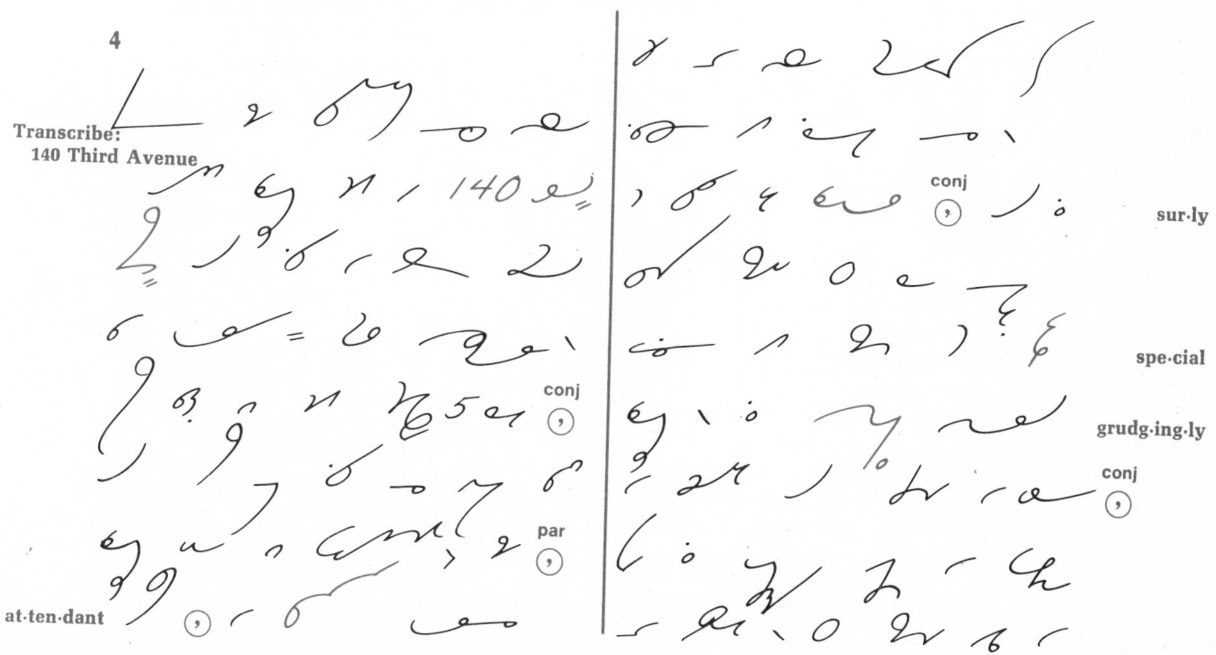

conj

intro

quite an·noyed

else·where

[148]

5

nonr

zon·ing

Transcribe: four

three-block hyphenated before noun

intro

res·i·den·tial

par

com·mer·cial thor·ough·fare

intro

[149]

6

and o

cour·te·ous

intro

as·sis·tance

res·i·dents intro

nc

al·ready

re·gard·less

intro

con·ges·tion par

[135]

7

as

se·vere

na·tion's

al·ter·na·tive

Transcribe: $30 million

intro

30

conj

intro

intro re·al·ly

intro

[180]

8

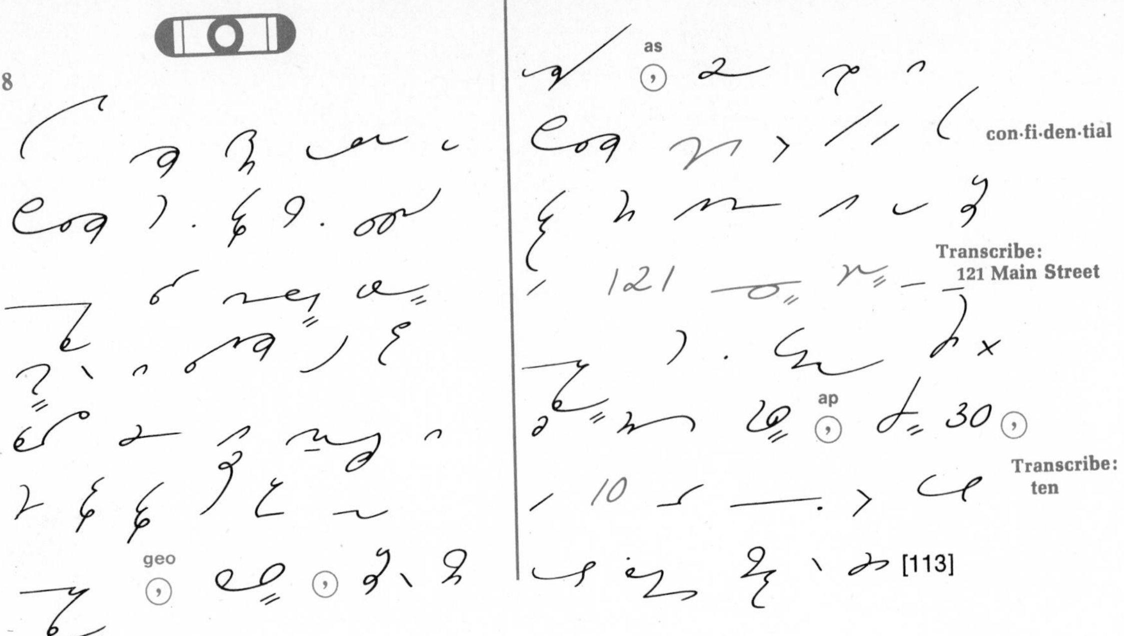

9 **Transcription Quiz** For you to supply: 3 commas—1 comma geographical, 1 comma apposition, 1 comma *as* clause; 1 semicolon no conjunction; 2 missing words.

[98]

Developing Word-Building Power

1 Word Beginnings and Endings

Ex-

Enter-, Entr-

-cient, -ciency

-gram

1 Export, express, exert, explain, expense, except, excel, expert.
2 Enter, entertain, entertainment, entered, entrance, entrances.
3 Efficient, sufficient, deficient, efficiency, sufficiency, deficiency, inefficiency.
4 Telegram, program, diagram, cablegram, radiogram.

Building Transcription Skills

2 GRAMMAR CHECKUP ● doesn't, don't

Use *doesn't* in the third person singular.

She doesn't *want to leave her present job.*

He doesn't *need any additional supplies.*

It doesn't *seem to be the right time to change positions.*

Very few people ever make the mistake of using *doesn't* for *don't.* Seldom do you hear anyone say, "I doesn't." However, many people mistakenly use *don't* for *doesn't.* It is not uncommon to hear someone say, "he don't," "she don't," or "that don't." Be extremely careful *never* to make this mistake.

3 Business Vocabulary Builder

maintenance The care and upkeep of property or equipment.

dispatch *(noun)* Promptness; efficiency.

depleted Decreased; used up.

Reading and Writing Practice

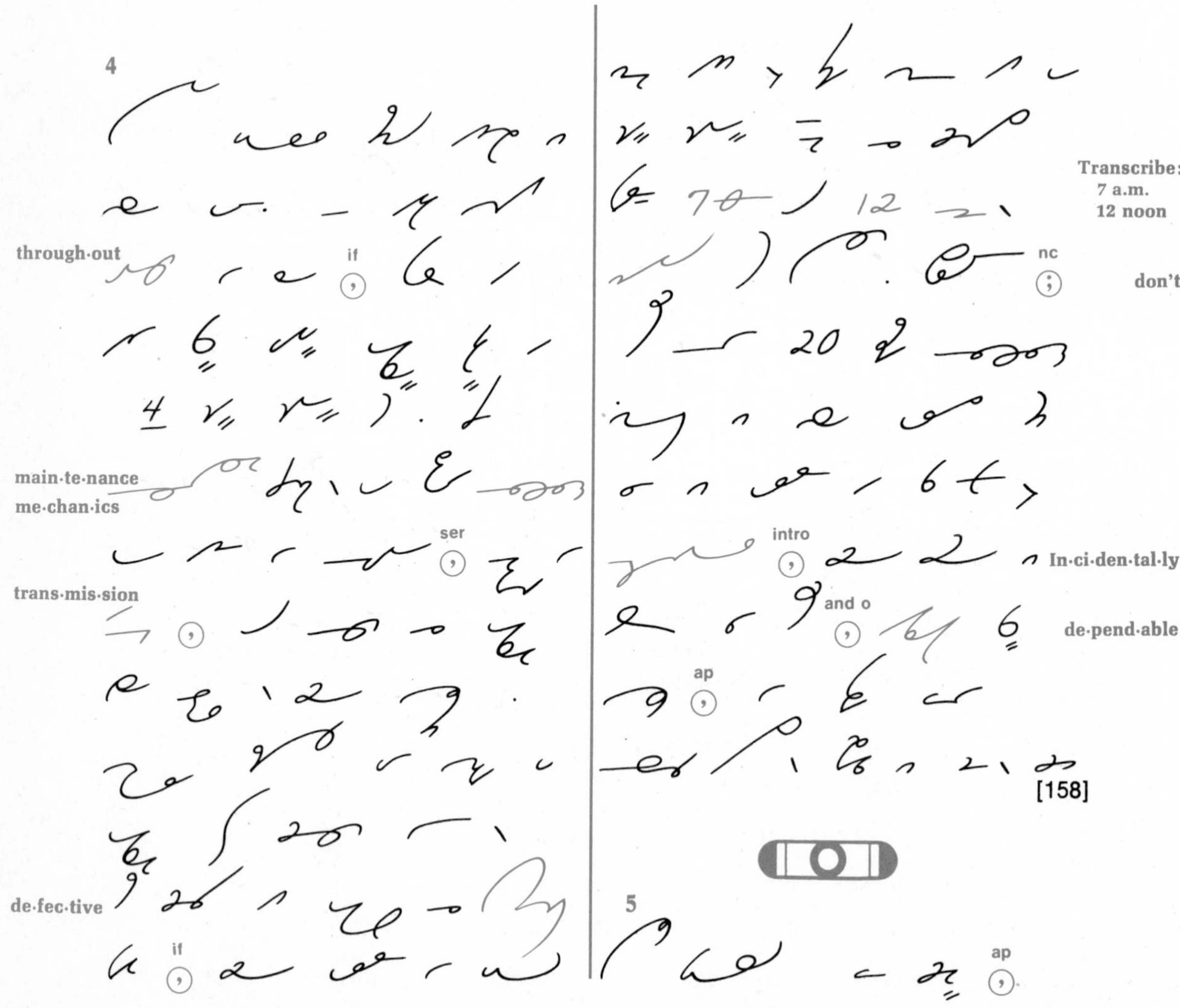

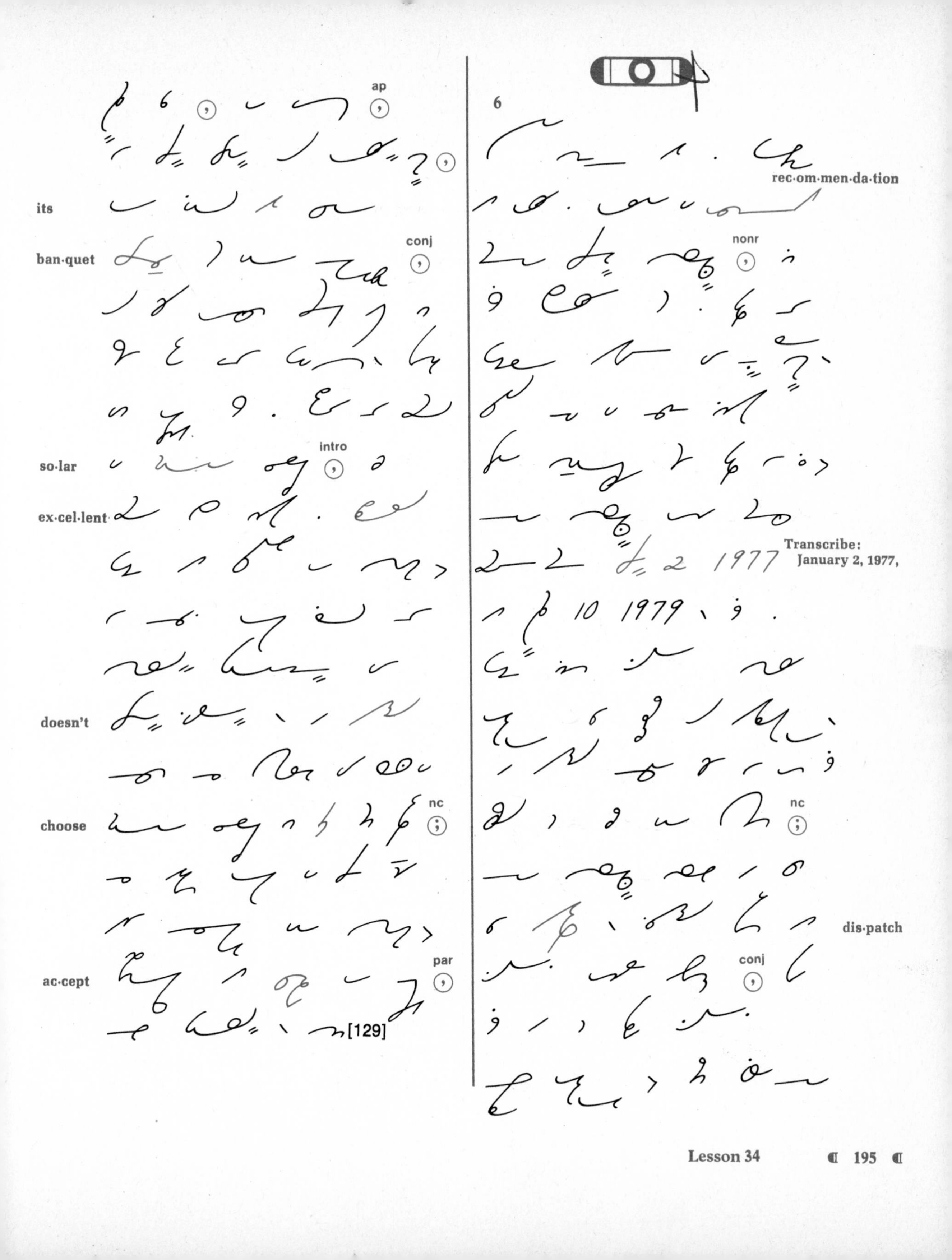

ap

its

ban·quet

conj

intro

so·lar

ex·cel·lent

doesn't

choose

nc

ac·cept

par

[129]

6

rec·om·men·da·tion

nonr

Transcribe: January 2, 1977,

nc

dis·patch

conj

if

[158]

7

intro

intro

[86]

8

na·tion's

de·plet·ed

in·suf·fi·cient

par

Transcribe: five

long-term hyphenated before noun

par [186]

9 Transcription Quiz For you to supply: 5 commas—2 commas apposition, 2 commas parenthetical, 1 comma conjunction; 2 missing words.

[110]

Many people who have special talents or interest in drama, music, art, journalism, politics, and so on, have found that secretarial training works almost like magic in gaining entrance to these areas of work.—*John Robert Gregg*

Developing Word-Building Power

1 Shorthand Vocabulary Builder

Ow

1

W

2

Wh

3

Abbreviated Words

4

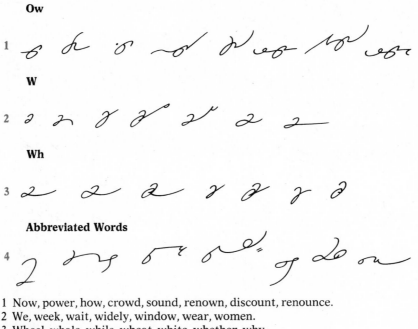

1 Now, power, how, crowd, sound, renown, discount, renounce.
2 We, week, wait, widely, window, wear, women.
3 Wheel, whale, while, wheat, white, whether, why.
4 Convenient-convenience, significant-significance, atmosphere, Atlantic, anniversary, variety, ecology.

Building Transcription Skills

2 Business Vocabulary Builder

endeavors *(noun)* Efforts.

flourished Succeeded; grew.

inexhaustible Incapable of being used up; never ending.

ecology The science of the relation of people to the environment.

Reading and Writing Practice

3 Energy To Run the World

par intro

de·pen·dent

beasts

hu·man·kind

gi·gan·tic

per·son's

ser

nonr

mus·cles

abun·dant

intro

ser

suf·fi·cient

intro

ar·tis·tic en·deav·ors

in·ad·e·quate

However,

People

ser

intro

whale's

ex·tinct

world's

conj

prac·ti·ca·ble

intro

flour·ished

pre·dom·i·nant

After

intro

wide·ly used
no hyphen
after ly

in·ex·haust·ible

intro

cu·bic

par

conj

While

intro

de·plet·ed

conj

par

nc

intro

conj

ecol·o·gy

if

its

pol·lute

intro

ser

intro

and o

[677]

8 REAL ESTATE

Developing Word-Building Power

1 Brief Forms and Derivatives

1 Than, thank, thanks, thanking, them, themselves.
2 There (their), thing-think, things-thinks, this, throughout, time.
3 Timing, timed, underneath, undergo, usual, unusual.
4 Valuable, valueless, valued, were, when, where.
5 Will-well, willing, willingly, wish, wished, wishing.
6 World, worth, worthy, yesterday, you-your, yours.

Building Transcription Skills

2 Business Vocabulary Builder

exterior The outside surface or area of something.
options Choices; alternatives.
competent Capable; well qualified.
exclusive contract The only agreement made.

Reading and Writing Practice

3 Brief-Form Letter

555-7244 nc ;

[134]

suit·able

three-bed·room hyphenated before noun

nonr ,

ser ,

intro ,

conj ,

hour's

com·mut·ing

qui·et

ser ,

trans·por·ta·tion

cr .

if ,

(901)

4

ap ,

Wednes·day

geo ,

40 95

Transcribe: $40,000

ser ,

de·sir·able

some·what

nonr

intro

intro

alu·mi·num

nonr

ex·te·ri·or

when

[219]

5

if

ap

ser

as·pect

com·pe·tent

gen·u·ine

when

par

par

[218]

conj

mul·ti·ple-list·ing = hyphenated before noun

when

[130]

6

ser

de·pend·able

conj

par

com·mit·ment

7

rec·om·men·da·tion

nonr

conj

[85]

8 Transcription Quiz For you to supply: 5 commas—1 comma *if* clause, 2 commas parenthetical, 2 commas introductory; 1 semicolon no conjunction; 2 missing words.

[235]

Building Phrasing Skill

1 Useful Business-Letter Phrases

To Before a Downstroke

1

Want

2

Ago

3

I Hope

4

You Will

5

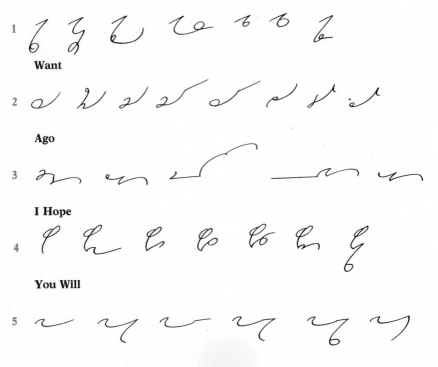

1 To buy, to purchase, to build, to plan, to see, to say, to join.
2 I want, if you want, we want, we wanted, I wanted, they want, she wants, he wants.
3 Weeks ago, years ago, some time ago, months ago, hours ago.
4 I hope, I hope you will, I hope to, I hope that, I hope that the, I hope you can, I hope to be able.
5 You will, you will be, you will not, you will not be, you will not be able, you will have.

2 Geographical Expressions

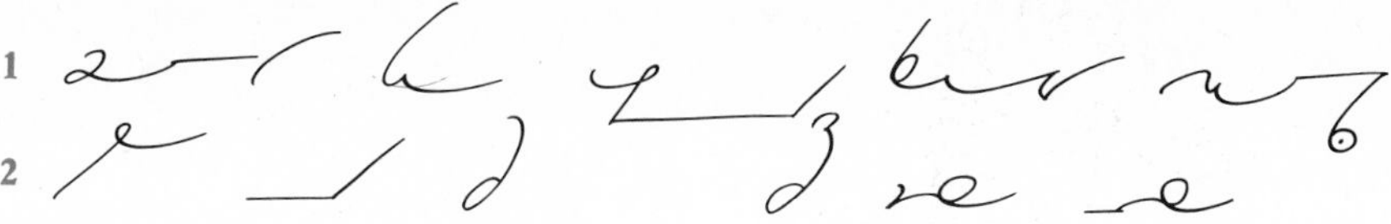

1 Wilmington, Baltimore, Richmond, Charleston, Columbia.
2 Delaware, Maryland, Virginia, West Virginia, South Carolina, North Carolina.

Building Transcription Skills

3 SIMILAR-WORDS DRILL ● quite, quiet, quit

quite Very.

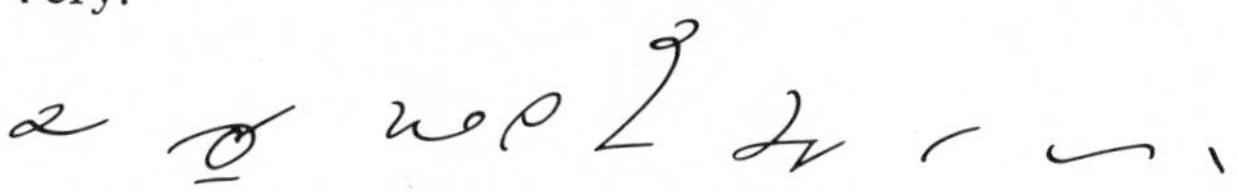

We are quite *sorry that we have not finished the work.*

quiet Silent; without noise.

The house is located on a quiet *street.*

quit To stop; to release from.

Quit *risking your valuable savings in an uncertain market.*

4 Business Vocabulary Builder

prior to Before.
per annum In each year; annually.
duplexes Two-family houses.
utilized Used.

Reading and Writing Practice

5 Phrase Letter

pre·lim·i·nary

cor·ner

geo

ab·stract

conj

quite

per·son·al·ly

par

cr

conj

clear

[114]

6

274 275

geo

qui·et

Pri·or

par

thor·ough

ser

intro

ter·mites

if

touch

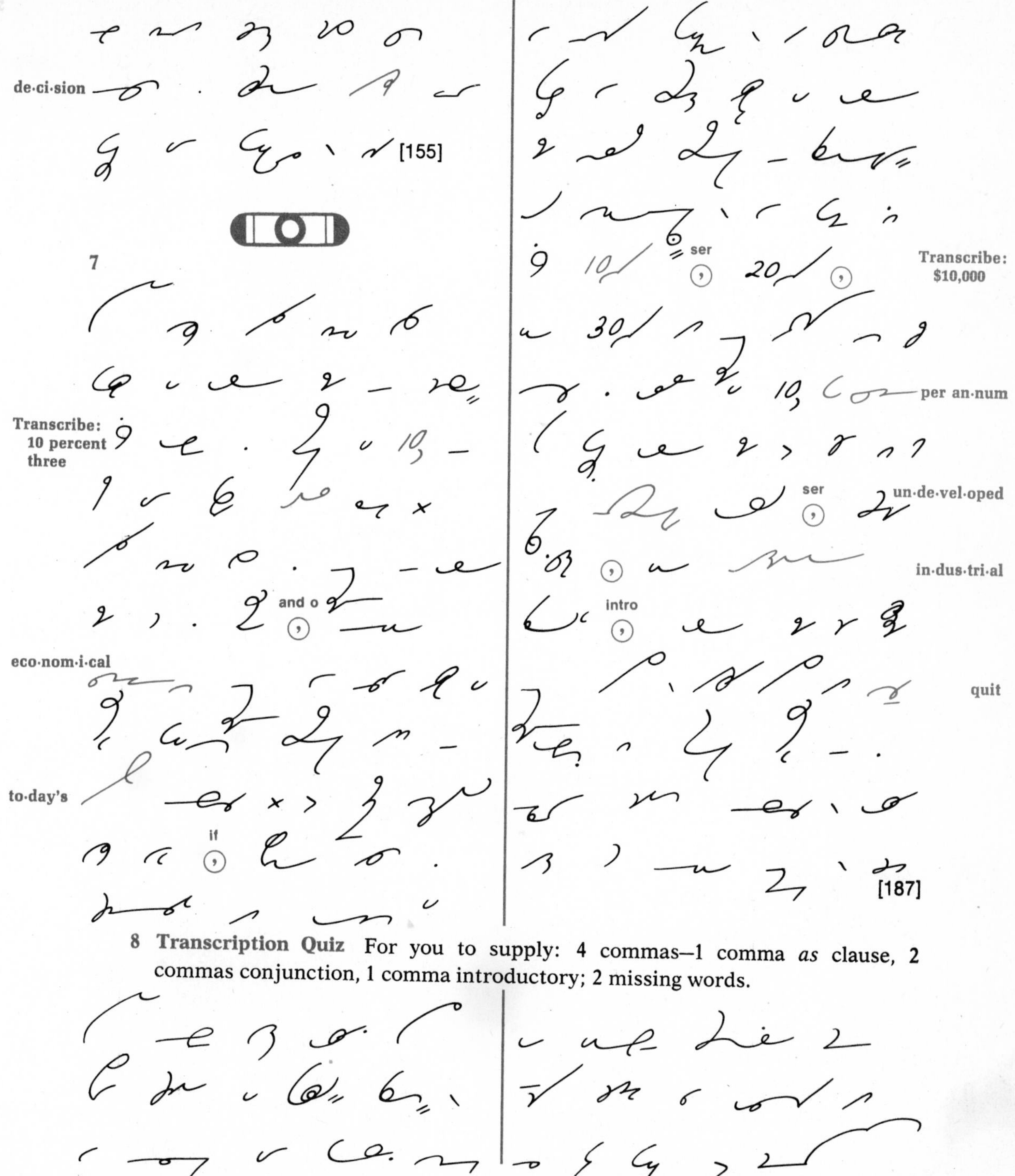

8 Transcription Quiz For you to supply: 4 commas—1 comma *as* clause, 2 commas conjunction, 1 comma introductory; 2 missing words.

[259]

Developing Word-Building Power

1 Word Families

-form

1

-cation

2

-serve

3

-point

4

1 Form, inform, information, reform, reforming, uniform.
2 Vacation, vocation, vocational, location, allocation, educational.
3 Serve, servant, service, servicing, reserve, reserved, servile.
4 Point, pointed, points, disappoint, appointment, reappoint.

Building Transcription Skills

2 SPELLING FAMILIES ● silent e dropped before -ment

Most words ending in *e* retain the *e* before the ending *-ment*.

ad-ver-tise-ment **ar-range-ment** **man-age-ment**

an-nounce-ment **en-cour-age-ment** **re-quire-ment**

amaze-ment **en-gage-ment** **state-ment**

However, there are some words in which the final *e* is dropped before the word ending *-ment*. Remember these three in particular.

ac-knowl-edg-ment **judg-ment** **ar-gu-ment**

3 Business Vocabulary Builder

accessible Able to be reached.

vacate To leave; to move out.

residential Relating to a living area, as a neighborhood.

Reading and Writing Practice

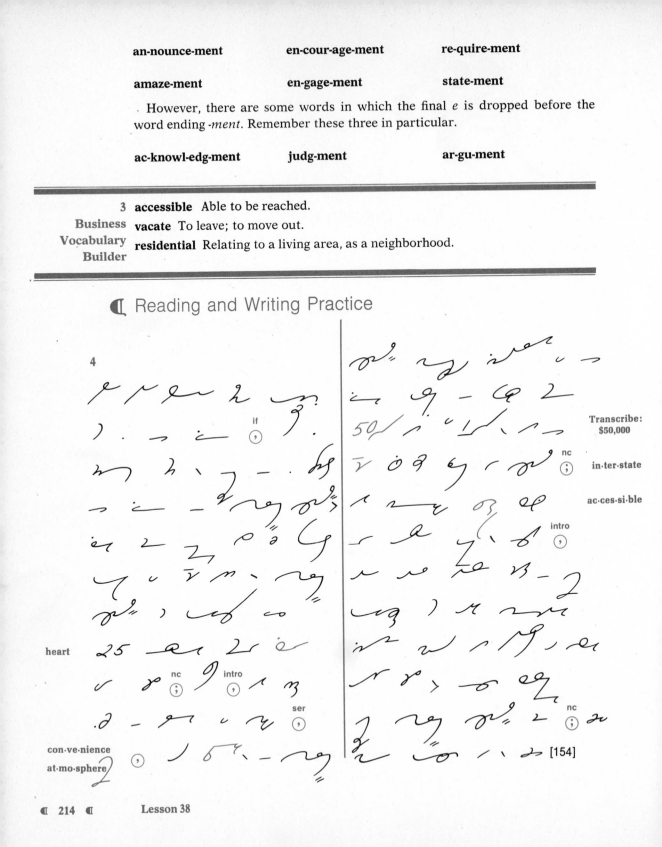

4

if

heart 25

nc intro

ser

con·ve·nience

at·mo·sphere

50

Transcribe: $50,000

nc

in·ter·state

ac·ces·si·ble

intro

nc

[154]

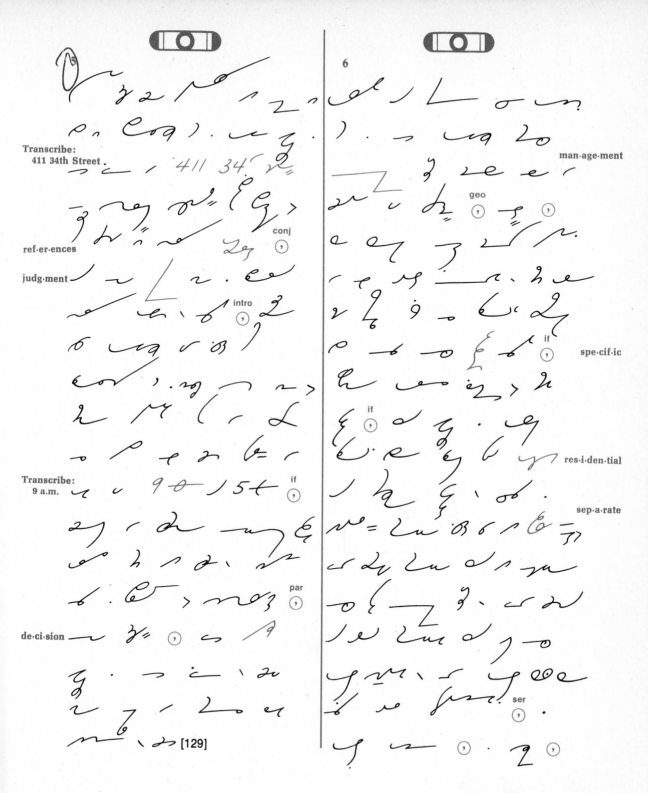

5

Transcribe: 411 34th Street

ref·er·ences

conj

judg·ment

intro

Transcribe: 9 a.m.

if

par

de·ci·sion

[129]

6

man·age·ment

geo

if

spe·cif·ic

if

res·i·den·tial

sep·a·rate

ser

if

pho·to·graphs

[158]

21

ap

23

cr

[131]

7

geo

im·pressed

if

if

ar·range·ments

ap

8

re·al

conj

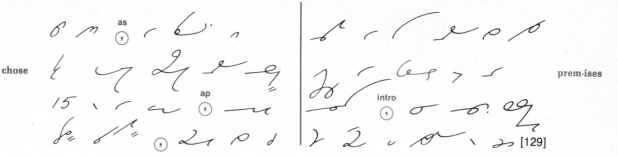

as

chose

ap

prem·ises

intro

[129]

9 Transcription Quiz For you to supply: 6 commas—1 comma geographical, 1 comma introductory, 1 comma *when* clause, 2 commas series, 1 comma conjunction; 2 missing words.

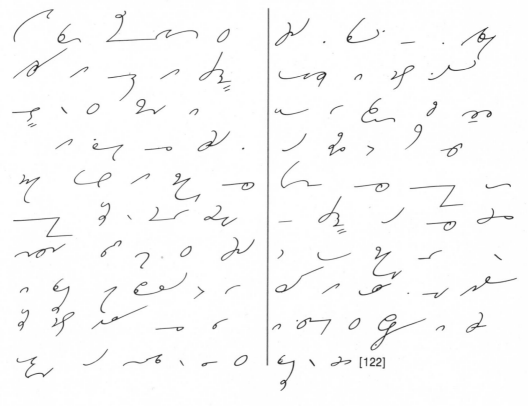

[122]

Developing Word-Building Power

1 Word Beginnings and Endings

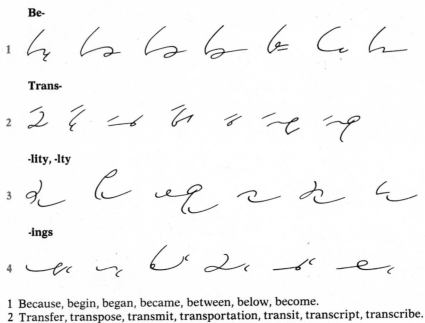

Be-

1

Trans-

2

-lity, -lty

3

-ings

4

1 Because, begin, began, became, between, below, become.
2 Transfer, transpose, transmit, transportation, transit, transcript, transcribe.
3 Facility, ability, reliability, quality, faculty, penalty.
4 Listings, workings, buildings, failings, meetings, mailings.

Building Transcription Skills

2 GRAMMAR CHECKUP ● pronoun I or me after a preposition

Secretaries seldom make errors with a single pronoun after a preposition.

Will you do the work for me? (*not* I)

However, when other words come between the preposition and the pronoun, trouble sometimes occurs.

Please go with Mr. Case and me. (*not* I)

You can quickly decide whether to use *I* or *me* by mentally eliminating the words between the preposition and the pronoun.

Please go with . . . me. (*not* I)

3 Business Vocabulary Builder

realty Real estate; property.

literally Actually; really.

ample Enough; sufficient.

Reading and Writing Practice

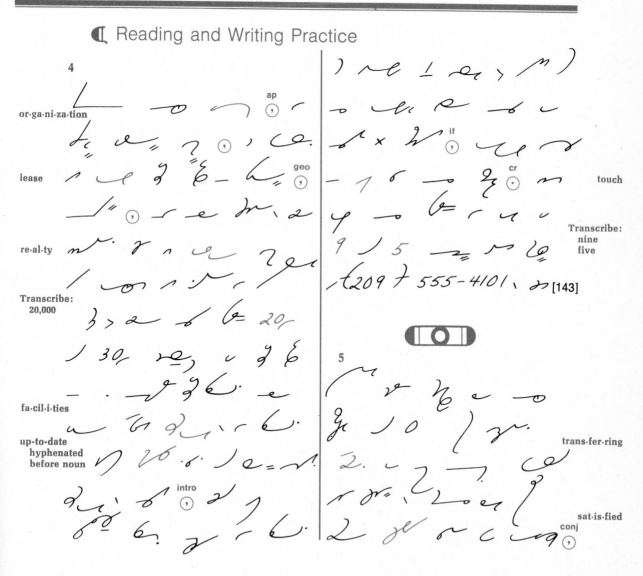

4

or·ga·ni·za·tion

ap

lease

geo

re·al·ty

Transcribe: 20,000

20,000 30,000

fa·cil·i·ties

up-to-date hyphenated before noun

intro

if

touch

cr

Transcribe: nine five

9 5

(209) 555-4101 [143]

5

trans·fer·ring

sat·is·fied

conj

too

conj

suit·able

50

50

if

lose
al·most

par

if

[161]

6

its

when

lit·er·al·ly

arise

par

mis·take

chose

25

well-trained
hyphenated
before noun

ser

intro

if

[177]

7 Transcription Quiz For you to supply: 5 commas—2 commas geographical, 1 comma introductory, 2 commas series; 1 period courteous request; 2 missing words.

[136]

Developing Word-Building Power

1 Shorthand Vocabulary Builder

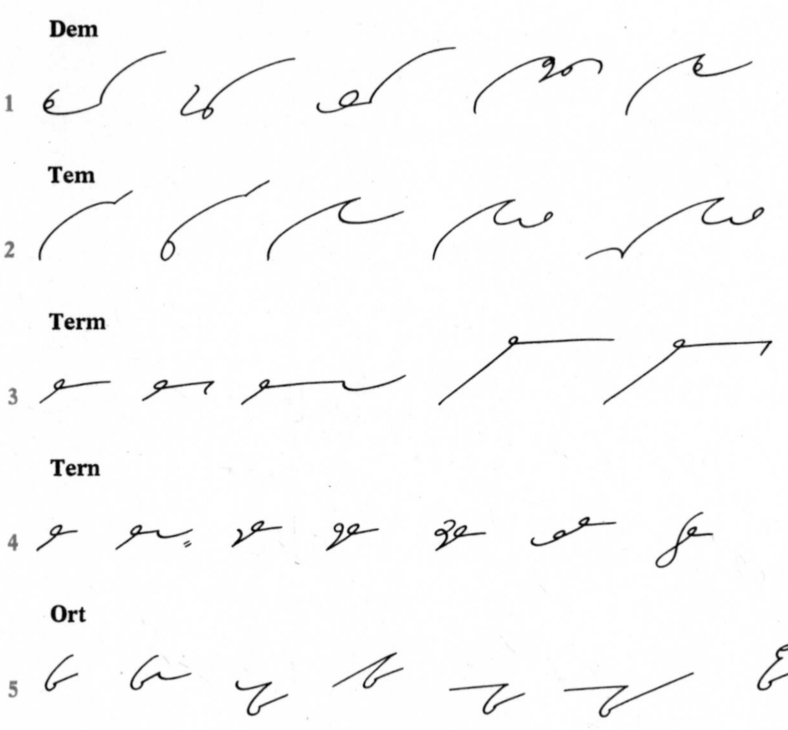

1 Seldom, freedom, random, domestic, domicile.
2 Tempt, attempt, temple, temporary, contemporary.
3 Term, terms, terminal, determine, determination.
4 Turn, Turner, stern, eastern, western, return, pattern.
5 Port, porter, report, deport, import, imported, export.

Building Transcription Skills

2 Business Vocabulary Builder

gross income Income before deductions, such as taxes, have been made.

unwary Not alert; easily fooled.

induced Persuaded.

Reading and Writing Practice

3 Investing in Real Estate

when

intro

and o

intro

in·ves·tor

do·mes·tic

conj

de·duct·ible

def·i·nite·ly

par

intro

intro

Transcribe: $1,000

ser

course

Transcribe: 20 percent

if

bor·rowed

par

intro

Over the

intro

Transcribe:
10 percent

10, 15,

intro

year's

quite

But

over·night

conj

ex·cep·tion
un·wary

in·duced

even·tu·al·ly
when

worth·less

mid·dle

ser

des·ert

ac·cess

Before

intro

An investment

conj

conj

conj

bur·den

[680]

Secretaries with an eye to the future take their responsibilities seriously; they willingly give their very best to every assignment.

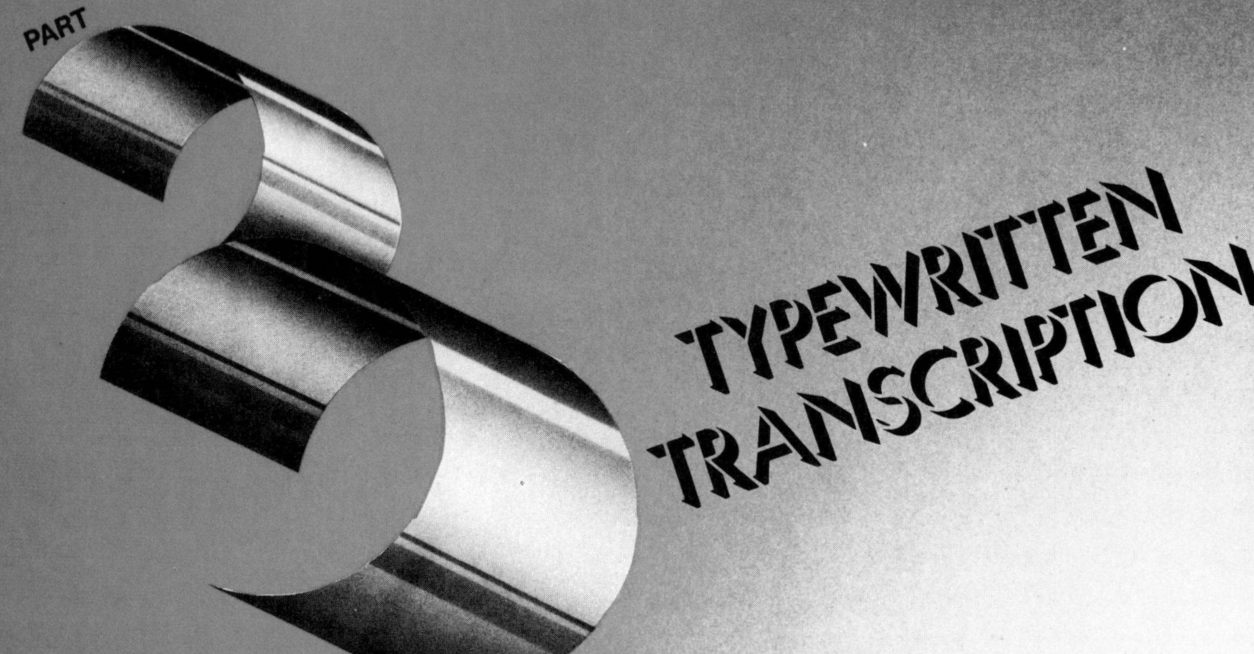

If you have practiced regularly and have completed your assignments correctly, your skill has probably grown to the point that you are ready to transcribe on the typewriter.

Making the transition from transcribing in longhand to transcribing on the typewriter is easy and simple if you remember a few things. Do not expect your first attempt at transcribing on the typewriter to produce mailable letters. On your first few tries you will probably type easy, familiar letters from the shorthand plates in this textbook. At this stage, you should pay little attention to letter form, typing style, or typographical errors. The idea is simply to type all of the material. When you can transcribe the notes in your textbook easily and quickly on your typewriter, your teacher will probably introduce transcription from your homework notes or from material dictated in class. As your skill develops, your teacher will likely add the other elements of transcription one at a time — typing in letter form, correcting errors, producing mailable copy, and so on.

It is very important in transcription to keep your work station properly organized. You should select a place to keep your textbook, your typewriter paper, your pen, and any other supplies you will need. If these things are always in the same place, you will be able to find them easily.

When you are taking dictation for transcription, it is a good idea to date each page of your notebook at the bottom. In this way, you will be able to find your shorthand notes quickly if you should need them for future reference. After you have transcribed a letter, you should draw a diagonal line through the notes. This will tell you at a glance that you have finished transcribing that particular letter.

When you take dictation for transcription, remember that producing mailable letters is your final goal, but that transcription skill grows slowly—a little every day. Do not demand perfection of yourself in the early stages, but be sure that your work improves each day. By the end of the term, you should be able to produce business letters from your own shorthand notes that a business executive would be happy to sign!

9 FOOD

Developing Word-Building Power

1 Brief Forms and Derivatives

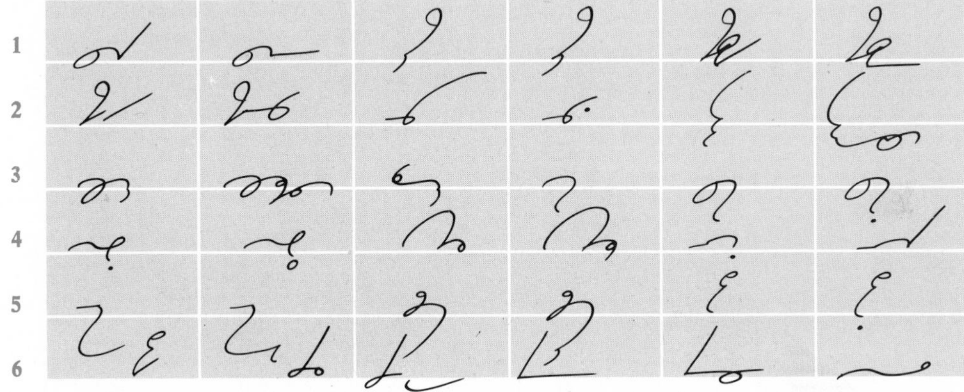

1 Acknowledged, acknowledgment, advantages, advantageous, advertised, advertisement.
2 Afterward, aftermath, anytime, anything, businesses, businesslike.
3 Characters, characteristic, circulars, company, accompany, accompanying.
4 Corresponding, correspondingly, difficulty, difficulties, enclosing, enclosed.
5 Envelope, envelopes, executive, executives, experience, experiencing.
6 Experienced, generally, generality, gentlemen, gentleman, gladly.

Building Transcription Skills

2 TYPING STYLE STUDY ● short letters

In this lesson you will learn how to place by judgment short letters of approximately 100 words. The following illustration shows a short letter as it was written in shorthand and transcribed. The letter was typed on a machine that had elite (small) type.

The shorthand required a little more than half a column in the notebook. When a letter takes about half a column in your notebook, you should do these things:

☐ 1 Set your typewriter for a 2-inch left margin and a 2-inch right margin.

☐ 2 Insert a sheet of letterhead paper.

☐ 3 Type the date on the third line below the last line of the letterhead, beginning at the horizontal center of the page.

☐ 4 Begin the address at the left margin about 10 lines below the date. (If you use a machine with pica (large) type, begin 8 lines below the date.)

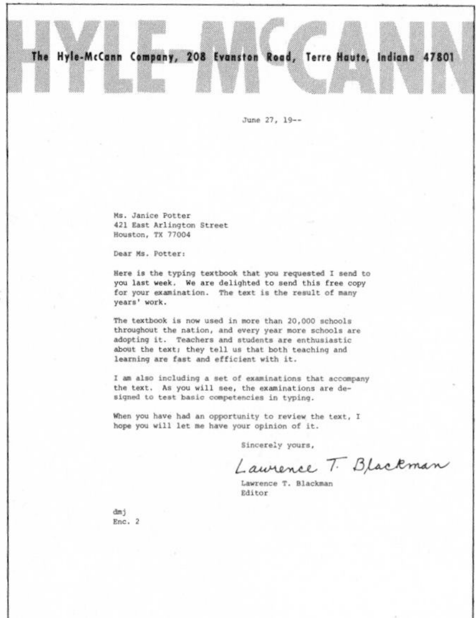

HYLE-McCANN

The Hyle-McCann Company, 208 Evanston Road, Terre Haute, Indiana 47801

June 27, 19--

Ms. Janice Potter
421 East Arlington Street
Houston, TX 77004

Dear Ms. Potter:

Here is the typing textbook that you requested I send to you last week. We are delighted to send this free copy for your examination. The text is the result of many years' work.

The textbook is now used in more than 20,000 schools throughout the nation, and every year more schools are adopting it. Teachers and students are enthusiastic about the text; they tell us that both teaching and learning are fast and efficient with it.

I am also including a set of examinations that accompany the text. As you will see, the examinations are designed to test basic competencies in typing.

When you have had an opportunity to review the text, I hope you will let me have your opinion of it.

Sincerely yours,

Lawrence T. Blackman

Lawrence T. Blackman
Editor

dmj
Enc. 2

SHORT LETTER

---

3 Business Vocabulary Builder

keenly Sharply; intensely.

hold the line To operate within certain limits.

deteriorated Worsened.

converted Changed; remade.

Reading and Writing Practice

4 Brief-Form Letter

keen·ly

ris·ing

whole·sale

par

Nev·er·the·less

intro

nonr

Transcribe:
400 Worth Street

[147]

5

first-class
hyphenated
before noun

par

sub·stan·dard

conj

veg·e·ta·bles

intro

stale

taste·less

per·plexed

intro

nc

rise

if

[134]

com·pet·i·tors

6

quan·ti·ties

nc

intro

and o

fam·i·ly-sized hyphenated before noun

nc

Transcribe: 15 percent

15,

[150]

7

ad·ver·tise·ment

when

par·tic·u·lar·ly

gro·cery

com·mu·ni·ty

con·vert·ed

bulk-quan·ti·ty hyphenated before noun

and o

intro

elim·i·nat·ing

par

conj

re·in·state

[158]

8 Transcription Quiz For you to supply: 9 commas—1 comma apposition, 6 commas parenthetical, 1 comma conjunction, 1 comma introductory; 1 semicolon no conjunction; 2 missing words.

[150]

Building Phrasing Skill

1 Useful Business-Letter Phrases

On

1

Omission of Words in Phrases

2

Very

3

Month

4

1 On the, on that, on that date, on which, on time, on this, on our.
2 One or two, two or three, three or four, one of the, some of these, none of them, many of the.
3 Very much, very well, very glad, very good, very important, very many.
4 Each month, every month, months ago, several months ago.

2 Geographical Expressions

1
2

1 Spokane, Provo, Cleveland, Cincinnati, Lynn, Salem, Helena.
2 Washington, Utah, Hawaii, Illinois, Ohio, Massachusetts, Montana.

Building Transcription Skills

3 Business Vocabulary Builder

changeover Use of a different method; transfer.

cooperative *(noun)* An organization owned by the users of its services.

predicted Foretold; declared in advance.

Reading and Writing Practice

4 Phrase Letter

geo

geo

Transcribe: 15th of August

in·sti·tute

ser

its

pro·ceed

intro

[147]

5

geo

5

co·op·er·a·tive

intro

sub·stan·tial

whole·sale

Transcribe: $5

full-time hyphenated before noun

ap

nonr

en·roll

unique

[173]

6

Transcribe: 1,000

conj

Transcribe: $100,000

pro·ce·dures

conj

oc·ca·sions

if

[133]

7

mu·tu·al

ap

pro·mot·ed

po·si·tion

geo

Con·grat·u·la·tions

nc

de·serve

nonr

dis·trict

busy

when

al·low

[135]

8

ap

Transcribe:
April 8

nonr

for·mal

nonr

par

intro

[217]

9 Transcription Quiz For you to supply: 2 commas—1 comma introductory, 1 comma *when* clause; 1 semicolon no conjunction; 2 missing words.

[90]

Developing Word-Building Power

1 Word Families

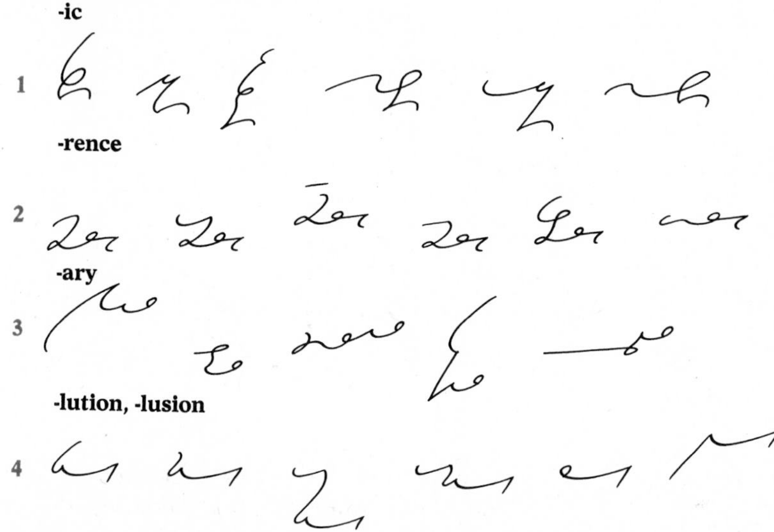

1 Basic, topic, specific, graphic, logic, classic.
2 Conference, reference, interference, inference, preference, occurrence.
3 Temporary, necessary, secretary, budgetary, monetary.
4 Pollution, solution, revolution, resolution, illusion, delusion.

Building Transcription Skills

2 SPELLING FAMILIES ● **words in which y is changed to i in the past tense and in the s form**

ap-ply	**ap-plies**	**ap-plied**
re-ply	**re-plies**	**re-plied**
im-ply	**im-plies**	**im-plied**
com-ply	**com-plies**	**com-plied**
sup-ply	**sup-plies**	**sup-plied**

3 Business Vocabulary Builder	**utensils** Tools.
	amenities Comforts; pleasantries.
	financially pressed Short of money.

Reading and Writing Practice

4

plan·ning

res·tau·rant

Mall

al·ready

geo

if

ap

ser

ser

uten·sils

as

nonr

nonr

pref·er·ence

intro

42

10

[184]

5

ac·cept·ed

intro

intro

conj

bud·get·ary

intro

par

con·sult·ing

cr

rec·om·mend

[174]

6

ef·fect

to·day's

high-qual·i·ty hyphenated before noun

ame·ni·ties

ap·plies

nc

suc·ceed·ing

fi·nan·cial·ly pressed
no hyphen
after ly

con·fer·ence

Transcribe:
9 a.m.

ap

410

ap

Transcribe:
555-1401

555-1401

[238]

7

as

en·act·ed

city's

san·i·tary

ser

ap

some·time

intro

hour's

par

[174]

8 Transcription Quiz For you to supply: 4 commas—1 comma introductory, 1 comma *if* clause, 2 commas parenthetical; 1 semicolon no conjunction; 2 missing words.

140

75

[148]

Developing Word-Building Power

1 Word Beginnings and Endings

Self-

1

Sub-

2

-rity

3

-ship

4

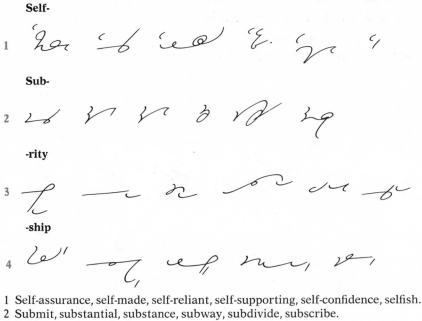

1 Self-assurance, self-made, self-reliant, self-supporting, self-confidence, selfish.
2 Submit, substantial, substance, subway, subdivide, subscribe.
3 Majority, minority, security, integrity, authorities, maturity.
4 Friendship, membership, relationship, scholarship, steamship.

Building Transcription Skills

2 SIMILAR-WORDS DRILL ● suite, suit

suite (pronounced *swēt*) A group of rooms occupied as a unit.

We reserved a *suite* of rooms.

suit (*noun*) A set of clothing.

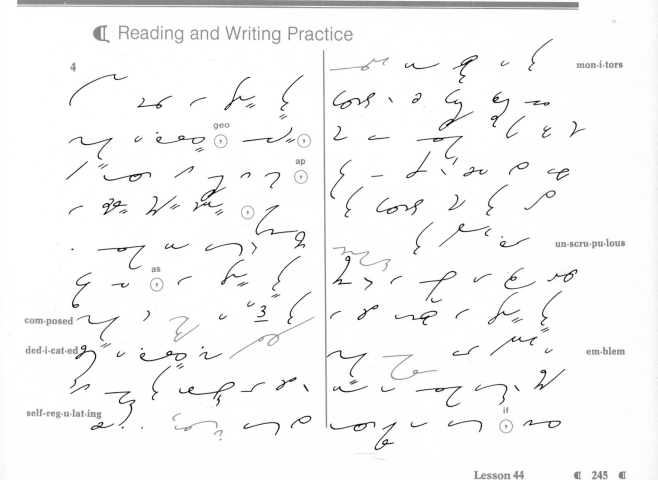

I need a new brown *suit*.

suit (*verb*) To meet the requirements of.

Did the work *suit* you?

3 Business Vocabulary Builder

monitors *(verb)* Observes; checks.
emblem Symbol; identifying mark.
strive To work diligently.
accommodate To make room for; to supply.

Reading and Writing Practice

4

geo

ap

as

com·posed

ded·i·cat·ed

self-reg·u·lat·ing

mon·i·tors

un·scru·pu·lous

em·blem

if

com·plet·ing

self-ad·dressed

[186]

5

ide·als
suit

nc

con·sis·tent

top-qual·i·ty
hyphenated
before noun

sub·mit·ting

[99]

6

ap

ap

Feb·ru·ary

an·nu·al

geo

ac·com·mo·date

10

suite

if

[99]

7

conj

ref·er·ence

cr

self-re·li·ant

intro

in·teg·ri·ty

if

if

[140]

8

ap

par

conj

Transcribe: 432 21st Avenue

intro

intro

intro

[140] mem·o·ra·ble

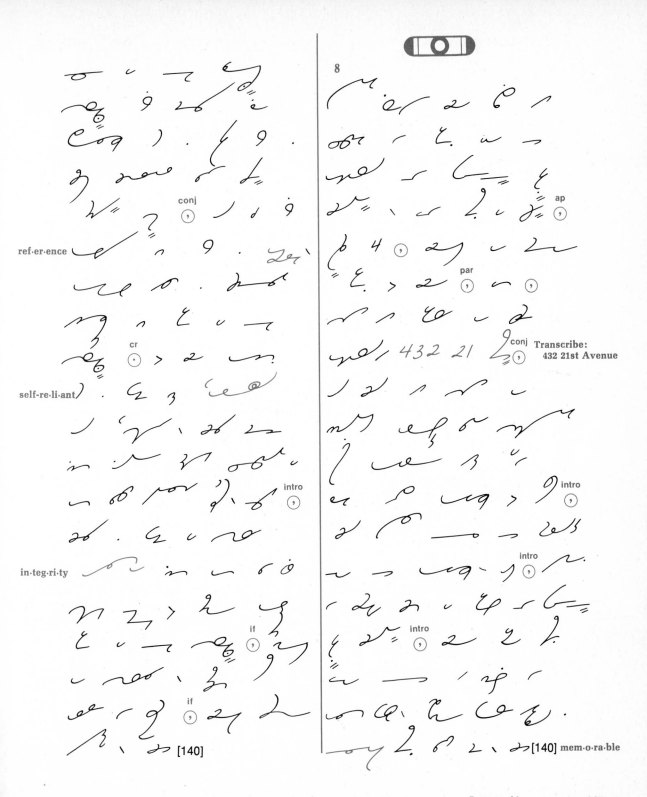

9 Transcription Quiz For you to supply: 4 commas—2 commas series, 2 commas parenthetical; 2 missing words.

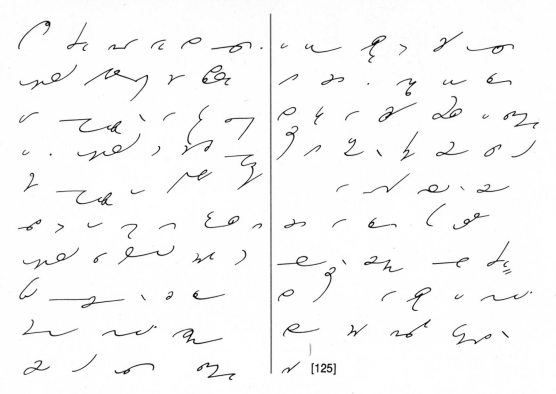

[125]

Today's executives want truly competent, responsible assistants. As a result of the increasing pace of business, executives must now depend on secretaries to handle many important matters for them. If you are a competent, responsible worker, you are sure to be more than welcome in any business office.

Developing Word-Building Power

1 Shorthand Vocabulary Builder

Oi

1

Ye-, Ya-

2

Ten

3

Nt

4

1 Oil, soil, boiler, loyal, coin, employ.
2 Year, yet, yellow, yard, yarn, Yale.
3 Tennis, attention, retention, intended, distance, standards, stand, continue.
4 Sent, center, central, rent, different, independent, continent.

Building Transcription Skills

2 Business Vocabulary Builder

consultation Conference; discussion.
disposable Designed to be thrown away after use.
recycle To process material for reuse.

Reading and Writing Practice

3 Franchising Food

rad·i·cal·ly

suf·fered

flour·ished

nc ;

intro ,

intro ,

fast-food hyphenated — before noun

and o ,

de·signed

ex·treme·ly

intro ,

intro ,

signs

rec·og·nize

intro ,

ac·cep·tance

geo·graph·ic

intro ,

fa·mil·iar

intro ,

weeks'

ser

warn·ing

de·fi·cien·cies

Franchise

in·de·pen·dent

par

con·sul·ta·tion

de·vice

ser

due

al·most

In a

when

trays

dis·pos·able

intro

du·ra·ble

re·cy·cle

intro

nc

intro

[666]

4 Learning To Cook

great

intro

ap·pren·tice chef

and o

intro

ap·pren·tice·ship

when

com·mand

In

dis·ap·peared

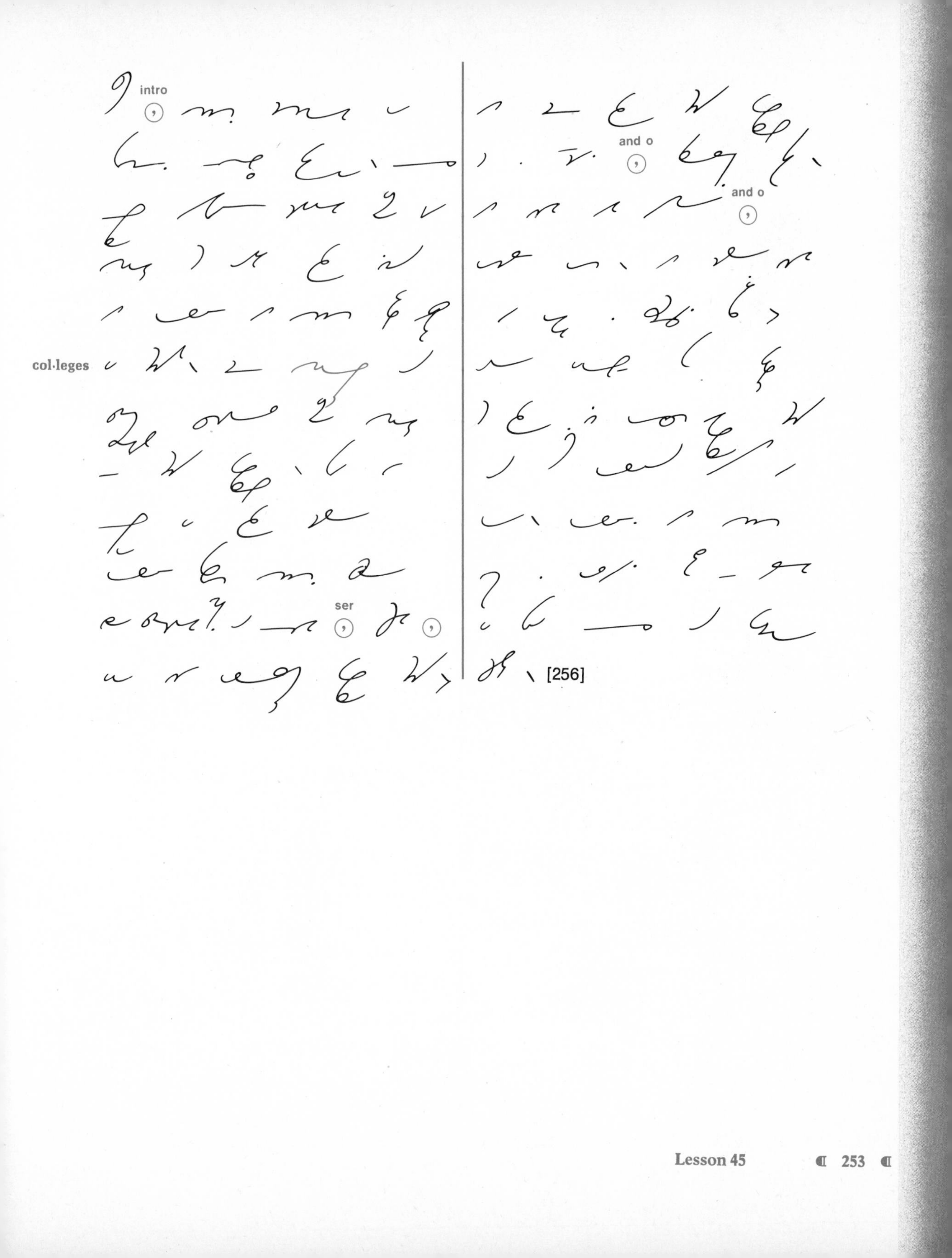

intro

col·leges

ser

and o

and o

[256]

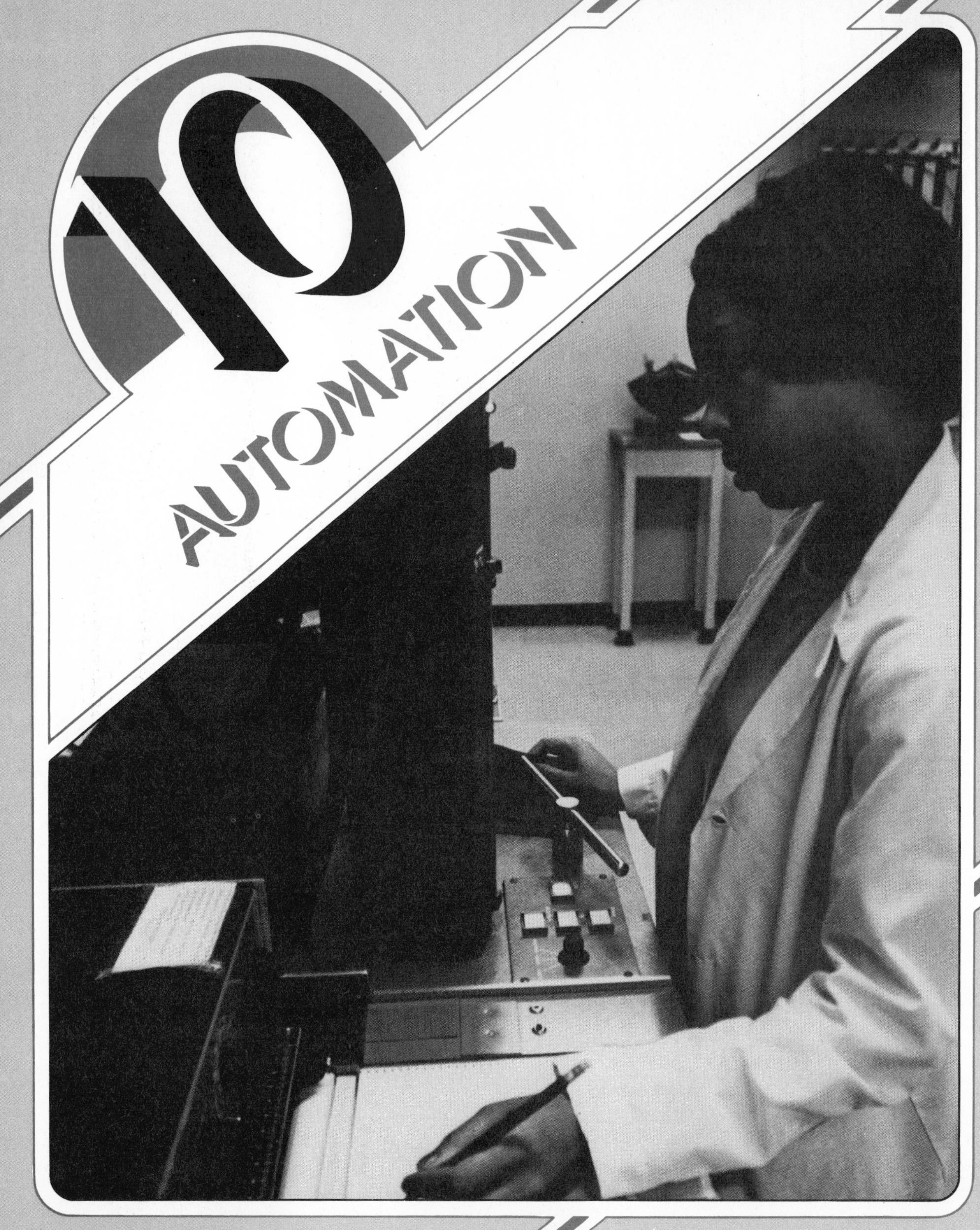
10
AUTOMATION

Developing Word-Building Power

1 Brief Forms and Derivatives

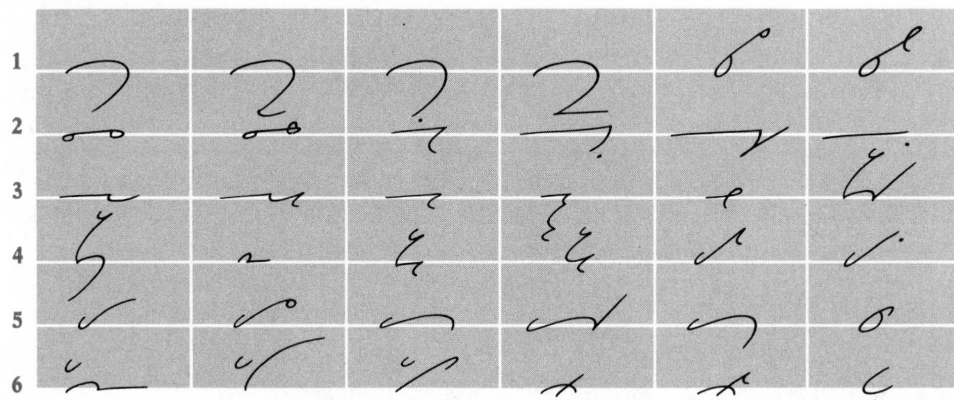

1 Govern, governor, governing, government, idea, ideas.
2 Immediate, immediately, importance-important, manufacturing, manufactured, morning.
3 Mr., Mrs., Ms., newspapers, next, objected.
4 Objective, one (won), opinions, opportunities, orders, ordering.
5 Ordinary, ordinarily, organize, organized, organization, out.
6 Overcome, overtime, overdo, quantity, quantities, present.

Building Transcription Skills

2 Business Vocabulary Builder

marvels Things that cause wonder or surprise.

affords Provides.

reschedule To set a new time.

Reading and Writing Practice

3 Brief-Form Letter

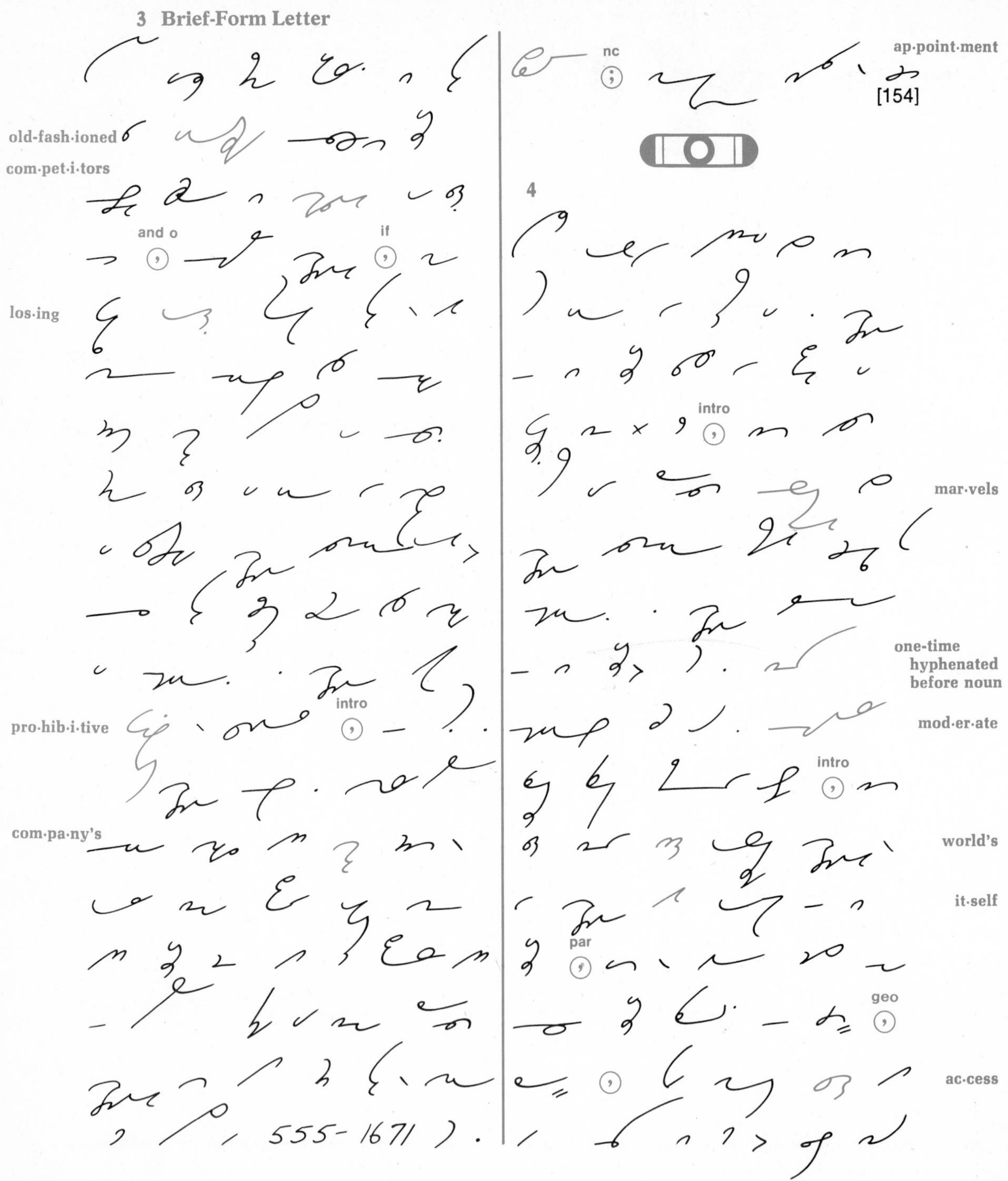

intro

nonr

as·sign

key·board

hours'

fac·to·ry-trained
hyphenated
before noun

ser

sign

re·ceive

when

[244]

5

nonr

due

intro

de·layed

when

re·main·der

can·celed

intro

intro

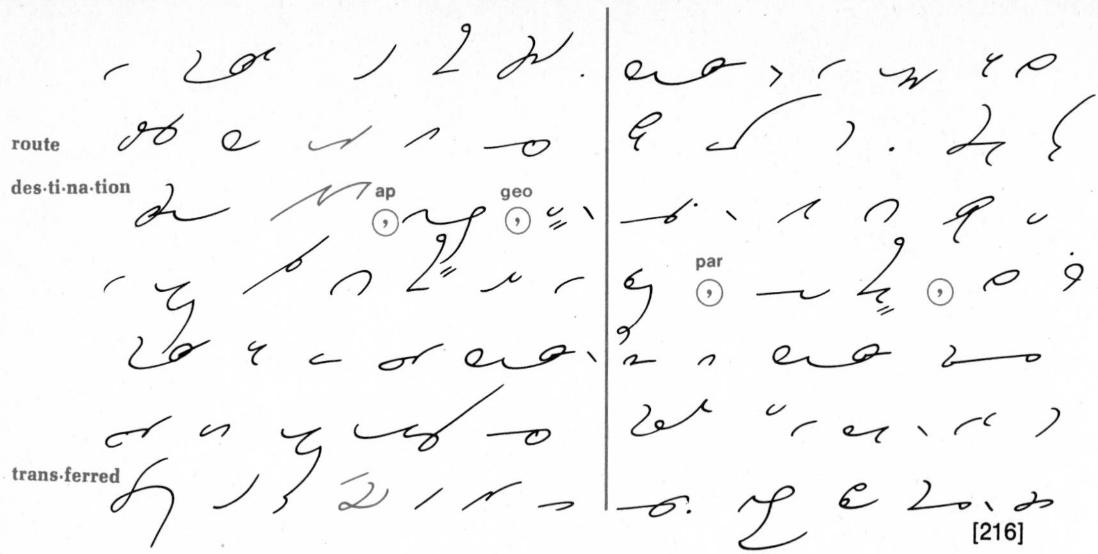

6 Transcription Quiz For you to supply: 5 commas—1 comma apposition, 1 comma conjunction, 1 comma introductory, 2 commas parenthetical; 1 semicolon no conjunction; 2 missing words.

[118]

Building Phrasing Skill

1 Useful Business-Letter Phrases

Done

Do Not

Words Omitted

Let Us

1 Have done, I have done, to be done, has done, should be done, will be done.
2 I do not, you do not, we do not, they do not, do not have, we do not have.
3 One of the most, one of the best, in the future, in the past, as a result, will you please.
4 Let us, let us have, let us know, let us make, let us say, let us see.

2 Geographical Expressions

1 San Antonio, El Paso, Odessa, Tucson, Tampa, Orlando.
2 Texas, New Mexico, Mississippi, Colorado, Florida, Georgia.

Building Transcription Skills

3 SIMILAR-WORDS DRILL ● real, reel

real Genuine; authentic; actual.

Our company charges you only for the *real* time you use our computer.

reel Spool.

The *reel* of computer tape must be handled carefully.

4 Business Vocabulary Builder

printout A record produced automatically, as by a computer.

offend To insult.

eventually Finally; ultimately.

Reading and Writing Practice

5 Phrase Letter

intro

dis·turbed

print·out

high-qual·i·ty hyphenated before noun

prompt·ly

en·ti·tled

re·al

intro

intro

min·utes'

ex·act·ly

cr

[184]

6

intro

man·age·ment

as

conj

intro

state·ments

even·tu·al·ly

conj

intro

conj

intro

[180]

7

poor-qual·i·ty hyphenated before noun

if

treat·ed

conj

com·plete

as

reels

un·til

lose

valu·able

nc

trans·fer

if

geo

[149]

8

geo

suede

when

tear

sleeve

conj

intro

par

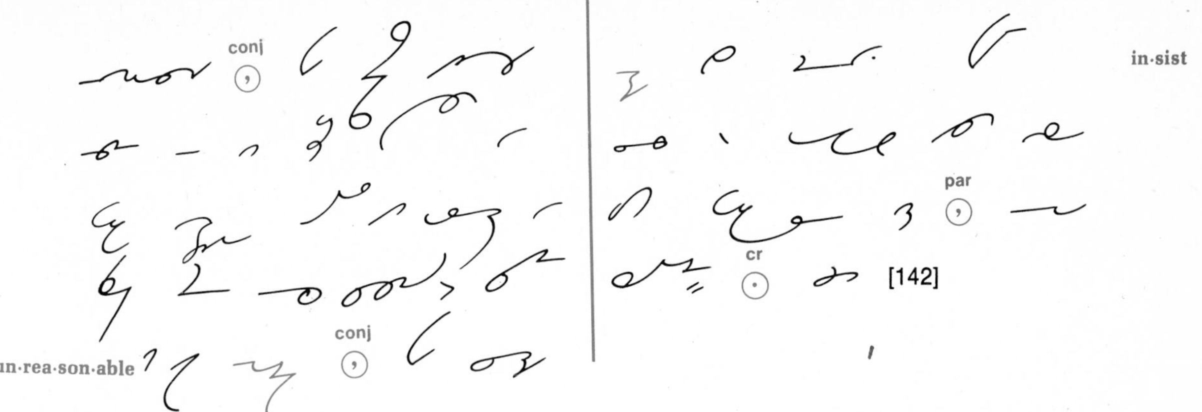

9 Transcription Quiz For you to supply: 3 commas—1 comma introductory, 1 comma *as* clause, 1 comma *and* omitted; 1 semicolon no conjunction; 2 missing words.

[120]

Developing Word-Building Power

1 Word Families

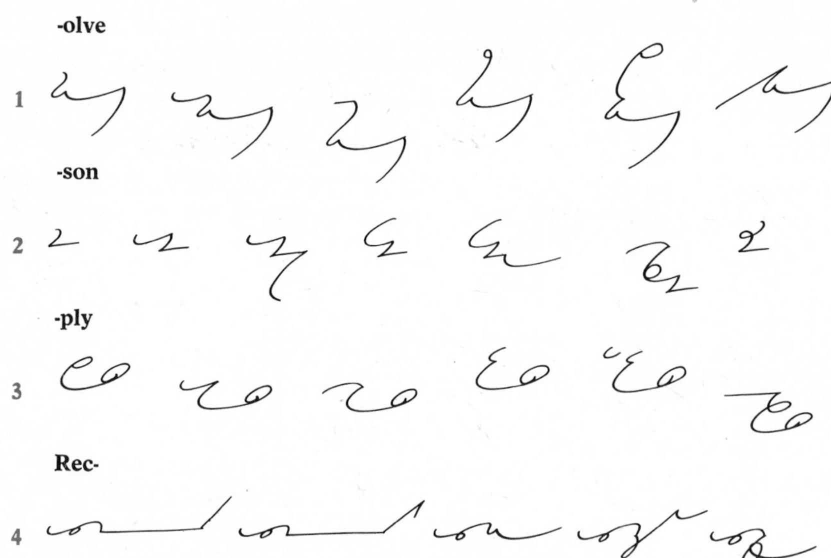

1 Solve, resolve, involve, evolve, absolve, dissolve.
2 Son, reason, reasonable, person, personal, comparison, season.
3 Apply, reply, comply, supply, oversupply, misapply.
4 Recommend, recommendation, recall, reconsider, reconcile.

Building Transcription Skills

2 COMMON PREFIXES ● ex-

ex- In many words the prefix *ex* means *out* or *out of.*

exit A way out.

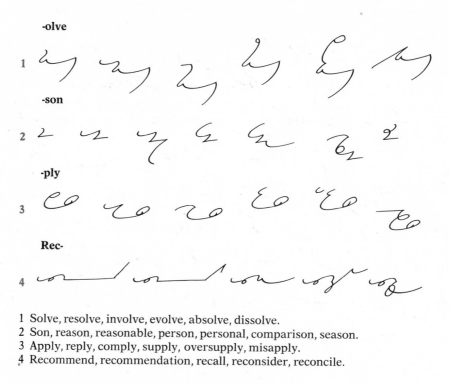

expand	To spread out.
expenditure	That which is paid out.
exterior	The outside of something.
external	On the outside.

3 Business Vocabulary Builder

records-retention system A carefully planned filing system.

color scheme A planned combination of colors.

reassess To evaluate again.

Reading and Writing Practice

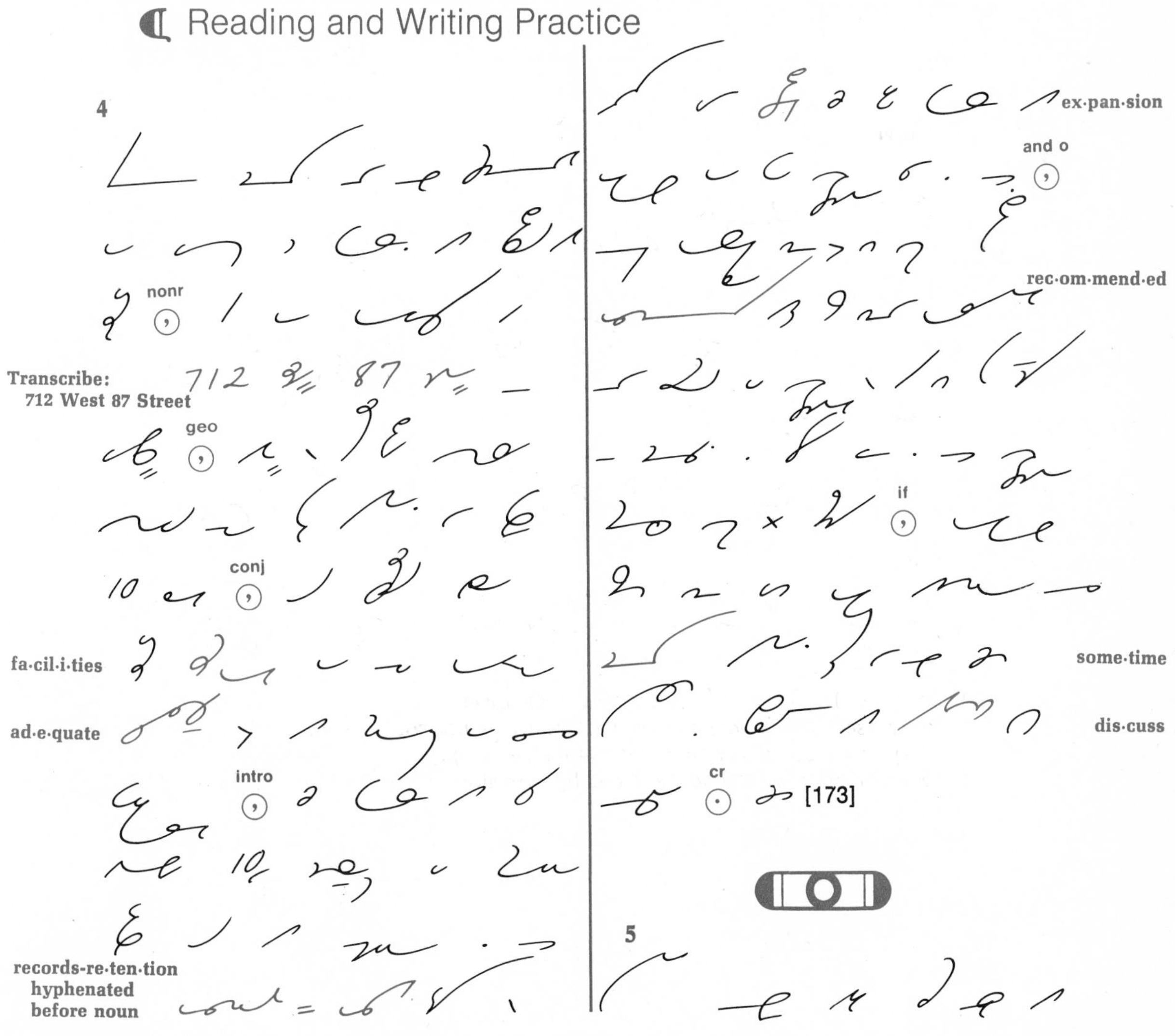

per·son·nel

well-run hyphenated before noun

compact

ex·te·ri·or

scheme

avoid
ini·tial

ex·pen·di·ture

intro

conj

intro

re·mod·el·ing

par

ser

[206]

6

Transcribe:
400 State Street

intro

min·i·mum
safe·ty

intro

par ,

,

complete·ly new
no hyphen
after ly

intro ,

intro ,

di·rect·ly

conj ,

Transcribe:
10 percent

intro ,

ex·tin·guish·ers

par ,

,

conj ,

[208]

7

ex·its

nc ;

com·ply

intro ,

ap ,

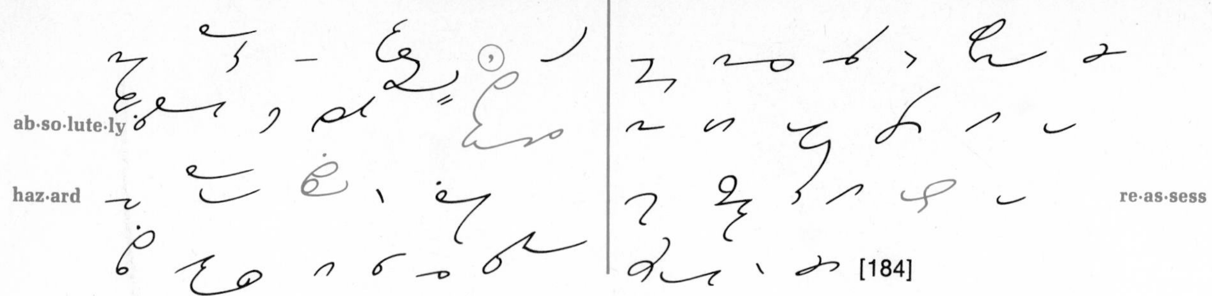

8 Transcription Quiz For you to supply: 3 commas—1 comma conjunction, 1 comma introductory, 1 comma *if* clause; 2 missing words.

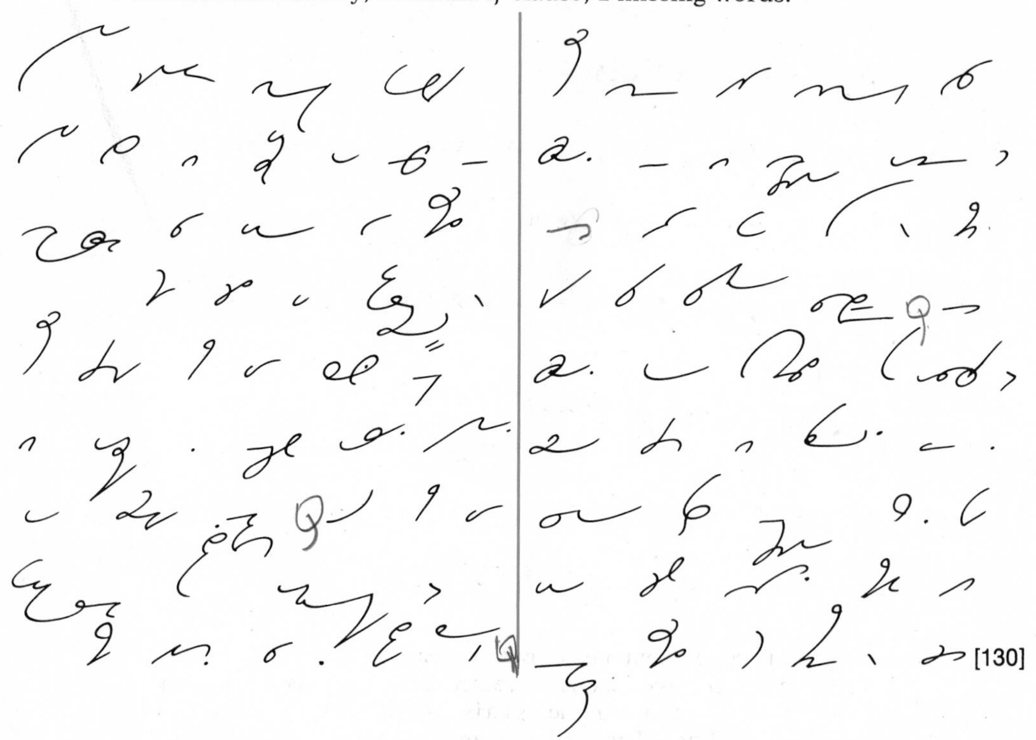

Get your day off to a good start by greeting everyone with a cheerful and sincere "Good morning!"

Developing Word-Building Power

1 Word Beginnings and Endings

Con-, Com- Followed by a Vowel

1

In-, Im-, Etc., Followed by a Vowel

2

-ily

3

-self, -selves

4

1 Connect, connection, connote, commerce, commercial, committee.
2 Innovation, inexpensive, inaugurate, enact, enable, emotion, immodest.
3 Steadily, readily, temporarily, necessarily, easily, family.
4 Myself, yourself, himself, yourselves, themselves, ourselves.

Building Transcription Skills

2 SPELLING FAMILIES ● des-, dis-, dec-

Words beginning *des, dis,* and *dec* are often pronounced in a similar way. The stenographer should be very careful to spell such words correctly. Study the words in the following lists carefully so that you will be able to spell them without hesitation.

Des-

de-sire	**de-stroy**	**de-spite**
de-scribe	**de-serve**	**de-sign**

Dis-

dis-turb	**dis-agree**	**dis-burse**
dis-ap-point	**dis-cuss**	**dis-card**
dis-cern	**dis-charge**	**dis-cov-er**

Dec-

de-ci-sion	**de-ceit**	**de-ceive**
de-cent	**de-cide**	**dec-i-mal**

3 Business Vocabulary Builder

effect *(verb)* To cause to happen.
inaugurate To begin.
discharge *(verb)* To let go; to dismiss.

Reading and Writing Practice

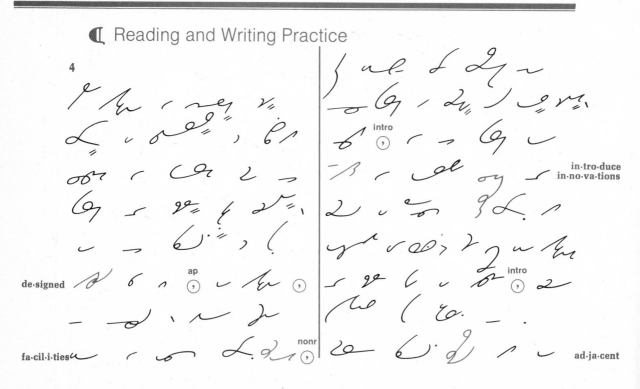

4

de·signed ap intro fa·cil·i·ties nonr intro in·tro·duce in·no·va·tions intro ad·ja·cent

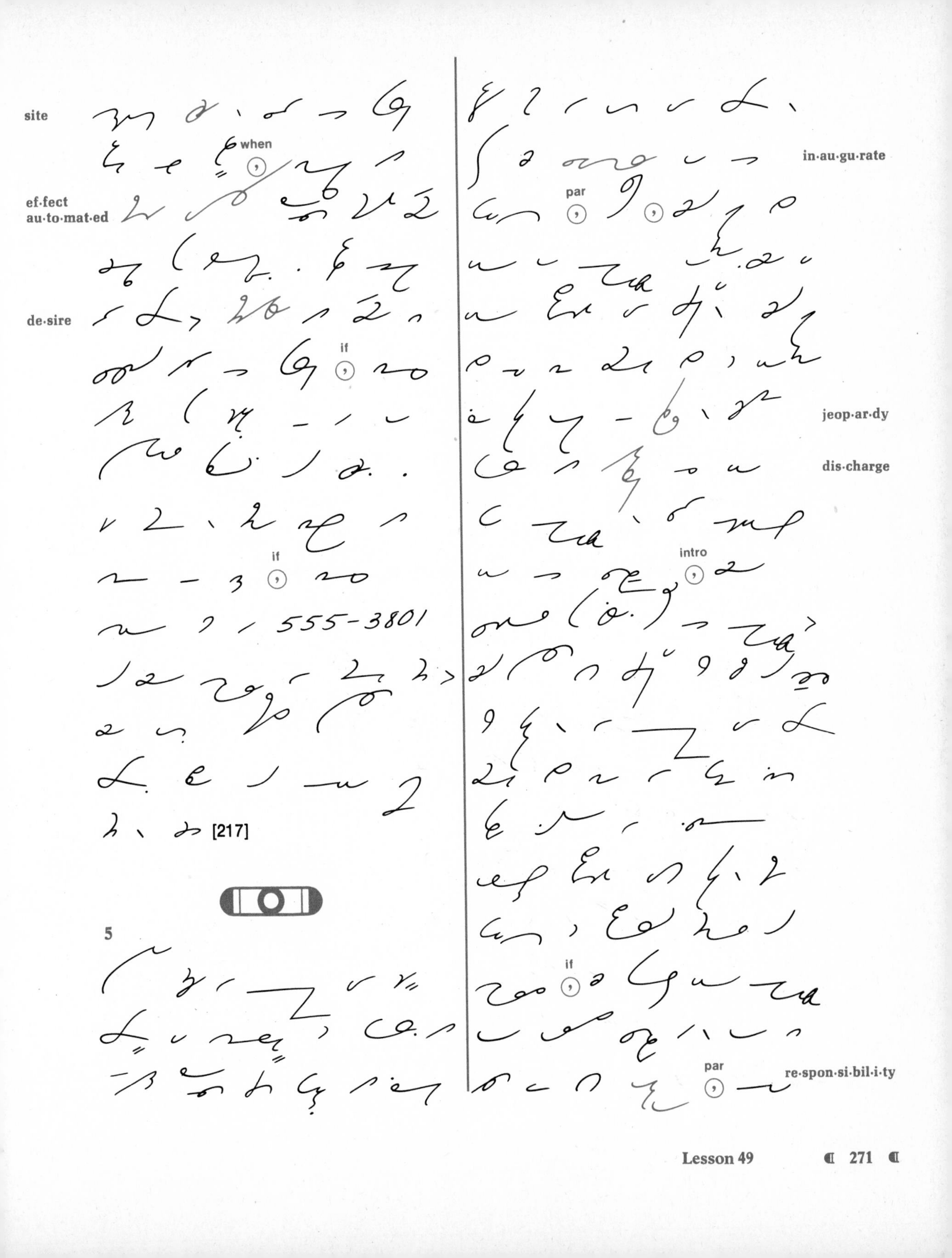

site

when

ef·fect
au·to·mat·ed

de·sire

if

if

555-3801

[217]

5

in·au·gu·rate

par

jeop·ar·dy

dis·charge

intro

if

par

re·spon·si·bil·i·ty

de·cide

intro

intro

rec·om·mend

dis·cuss

cr

[221]

6

Transcribe:
110 West Main Street

geo

conj

in·stal·la·tion

par

if

Transcribe:
9 a.m.
5 p.m.

par

[156]

7

nonr

cat·a·log

de·scribes

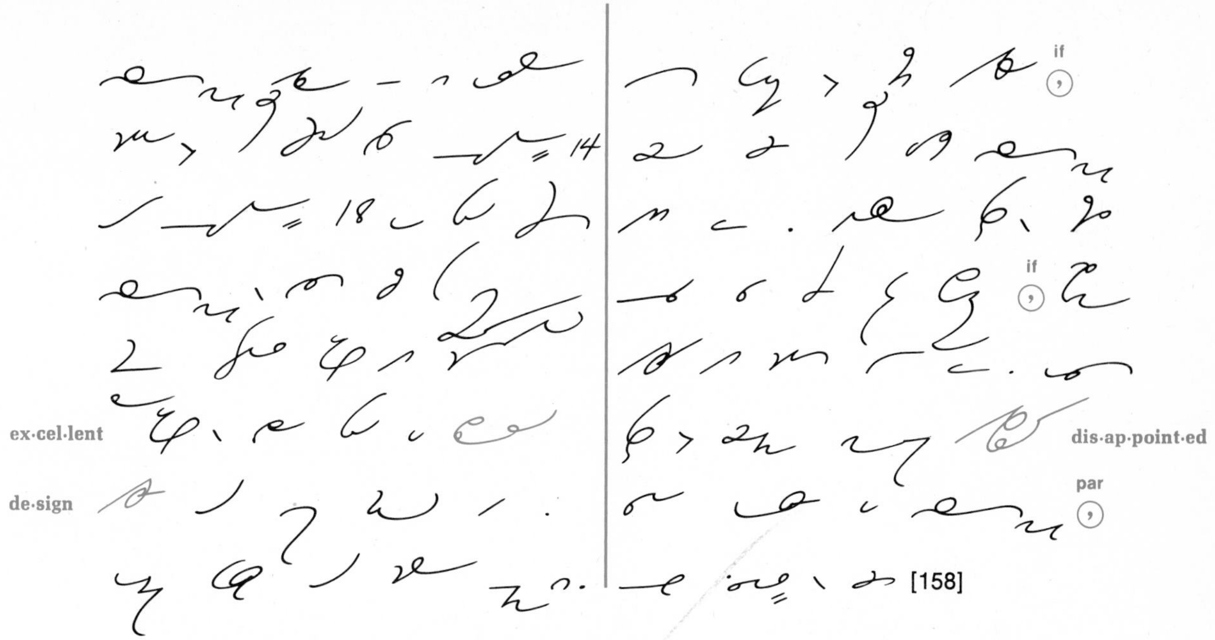

8 Transcription Quiz For you to supply: 9 commas—1 comma geographical, 1 comma *as* clause, 2 commas introductory, 4 commas apposition, 1 comma *if* clause; 2 missing words.

[130]

Developing Word-Building Power

1 Shorthand Vocabulary Builder

W Dash

Amounts

Abbreviation -quire

Abbreviation -graph

1 Quiet, quick, square, twice, Broadway, equipped.
2 5 percent; $100,000; 2 million; $3,000; 400; several hundred; a dollar.
3 Acquire, acquired, require, required, inquire, esquire.
4 Telegraph, monograph, stenographer, paragraph, paragraphed.

Building Transcription Skills

2 Business Vocabulary Builder

artisans Skilled workers in trade.
crude Rough; not expert.
drastically Extremely; radically.

Reading and Writing Practice

3 The New Industrial Revolution

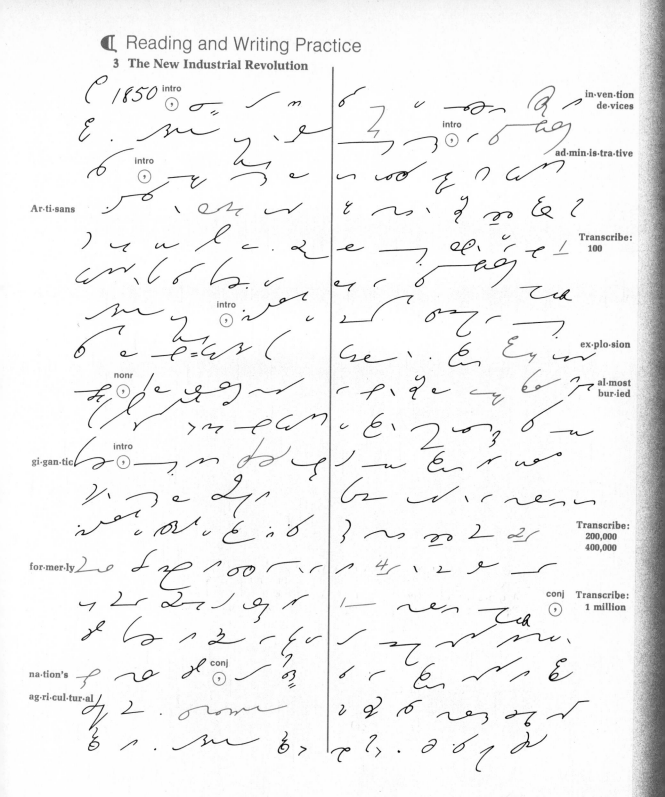

1850 intro

intro

Ar·ti·sans

intro

nonr

intro

gi·gan·tic

for·mer·ly

conj

na·tion's

ag·ri·cul·tur·al

in·ven·tion

de·vices

intro

ad·min·is·tra·tive

Transcribe: 100

ex·plo·sion

al·most

bur·ied

Transcribe: 200,000 400,000

conj

Transcribe: 1 million

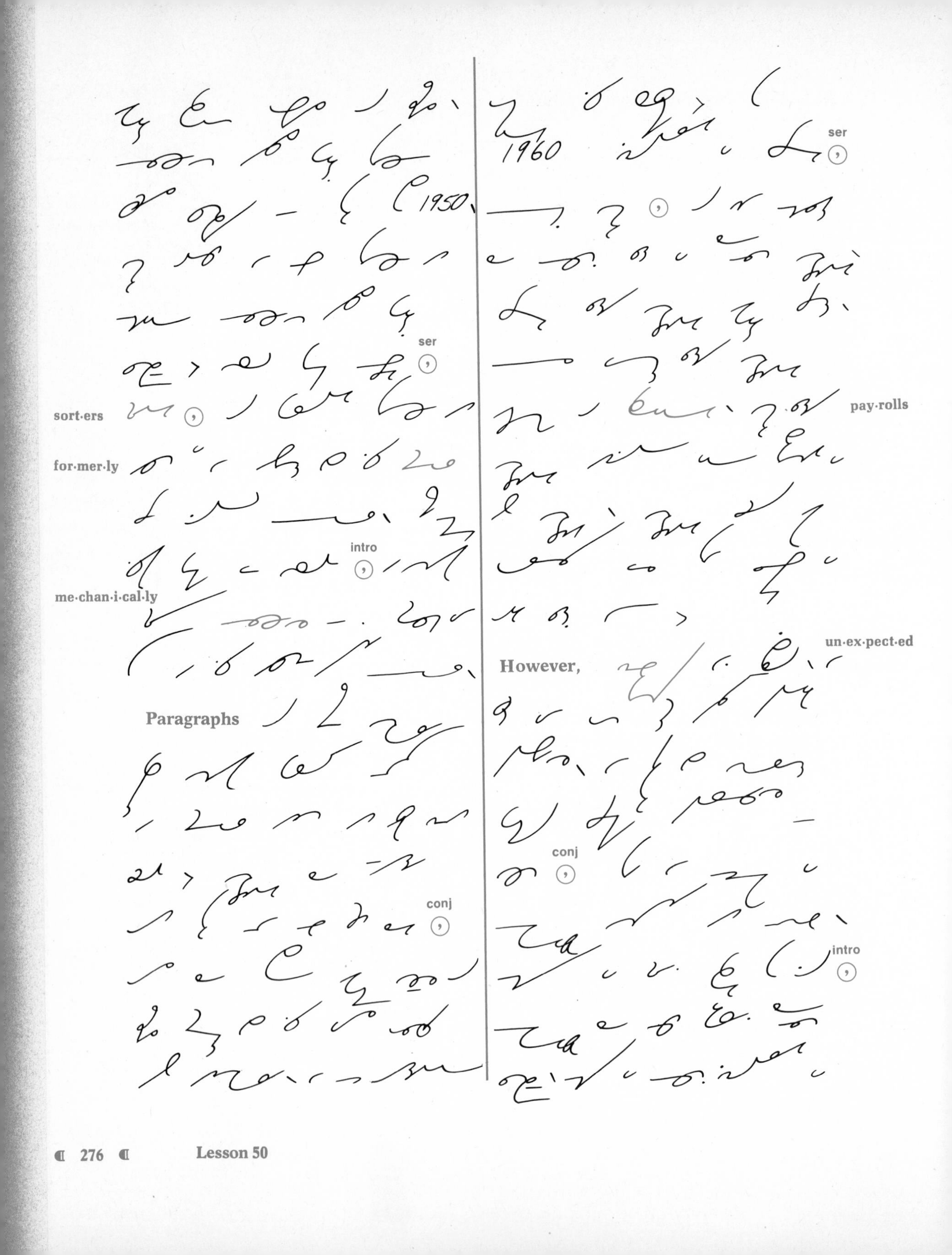

1950

1960

ser

sort·ers

for·mer·ly

intro

me·chan·i·cal·ly

Paragraphs

conj

pay·rolls

un·ex·pect·ed

However,

conj

intro

intro

intro

1970 par

ap·par·ent

intro

re·leased

chal·leng·ing

and o

Today

conj

It is

5 10

[759]

Those who stand out in a crowd show that they are willing to accept responsibility. They can think for themselves, and they possess the initiative to work out problems on their own.

11
TRAVEL

Developing Word-Building Power

1 Brief Forms and Derivatives

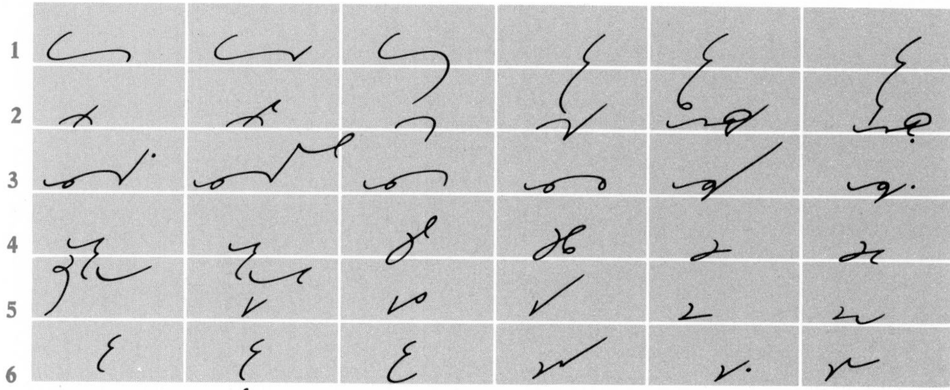

1 Progress, progressed, progressive, public, publicly, publish-publication.
2 Quantity, quantities, question, questioned, recognized, recognizing.
3 Regarding, regardless, regular, regularly, requested, requesting.
4 Responsibility, responsibilities, satisfy-satisfactory, satisfactorily, send, sends.
5 Several, short, shortly, should, soon, sooner.
6 Speak, speaking, speaker, stated, stating, street.

Building Transcription Skills

2 Business Vocabulary Builder

strenuously Strongly; with great energy.
anguish Sorrow; distress.
overbook To issue reservations in excess of the space available.
denied Refused.

Reading and Writing Practice

3 Brief-Form Letter

when

ap

busy

con·ti·nent

Orient

if

nonr

for·mer

if

nonr

res·i·dent

ser

if

born

nonr

as·sis·tance

out-of-the-way hyphenated before noun

555-9923

par

[190]

4

121

21

heavy

when

plane

ca·pac·i·ty

stren·u·ous·ly

conj

al·low

intro

Need·less

intro

an·guish

in·ci·dent

cr

[183]

5

ap·pear

par

intro

va·ca·tion·ers

iso·lat·ed

val·id

10

re·ceive
yes·ter·day's

if

nc

des·ti·na·tion

ap

le·git·i·mate

if

if

nonr

can·cel

res·i·dents

intro

par

par

fur·ther

nonr

[250]

6

Transcribe:
nine
five

mu·tu·al·ly

Yale's

5 5 5 - 8102

[214]

7

[197]

year's

ten·ta·tive·ly

sights

weeks'

re·main·der

8 Transcription Quiz For you to supply: 10 commas—2 commas conjunction, 2 commas apposition, 2 commas series, 3 commas parenthetical, 1 comma *if* clause; 3 semicolons no conjunction; 2 missing words.

[193]

Building Phrasing Skill

1 Useful Business-Letter Phrases

Time

To Omitted in Phrases

We will

We can

1 In time, on time, at this time, at that time, at the time, for the time.
2 Glad to hear, glad to see, able to say, in addition to the, up to date, up-to-the-minute.
3 We will, we will be, we will be able, we will not be able, we will have, we will not have.
4 We can, we cannot, we can have, we cannot have, we can be, we cannot be, we can get.

2 Geographical Expressions

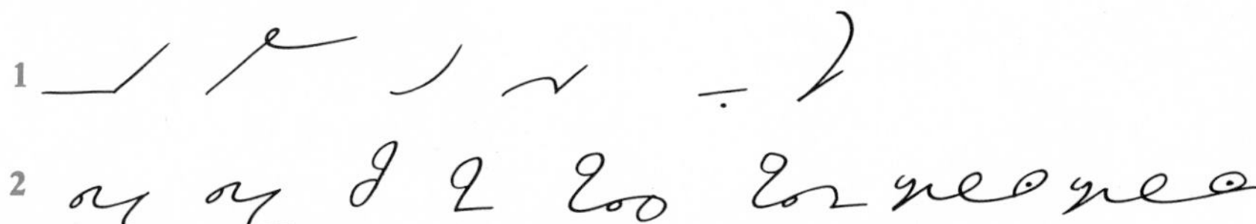

1 Maryland, Delaware, Indiana, Connecticut, New Hampshire, Vermont.
2 Europe, European, Asia, Asian, Africa, African, Australia, Australian.

3 TYPING STYLE STUDY ● average letters

By this time you should be able to place short letters by judgment. You will now learn to place by judgment average-length letters (those that contain about 150 words).

If your shorthand is similar in size to that which appears in this book, you will use almost an entire column in your notebook for an average-length letter.

When a letter takes approximately one column in your notebook, you should do three things:

☐ **1** Set the margin stops on the typewriter for a 1½-inch margin at the left and a 1½-inch margin at the right.

☐ **2** Type the date on the third line below the last line of the letterhead.

☐ **3** Start the address on the eighth line below the date. If your typewriter has pica (large) type, start the inside address on the sixth line below the date.

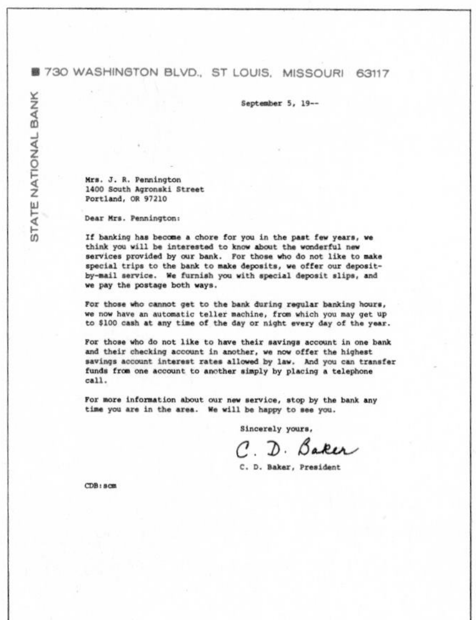

STATE NATIONAL BANK

■ 730 WASHINGTON BLVD., ST LOUIS, MISSOURI 63117

September 5, 19--

Mrs. J. R. Pennington
1400 South Agronski Street
Portland, OR 97210

Dear Mrs. Pennington:

If banking has become a chore for you in the past few years, we think you will be interested to know about the wonderful new services provided by our bank. For those who do not like to make special trips to the bank to make deposits, we offer our deposit-by-mail service. We furnish you with special deposit slips, and we pay the postage both ways.

For those who cannot get to the bank during regular banking hours, we now have an automatic teller machine, from which you may get up to $100 cash at any time of the day or night every day of the year.

For those who do not like to have their savings account in one bank and their checking account in another, we now offer the highest savings account interest rates allowed by law. And you can transfer funds from one account to another simply by placing a telephone call.

For more information about our new service, stop by the bank any time you are in the area. We will be happy to see you.

Sincerely yours,

C. D. Baker

C. D. Baker, President

CDB:scm

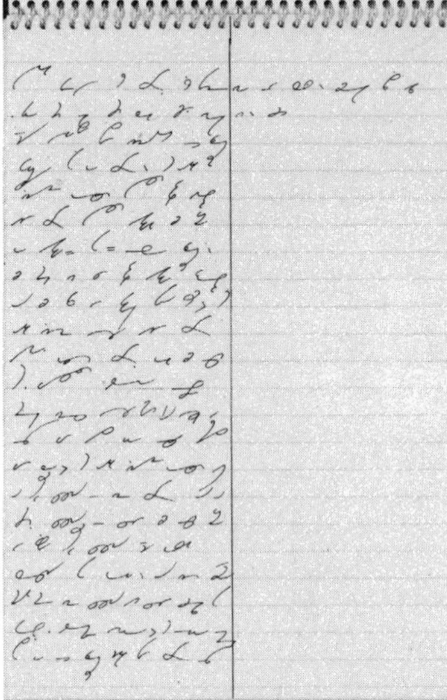

AVERAGE-LENGTH LETTER

4 Business Vocabulary Builder

implies Suggests.

guarantee *(verb)* To back up; to assure.

symbol An identifying mark.

Reading and Writing Practice

5 Phrase Letter

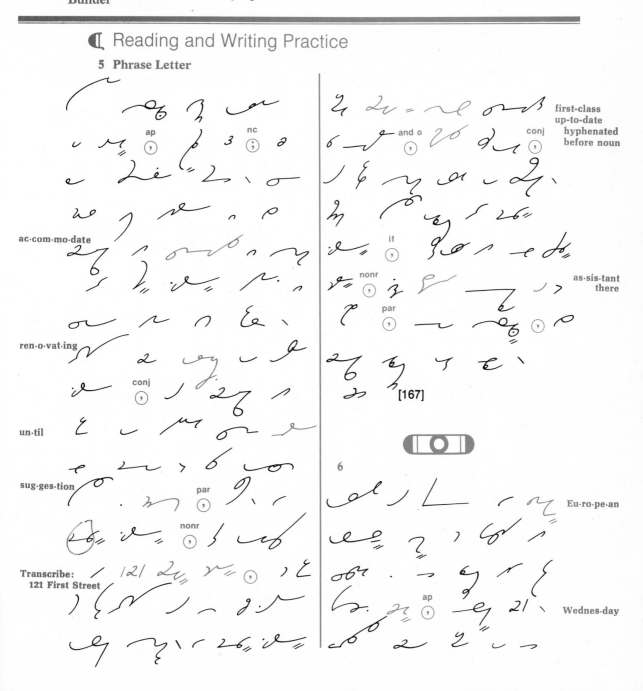

ap nc

ac·com·mo·date

ren·o·vat·ing

conj

un·til

sug·ges·tion

par

nonr

Transcribe: 121 First Street

first-class up-to-date hyphenated before noun

and o conj

if

nonr

as·sis·tant there

par

[167]

6

Eu·ro·pe·an

ap

Wednes·day

im·plies

al·most

ser

fur·ther

intro

re·turn

[137]

7

its

co·op·er·at·ing

conj

Transcribe: $500

if

nc ; conj , [178]

Transcribe:
9 a.m.
3 p.m.

8 Transcription Quiz For you to supply: 4 commas—2 commas series, 1 comma conjunction, 1 comma introductory; 1 semicolon no conjunction; 2 missing words.

[111]

The best aids to success and advancement are hard work and a genuine interest in your job. No one starts at the top of the ladder, and you should not be discouraged if your first business position does not seem to be too important to you. Remember, every job—no matter what level—is of value.

Developing Word-Building Power

1 Word Families

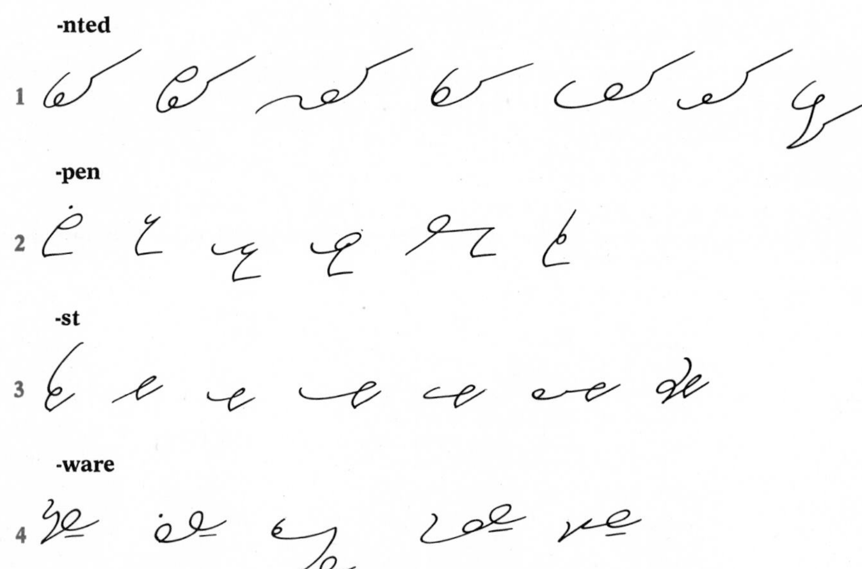

1 Pointed, appointed, granted, painted, planted, rented, prevented.
2 Happen, open, reopen, ripen, dampen, cheapen.
3 Best, test, rest, list, honest, earnest, fastest.
4 Software, hardware, silverware, flatware, stoneware.

Building Transcription Skills

2 SPELLING FAMILIES ● for-, fore-

Be very careful when you transcribe a word beginning with the sound *for.* Sometimes it is spelled *for;* sometimes, *fore.*

For-

for-ward	**for-give**	**for-bid**
for-mal	**for-get**	**for-got**

Fore-

fore-cast	**fore-thought**	**fore-ground**
fore-most	**fore-word**	**fore-close**

In addition, you should give special care when you spell the following words, which are related to the number *four*.

four	**four-teen**	**fourth**	**for-ty**

3 Business Vocabulary Builder

net profit Money earned after deductions are made.
routes (*noun*) Lines of travel; courses.
consecutive Following one after the other.

Reading and Writing Practice

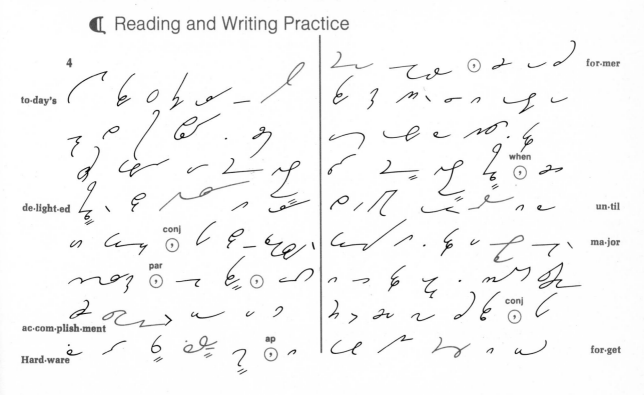

4

to·day's

de·light·ed

conj

par

ac·com·plish·ment

Hard·ware

ap

for·mer

when

un·til

ma·jor

conj

for·get

if

[172]

5

ho·nest·ly

Transcribe: four

intro

short-range long-range hyphenated before noun

months'

com·pa·ny's

nonr

Transcribe: 410 Fourth Avenue

nonr

[164]

6

as

rec·ord-set·ting hyphenated before noun

Transcribe: 5,000 $500,000

conj

year's

fourth

con·sec·u·tive

fore·cast

forth

intro

conj

if

par

[149]

7

routes

ap

in·au·gu·rate

up-to-date hyphenated before noun

and o

ef·fi·cient

oc·ca·sion

if

cour·te·ous

555-1701

nc

[144]

8

intro

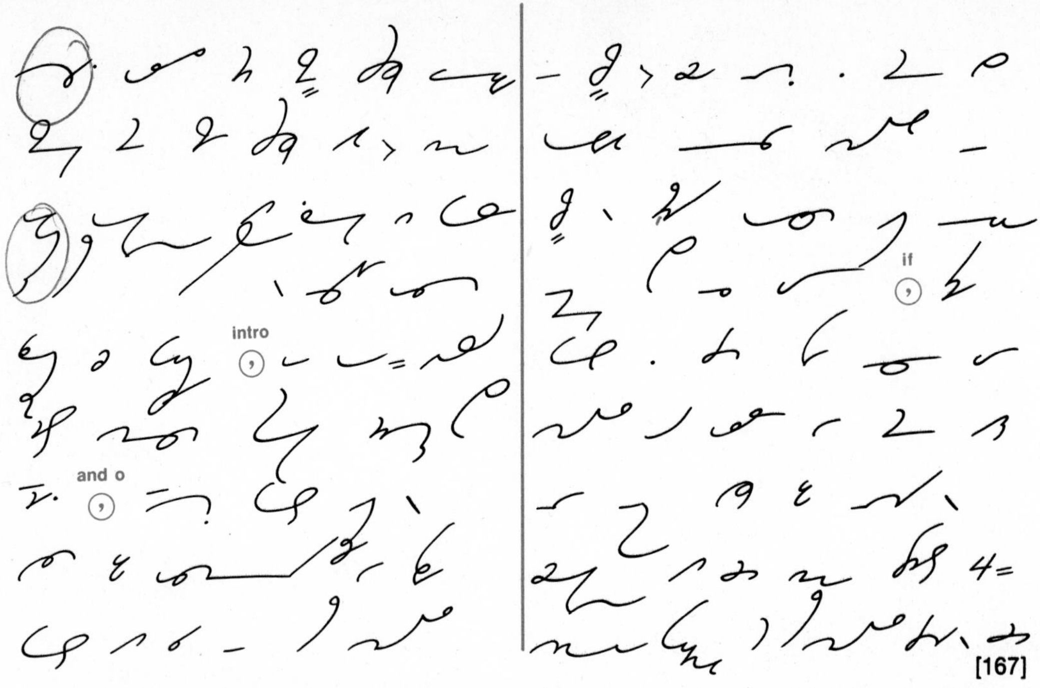

9 Transcription Quiz For you to supply: 9 commas—2 commas apposition, 1 comma geographical, 1 comma nonrestrictive, 4 commas parenthetical, 1 comma introductory; 2 missing words.

[133]

Developing Word-Building Power

1 Word Beginnings and Endings

Fur-

1

Inter-, Intr-

2

-ual

3

-tion

4

1 Furnish, furniture, furnishings, further, furthermore, furnace.
2 Interest, interested, interfere, interview, introduce, introduction.
3 Annual, manual, gradual, natural, mutual.
4 Recreation, action, reaction, nation, vacation, promotion, variation.

Building Transcription Skills

2 COMMON PREFIXES ● dis-

dis- In many words the prefix *dis-* means *not, in the absence of*, or *the opposite of*.

distrust *(noun)* Absence of trust; lack of confidence; suspicion.

dislike *(verb)* To disapprove; opposite of like.

disregard *(verb)* To pay no attention to; opposite of regard.
disrespect Absence of respect or regard.
disloyal Not loyal; unfaithful.

3 **Business Vocabulary Builder**

en route On or along the way.
double occupancy Two persons per room.
fluently Effortlessly; flowing easily.

Reading and Writing Practice

4

if
if
ser
intro
dis·loy·al
dis·ap·point·ment
whose

par
years'
ser
plac·ing
when
ser
when

if

conj

intro

if

per·son's

self-in·ter·est

if

Transcribe:
nine
four

[272]

5

employ·ees'

ap

four-week
hyphenated
before noun

ser

intro

en route

and o

world's

un·usu·al

fur·nish

ser

lodg·ing

intro

Transcribe:
$2,000

oc·cu·pan·cy

nonr

bal·ance
due

nc

mis·take

[176]

6

mu·tu·al

ap

over·seas

ap

fluent·ly

if

[153]

7

if

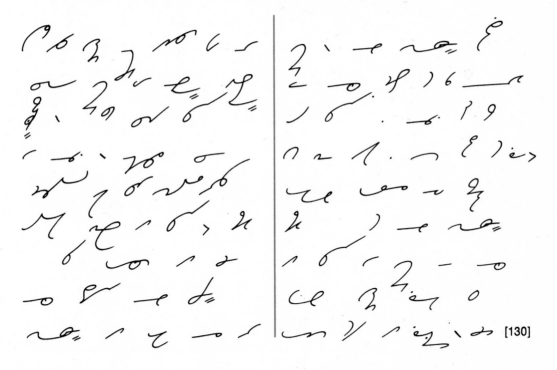

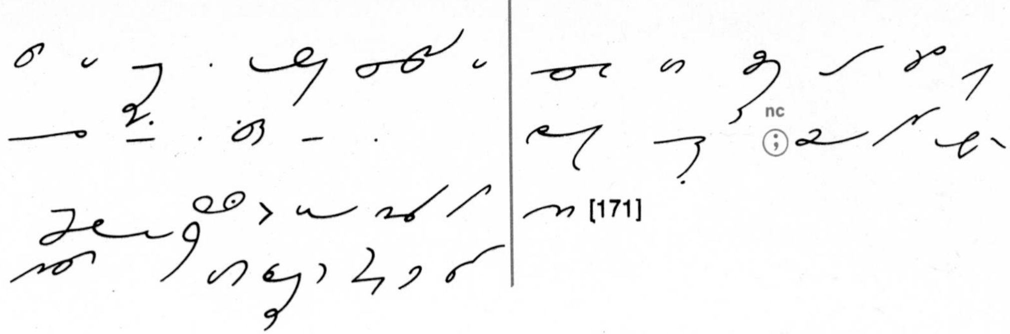

8 **Transcription Quiz** For you to supply: 5 commas—1 comma introductory, 1 comma *if* clause, 2 commas apposition, 1 comma conjunction; 1 period courteous request; 1 semicolon no conjunction; 2 missing words.

[130]

Developing Word-Building Power

1 Shorthand Vocabulary Builder

Contractions

1

Abbreviations -titute, -titude

2

Abbreviation -quent

3

Abbreviations

4

1 Haven't, don't, wouldn't, doesn't, shouldn't, couldn't, weren't.
2 Substitute, institute, constitute, aptitude, gratitude, attitude.
3 Frequent, frequently, consequent, consequences, eloquent, subsequently.
4 Memorandum, statistics, statistical, equivalent, reluctant, privilege.

Building Transcription Skills

2 Business Vocabulary Builder

bland Dull; without flavor or interest.
staples Basic, common foods.
immensely Greatly.
thriving Prospering; succeeding.

Reading and Writing Practice

3 Exploring the World

there

their

fre·quent·ly

ev·ery·day

and o

broad·en
one's

Travel

par

for·eign

conj

peo·ple's

af·fect
ac·cent

intro

ad·just

conj

intro

im·i·tate

nc ;

high·ly sea·soned
no hyphen
after ly

In

ed·i·ble

sta·ples

un·touched

conj ,

if ,

intro ,

im·mense·ly

At nonr ,

1965 ,

ac·cept·ed

per·ma·nent

role

conj

equal·ly

nc

wom·en's

in·tri·cate·ly

nc

men's

ser

sig·ni·fi·cant·ly

par

ser

lan·guage

intro

tru·ly

[737]

12 TRANSPORTATION

Developing Word-Building Power

1 Brief Forms and Derivatives

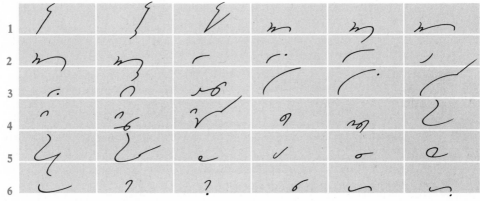

1 Subject, subjects, subjected, success, successful, suggest.
2 Suggestion, suggestions, than, thank, them, there (their).
3 Think-thing, this, throughout, time, timing, timed.
4 Under, underneath, understand, usual, unusual, value.
5 Valuable, valued, were, what, when, where.
6 Will-well, wish, wishing, with, work, working.

Building Transcription Skills

2 TYPING STYLE STUDY ● interoffice memorandums

In this lesson you will learn how to type an interoffice memorandum. Following you will see a memorandum as it was written in shorthand and transcribed. The transcript was typed on a machine that had elite (small) type.

The shorthand required a little more than half a column in the notebook. When a memorandum requires about half a column in the notebook, you should do these things:

☐ **1** Set the left margin 3 spaces after the longest guide word in the left side of the printed heading.

☐ **2** Set a tab stop 3 spaces after the longest guide word in the right side of the printed heading.

☐ **3** Set the right margin equal to the left margin.

☐ **4** Type the message single spaced beginning on the third line below the last line of the printed heading.

inter-office memorandum

To	James Brown	From	Mary Sims
Subject	New Employee	Date	January 14, 19--

When I was in Chicago three weeks ago, I interviewed Martha Kelly for the position of assistant to the director of personnel.

While she had an excellent background I felt that she did not have enough experience to handle a position of such great responsibility. Therefore, I recommended that we look further for a person for this important position.

I have now come to the conclusion that Ms. Kelly is indeed the best person for the position. Will you please call her and ask that she come to the office for a personal interview with you and the other members of your staff.

If you need any further information, I will be happy to supply it.

M. S.

mcb

INTEROFFICE MEMORANDUM

3 Business Vocabulary Builder

patrons Customers.

in the red At a loss; losing money.

subsidy A grant or gift of money.

refurbish To renovate; to make like new.

Reading and Writing Practice

4 Brief-Form Letter

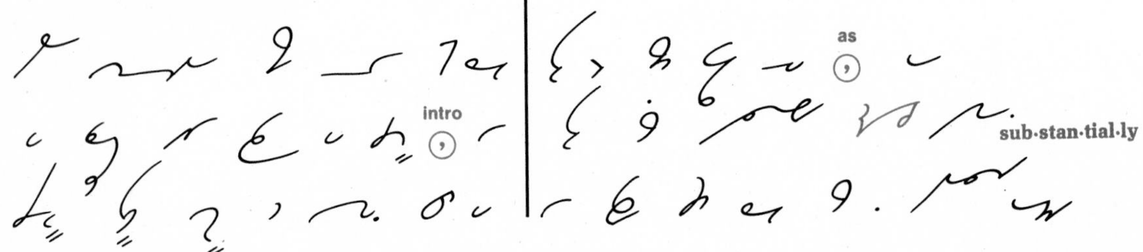

Al·though

faith·ful pa·trons

and o

intro

sub·si·dy

intro

un·fea·si·ble

par

dis·con·tin·ue

[160]

5

vir·tu·al·ly

first-class hyphenated before noun

se·vere

conj

de·clined

if

cur·tail·ment

par

conj

fares

ap·peal

as·sis·tance

cr [197]

6

as

con·ges·tion

Transcribe:
Fourth
Fifth

intro

re·mod·el·ing

intro

re·fur·bish

intro

bear

[108]

7 Transcription Quiz For you to supply: 5 commas—1 comma geographical, 3 commas introductory, 1 comma *if* clause; 2 missing words.

412

5:30

12

555-

310 [141]

Building Phrasing Skill

1 Useful Business-Letter Phrases

I Can

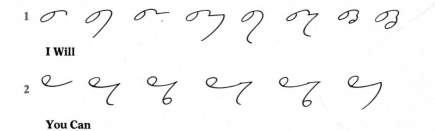

1

I Will

2

You Can

3

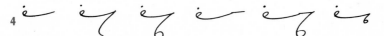

He Will

4

1 I can, I can have, I cannot, I cannot have, I can be, I cannot be, I can see, I can say.
2 I will, I will be, I will be able, I will not be, I will not be able, I will have.
3 You can, you can have, you can be, you cannot have, you cannot be, you can make, you cannot.
4 He will, he will be, he will be able, he will not, he will not be able, he will see.

2 Geographical Expressions

1

2

1 Bennington, Burlington, Lexington, Washington, Huntington, Wilmington.
2 Arkansas, Kentucky, North Carolina, Montana, American, United States.

Building Transcription Skills

3 TYPING STYLE STUDY ● mailability

A letter is not usually judged on the number of errors it contains or on the number of erasures it has. It is not judged on any one particular thing. Rather, it is judged *as a whole* for *mailability.*

Mailability simply means this: A business executive would be willing to sign the letter and mail it.

To judge your letters for mailability, you should do these three things:

□ **1** Check to see if the content is accurate. It is not always necessary to follow the dictator's words exactly. What is important, however, is to follow the *meaning* exactly.

□ **2** Check to see if the letter looks nice. A letter may be accurate in nearly every detail but be so unattractively arranged on the page that an executive would not sign it. If your letter is too high or too low or if the margins are obviously uneven, it will create a poor impression.

□ **3** Check to see that any errors you might have made are corrected neatly. Sometimes you will make an error in transcription that you can correct easily. Take the time and effort to make the correction as neatly as possible. Be certain that if you have made an error, you have corrected it.

Whenever you type a letter, always ask yourself, "Is this letter *mailable?*"

4 Business Vocabulary Builder

associate *(noun)* A co-worker.

invaluable Priceless.

keynote address The first speech given at a meeting or convention.

Reading and Writing Practice

5 Phrase Letter

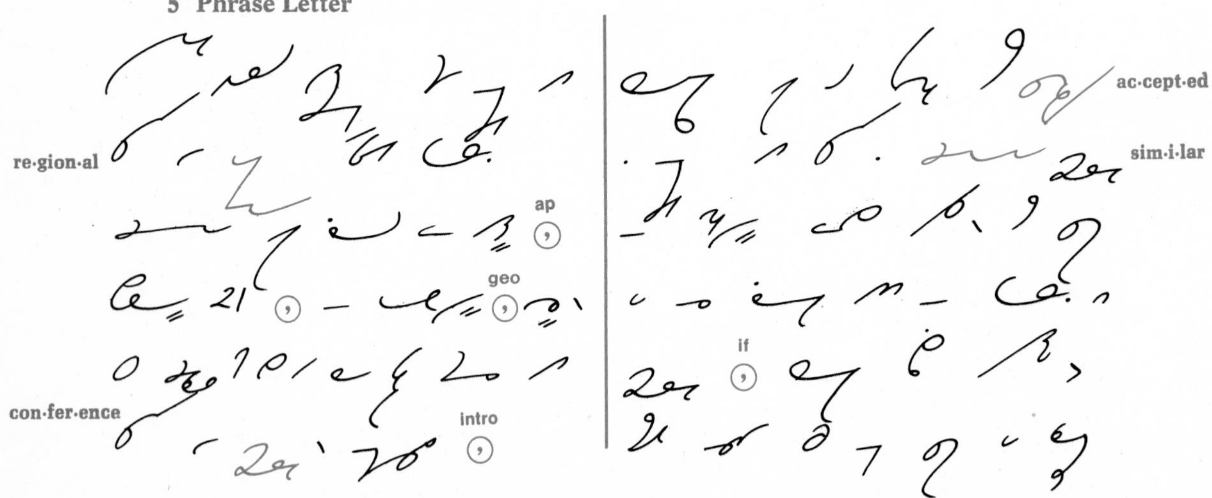

if

Transcribe:
nine
five

[138]

6

cor·re·spon·dent

ver·i·fy

cr

intro

com·pe·tent

and o

de·pend·able

suc·cess·ful·ly

par

[130]

7

conj

intro

afraid

ap

for·mer

if

touch

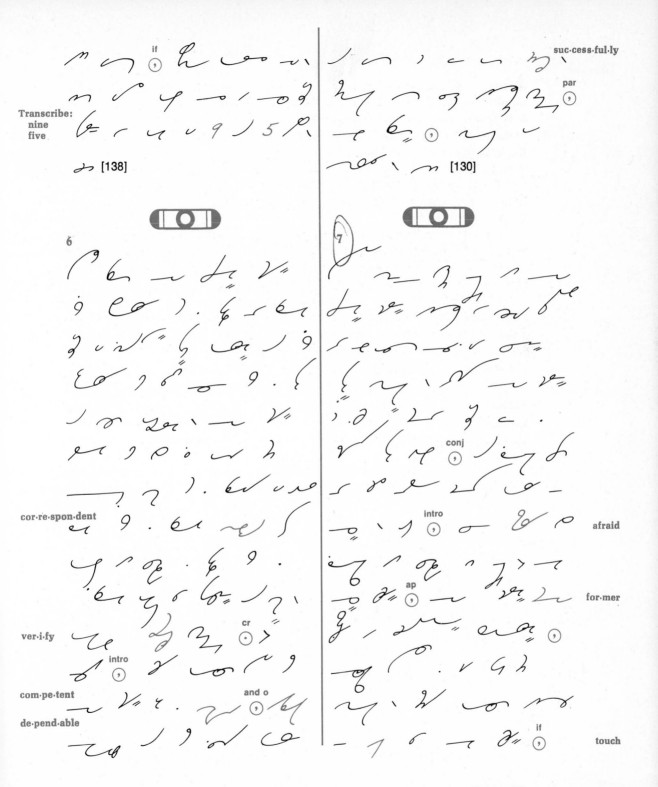

Transcribe: 211 West 81 Street

geo

conj

[141]

8

as

par

in·valu·able

pro·fes·sion·al

ser

Transcribe: 100

Transcribe: 50

conj

when

au·to·mat·i·cal·ly

par

[158]

9

conj

[108]

10 Transcription Quiz For you to supply: 5 commas—2 commas introductory, 1 comma *when* clause, 2 commas parenthetical; 1 semicolon no conjunction; 2 missing words.

[149]

Developing Word-Building Power

1 Word Families

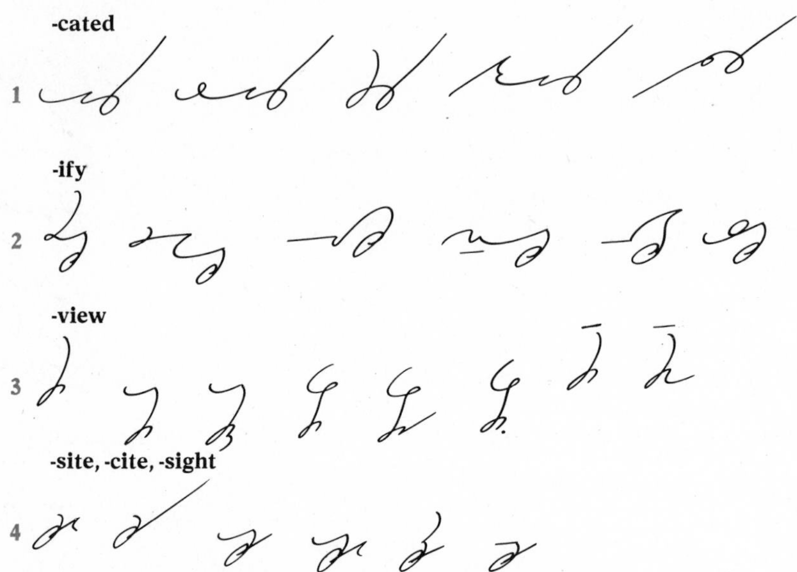

1 Located, relocated, vacated, dislocated, dedicated.
2 Verify, simplify, modify, qualify, intensify, ratify.
3 View, review, reviews, preview, previewed, previewing, interview, interviewer.
4 Sites, cited, recite, recites, foresight, insight.

Building Transcription Skills

2 COMMON PREFIXES ● con-

con- In many words the prefix *con* means *with* or *together.*

connect To join one thing with another.

concerted Planned together.

concord	Agreement with; harmony.
concur	To come together; to agree.
conduct	To go with; to lead.
conference	A meeting together.

3 Business Vocabulary Builder

portals Doors.

razing Destroying.

adopted Accepted and put into use.

surface transportation Vehicles that run on land.

Reading and Writing Practice

4

ap·par·ent

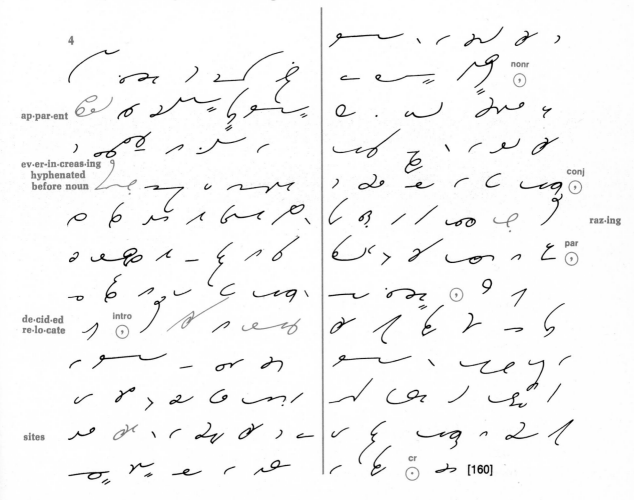

ev·er-in·creas·ing hyphenated before noun

de·cid·ed re·lo·cate intro

sites

nonr

conj

raz·ing

par

cr [160]

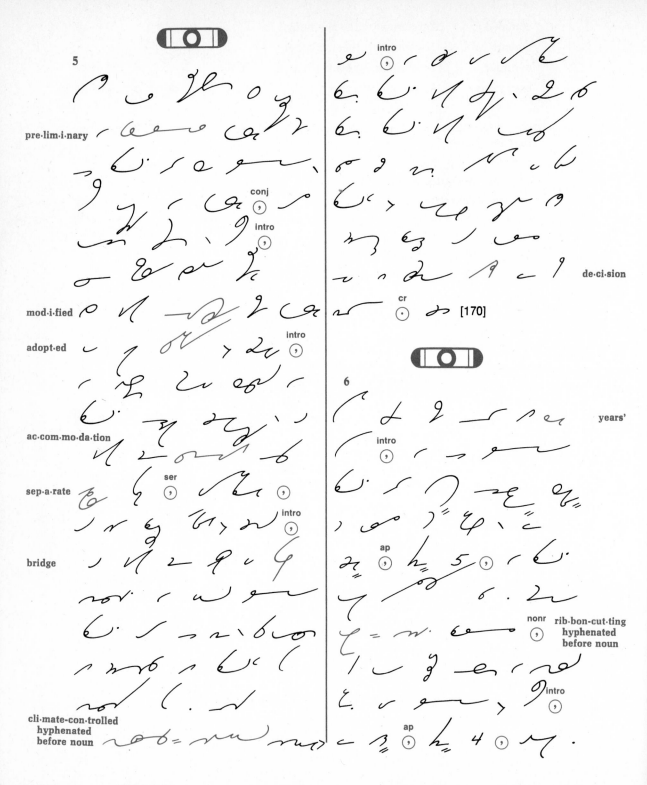

5

pre·lim·i·nary

conj

intro

mod·i·fied

adopt·ed

intro

ac·com·mo·da·tion

sep·a·rate

ser

intro

bridge

cli·mate-con·trolled hyphenated before noun

intro

de·ci·sion

cr

[170]

6

years'

intro

ap

nonr

rib·bon-cut·ting hyphenated before noun

intro

ap

par

Transcribe: 9 a.m.

self-ad·dressed

cr

[156]

7

ar·ti·cle

in·sight

too

con·clu·sion

if

[156]

8

ap

com·mut·er

conj

intro

intro

con·ges·tion

conj

and o

tem·po·rary

[115]

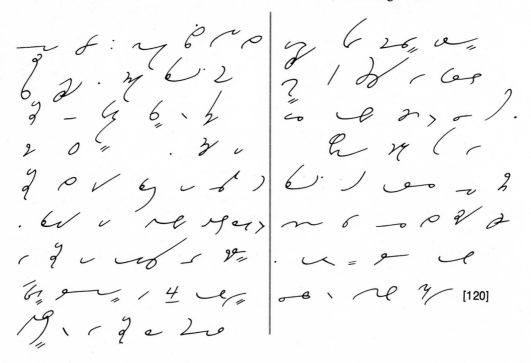

9 Transcription Quiz For you to supply: 3 commas—1 comma geographical, 1 comma nonrestrictive, 1 comma *when* clause; 2 missing words.

[120]

Developing Word-Building Power

1 Word Beginnings and Endings

1 Misinform, misinformed, misunderstand, misunderstood, mistake, mystery.
2 Direct, directly, direction, directed, directive, director.
3 Seemingly, willingly, unwillingly, knowingly, unknowingly, exceedingly, satisfyingly.
4 Other, neither, brother, mother, father, either, rather, leather.

Building Transcription Skills

2 SIMILAR-WORDS DRILL ● choose, chose

choose To select.

Did you *choose* a new suit?

chose (past tense of *choose*) Selected.

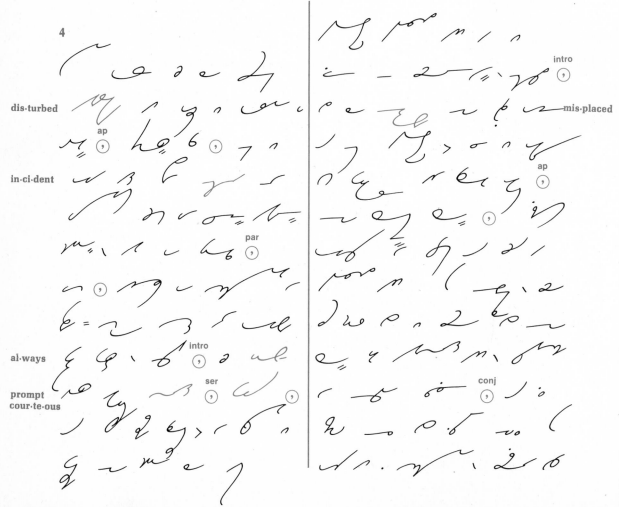

I *chose* a new pair of shoes yesterday.

3 Business Vocabulary Builder

restored Returned; renewed.

rational Logical; reasonable.

harsh Severe; rough.

trying *(adjective)* Difficult; annoying.

Reading and Writing Practice

4

dis·turbed

ap

in·ci·dent

par

al·ways

intro

prompt

cour·te·ous

ser

intro

mis·placed

ap

conj

intro

par

and o

[237]

5

ex·press·ing

nc

ne·ces·si·ty

Transcribe:
seven
nine

ser

def·i·nite·ly

conj

choose

de·pend·able

[178]

6

ser

par

intro

as

ra·tio·nal

worst

hours'

when

can·cel

intro

intro

[200] prin·ci·pal

7

com·plaint

ser

par

nc

cen·sure

ap

com·men·da·tion

nonr

quite

intro

ap

intro

[205]

8 Transcription Quiz For you to supply: 8 commas—2 commas apposition, 1 comma introductory, 1 comma conjunction, 4 commas parenthetical; 2 missing words.

[107]

Developing Word-Building Power

1 Shorthand Vocabulary Builder

Tain

1

Den

2

Sw

3

Th

4

1 Contain, container, retain, maintain, certain, captain.
2 Deny, denied, sudden, wooden, evidence, president, dental.
3 Sweet, swift, swell, sway, swear, swore, sweater, swim.
4 Thick, thin, bath, death, though, those, thought, thoughtless.

Building Transcription Skills

2 Business Vocabulary Builder

gaze To look.
intercontinental Between continents.
excursion Trip.

Reading and Writing Practice

3 Our Shrinking World

Broth·ers'

his·tor·ic

shrink·ing

al·most

ven·tured

across

wing·span

geo·graph·ic

for·tu·nate

young·sters

intro intro conj intro intro conj nc par intro intro

That

Though

Su·per·son·ic

sun·rise

ser

par

too

It

sleek

mir·a·cle

com·mon·place

intro

and o

fresh·ly cut
no hyphen
after ly

ex·cur·sion

Sometimes

routes

vig·or·ous·ly

intro

fares

intro

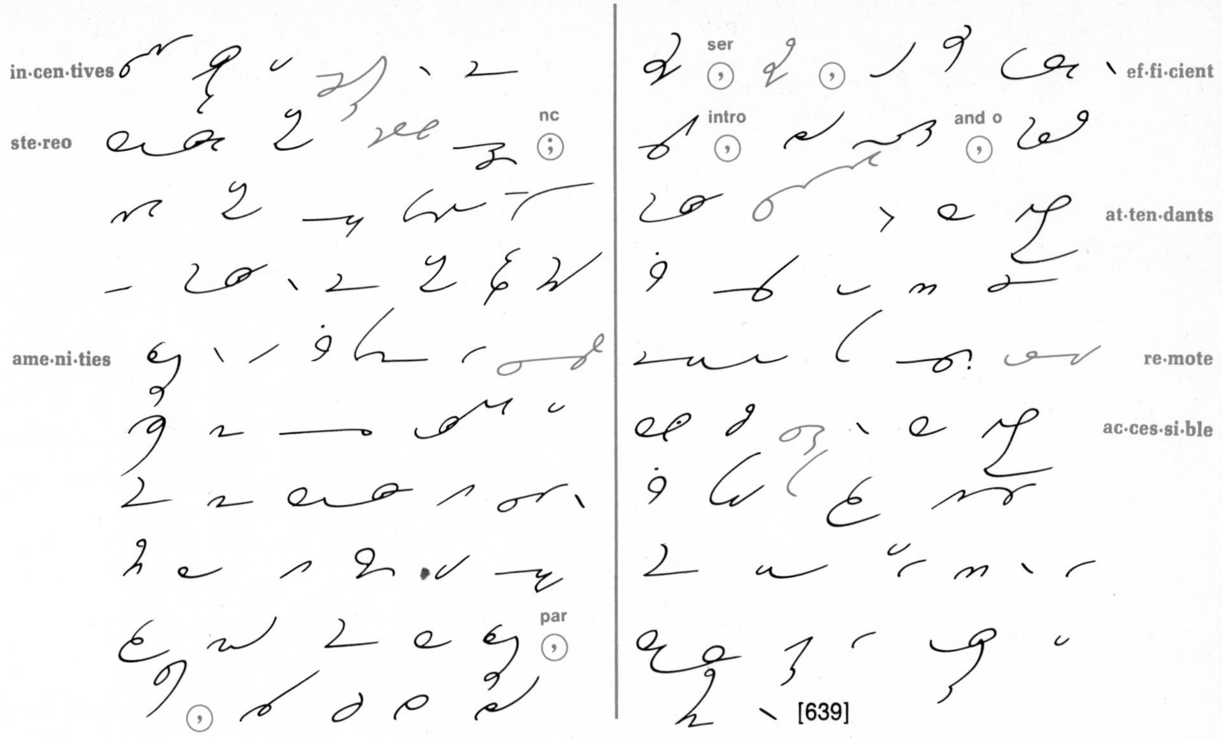

in·cen·tives

ste·reo

ame·ni·ties

ef·fi·cient

at·ten·dants

re·mote

ac·ces·si·ble

[639]

The secretary who can type letters that an executive can sign with confidence is extremely valuable—the busy executive does not have time to read each piece of correspondence that leaves the office.

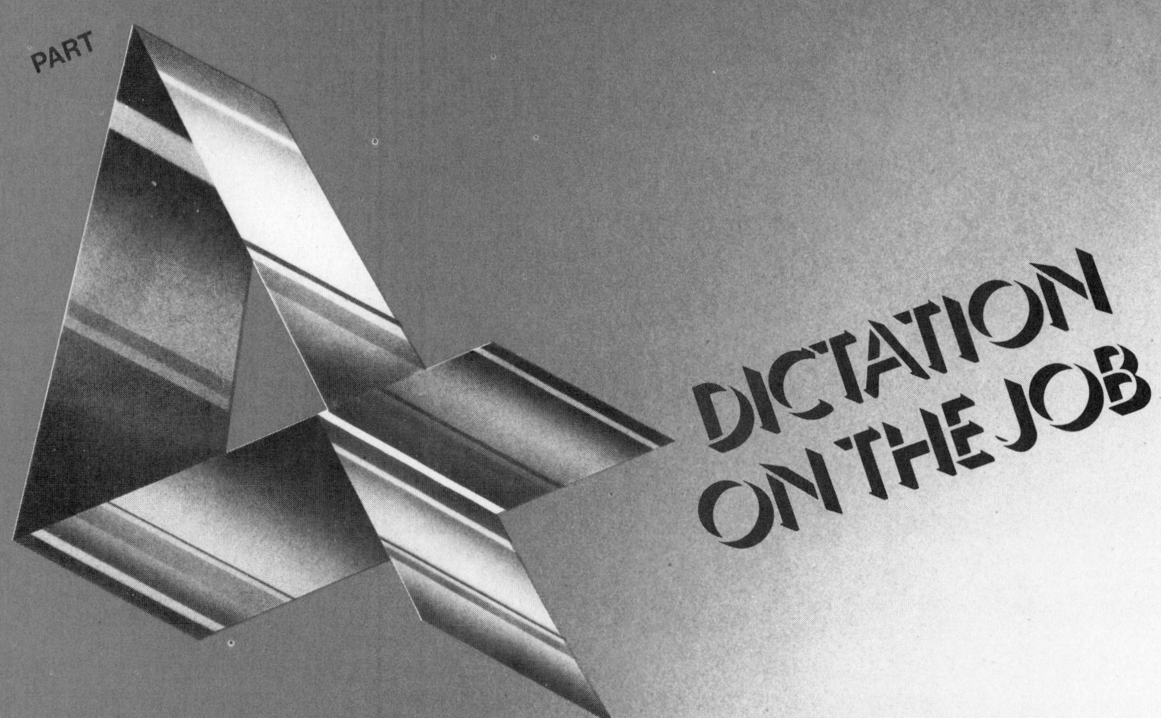

You have read and written thousands of words. You have also taken thousands of words of dictation on familiar material as well as new material. Therefore, your shorthand skill has grown considerably—probably much more than you realize. You could now take dictation in a business office, provided the dictation was not too fast or too difficult.

Until now, your study of shorthand has been carefully controlled. The dictation has been given under ideal conditions. It has been given smoothly and evenly because your skill develops best in that way. Most of the dictation you have taken has been timed, enabling you to progress easily from one level to the next. The timing has also made measurement of your skill possible. You will find, however, that taking dictation in an office is quite different from taking dictation in the classroom.

Office-Style Dictation

Employers are not concerned with the development of your shorthand speed. They assume that you have adequate skill the first day that you report for work. In order to keep up with the dictation, it is very important for you to develop your shorthand speed to the highest possible level.

Business executives do not always dictate smoothly and evenly. Depending on the flow of their thoughts, their dictation will be slow at times and very fast at other times. Your responsibility will be to keep up with the dictation regardless of the speed. It is essential that you have a reserve which will enable you to take even the fastest dictation. You will quickly become accustomed to office-style dictation if you have sufficient speed. The more speed you possess, the easier office-style dictation will be for you.

Sometimes a business executive will decide to change a sentence during dictation or after the dictation is finished. At other times the executive may ask that you take out a word, a sentence, or an entire paragraph. After the dictation has been completed, the executive may ask that a word or more be inserted or transposed. And the dictation will never be timed! This type of dictation is normal in every business office, and you must learn to make changes in your notes easily and quickly.

In order to help you learn to take office-style dictation, beginning with Lesson 61 — and in a number of lessons that follow — you will study some of the problems you will meet when you take dictation in a business office.

You will learn how to make short deletions during dictation and after the dictation has been completed. You will learn the easiest way to make insertions in your shorthand notes in case the dictator wants to add something after a sentence has been dictated. You will also learn the most efficient way to restore words, phrases, or sentences to your shorthand notes if the dictator decides to put back something that had been deleted. You will also learn the best way to handle both short and long transpositions if the dictator decides to change the order of words, phrases, or sentences.

By following the instructions given in the lessons, you will soon be able to take and transcribe office-style dictation efficiently and accurately.

13
PUBLIC RELATIONS

Developing Word-Building Power

1 Brief Forms and Derivatives

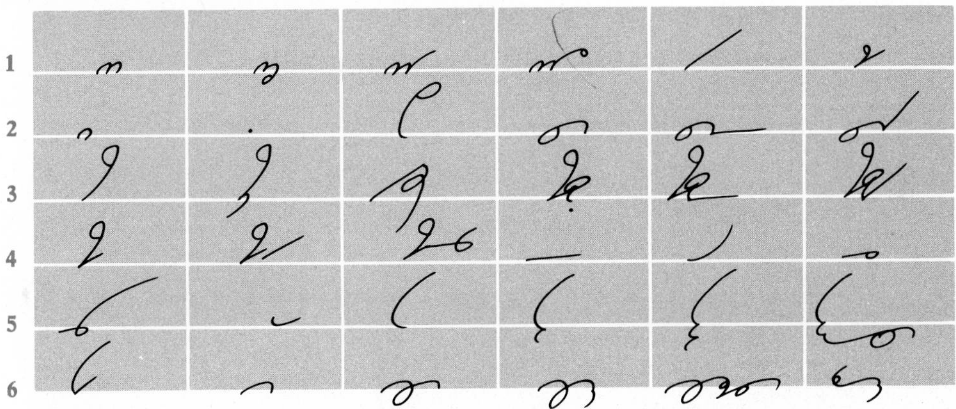

1 World, worldly, worth, worthy, would, yesterday.
2 You-your, a-an, about, acknowledge, acknowledgment, acknowledged.
3 Advantage, advantageous, disadvantage, advertising, advertisement, advertised.
4 After, afterward, aftermath, am, and, any.
5 Anytime, are-our-hour, be-by, business, businesses, businesslike.
6 But, can, character, characters, characteristic, circulars.

Building Transcription Skills

2 OFFICE-STYLE DICTATION ● short deletions

An executive may decide to delete a word, a phrase, or a sentence that has been dictated. The dictator might say:

We have a dedicated, well-trained staff—no, take out **dedicated.**

To indicate that *dedicated* should be deleted, strike a heavy downward line through the word, thus:

Sometimes the executive may simply repeat the sentence without the word or phrase that should be omitted.

We have a dedicated and well-trained staff—no, **We have a well-trained staff.**

To indicate the deletion, strike out in your notes not only the word *dedicated* but the *and* as well.

If only a word or two must be taken out, use a heavy downward line; if several words are to be deleted, use a wavy line.

I have a large staff—oh, scratch that out.

In your notes you would show this deletion thus:

Illustration of Office-Style Dictation

3 Business Vocabulary Builder

orientation Explanation; introduction.

reluctance Unwillingness; hesitancy.

acquaint To become familiar with.

Reading and Writing Practice

4 Brief-Form Letter

ex·cel·lent

conj

add

when

nonr

ori·en·ta·tion

de·signed

if

Transcribe: 9 a.m.

[130]

5

hired

conj

great

con·fi·dence

ours

intro

in·teg·ri·ty

when

nc

[121]

6

rec·om·men·da·tion

nonr

ten·ure

intro

bright·est
de·pend·able

and o

ac·cept·ed

par

mis·take

if

[118]

7

for·mer

ap

intro

conj

Yale's

ap·par·ent·ly

intro

conj

con·fi·dent

par

[121]

8 Transcription Quiz Up to this time, you have been told what punctuation marks were necessary to punctuate each Transcription Quiz. In addition, you have been told how many missing words you were to supply. Beginning with this lesson, you must determine for yourself what punctuation marks are necessary and what words are missing.

[133]

Building Phrasing Skill

1 Useful Business-Letter Phrases

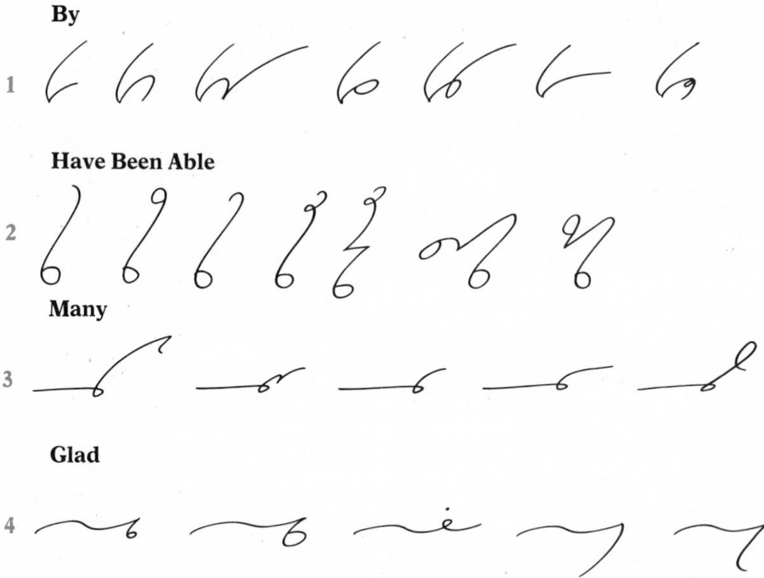

1 By the, by this, by this time, by that, by that time, by them, by these.
2 Have been able, I have been able, you have been able, we have been able, we have not been able, I could have been able, I should have been able.
3 Many times, many other, many of the, many of them, many days.
4 Glad to see, glad to say, glad to hear, glad to have, glad to be.

2 Geographical Expressions

1

2

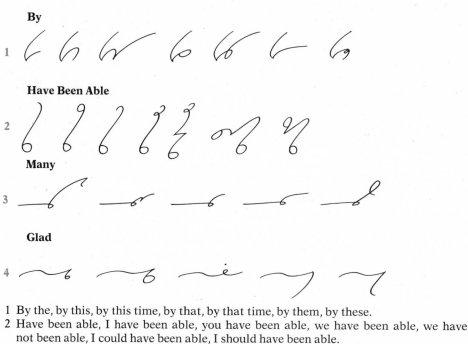

1 Framingham, Birmingham, Nottingham, Cunningham, Buckingham.
2 Iowa, Idaho, Missouri, South Carolina, Wisconsin, South Dakota, Oklahoma, Rhode Island.

Building Transcription Skills

3 SPELLING FAMILIES ● -al, -el, -le

Always be careful when you transcribe a word ending in the sound of *l;* the word may be spelled *-al, -el,* or *-le.*

-al	**lo-cal**	**per-son-al**	**to-tal**
	fi-nal	**vi-tal**	**an-nu-al**
-el	**can-cel**	**pan-el**	**tun-nel**
	la-bel	**par-cel**	**per-son-nel**
-le	**mid-dle**	**set-tle**	**an-gle**
	sam-ple	**cir-cle**	**am-ple**

4 Business Vocabulary Builder

public image Reputation.
phenomenal Remarkable.
substandard Below an acceptable level of quality.

Reading and Writing Practice

5 Phrase Letter

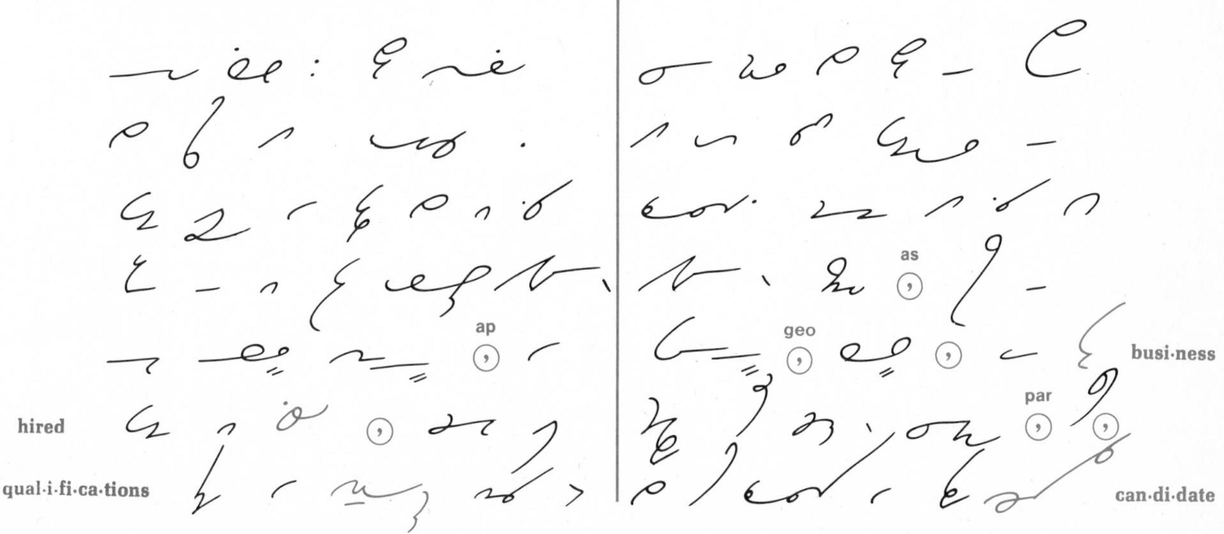

when

per·son·nel

[126]

6

com·pa·ny's

rep·re·sen·ta·tives

pro·spec·tive cli·ents

when

if

ap

spe·cial·izes

and o

pos·i·tive

nc

Transcribe: 20 percent

par

[193]

7

geo

ser

1601 if

[201]

Transcribe: ten

8

phe·nom·e·nal

par

bro·chure

intro

as

ap

years'

nc

intro

sub·stan·dard

Transcribe: $200,000 $2 million

care·less·ly

par

par cr [97]

9 Transcription Quiz Supply the necessary punctuation marks and the missing words.

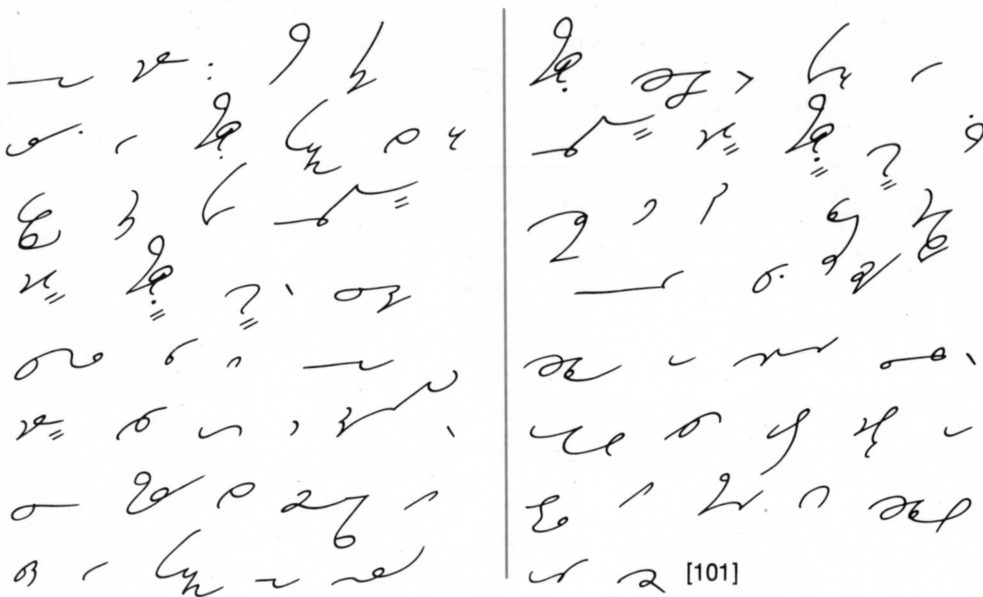

In order to obtain your major objectives, you must set small goals for yourself. If you check often to be sure you are meeting the small goals, the major ones will take care of themselves.

Developing Word-Building Power

1 Word Families

-per

-ually

Mem, Etc.

Post

1 Paper, bookkeeper, upper, proper, improper, cheaper, pauper, stopper.
2 Actually, mutually, punctually, annually, individually, factually.
3 Member, remember, memory, maximum, minimum.
4 Post, postage, postpone, postponed, postpaid, postscript, poster, postdated.

Building Transcription Skills

2 SIMILAR-WORDS DRILL ● fair, fare

fair Just; cloudless; a festival.

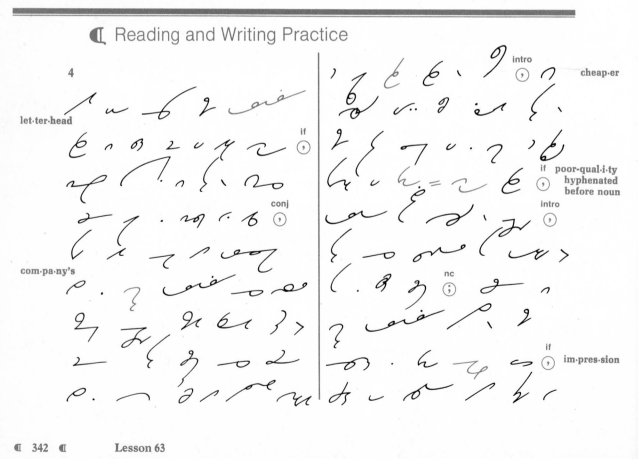

The examination was *fair*.
We will go only if the weather is *fair*.
We went to the county *fair*.

fare The price of transportation.

The bus *fare* was reasonable.

3 **Business Vocabulary Builder**

reams Packages of 500 sheets of paper.
exceed To go over; to go beyond a goal.
gross Twelve dozen.

Reading and Writing Practice

4

let·ter·head

if

conj

com·pa·ny's

intro

cheap·er

if poor-qual·i·ty hyphenated before noun

intro

nc

if im·pres·sion

de·sign

post·age-paid hyphenated before noun

nc

[184]

5

fair judge

intro

sta·tio·nery

top-qual·i·ty hyphenated before noun

intro

pack·et

intro

post·al

[124]

6

year's

yours

high-qual·i·ty hyphenated before noun

nonr

fair·grounds

world's

intro

ef·fi·cient

and o

fares

ac·cept

week·end

[174]

7

one-year hyphenated before noun

reams

ser

pen·cils

nonr

Transcribe: $2,000

fair

intro

re·ceived

ex·ceed

Transcribe: 3 percent

conj

nc

intro

else's

cr

[198]

8

al·ways

pur·su·ing

and o

knowl·edge

ser

when

ser

ap·pli·cants

intro

conj

par

[246]

9 Transcription Quiz Supply the necessary punctuation and the missing words.

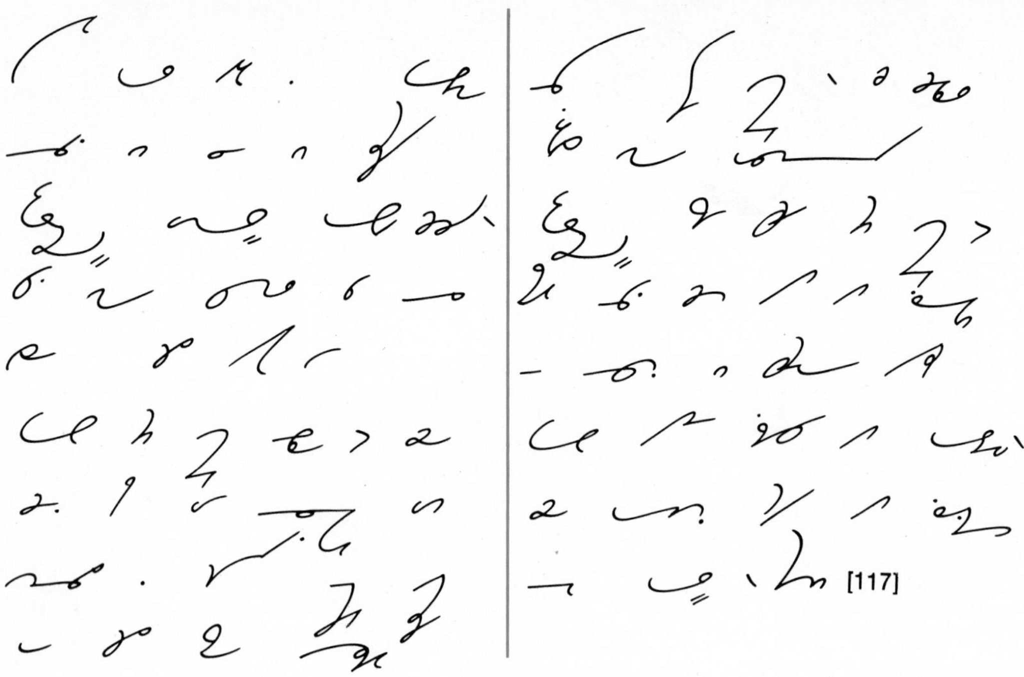

[117]

Using the telephone, greeting visitors, and working with others give the secretary valuable practice in developing good human relations skills.

Developing Word-Building Power

1 Word Beginnings and Endings

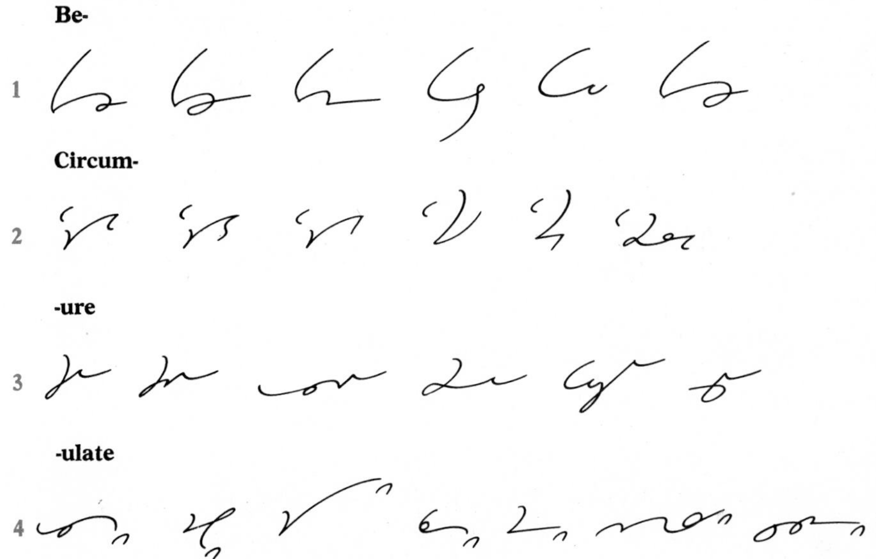

1 Begin, became, become, believe, below, began.
2 Circumstance, circumstances, circumstantial, circumvent, circumvention, circumference.
3 Feature, future, lecture, failure, procedure, nature.
4 Regulate, stipulate, stimulate, circulate, formulate, congratulate, accumulate.

Building Transcription Skills

2 COMMON PREFIXES ● in-

in- As a prefix *in* frequently means *not*.

informal Not formal; casual.

incapable Not capable; without ability.

insincere	Not sincere.
inconvenient	Not convenient.
indisposed	Not well; ill.

3 Business Vocabulary Builder

appealing *(adjective)* Pleasing.

auditors Individuals who verify accounts.

inconsistencies Items that do not agree with each other.

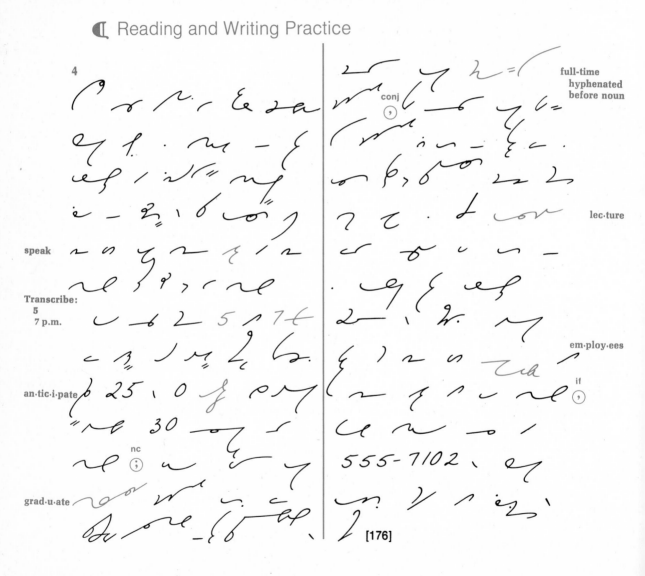

Reading and Writing Practice

4

speak

Transcribe: 5 7 p.m.

an·tic·i·pate

30

nc ;

grad·u·ate

conj ,

full-time hyphenated before noun

lec·ture

em·ploy·ees

if ,

555-7102

[176]

5

Transcribe: four

conj

en·rolled

conj

well-known hyphenated before noun

intro

part time no noun, no hyphen

ap

ref·er·ence

com·plete

if

nc

[199]

6

com·ments

par

par·tic·i·pants

sim·i·lar

year's

[103]

7

as

all-out hyphenated before noun

an·nu·al·ly

conj

econ·o·my

site

per·suade

if

em·pha·size

ser

ex·cel·lent

vi·cin·i·ty

fares

[175]

ven·ture

8

au·di·tors

in·con·sis·ten·cies

dis·cuss

ap 14 10

if

in·con·ve·nient

[99]

9

re·sponse

conj

ap·pli·cant

if

19

par

5 555-9208

[115]

10

ap

conj

intro

def·i·nite·ly

conj

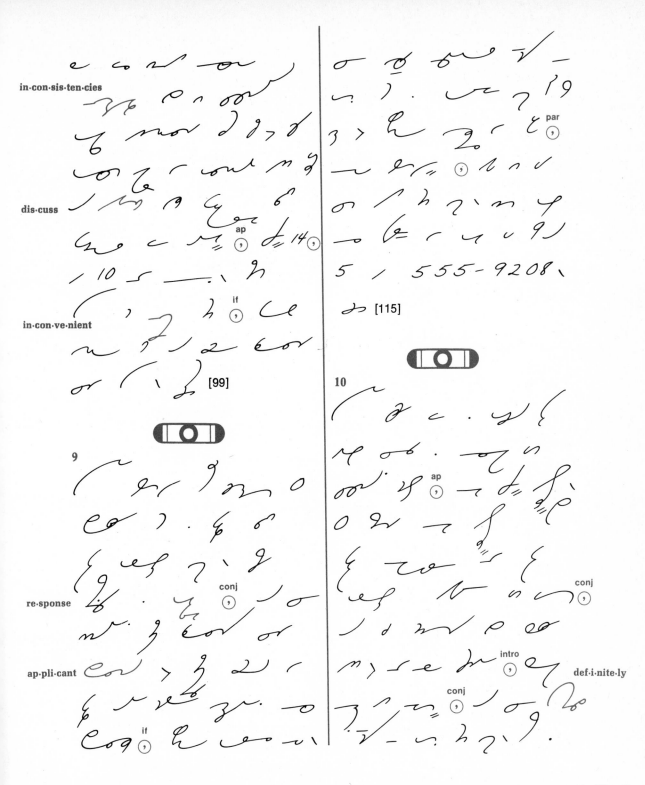

com·plete

par
,

[148]

11 Transcription Quiz Supply the necessary punctuation and the missing words.

10

10

436

[199]

Developing Word-Building Power

1 Shorthand Vocabulary Builder

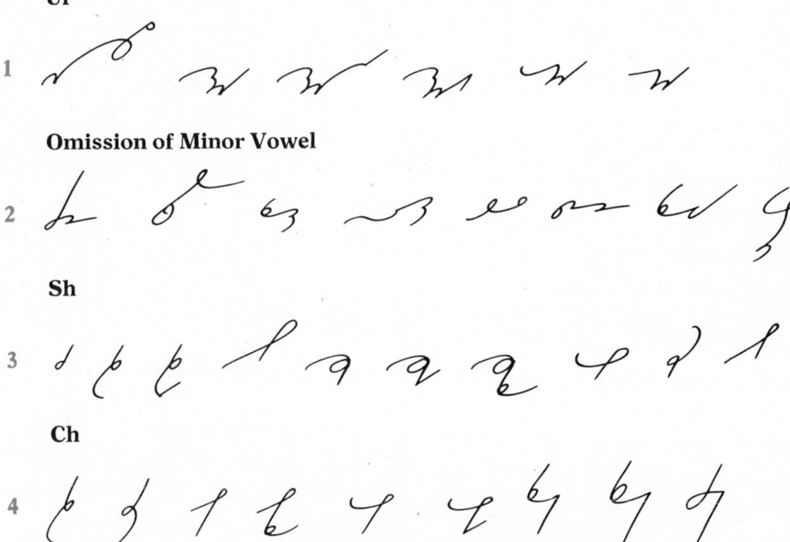

1 Ultimately, consult, consultant, consultation, result, insult.
2 Genuine, ideal, serious, courteous, theory, union, period, previous.
3 She, ship, shipped, dash, cash, cashed, cashier, rash, fish, dish.
4 Cheap, chief, teach, teacher, reach, reached, church, charge, change.

Building Transcription Skills

2 Business Vocabulary Builder

vast Large.
perceives Views; understands.
multinational Conducting business in more than one country.

Reading and Writing Practice

3 Public Relations

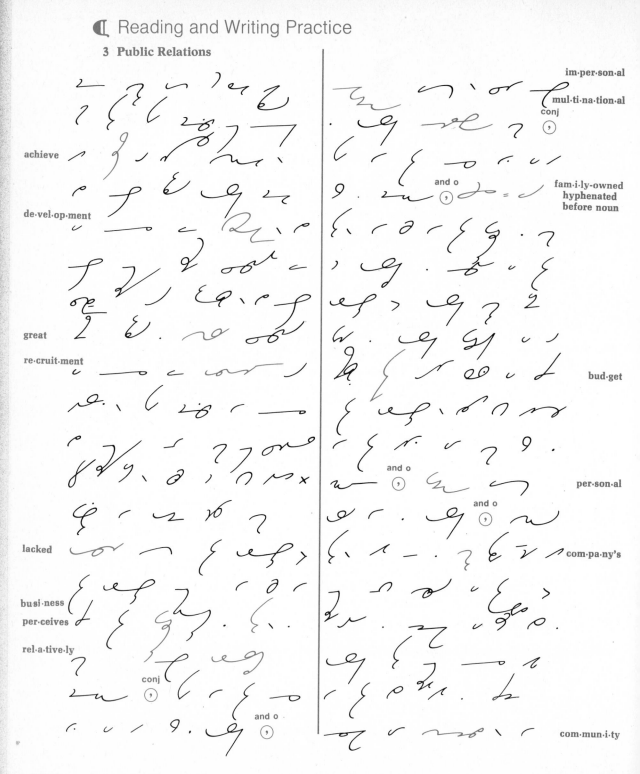

achieve

de·vel·op·ment

great

re·cruit·ment

lacked

busi·ness

per·ceives

rel·a·tive·ly

conj

and o

im·per·son·al

mul·ti·na·tion·al

conj

and o

fam·i·ly-owned hyphenated before noun

bud·get

and o

per·son·al

and o

com·pa·ny's

com·mun·i·ty

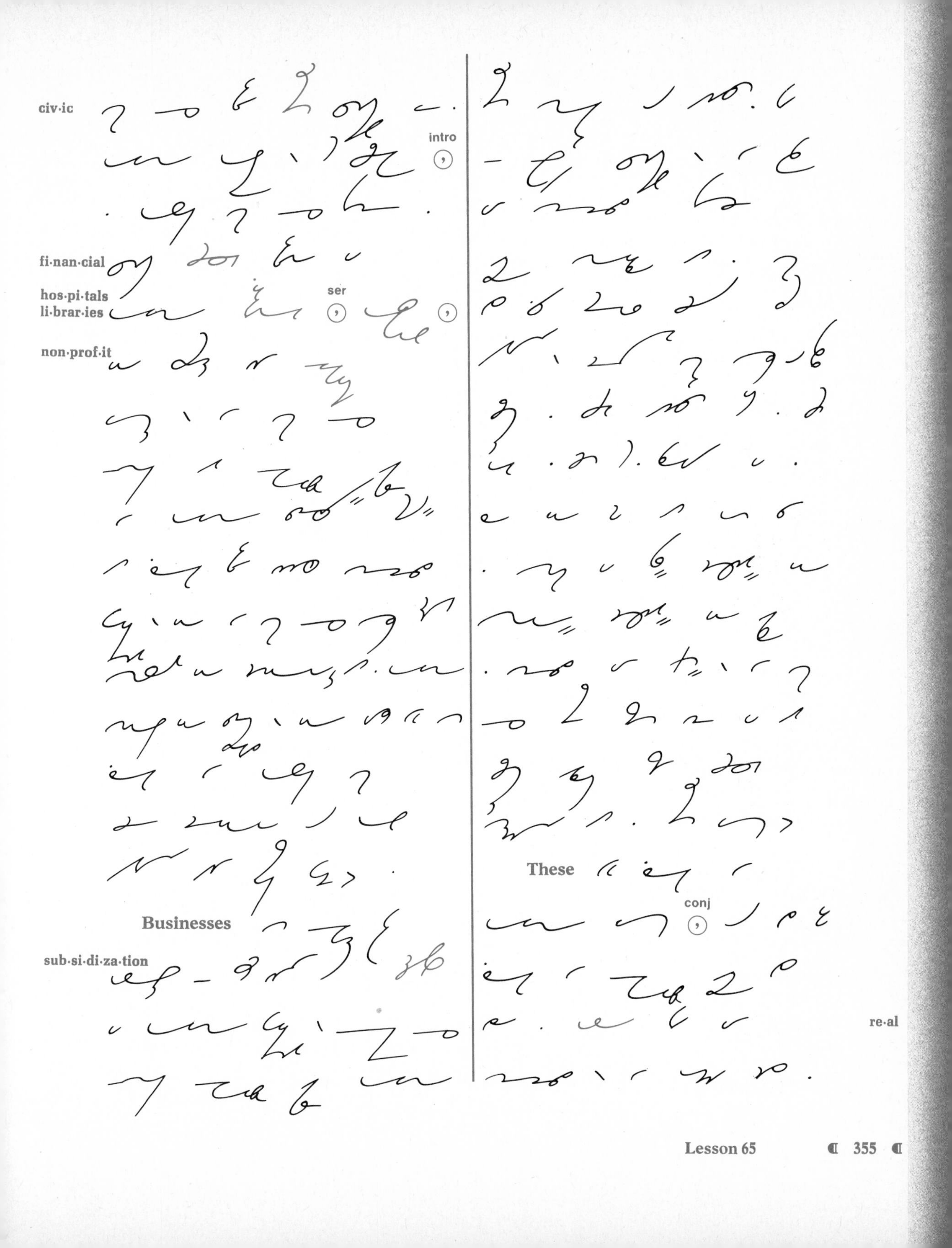

civ·ic

intro

fi·nan·cial

hos·pi·tals

ser

li·brar·ies

non·prof·it

Businesses

sub·si·di·za·tion

These

conj

re·al

sen·si·tive

[543]

4 A Career in Public Relations

glam·or·ous

par

pa·tience

The

knowl·edge·able

ser

intro

psy·chol·o·gy

intro

conj

It is

par

in·ter·pret·ed

par

al·ways

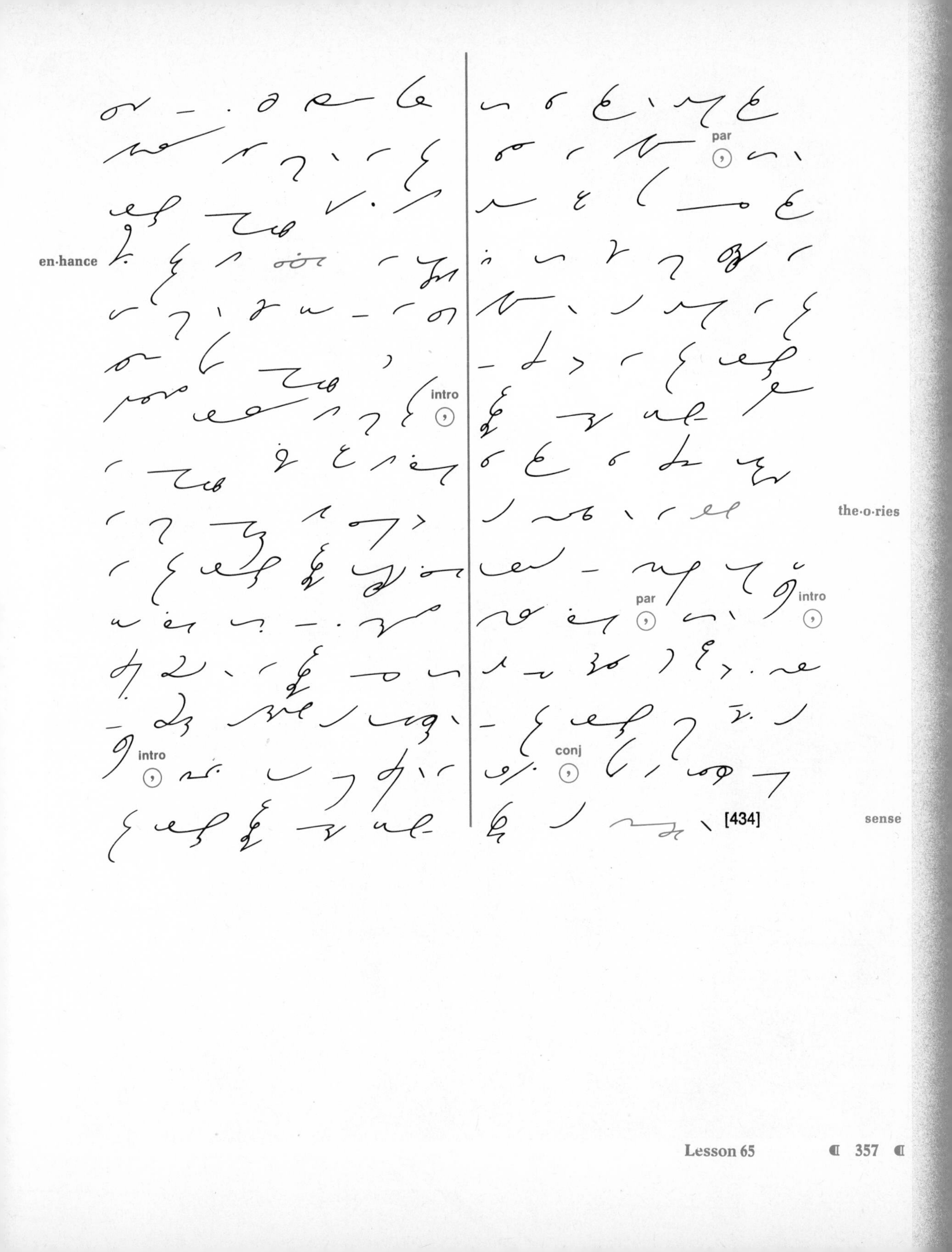

en·hance

intro

intro

par

the·o·ries

par

intro

conj

[434]

sense

14 PUBLISHING

Developing Word-Building Power

1 Brief Forms and Derivatives

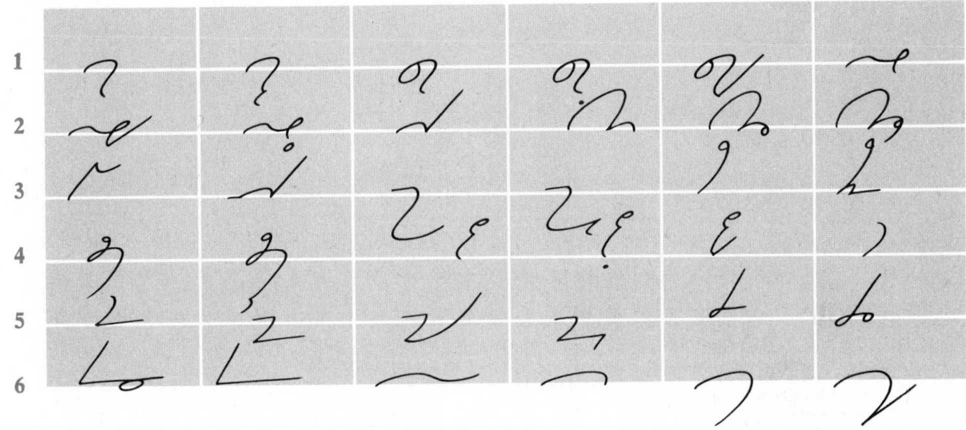

1 Company, companies, accompany, accompanying, accompanied, correspond-correspondence.
2 Corresponded, correspondingly, could, difficult, difficulty, difficulties.
3 Dr., enclosed, envelope, envelopes, ever-every, everyone.
4 Executive, executives, experience, experiencing, experienced, for.
5 Form, inform, informed, information, general, generally.
6 Gentleman, gentlemen, glad, good, govern, governed.

Building Transcription Skills

2 OFFICE-STYLE DICTATION ● short insertions and changes

A dictator may decide to change a word or phrase after completing a sentence.

Please buy a cheap gift—change **cheap** *to* **inexpensive.**

Indicate this change in your notes this way:

The dictator may wish to insert a word or a phrase.

Please buy an inexpensive gift—make that **small,** *inexpensive gift.*

You must be very alert to make the insertion. Quickly find the point at which the addition is to be made and insert the word or phrase with a caret, just as you would in longhand, thus:

Illustration of Office-Style Dictation

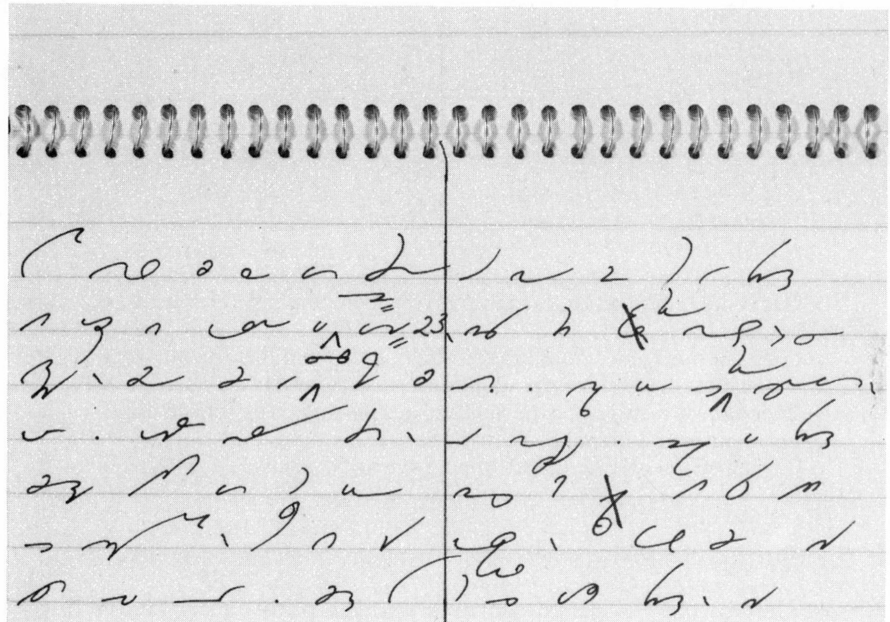

3 Business Vocabulary Builder

groundwork Foundation; basis.

master's degree College degree granted after graduate study.

perseverance The ability to keep trying.

Reading and Writing Practice

4 Brief-Form Letter

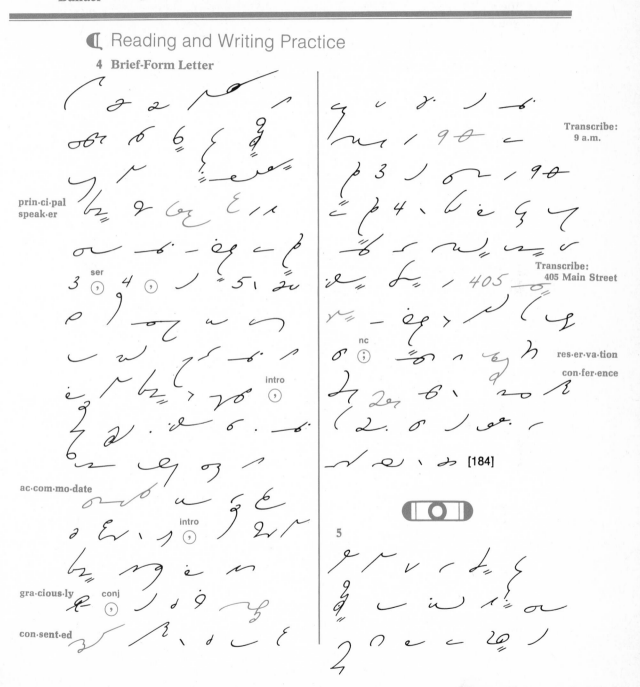

prin·ci·pal
speak·er

ser

intro

ac·com·mo·date

intro

gra·cious·ly

conj

con·sent·ed

Transcribe: 9 a.m.

Transcribe: 405 Main Street

nc

res·er·va·tion

con·fer·ence

[184]

5

ap

Transcribe:
275 State Street

geo

fea·tured
year's

nonr

gov·ern·ment

at·ten·dance

intro

Transcribe:
$65

[166]

6

ap

for·mer

morn·ing's

as·sign·ments

ser

per·se·ver·ance

conj

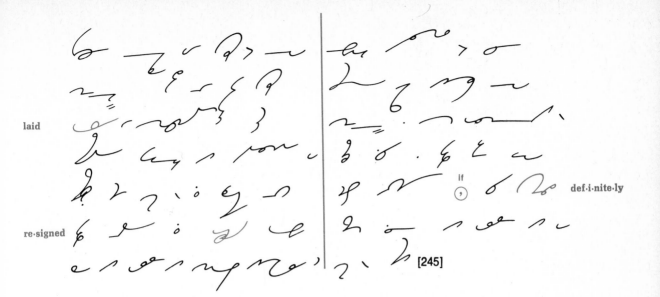

laid

re·signed

if

def·i·nite·ly

[245]

7 **Transcription Quiz** Supply the necessary punctuation and the missing words.

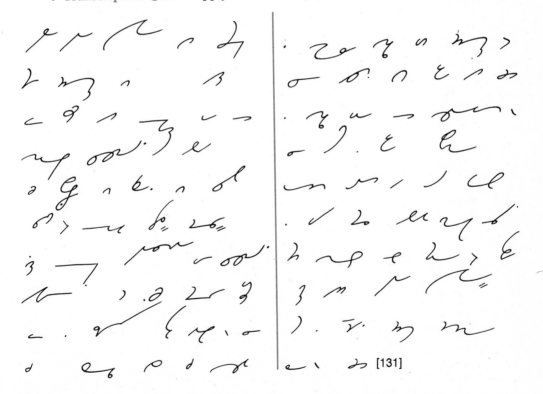

[131]

Building Phrasing Skill

1 Useful Business-Letter Phrases

Have Done

1

Do Not

2

Words Omitted

3

Let Us

4

1 Have done, I have done, we have done, could have done, they have done.
2 Do not, do not have, I do not have, we do not, we do not have, they do not.
3 One of the, one of the most, one of the best, in the future, in the past, as a result, will you please.
4 Let us, let us have, let us see, let us say, let us know, let us make.

2 Geographical Expressions

1

2

1 Harrisburg, Vicksburg, Pittsburgh, Fitchburg, Greensburg, Plattsburgh, Lynchburg, Newburgh.
2 Louisiana, Tennessee, Georgia, Kansas, Nevada, Virginia, West Virginia, Wyoming.

Building Transcription Skills

3 SPELLING FAMILIES ● -ant, -ent

Words Ending in -ant

re-li-ant	**pli-ant**	**in-stant**
self-re-li-ant	**as-sis-tant**	**con-stant**

Words Ending in -ent

dif-fer-ent	**sub-se-quent**	**si-lent**
con-cur-rent	**ab-sent**	**ex-cel-lent**
fre-quent	**el-o-quent**	**re-cent**

4 Business Vocabulary Builder

systematic Orderly.
compiling Gathering; collecting.
adopting (*as a textbook*) Choosing for required study.

Reading and Writing Practice

5 Phrase Letter

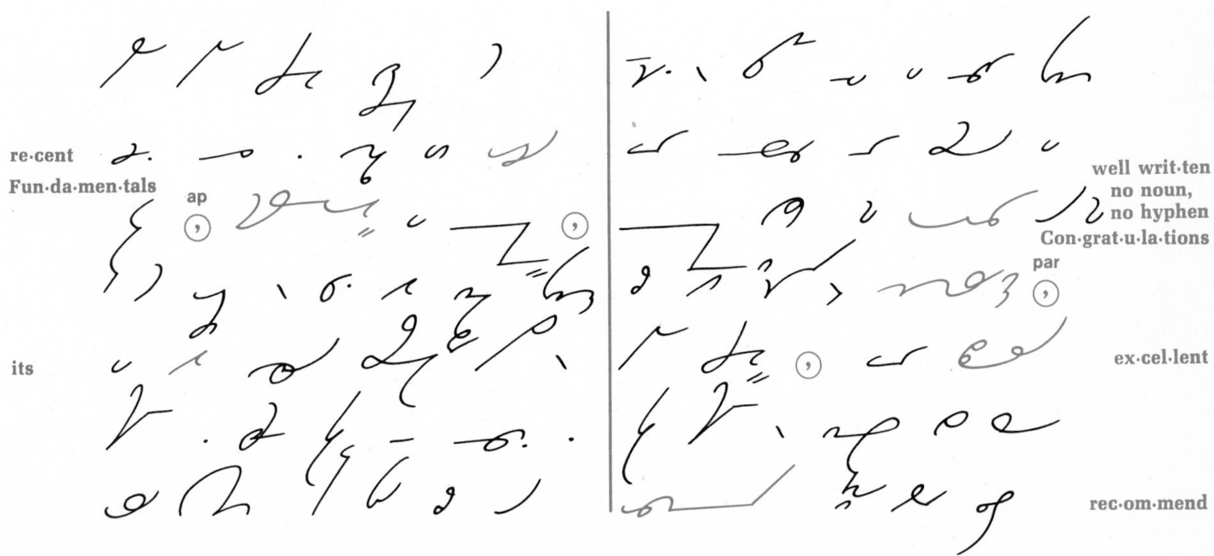

oc·ca·sion [111]

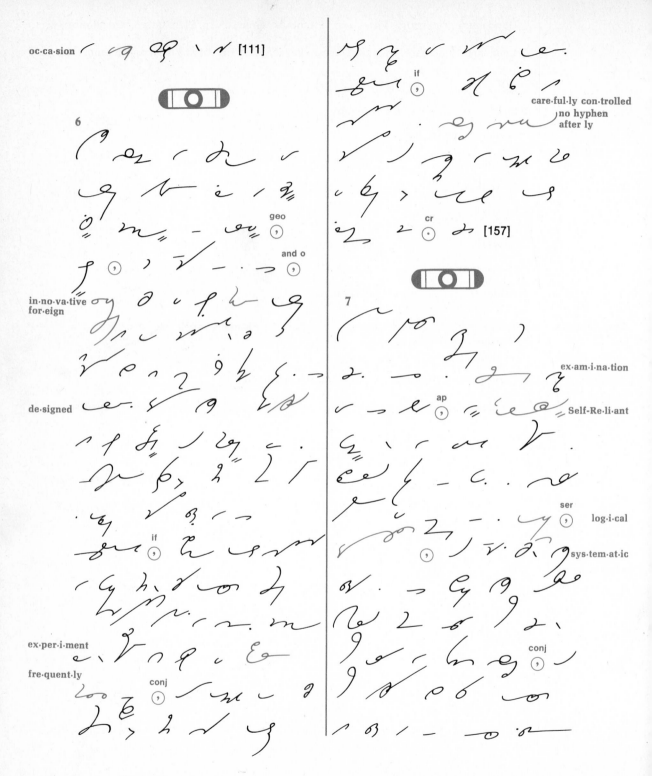

6

geo

and o

in·no·va·tive
for·eign

de·signed

if

ex·per·i·ment

fre·quent·ly

conj

if

care·ful·ly con·trolled
no hyphen
after ly

cr [157]

7

ex·am·i·na·tion

ap

Self-Re·li·ant

ser

log·i·cal

sys·tem·at·ic

conj

Transcribe: three

intro

book·store

geo cr

conj ap

[173]

8

writ·ten

ap

ap

as

as·sis·tant

intro

com·pil·ing

conj

and o

up-to-date hyphenated before noun

if

adopt·ing

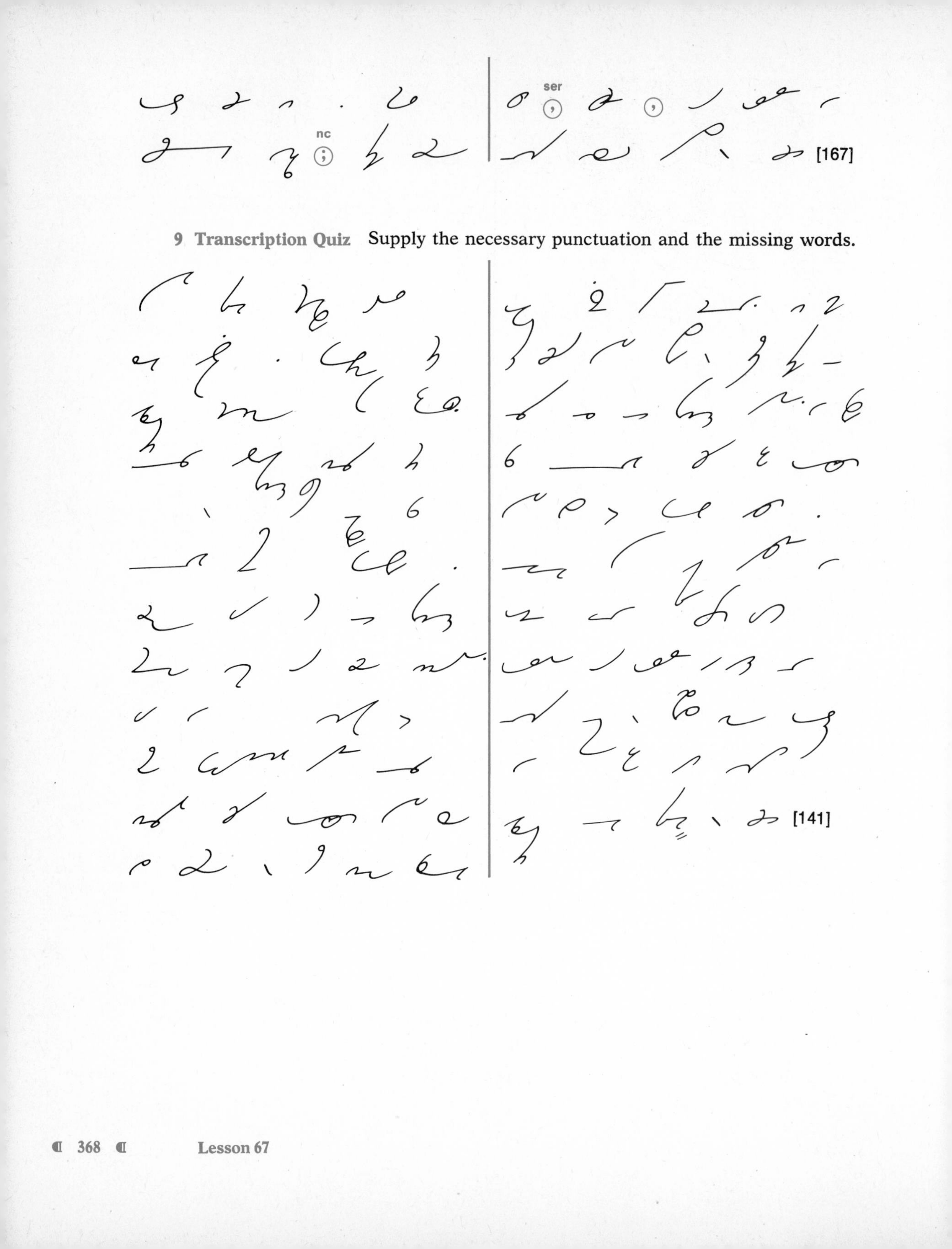

[167]

9 Transcription Quiz Supply the necessary punctuation and the missing words.

[141]

Developing Word-Building Power

1 Word Families

-ol

1

-sume

2

-room

3

-book

4

1 All, small, call, recall, collect, stall, ball.
2 Assume, assumes, presume, presuming, consumer, consuming.
3 Room, bedroom, playroom, showroom, stateroom.
4 Book, textbook, workbook, handbook, notebook, bankbook, yearbook, passbook.

Building Transcription Skills

2 COMMON PREFIXES ● co-

co- means *with, together, jointly.*

cooperation	The act of working together.
cooperative *(adjective)*	Willing to work together.
co-worker	A person who works with another.

coincidence	Seemingly connected occurrence of events.
coinsurance	Insurance in which the insurance company and the policyholder each assume partial risk.

3 Business Vocabulary Builder

splendid Excellent.
format *(noun)* A plan or layout.
concise Short; brief.

Reading and Writing Practice

4

Co·op·er·a·tive
re·ceive
care·ful·ly
en·ter·prise
role

care·ful·ly se·lect·ed no hyphen after ly
up-to-date hyphenated before noun
de·cide
lo·cal
ac·cept

[181]

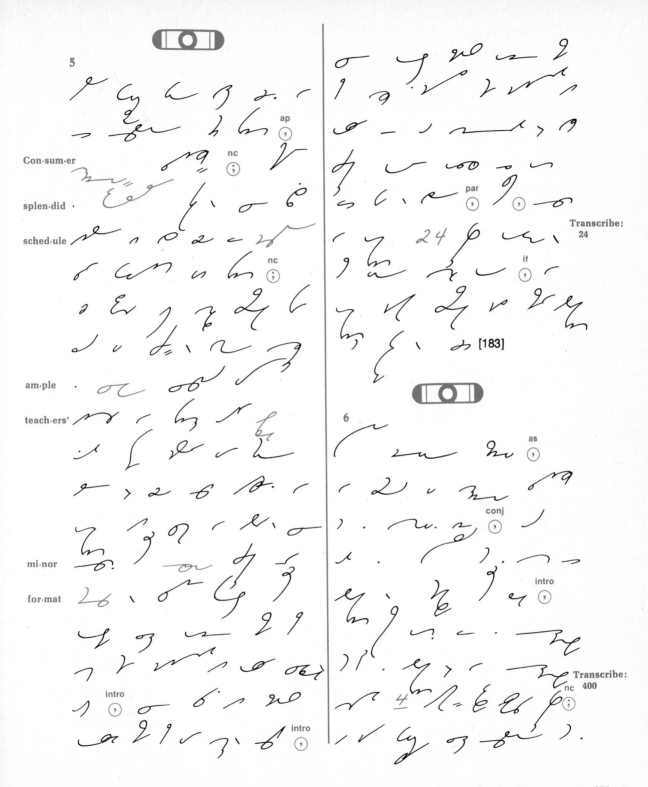

5

Con·sum·er ; nc

splen·did

sched·ule ; nc

am·ple

teach·ers'

mi·nor

for·mat

, intro

, intro

, ap

, par ,

Transcribe: 24

, if

[183]

6

, as

, conj

, intro

Transcribe: 400

; nc

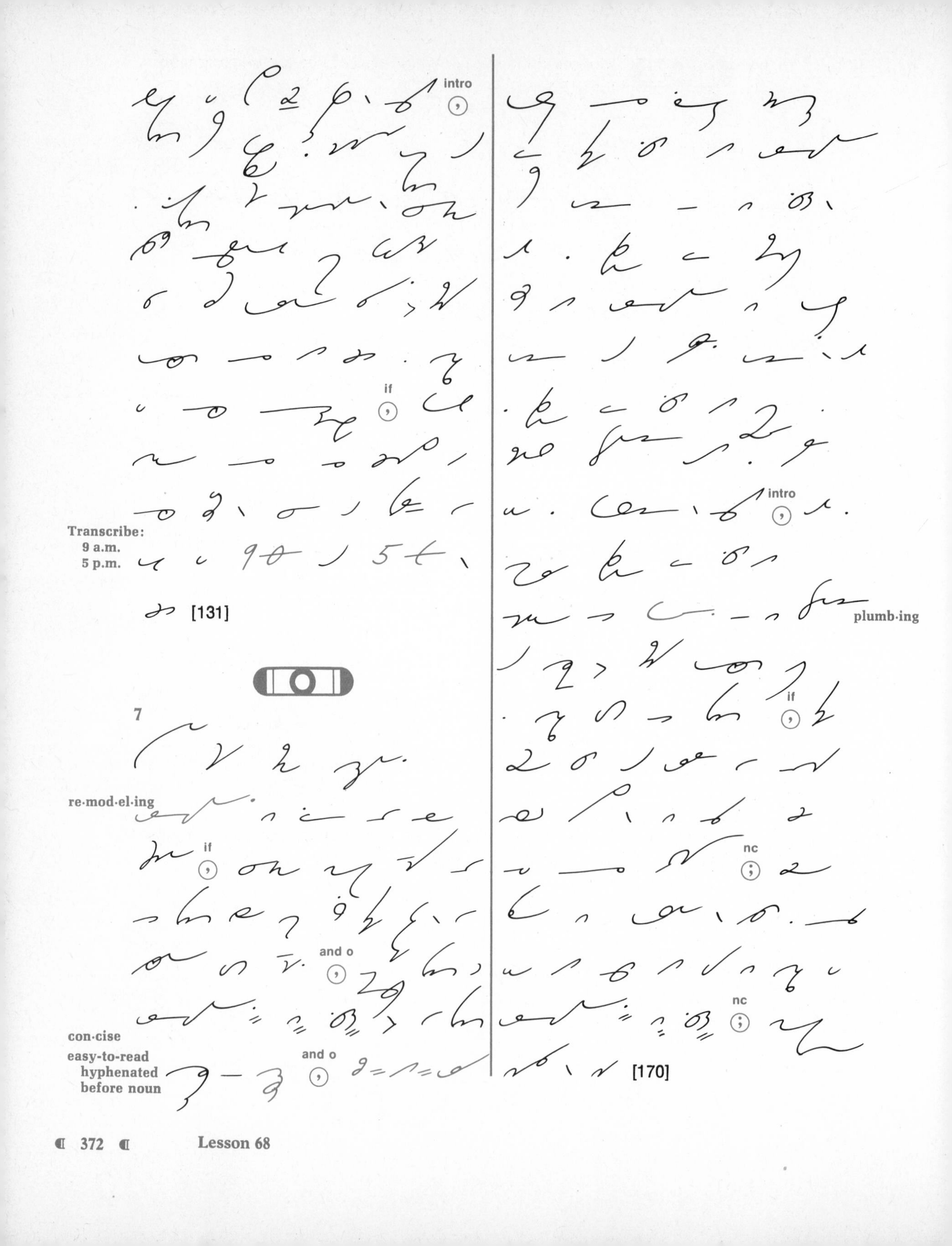

intro

if

Transcribe:
9 a.m.
5 p.m.

[131]

7

re·mod·el·ing

if

and o

con·cise

easy-to-read
hyphenated
before noun

and o

intro

plumb·ing

if

nc

nc

[170]

8 Transcription Quiz Supply the necessary punctuation and the missing words.

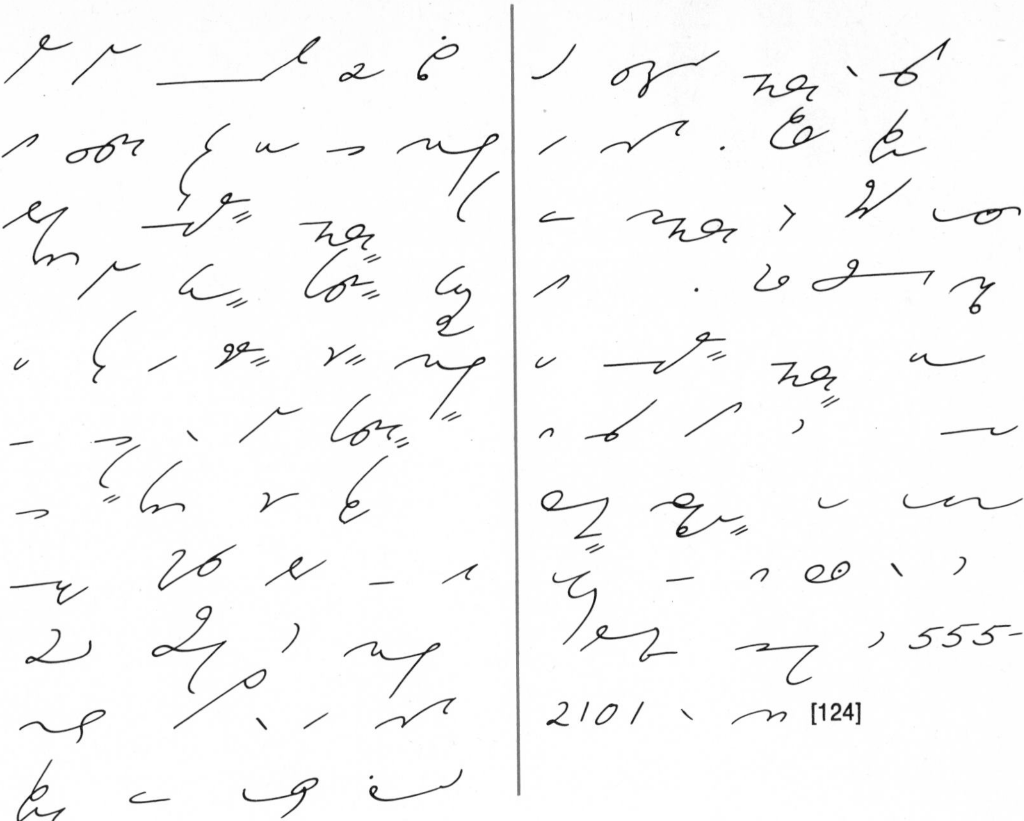

The secretary *never* speaks about confidential company matters outside the office. Even casual remarks can lead to trouble.

Developing Word-Building Power

1 Word Beginnings and Endings

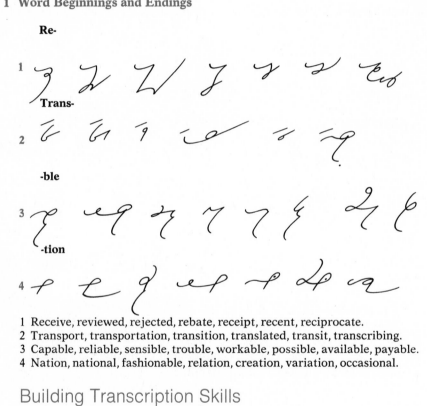

Re-

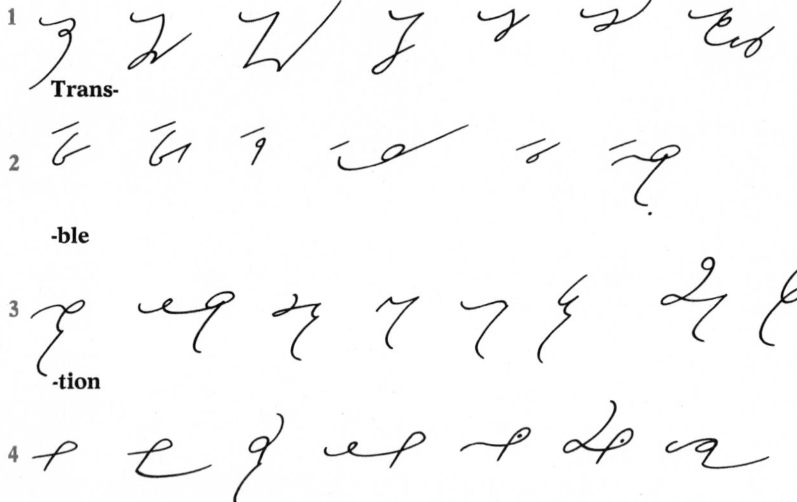

1 Receive, reviewed, rejected, rebate, receipt, recent, reciprocate.
2 Transport, transportation, transition, translated, transit, transcribing.
3 Capable, reliable, sensible, trouble, workable, possible, available, payable.
4 Nation, national, fashionable, relation, creation, variation, occasional.

Building Transcription Skills

2 SIMILAR-WORDS DRILL ● forward, foreword

forward To or toward what is ahead.

We look *forward* to seeing the play.

foreword Preface.

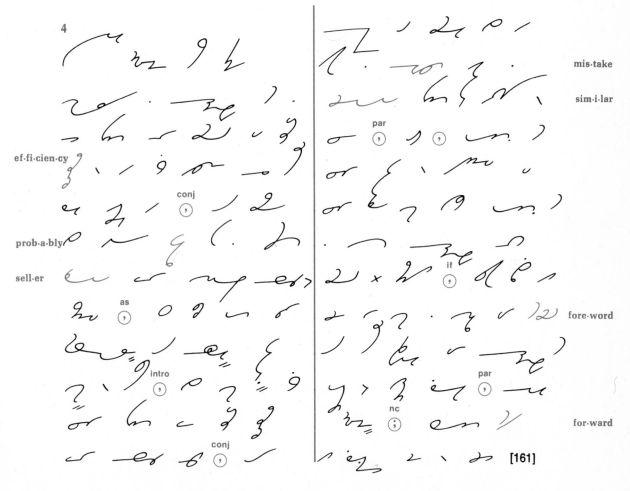

Please read the *foreword* of the book before the next class.

3 Business Vocabulary Builder

typesetting Putting into type for printing.

goodwill A friendly attitude.

devoted *(verb)* Concentrated; dedicated.

Reading and Writing Practice

4

ef·fi·cien·cy

conj

prob·a·bly

sell·er

as

intro

conj

mis·take

sim·i·lar

par

if

fore·word

par

nc

for·ward

[161]

5

Re·li·able

ap

if

intro

intro

if

intro

ap·pro·pri·ate

signed

par

[129]

6

can·celed

ap

Transcribe: four

nonr

par

oc·ca·sions

intro

intro

stopped

nc

intro

re·ceive

cr

[157]

7

ap

De·sign

par

intro

intro

ser

sen·si·ble

help·ful

[109]

8

ap

Pro·ce·dures

well writ·ten
no noun,
no hyphen

conj

and o

thor·ough

par

intro

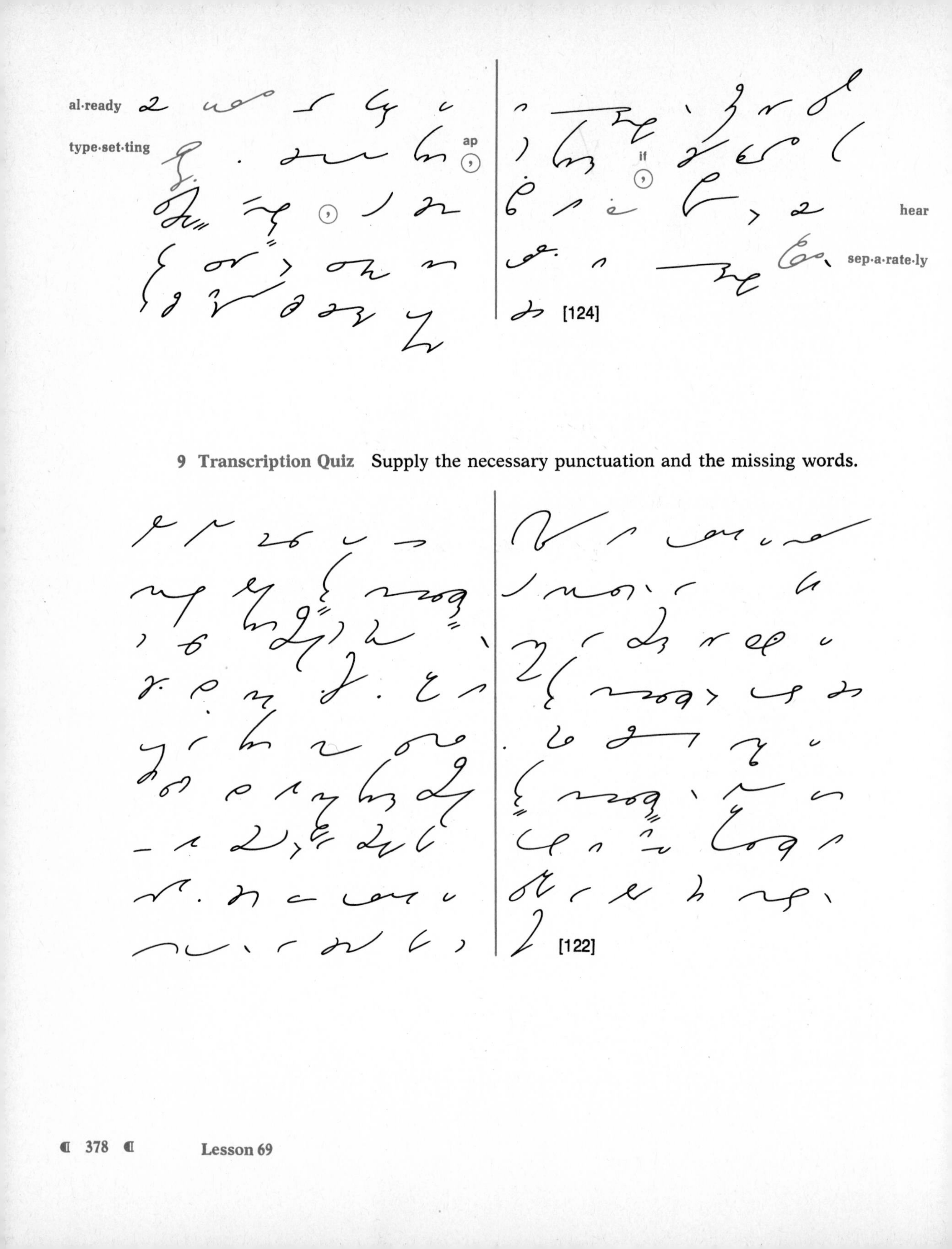

al·ready

type·set·ting

ap

if

hear

sep·a·rate·ly

[124]

9 Transcription Quiz Supply the necessary punctuation and the missing words.

[122]

Developing Word-Building Power

1 Shorthand Vocabulary Builder

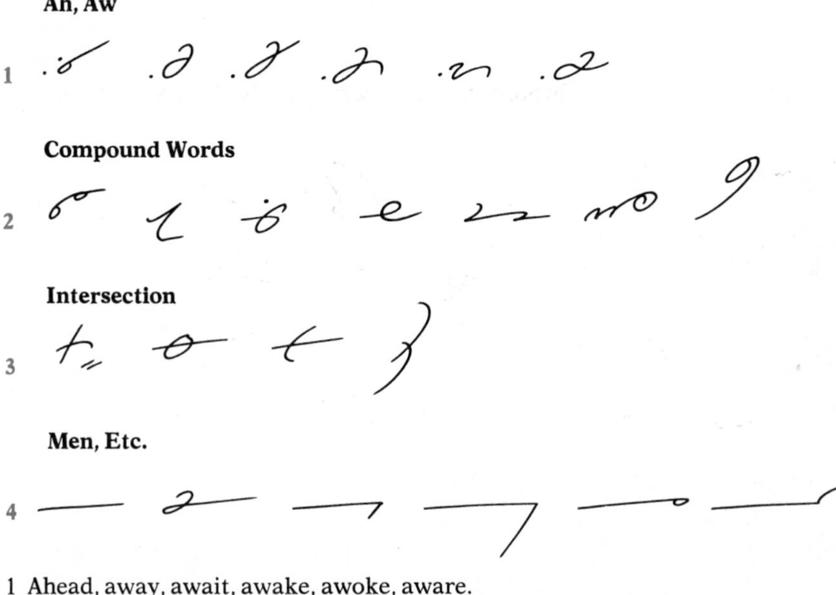

1 Ahead, away, await, awake, awoke, aware.
2 Within, thereupon, anyhow, anywhere, someone, worthwhile, however.
3 Chamber of Commerce, a.m., p.m., vice versa.
4 Men, women, mention, manage, money, month.

Building Transcription Skills

2 Business Vocabulary Builder

myth Legend.
marginal Closer to low quality than to high quality.
remuneration Pay; salary.

Reading and Writing Practice

3 A Job as a Newspaper Reporter

intro

great

dra·mas

cin·e·ma

A myth

glam·or·ous

ac·tu·al·i·ty

par

nei·ther

and o

te·dious

care·ful

Transcribe: 6 a.m.

Many

jour·nal·ism

quite

pre·con·ceived

dis·cour·ag·ing

conj

intro

en·deav·or

and o

de·pend·able

and o

Just

intro

sal·a·ries

nonr

intro

whose

mar·gin·al

re·mu·ner·a·tion

above-av·er·age hyphenated before noun

conj

months'

intro

conj

ma·nip·u·lat·ed

read·er's

Sen·sa·tion·al·ism

par

intro

in·trigu·ing

In the

intro

per·ti·nent

and o

conj

par

chal·leng·ing

par

and o

[618]

4 Publishing a Book

intro

as

aware

There

par

ap·pear

intro

high·ly trained
no hyphen
after ly

judged

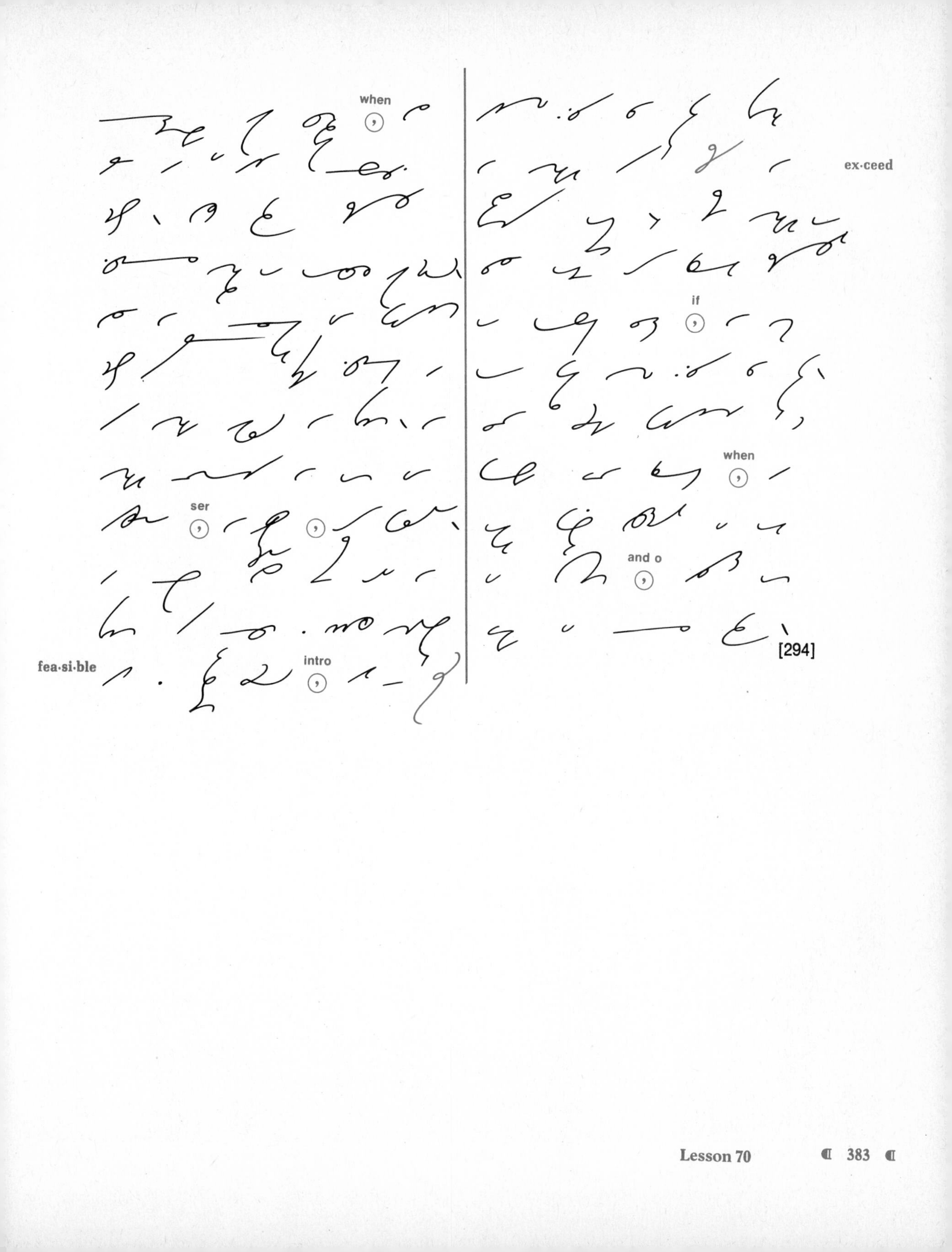

when

ex·ceed

if

when

ser

and o

[294]

fea·si·ble

intro

15 ADVERTISING

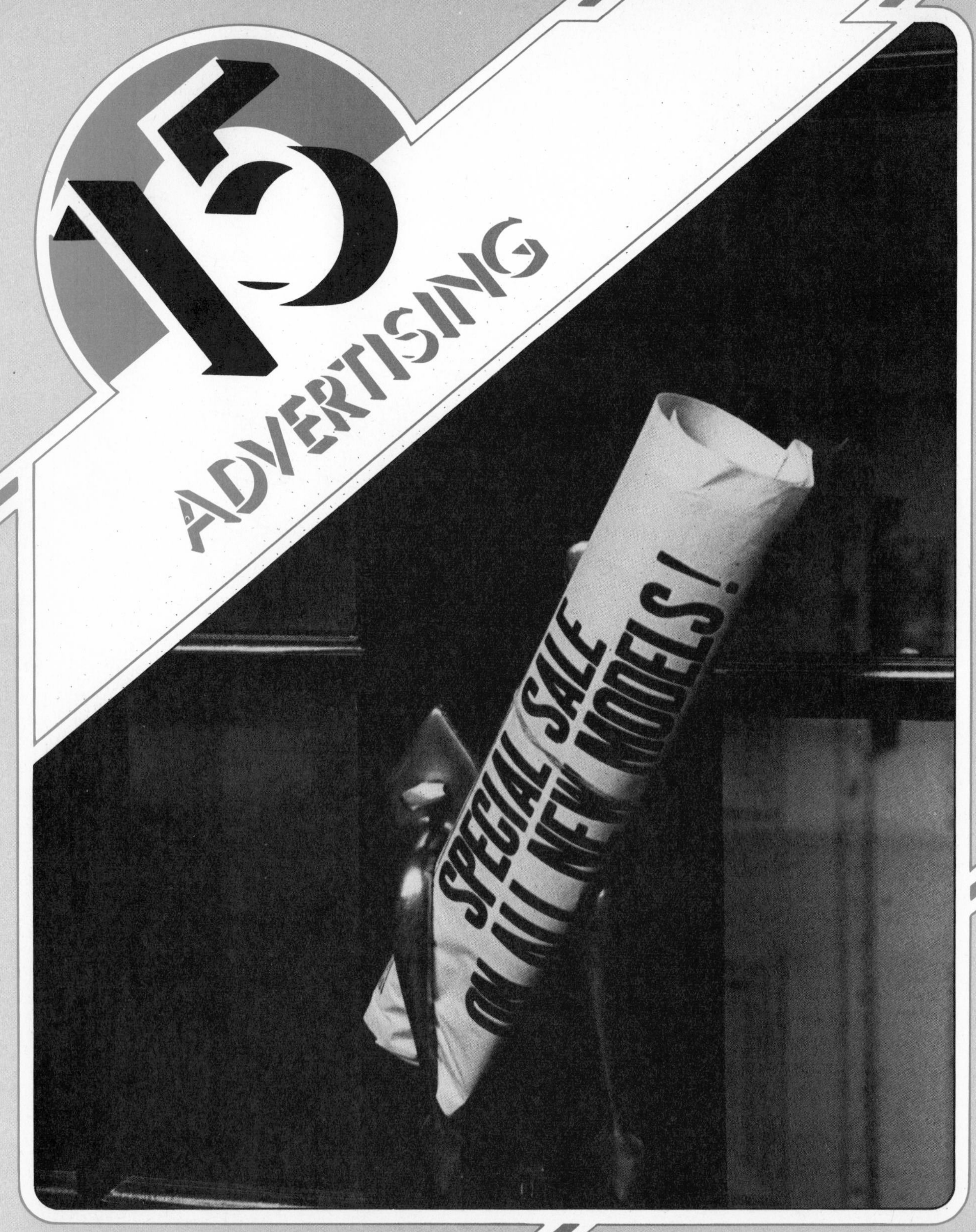
SPECIAL SALE
ON ALL NEW MODELS!

Developing Word-Building Power

1 Brief Forms and Derivatives

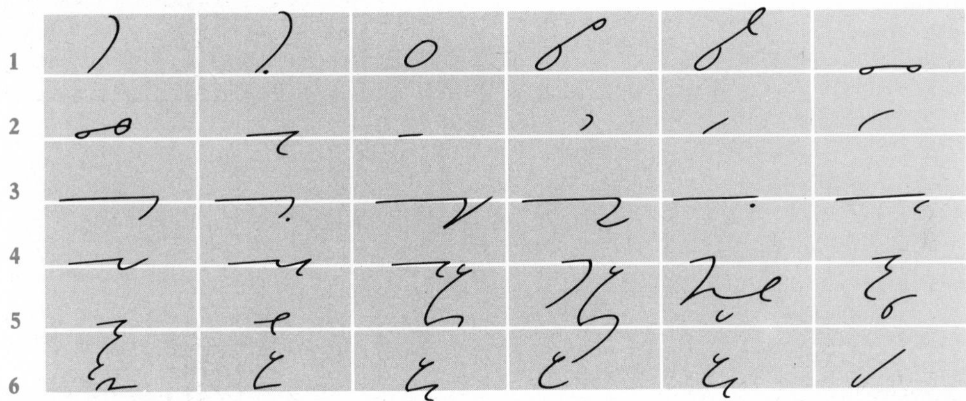

1 Have, having, I, idea, ideas, immediate.
2 Immediately, important-importance, in-not, is-his, it-at, the.
3 Manufacture, manufacturing, manufactured, manufacturer, morning, mornings.
4 Mr., Mrs., Ms., never, nevertheless, newspaper.
5 Newspapers, next, object, objective, of, with.
6 One (won), opinion, opinions, opportunity, opportunities, order.

Building Transcription Skills

2 OFFICE-STYLE DICTATION ● restorations

An executive may dictate a word or phrase and then change it. Upon reflection, however, the dictator may decide that the original word or phrase was better.

The work is satisfactory—no, **adequate;** *oh, maybe* **satisfactory** *is better.*

Write the restored word or phrase as though it were a completely new form.

Write the word *satisfactory;* then strike it out and write *adequate.* Strike out *adequate* and rewrite *satisfactory.* The shorthand notes would look like this:

Do not try to indicate that the original outline for *satisfactory* is to be restored. This could make your notes difficult to read.

Illustration of Office-Style Dictation

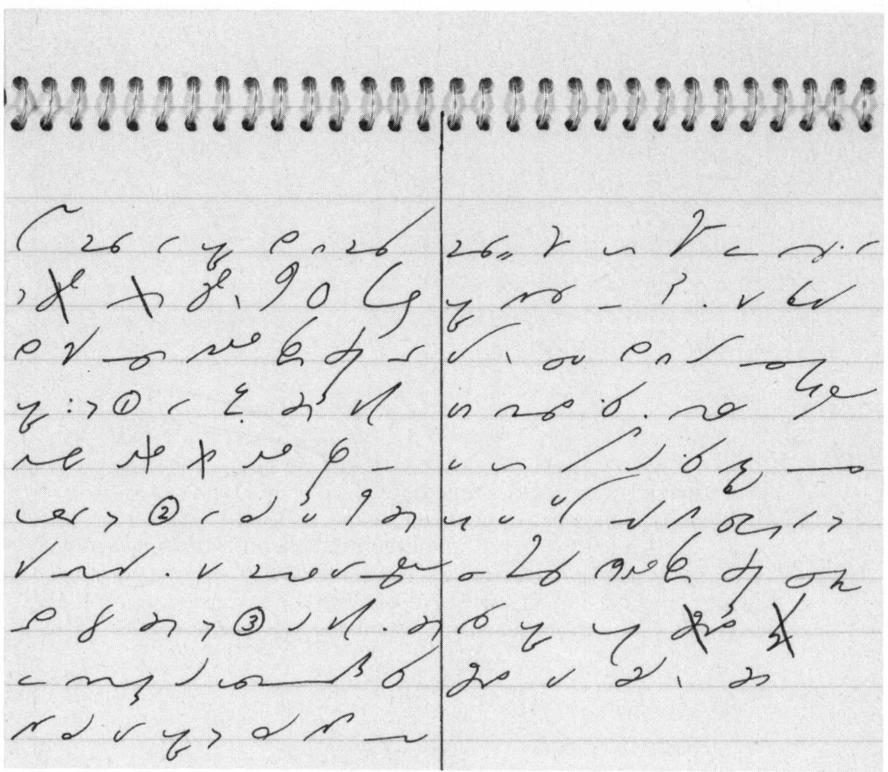

3 Business Vocabulary Builder	**clients**	Customers.
	impact	Influence; effect.
	effective	Capable of producing or accomplishing.

Reading and Writing Practice

4 Brief-Form Letter

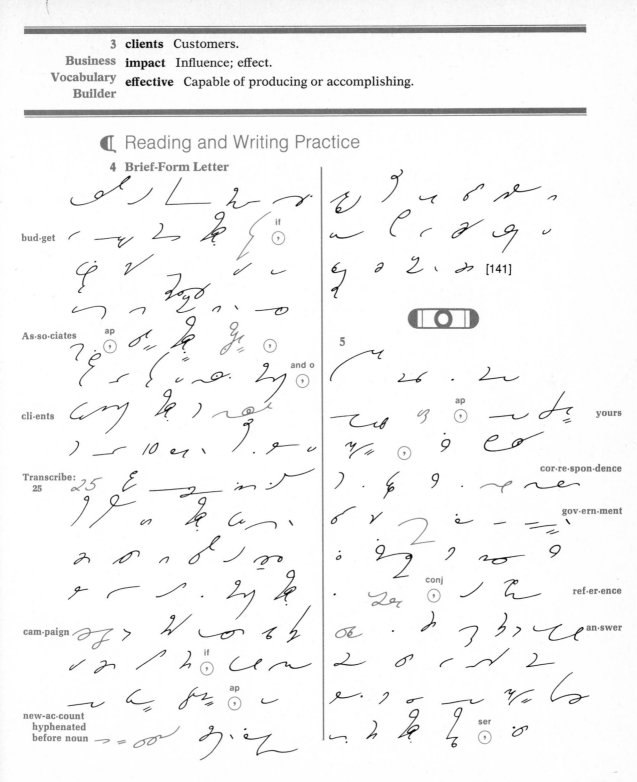

bud·get

if

As·so·ciates

ap

and o

cli·ents

Transcribe: 25

cam·paign

if

ap

new-ac·count hyphenated before noun

[141]

5

ap

yours

cor·re·spon·dence

gov·ern·ment

conj

ref·er·ence

an·swer

ser

cr

ser

char·ac·ter

ini·tia·tive

clear·ance

com·plete

[144]

6

de·vel·op·ing

intro

Transcribe:
15 percent
re·mark·able

nonr

15,

conj

intro

nonr

half-page
hyphenated
before noun

cr

[218]

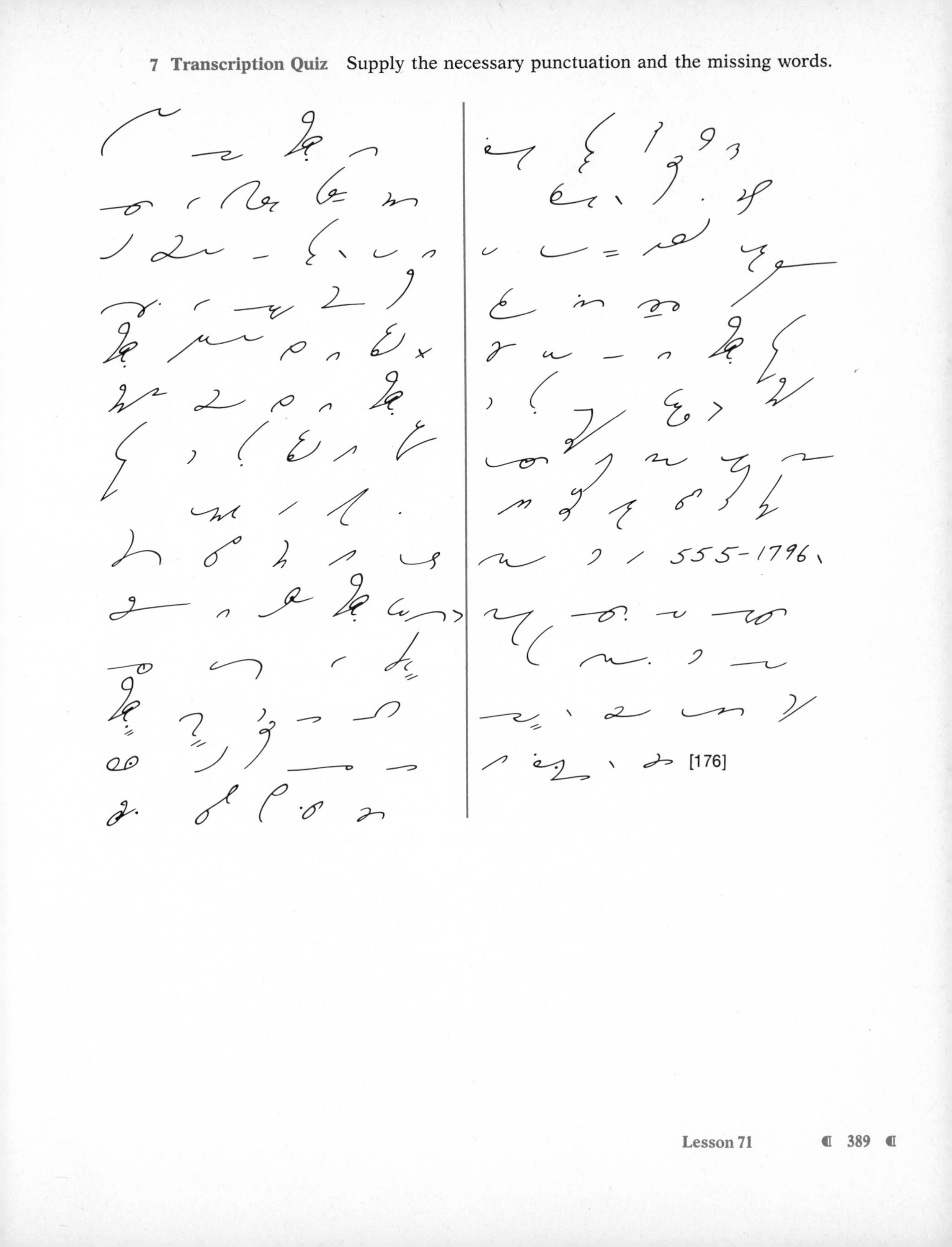

7 Transcription Quiz Supply the necessary punctuation and the missing words.

555-1796

[176]

Building Phrasing Skill

1 Useful Business-Letter Phrases

Will

1

Can

2

In

3

From

4

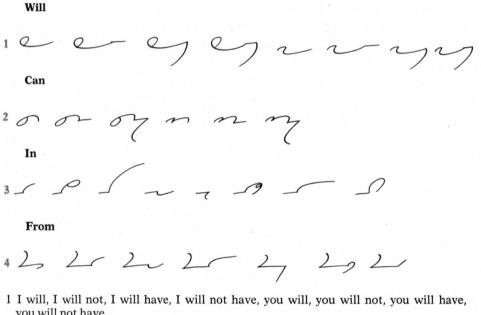

1 I will, I will not, I will have, I will not have, you will, you will not, you will have, you will not have.
2 I can, I cannot, I cannot be, you can, you cannot, you cannot be.
3 In the, in that, in time, in our, in his, in these, in them, in this.
4 From you, from the, from our, from them, from which, from us, from it.

2 Geographical Expressions

1

2

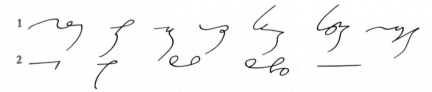

1 Greenville, Nashville, Knoxville, Louisville, Bronxville, Brownsville, Crawfordsville.
2 Michigan, Nebraska, Alabama, Alaska, Minnesota.

Building Transcription Skills

3 GRAMMAR CHECKUP ● all right

This expression should always be written as two words. Some transcribers mistakenly spell it as one. They are probably influenced by the spelling of such words as *altogether, always,* and *already.*

A way to remember that *all right* is spelled as two words is to keep in mind its opposite, *all wrong,* is also spelled as two words.

Will it be all right *with you?*

4 Business Vocabulary Builder

preliminary Introductory; preparatory.
eliminating Removing.
comprehensive Highly detailed; total.

Reading and Writing Practice

5 Phrase Letter

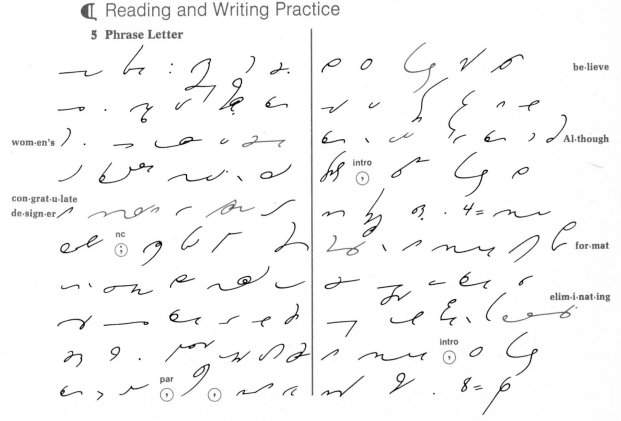

wom·en's

con·grat·u·late

de·sign·er

nc

par

be·lieve

Al·though

intro

for·mat

elim·i·nat·ing

intro

pre·lim·i·nary

eval·u·ate

[176]

6

yours

well-trained hyphenated before noun

Transcribe: 10 percent

weeks'

402 14

555-1682

all right

[194]

7

intro

par

some·time

if

[116]

8

ap

Transcribe: 10 percent

intro

nonr

fall·en

leads

long-term hyphenated before noun

if

nc

for·ward

[137]

9

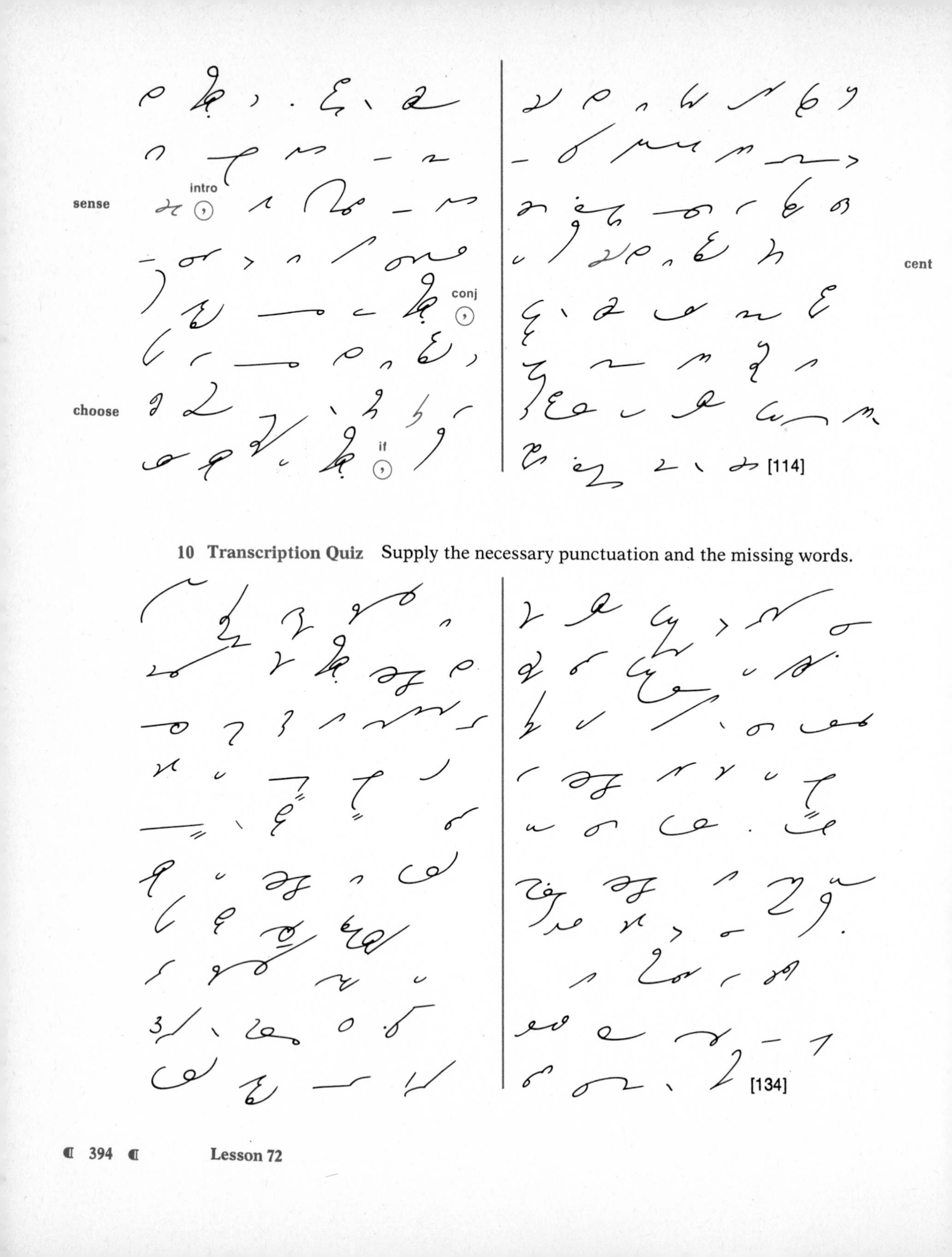

sense intro

conj

choose

if

cent

[114]

10 **Transcription Quiz** Supply the necessary punctuation and the missing words.

[134]

Developing Word-Building Power

1 Word Families

-count

1

-or

2

-sist

3

-est

4

1 Count, account, accountant, discount, miscount, recount.
2 Or, nor, more, store, ignore, floor.
3 Assist, insist, resist, consist, persist, pharmacist, consistent.
4 Latest, fastest, honest, earnest, fullest, oldest, finest.

Building Transcription Skills

2 SPELLING FAMILIES ● -ize, -ise, -yze

Words Ending in -ize

re-al-ize	**sum-ma-rize**	**or-ga-nize**
apol-o-gize	**crit-i-cize**	**mod-ern-ize**

Words Ending in -ise

ad-vise	**en-ter-prise**	**com-pro-mise**
ad-ver-tise	**com-prise**	**mer-chan-dise**

Words Ending in -yze

an-a-lyze	**par-a-lyze**

3 Business Vocabulary Builder

bid *(noun)* The price offered.
launch *(verb)* To start.
attributed Explained by indicating a cause.

Reading and Writing Practice

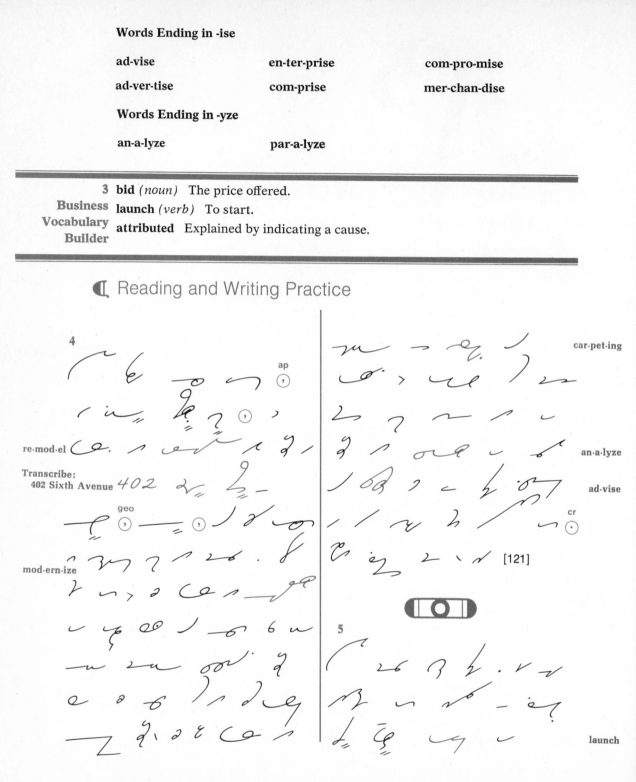

4

ap

re·mod·el

Transcribe: 402 Sixth Avenue

402

geo

mod·ern·ize

car·pet·ing

an·a·lyze

ad·vise

cr

[121]

5

launch

as

nonr

at·tempt·ed

suc·cess·ful

suf·fi·cient

conj

at·trib·ut·ed

[115]

6

dol·lar

if

and o

com·pre·hen·sive

conj

and o

mon·ey-mak·ing hyphenated before noun

intro

enough

and o

con·tinu·ing

long-term hyphenated before noun

ser

min·i·mum

self-in·ter·est

nc

555-8020

[161]

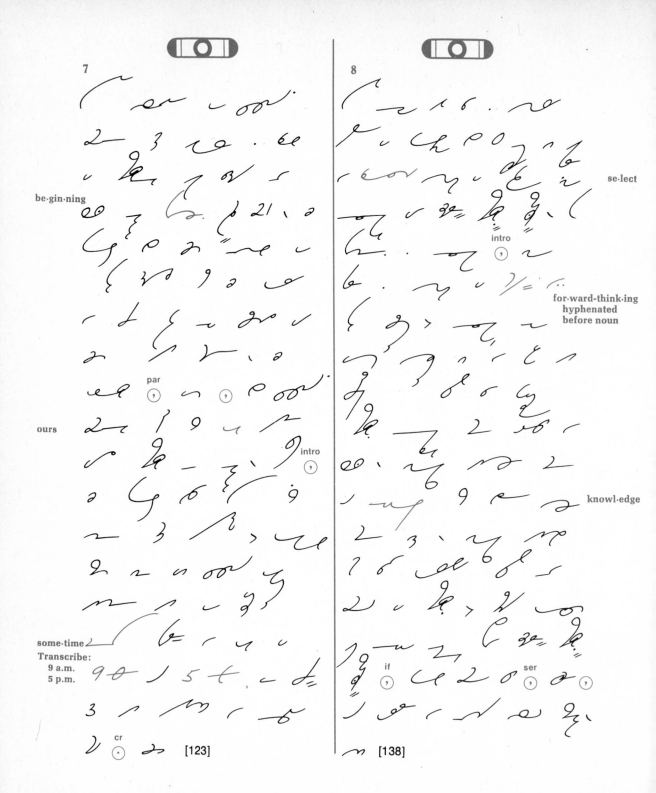

7

be·gin·ning

par

intro

ours

some·time

Transcribe:

9 a.m.

5 p.m.

cr

[123]

8

se·lect

intro

for·ward-think·ing hyphenated before noun

knowl·edge

if

ser

[138]

9 Transcription Quiz Supply the necessary punctuation and the missing words.

16 17

23

[144]

A smile has an amazing effect. When you deal with people, the best approach is a polite, interested manner accompanied by a smile—even over the phone!

Developing Word-Building Power

1 Word Beginnings and Endings

Des-

1

En-

2

-rity

3

-lty

4

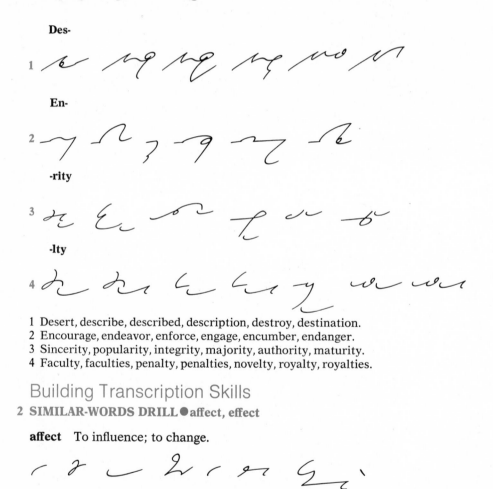

1 Desert, describe, described, description, destroy, destination.
2 Encourage, endeavor, enforce, engage, encumber, endanger.
3 Sincerity, popularity, integrity, majority, authority, maturity.
4 Faculty, faculties, penalty, penalties, novelty, royalty, royalties.

Building Transcription Skills

2 SIMILAR-WORDS DRILL ● affect, effect

affect To influence; to change.

The weather will *affect* the team's performance.

effect *(noun)* Outcome; result.

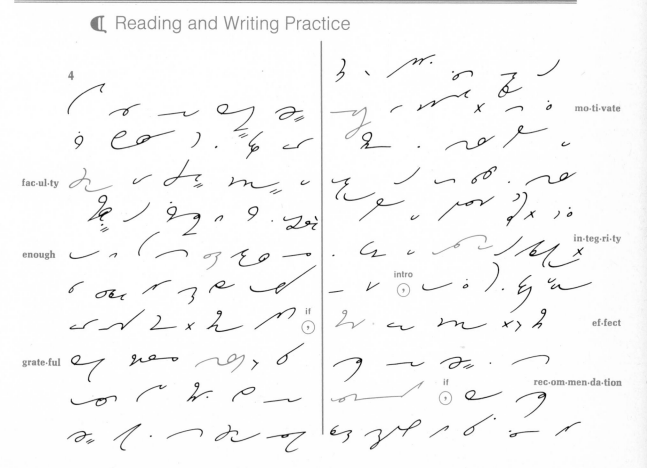

I did not believe the *effect* of inflation would be so great.

effect *(verb)* To bring about; to accomplish.

We will *effect* a settlement of the problem.

3 Business Vocabulary Builder

return on investment The amount earned from the amount invested.

justly With cause; deservedly so.

devise To invent.

ingenuity Skill; cleverness.

Reading and Writing Practice

4

fac·ul·ty

enough

if

grate·ful

mo·ti·vate

in·teg·ri·ty

intro

ef·fect

if

rec·om·men·da·tion

[158]

5

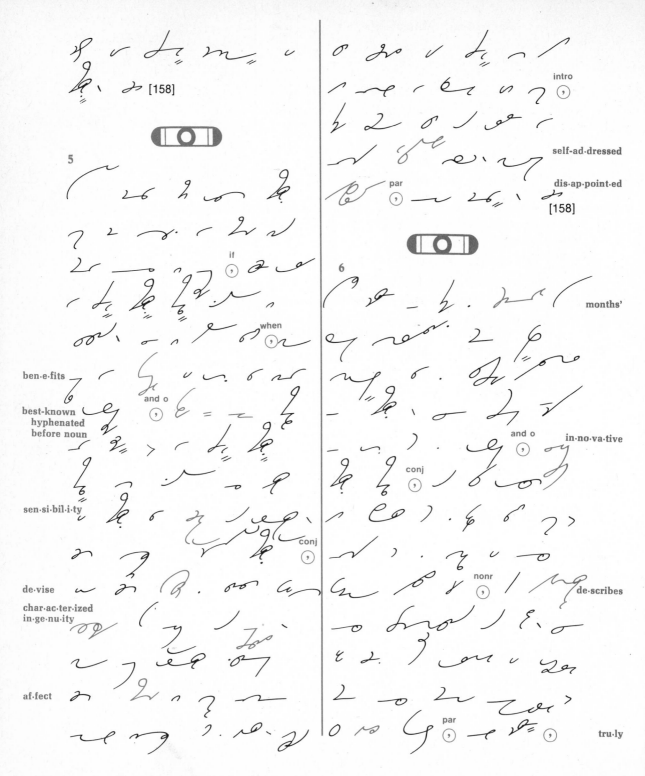

ben·e·fits

best-known hyphenated before noun

sen·si·bil·i·ty

de·vise

char·ac·ter·ized

in·ge·nu·i·ty

af·fect

if

when

and o

conj

intro

self-ad·dressed

dis·ap·point·ed

par

[158]

6

months'

in·no·va·tive

and o

conj

nonr

de·scribes

par

tru·ly

ef·fect

re·al

cr

[127]

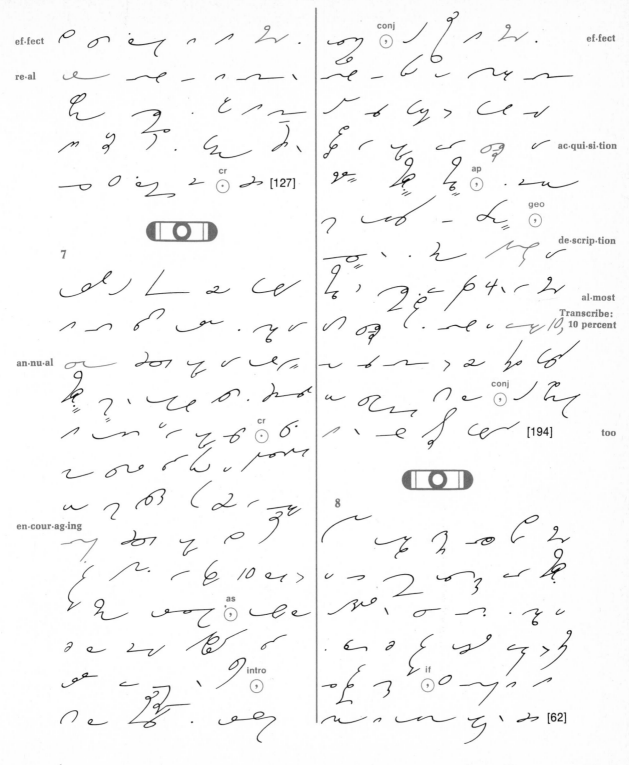

7

an·nu·al

cr

en·cour·ag·ing

as

intro

conj

ef·fect

ac·qui·si·tion

ap

geo

de·scrip·tion

al·most

Transcribe: 10 percent

conj

[194]

too

8

if

[62]

9 Transcription Quiz Supply the necessary punctuation and the missing words.

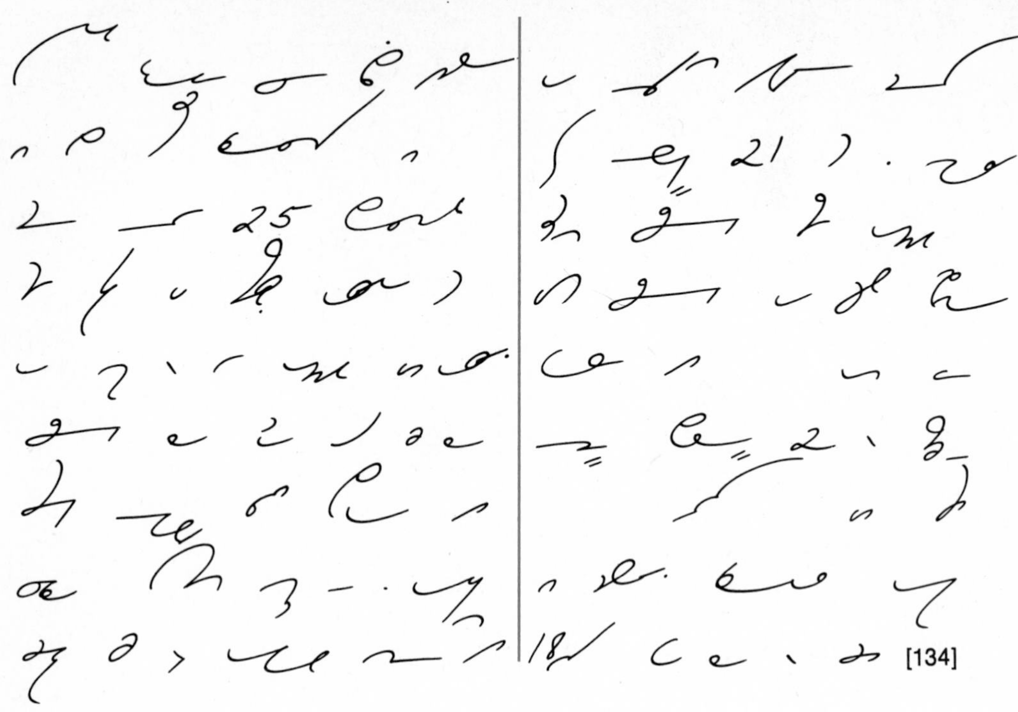

Keeping up to date on what is going on in the world—and in your own company—helps make you an interesting person and a valuable employee.

75

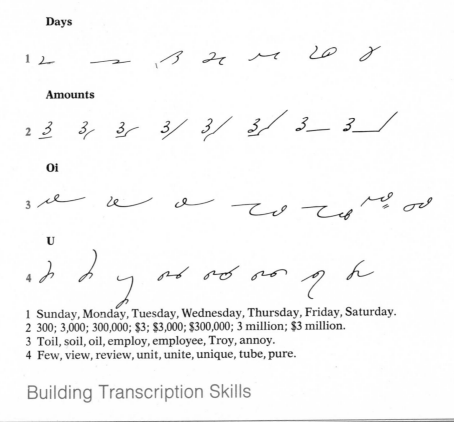

Developing Word-Building Power

1 Shorthand Vocabulary Builder

Days

1 

Amounts

2 

Oi

3 

U

4 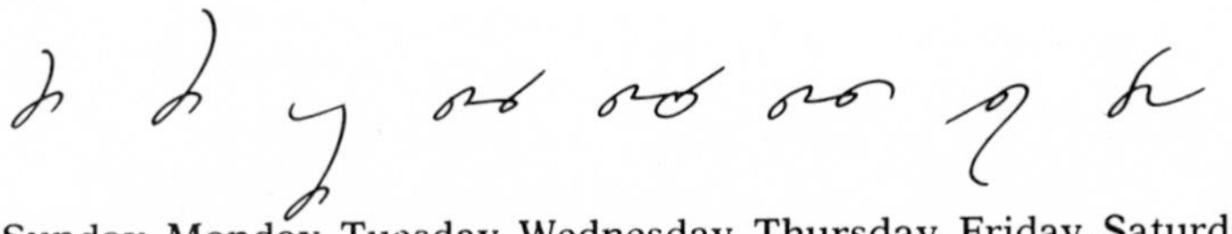

1 Sunday, Monday, Tuesday, Wednesday, Thursday, Friday, Saturday.
2 300; 3,000; 300,000; $3; $3,000; $300,000; 3 million; $3 million.
3 Toil, soil, oil, employ, employee, Troy, annoy.
4 Few, view, review, unit, unite, unique, tube, pure.

Building Transcription Skills

2 Business Vocabulary Builder

abundant Plentiful; amply supplied.
commodity An item; a product.
idle Not busy.

Reading and Writing Practice

3 Advertising—A Window for Business

their
opin·ion

if

Transcribe:
$1,000

sur·vey

Transcribe:
1 million

intro

Transcribe:
50 percent

50,

con·sum·er

fur·ther

Consider

ceased

abun·dant

nonr

com·mod·i·ty

conj

The

intro

conj

sup·pose

ser

edi·tions

Transcribe:
5,000

if

great
in·volved

when

low·er-priced
hyphenated
before noun

shelves

When

when

idle

conj

par

ef·fect

After

intro

nc

intro

across

[554]

4 Advertising Today

par

Transcribe: 1,000 40

ser

Transcribe: $1 million

intro

through

if

suc·ceed

and o

po·ten·tial

conj

People

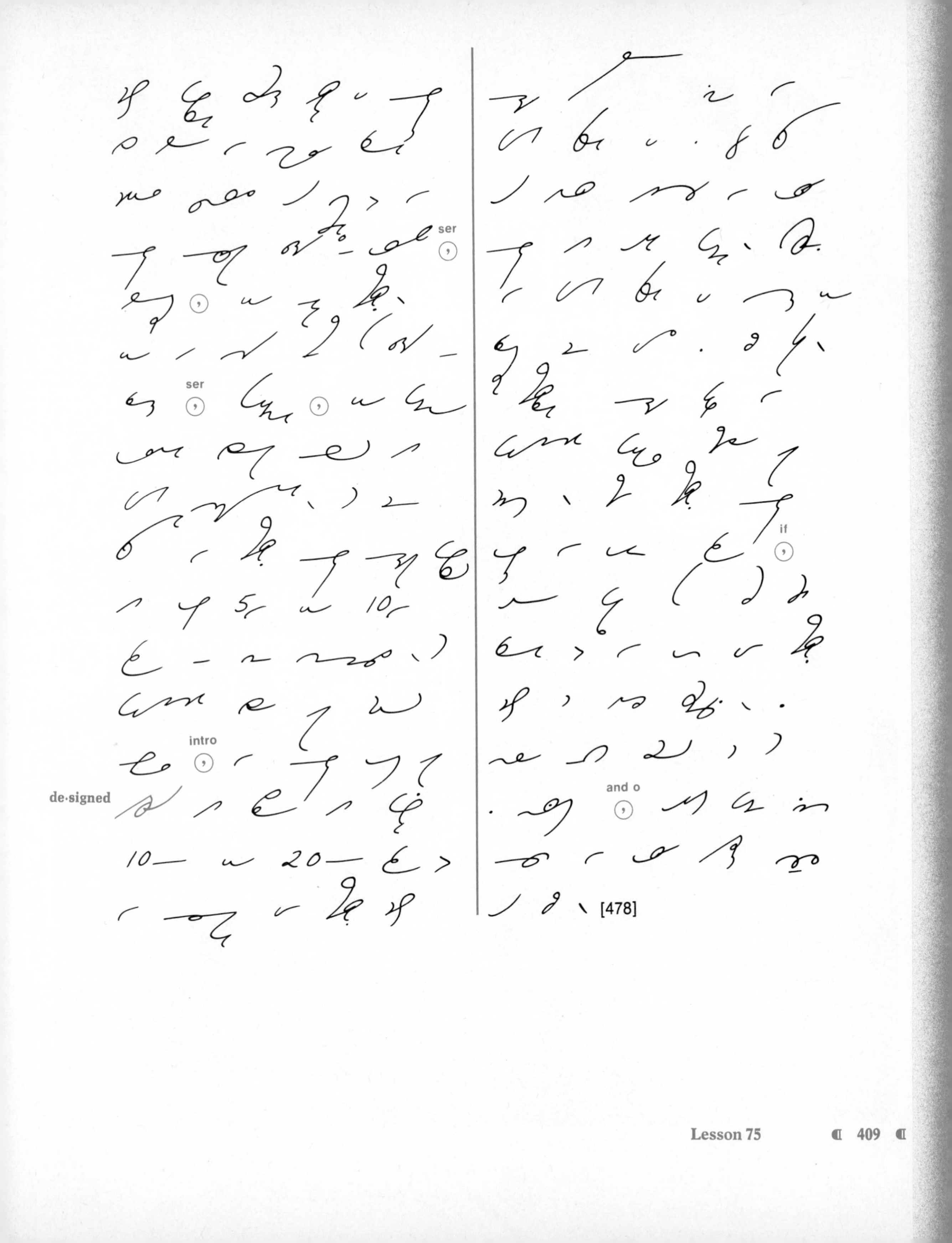

ser

ser

intro

de·signed

if

and o

[478]

16 INSURANCE

Developing Word-Building Power

1 Brief Forms and Derivatives

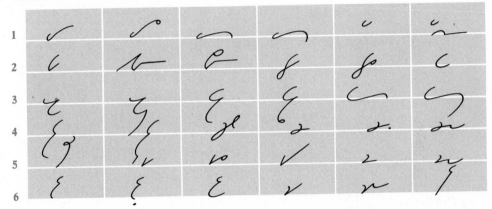

1 Ordinary, ordinarily, organize, organization, over, overcome.
2 Part, department, apartment, particular, particularly, present.
3 Represent, representative, probable, probably, progress, progressive.
4 Public, publish-publication, satisfy-satisfactory, send, sending, sender.
5 Several, short, shortly, should, soon, sooner.
6 Speak, speaking, speaker, state, street, subject.

Building Transcription Skills

2 OFFICE-STYLE DICTATION ● transpositions

A dictator may decide to transpose words or phrases. A simple way to indicate the transposition of a word or phrase is to use the printer's sign for transposition.

The dictator might say:
Our representatives are well trained and experienced—Make that **experienced and well trained.**

In your shorthand, you would make the change in this way:

You would then be careful, when you transcribe, to type the word *and* after the word *experienced.*

Illustration of Office-Style Dictation

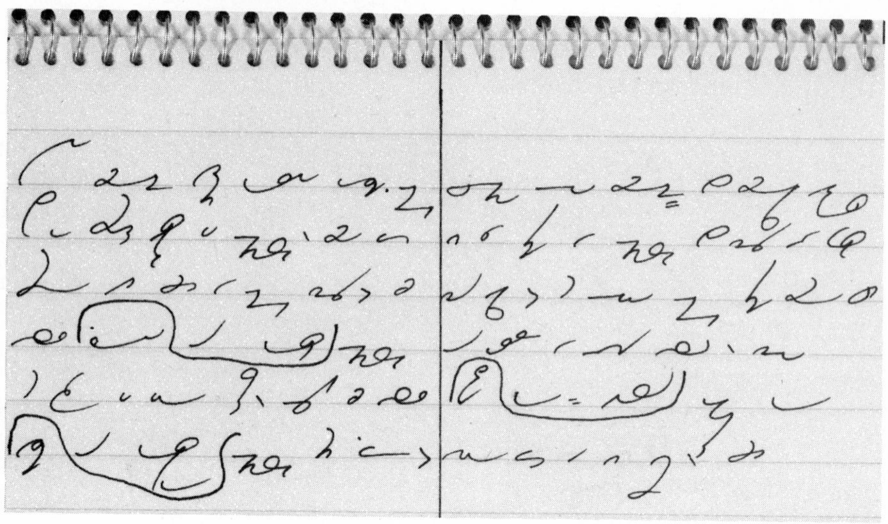

3 Business Vocabulary Builder

cooperative apartment An apartment building owned and operated by the tenants.

liability insurance Insurance against loss caused by damage to others or to their property.

Reading and Writing Practice

4 Brief-Form Letter

sub·urbs

intro

one-fam·i·ly hyphenated before noun

ser

theft

li·a·bil·i·ty

law·suit

if

[115]

5

re·ceipt

co·op·er·a·tive

quite

nc

intro

con·tents

intro

it·self

if

lose

intro

def·i·nite·ly

ser

bro·chure

[211]

6

conj

in·quire

par

ful·ly

ac·ci·dent

in·for·ma·tion

cr

[84]

7

conj

as

ap

Transcribe: $600

nc

par

par

dif·fer·ence

par

if

[155]

8

bev·er·age

ris·er

intro

after-din·ner hyphenated before noun

cr

Transcribe: 300

course

ser

[144]

9 Transcription Quiz Supply the necessary punctuation and the missing words.

[141]

Building Phrasing Skill

1 Useful Business-Letter Phrases

Thank

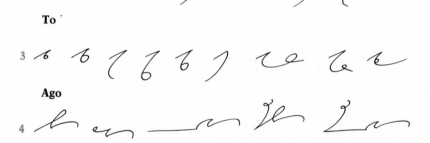

1

Hope

2

To

3

Ago

4

1 Thank you, thank you for, thank you for your, I thank you, I thank you for the, to thank you, we thank you, thank you for your order.
2 I hope, I hope you are, I hope you will, I hope you have, we hope, we hope you are, we hope you have, we hope to be.
3 To see, to say, to be, to be able, to pay, to have, to plan, to bring, to sell.
4 Days ago, years ago, months ago, several days ago, several months ago.

2 Geographical Expressions

1

2

1 Pittsburgh, Trenton, Camden, Paterson, Springfield, Harrisburg.
2 New Jersey, California, Pennsylvania, New York, Texas, United States, England, English.

Building Transcription Skills

3 GRAMMAR CHECKUP ● may, can

may Implies permission or possibility.

May *I leave now?*

can Implies ability or power.

We can *do the job.*

---

4 Business Vocabulary Builder

warranty A guarantee.
dispatcher One who assigns jobs to others.
reliable Dependable.

Reading and Writing Practice

5 Phrase Letter

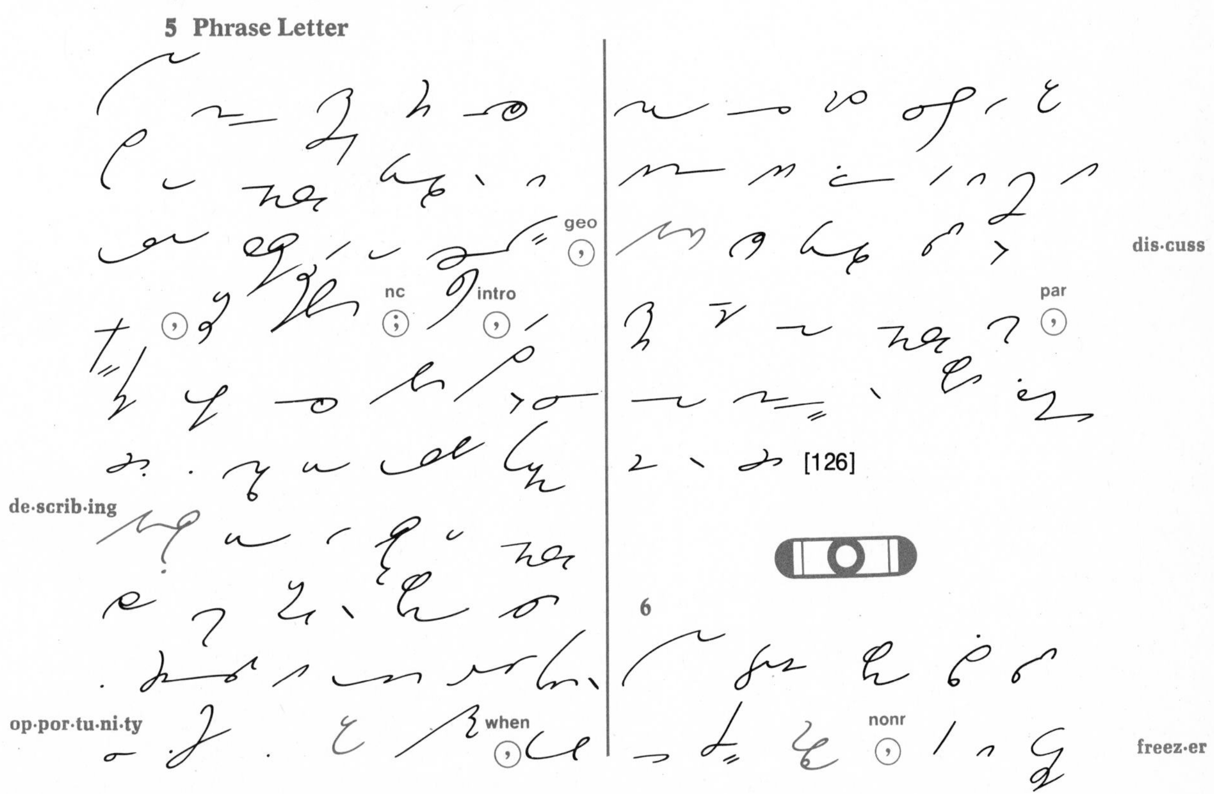

as

war·ran·ty

one-year
hyphenated
before noun

ex·tend·ed

Transcribe:
$50

50

re·place·ments

hid·den

conj

intro

ser

50

pro·vid·ed

if

nc

555-8020

[214]

7

re·pair

ad·just
bright·ness

conj

fad·ed

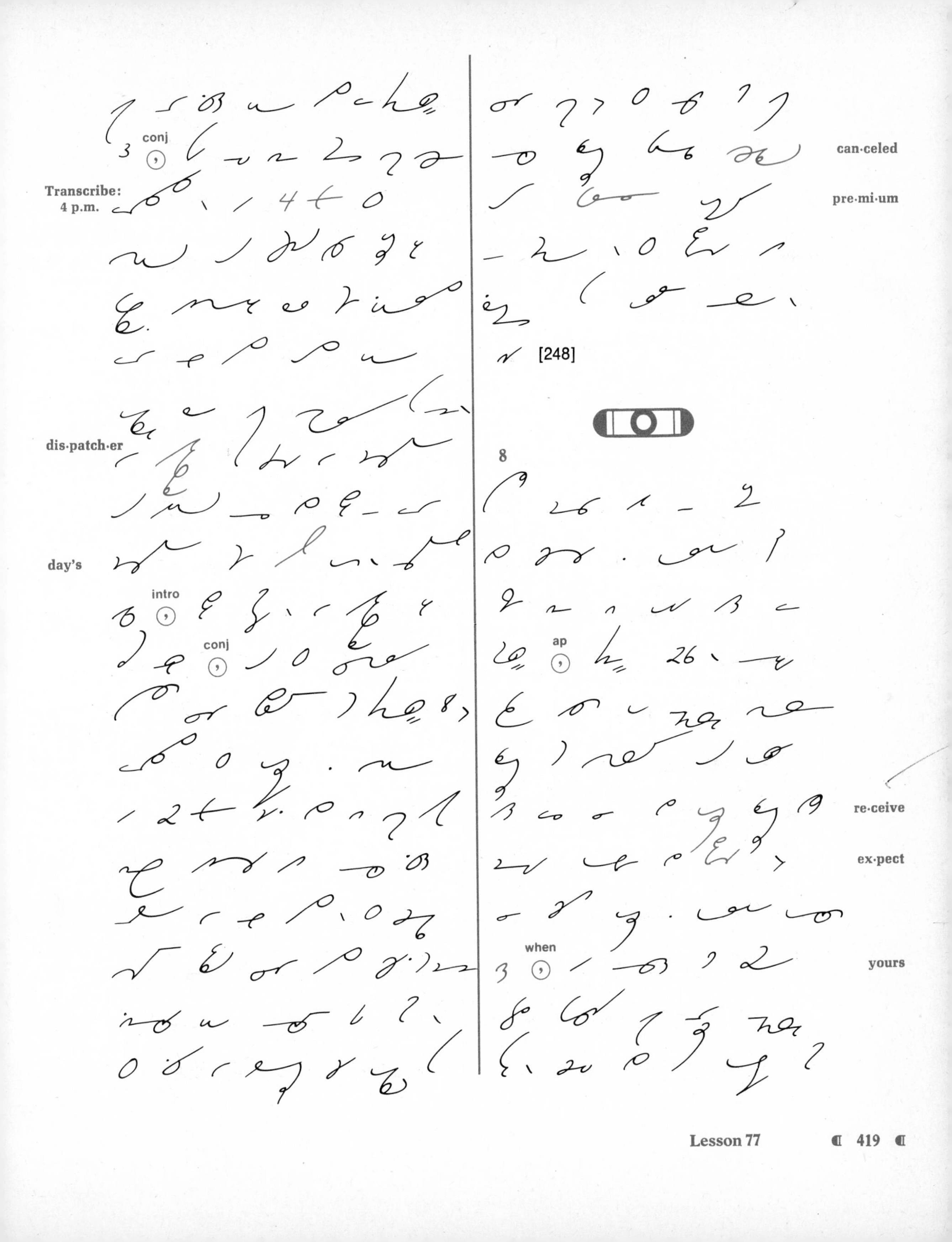

3 conj

Transcribe: 4 p.m.

dis·patch·er

day's

intro

conj

can·celed

pre·mi·um

[248]

8

ap

re·ceive

ex·pect

when

3

yours

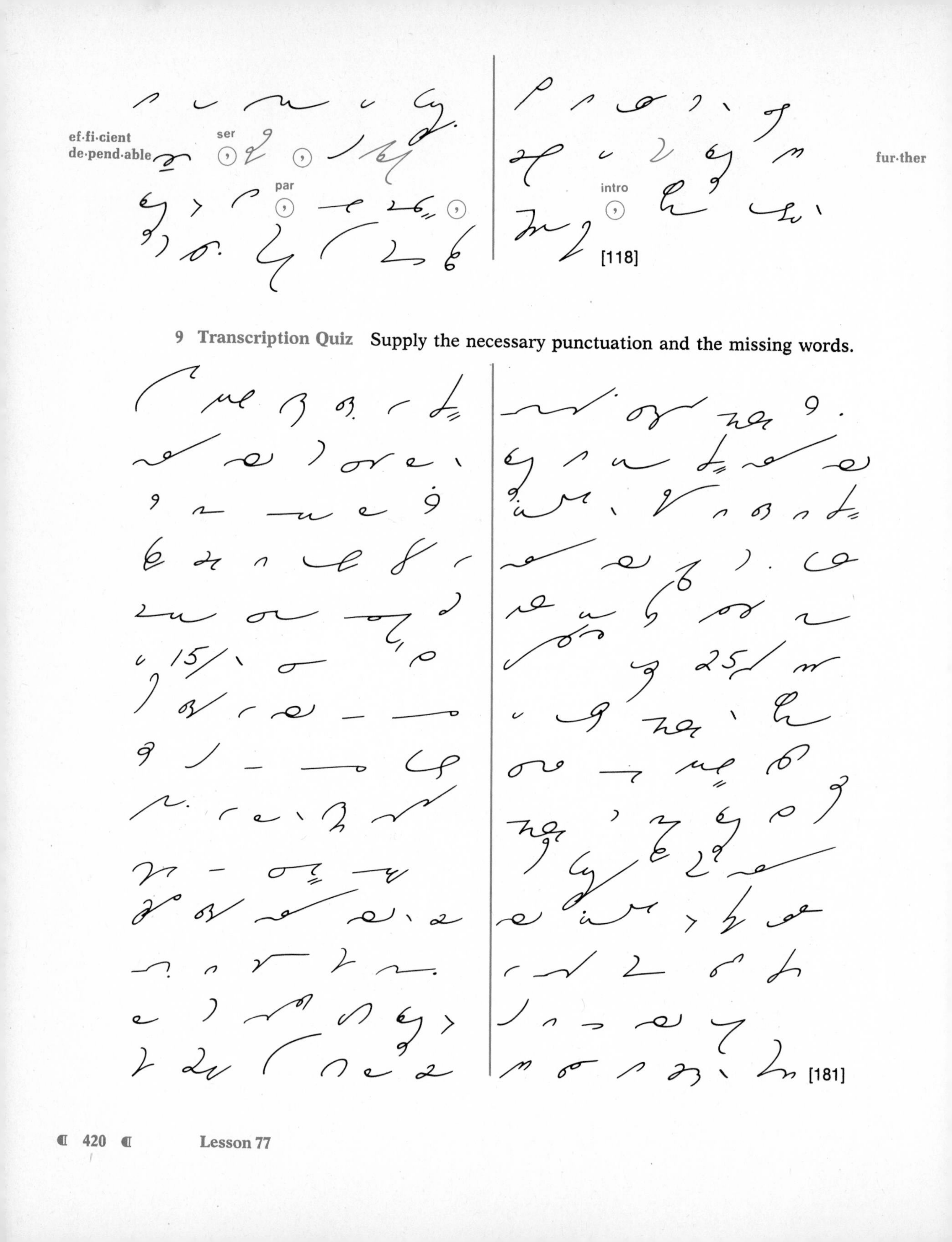

ef·fi·cient
de·pend·able

ser

par

intro

fur·ther

[118]

9 **Transcription Quiz** Supply the necessary punctuation and the missing words.

[181]

Developing Word-Building Power

1 Word Families

-sumption

-ciate, -tiate

-ally

-tive

1 Assumption, assumptions, resumption, consumption, presumption.
2 Appreciate, associate, depreciate, negotiate, substantiate, initiate.
3 Finally, totally, originally, personally, vitally, normally, legally.
4 Active, effective, creative, negative, positive, relative, alternative.

Building Transcription Skills

2 SPELLING FAMILIES ● -ight, -ite

Be careful when you transcribe a word ending in the sound *īt*. Sometimes it is spelled *ight;* at other times it is spelled *ite.*

might	**right**	**site**
sight	**night**	**cite**
de-light	**bright**	**write**

3 Business Vocabulary Builder

pamphlet A brochure; a booklet.

supplement (*verb*) To add to.

Medicare A government program of medical care.

Reading and Writing Practice

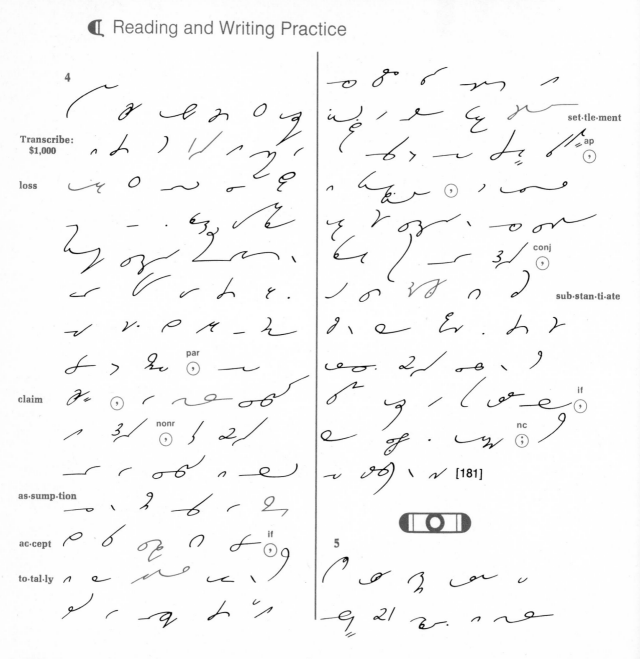

4

Transcribe: $1,000

loss

par

claim

nonr

as·sump·tion

ac·cept

if

to·tal·ly

set·tle·ment

ap

conj

sub·stan·ti·ate

if

nc

[181]

5

against

nonr

dis·cussed

length

conj

to·tal·ly

in·ter·sec·tion

pole
po·lice

sub·stan·ti·ates

intro

Transcribe:
$1,000

write

[136]

6

Transcribe:
3 cents

conj

hos·pi·tal

Transcribe:
$10

intro

sums

orig·i·nal·ly

par

might

if

con·ve·nience

per·son·al·ly

and o

up-to-date hyphenated before noun

555-1472

right

nc

par

[223]

7

if

de·scribes com·plete

ser

if

211

Transcribe: 211 West First Avenue

geo

conj

[131]

8

com·pa·ny's

intro

ben·e·fits

Transcribe: 10 percent

intro

Fi·nal·ly

conj

par

[145]

9 Transcription Quiz Supply the necessary punctuation and the missing words.

[119]

Developing Word-Building Power

1 Word Beginnings and Endings

Dis-

1

In-

2

-rity

3

-lity

4

1 Disappoint, disappointment, dismay, disappear, disapprove.
2 Insurance, incident, insight, injure, injury, involve.
3 Charity, authority, authorities, priority, priorities, integrity.
4 Liability, reliability, ability, stability, sensibility.

Building Transcription Skills

2 SIMILAR-WORDS DRILL ● prominent, permanent

prominent Standing out; noticeable.

She held a *prominent* position with the state government.

permanent Lasting; not subject to change.

The ink is *permanent;* it will not wash out.

3 Business Vocabulary Builder

similar Alike.

particularly Especially.

Reading and Writing Practice

4

dis·ap·point·ed

en·cour·age

ac·cept

re·luc·tant

nonr

par

conj

rec·om·mend

conj

al·ready

intro

in·teg·ri·ty

ser

intro

sin·cer·i·ty

prom·i·nent

per·ma·nent

ser

nc

[167]

5

nonr

intro

judg·ment

sim·i·lar

if

[138]

6

conj

pe·ri·od

di·rect

intro

pay·roll

[146]

7 **Transcription Quiz** Supply the necessary punctuation and the missing words.

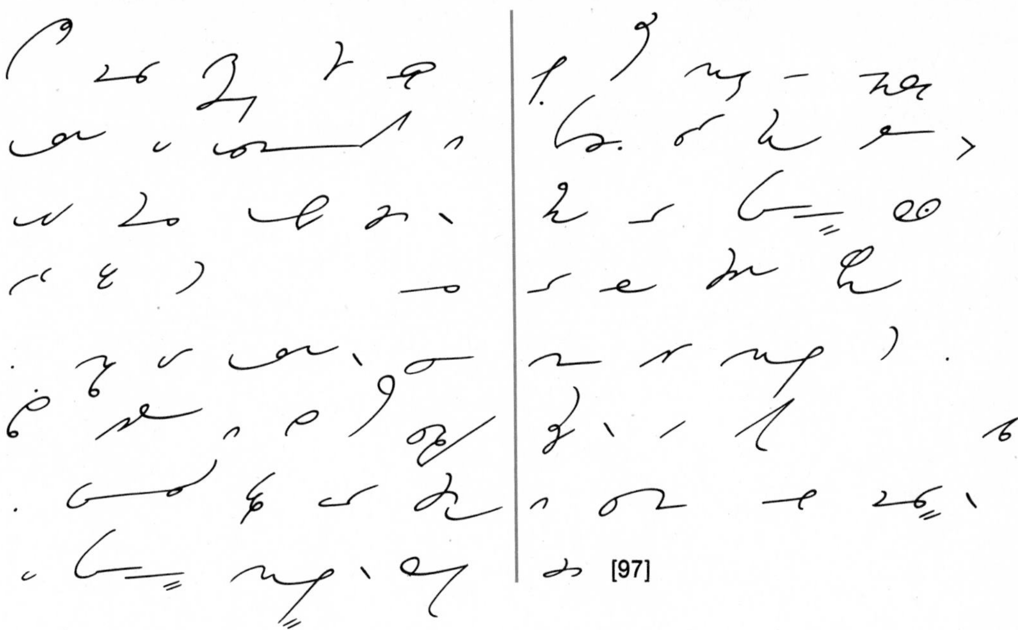

A pleasant disposition and a friendly tone of voice are easily communicated to others—cheerfulness is contagious.

Developing Word-Building Power

1 Shorthand Vocabulary Builder

Months

1

Ow

2

I

3

X

4

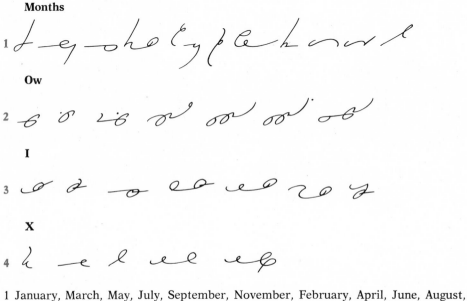

1 January, March, May, July, September, November, February, April, June, August, October, December.
2 Now, how, somehow, county, account, accounting, amount.
3 Write, sign, mine, align, rely, comply, resign.
4 Fox, mix, tax, relax, relaxation.

Building Transcription Skills

2 Business Vocabulary Builder

beneficiaries Persons named to receive payment.
redeem To get back.
collateral Something offered to guarantee payment of a debt.
monetary Relating to money.

Reading and Writing Practice

3 The Value of Insurance

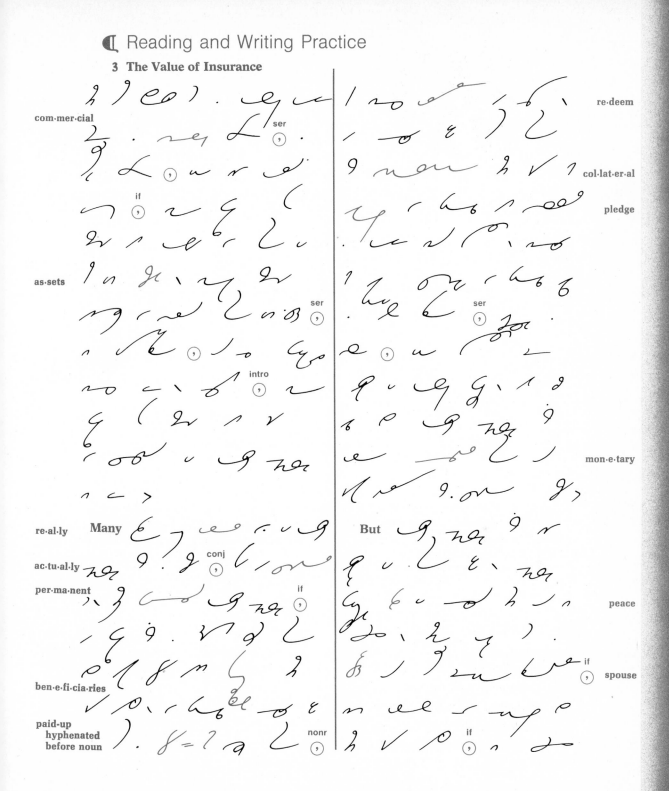

com·mer·cial

ser

if

as·sets

ser

intro

re·al·ly

Many

ac·tu·al·ly

conj

per·ma·nent

if

ben·e·fi·cia·ries

paid-up
hyphenated
before noun

nonr

re·deem

col·lat·er·al

pledge

ser

mon·e·tary

But

peace

if

spouse

if

Health

un·der·go

if

doc·tors'

ser

med·i·ca·tion

par

de·plete

fam·i·ly's

conj

sal·a·ry-con·tin·u·a·tion hyphenated before noun

bread·win·ner

if

One

nonr

sim·i·lar

dis·abil·i·ty

intro

if

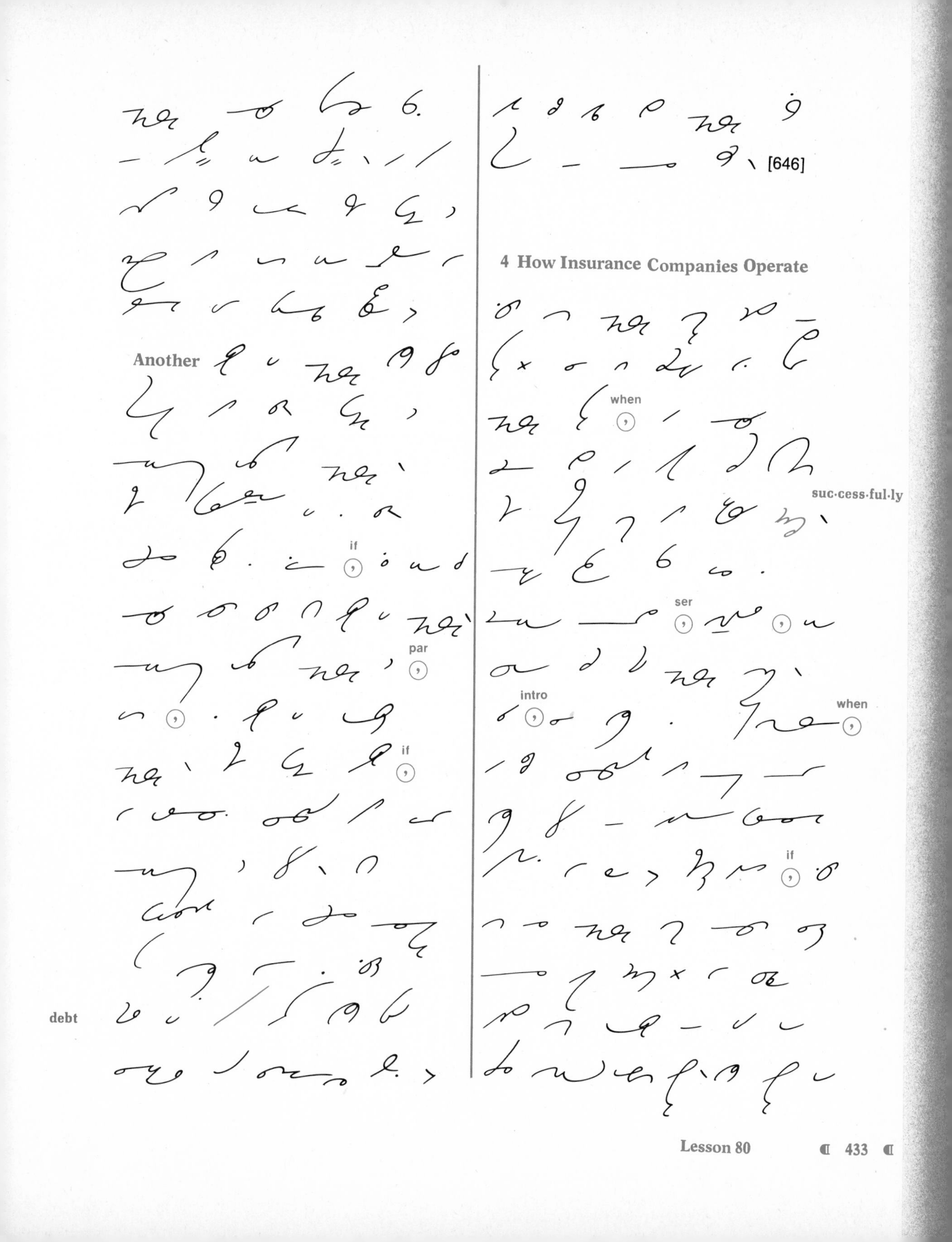

Another

debt

[646]

4 How Insurance Companies Operate

when

suc·cess·ful·ly

ser

intro

when

if

if

par

if

ser

Actuaries

cat·e·go·ries

ser

person's

when

com·piled

nc

The

up to date
no noun,
no hyphen

if

intro

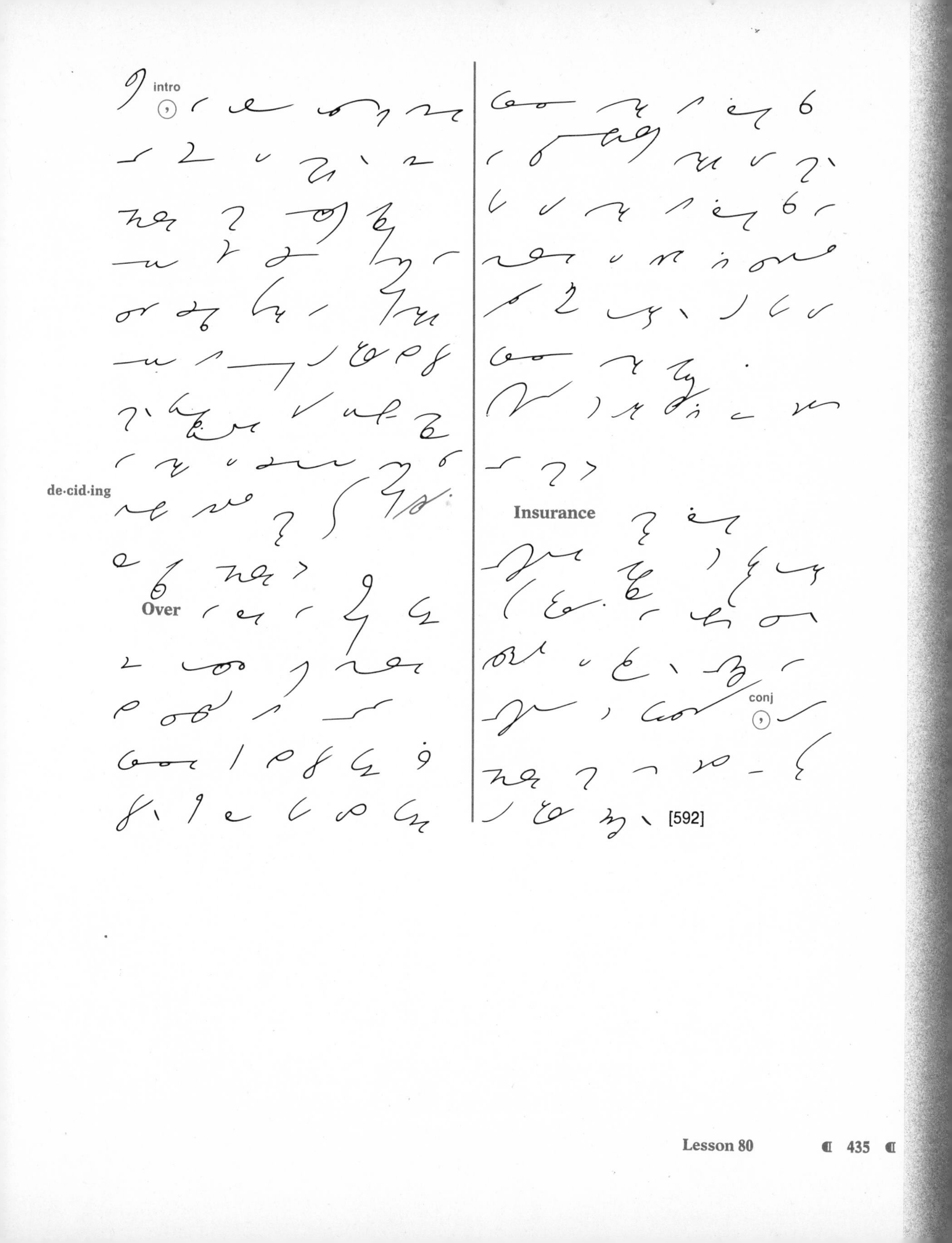

intro

de·cid·ing

Over

Insurance

conj

[592]

APPENDIX

Recall Drills

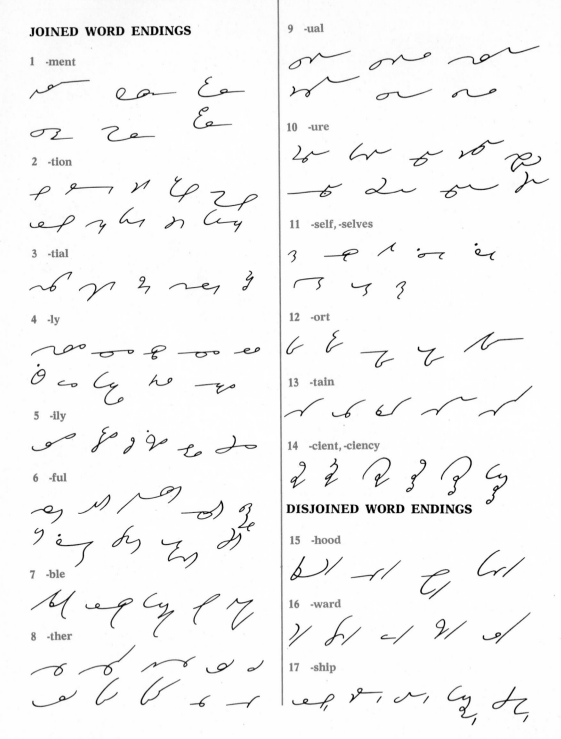

JOINED WORD ENDINGS

1 -ment

2 -tion

3 -tial

4 -ly

5 -ily

6 -ful

7 -ble

8 -ther

9 -ual

10 -ure

11 -self, -selves

12 -ort

13 -tain

14 -cient, -ciency

DISJOINED WORD ENDINGS

15 -hood

16 -ward

17 -ship

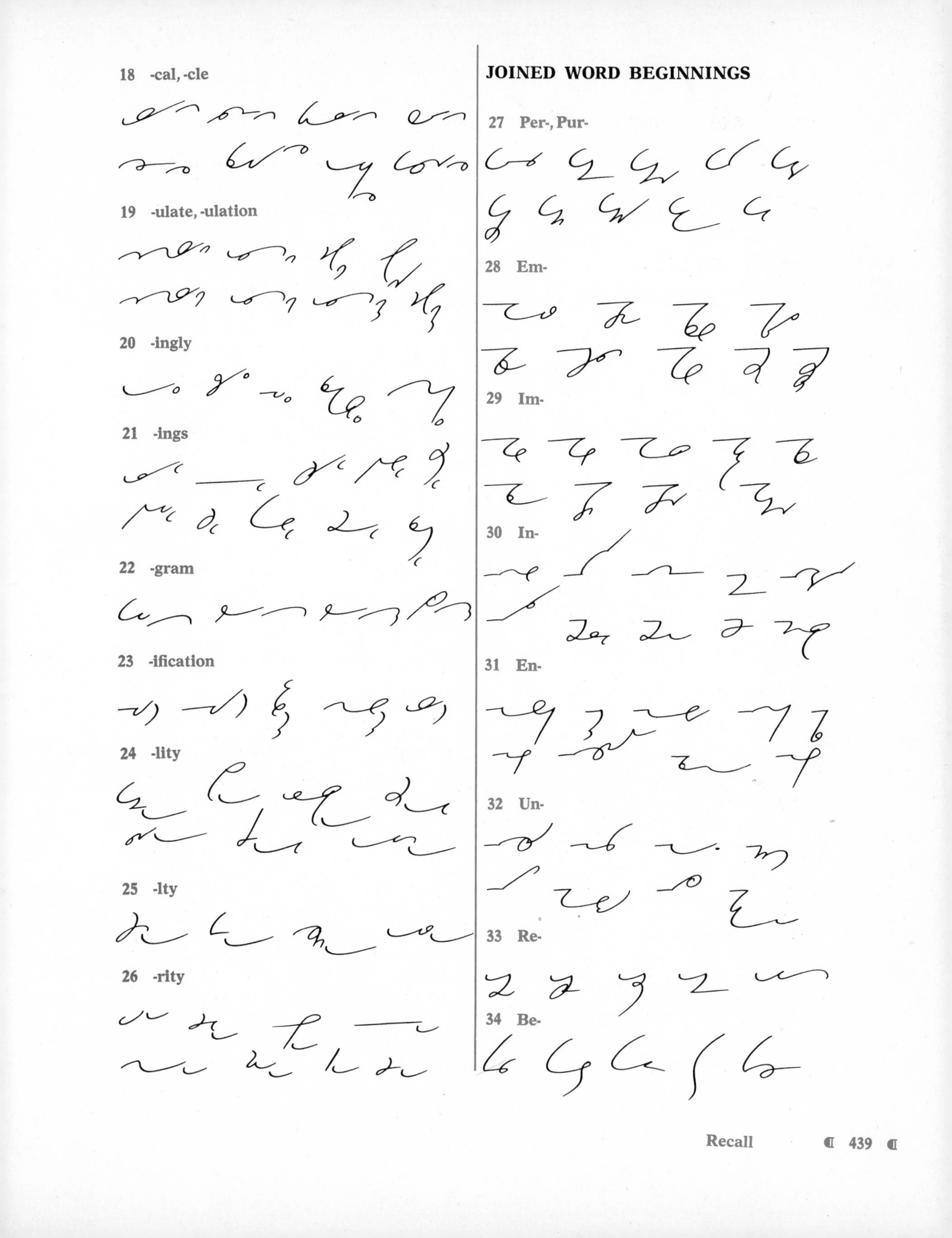

18 -cal, -cle

19 -ulate, -ulation

20 -ingly

21 -ings

22 -gram

23 -ification

24 -lity

25 -lty

26 -rity

JOINED WORD BEGINNINGS

27 Per-, Pur-

28 Em-

29 Im-

30 In-

31 En-

32 Un-

33 Re-

34 Be-

35 **De-, Di-**

36 **Dis-, Des-**

37 **Mis-**

38 **Ex-**

39 **Com-**

40 **Con-**

41 **Sub-**

42 **Al-**

43 **For-, Fore-**

44 **Fur-**

45 **Tern-, Etc.**

46 **Ul-**

DISJOINED WORD BEGINNINGS

47 **Inter-, Etc.**

48 **Electr-, Electric**

49 **Super-**

50 **Circum-**

51 **Self-**

52 **Trans-**

53 **Under-**

54 **Over-**

Addresses for Transcription

The numbers of the following names and addresses correspond to the numbers of the supplementary letters in the *Instructor's Handbook for Gregg Shorthand for Colleges, Volume Two, Series 90.*

CHAPTER 1

1 Mrs. R. T. Keith, National Wholesalers, Inc., 700 Central Avenue, Baltimore, MD 21233

2 Mr. Alexander Brown, 333 Beacon Street, Philadelphia, PA 17815

3 Mr. James Keith, 311 LaSalle Street, Chicago, IL 60644

4 Ms. Joan Winter, 1100 Central Boulevard, Orlando, FL 32801

5 Mr. Arnold Lang, Mason's Department Store, 12 Main Avenue, Austin, TX 76034

CHAPTER 2

6 Mr. William Morris, 110 West Riverside Drive, Trenton, NJ 07081

7 Miss Maryann Lee, 6 Lakeshore Drive, Dallas, TX 75214

8 Resident, 1010 Baylor Street, Lincoln, NE 68119

9 Mrs. Helen Lexington, 100 Pine Street, Newton, AL 36352

10 Ms. Irene Taylor, Madison Industries, 525 Southern Parkway, Portland, OR 97250

CHAPTER 3

11 Miss Wanda James, Superior Publishing Company, 5 Wilson Road, Troy, NY 12180

12 Mr. Benjamin White, 11 Franklin Avenue, St. Louis, MO 66111

13 Dr. Michael Jennings, 2000 Embassy Drive, Newport, KY 41071

14 Ms. Judy Cunningham, Personnel Director, Seattle Credit Corporation, 501 Skyline Drive, Seattle, WA 98101

15 Mr. Abraham Morris, 117 East Sutton Drive, Atlanta, GA 34600

CHAPTER 4

16 Mr. Robert Johnson, Brown Temporary Office Personnel, 1801 Wabash Drive, Chicago, IL 62904

17 Miss J. L. Edwards, Edwards Manufacturing Company, 1002 Main Drive, Little Rock, AR 72203

18 Miss Vanessa Brown, Vice President, Nelson Hardware Corporation, 100 Avenue A, Elkhart, IN 46514

19 Ms. Maureen Kelley, 123 Stevens Road, Bangor, ME 04401

20 Mr. Walter Jennings, Personnel Director, Madison Publishers, Inc., 750 Jefferson Avenue, Baltimore, MD 21205

CHAPTER 5

21 Mr. A. C. Stern, 53 North Brentwood Avenue, Troy, NY 10721

22 Mrs. Dolores Smith, 742 24th Street, Madison, OK 74104

23 Chamber of Commerce, One West 12 Street, Long Branch, NE 69217

24 Mr. Carl White, 857 Garden Lane, St. Paul, MN 55114

25 Resident, 903 Elm Drive, Greenburg, MO 66110

CHAPTER 6

26 Mr. R. J. Blank, Central State Bank, 11 South Street, Concord, NH 03303

27 Mr. Frank Carey, 340 South Pine Street, Seattle, WA 98101

28 Ms. Anita Temple, 210 Oak Street, Springfield, NJ 07093

29 Mrs. Ida Stern, 200 Fifth Avenue, New York, NY 10020

30 Miss V. R. Morris, 1101 State Street, Chicago, IL 62900

CHAPTER 7

31 Mr. Donald Jones, General Office Supplies, Inc., 211 Worth Place, Charlotte, NC 28216

32 Mr. M. R. Brown, President, General Construction Company of Detroit, 25 Harbor Avenue, Detroit, MI 48207

33 Mr. William Lexington, 2 Lee Street, Wheeling, WV 26003

34 Mr. Ira White, Regional Manager, General Power and Light Company, 120 Dade Boulevard, Miami, FL 33125

35 Mrs. Emma Park, P. O. Box 107, Springfield, OH 45387

CHAPTER 8

36 Miss Robin Stern, General Real Estate Company, 35 Primrose Lane, Denver, CO 80221

37 Mr. Thomas Lee, 83-24 Ford Avenue, Richmond, VA 23223

38 Mr. Arthur Brown, 13001 Day Street, Little Rock, AR 72203

39 Mrs. Isabel Stern, President, Madison Relocation Company, 1505 Park Avenue, New York, NY 10022

40 The Honorable I. R. Turner, Mayor of New Haven, New Haven, CT 06519

CHAPTER 9

41 Mr. D. M. Smith, 100 East Main Street, Newark, NJ 07118
42 Mr. Manuel Garcia, 12 Cliff Road, Lynn, MA 01906
43 Mr. Victor White, White's Restaurant, 212 Main Street, Medford, OH 45227
44 Mr. Sean Kelly, Personnel Director, General Food Company, 507 Commerce Street, Memphis, TN 38128
45 Resident, 2300 Beacon Street, Boston, MA 02143

CHAPTER 10

46 Miss Lynn Taylor, National Computer Products, Inc., 120 Broadway, Westport, WA 98411
47 Mr. Donald Gordon, 127 Broad Street, San Antonio, TX 75501
48 Mr. Albert Mason, Vice President, Odessa Insurance Company, 712 West 87 Street, Odessa, TX 79762
49 Mrs. Olive Golden, United Calculator Corporation, Mill Road, Hartford, CT 06531
50 Miss Jane Smith, P. O. Box 133, Jackson, AK 99762

CHAPTER 11

51 Mrs. Vera Buckingham, 59 First Avenue, New York, NY 10010
52 Miss Frances Hastings, Manager, Vermont Hotel, Mountain Road, Stowe, VT 05672
53 Mr. Frederic Foreman, 10 Westerly Road, Providence, RI 02891
54 Mr. Irving Smith, 1010 Third Avenue, Springfield, OH 45512
55 Ms. Linda Smith, 17 Broadway, Westport, WA 98411

CHAPTER 12

56 Memorandum from James Keith to Anita Short
57 Miss Fay Park, Director of Personnel, General Manufacturing Corporation, 35 Central Avenue, Bloomington, IN 46217
58 Memorandum from Alice Davis to William Madison
59 Miss Lorraine King, Public Relations Director, Suburban Railroad Company, 900 Lexington Avenue, Seattle, WA 98112
60 Miss Linda Taylor, 66 Baker Street, Atlanta, GA 34615

CHAPTER 13

61a Mr. Thomas Pace, Public Relations Director, Worth Advertising Company, 55 Ash Street, Scranton, PA 18509

61b Miss Nancy Short, 111 Laurel Drive, Scranton, PA 18505

62a Mrs. Ellen Hart, President, Superior Products Company, 15 Davis Drive, Madison, ME 04631

62b Memorandum from Kenneth Thompson to Jean Sweet

63a Miss Amy West, Office Manager, Central Insurance Agency, 1001 Cullen Drive, Houston, TX 77004

63b Mr. Laurence Green, Controller, Office Supplies, Inc., 67 York Avenue, Hartford, CT 06101

64a Dr. Fay Chan, Business Department, Huntington College, 156 Lincoln Boulevard, Racine, WI 53402

64b Mr. Alan Drake, 133 Cortelyou Avenue, Racine, WI 53402

65a Memorandum from John Reed to Patricia Tate

65b Mr. Bernard Chase, State Savings and Loan Association, 11 Bryan Avenue, Baltimore, MD 21221

CHAPTER 14

66a Mr. John O. Billings, 5554 Third Avenue, Erie, PA 16501

66b Dr. Thelma Tate, Secretary, General Publishing Association, 125 State Street, Chicago, IL 60670

67a Dr. Albert James, 4100 Beacon Street, Boston, MA 02215

67b Dr. Michael Turner, Secretarial Science Department, Smith College, 201 Elm Drive, Vicksburg, MS 39180

68a Mr. Wilbur Baker, American Publishing Corporation, 250 Eagen Street, Spokane, WA 99362

68b Miss Anne Taylor, 52 Woodward Drive, Detroit, MI 48207

69a Memorandum from Margaret Swanson to June Bennington

69b Mr. Francis O'Leary, 11 Mill Road, Casper, WY 82601

70a Mr. Carlos Lopez, Williams Publishing, Inc., 99 Rockdale Avenue, Los Angeles, CA 90041

70b Mr. Robert N. Billings, 17 Jasmine Place, Honolulu, HI 96818

CHAPTER 15

71a Miss Roberta Yale, Personnel Director, State Capitol, Santa Fe, NM 87501

71b Mr. T. M. Star, 1756 East Park Avenue, Jackson, MS 38949

72a Memorandum from Alvin Jones to Jane Lee

72b Mr. James T. White, Manager, Brownsville Shoe Store, The Mall, Brownsville, TN 38012

73a Mr. Peter Wilson, President, Hall Advertising Company, 402 Sixth Avenue, Minneapolis, MN 55805

73b Mr. Jonathon Bennington, Director of Marketing, General Enterprises, 3478 State Street, Montvale, NJ 07080

74a Mr. Matthew Stein, Personnel Director, James School of Adver[illegible]ing, 11 West 24 Street, Milwaukee, WI 53925

74b Mr. D. L. Davis, President, Lexington Advertising Company, 700 So[illegible] First Avenue, San Antonio, TX 75010

75a Ms. Rita Lopez, Vice President, Western Industries, Inc., 132 Lake Street, [illegible] kane, WA 98112

75b Mr. Adam Keith, Sanders Advertising Agency, 345 East 12 Street, New York, NY 10001

CHAPTER 16

76a Mrs. J. R. Smith, Smith & Donnelly Insurance Agency, 129 Glenview Drive, Missoula, MT 59801

76b Mr. Franklin Jones, 38 Dover Road, Baltimore, MD 21202

77a Mr. Richard Paterson, 195 Main Street, Reading, PA 19607

77b Mr. Gordon March, 778 Grayson Street, Birmingham, AL 35055

78a Mr. Walter Taylor, American Insurance, Inc., 65 Clark Street, Helena, MT 59601

78b Ms. M. V. Tate, Central Insurancy Agency, 211 West First Avenue, Harrisburg, PA 16507

79a Memorandum from Dave Wilson to May Torres

79b Ms. Olive Cunningham, Personnel Manager, Southwest Insurance, Inc., 19 Clearwater Circle, Las Vegas, NV 89117

80a Mr. Randolph Gates, 984 Valley Road, Burlington, IA 52601

80b Memorandum from Myrna Monroe to The Staff

Inde of Building Transcription Skills

Th number next to each entry refers to the page in the text on which the entry appears.

Brief Forms of Gregg Shorthand

IN ALPHABETICAL ORDER

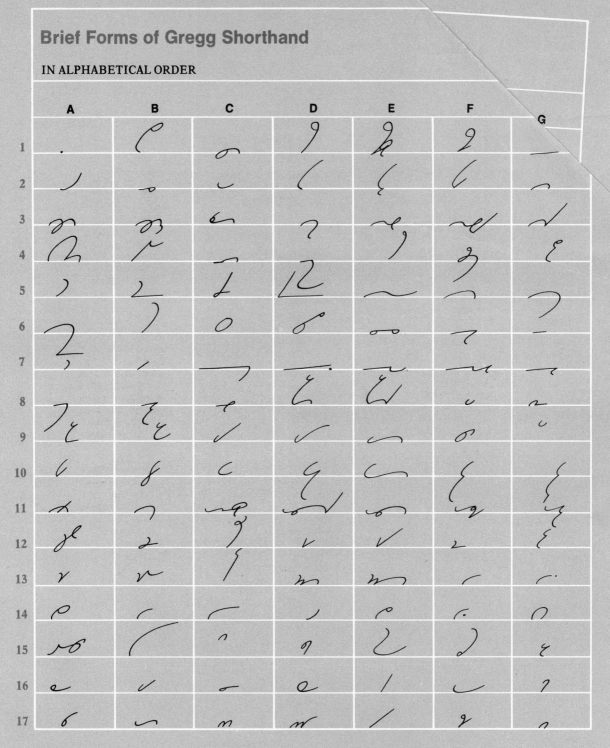

	A	B	C	D	E	F	G
1							
2							
3							
4							
5							
6							
7							
8							
9							
10							
11							
12							
13							
14							
15							
16							
17